THE NATURE
OF
REINFORCEMENT

THE NATURE
OF
REINFORCEMENT

Edited by

ROBERT GLASER

University of Pittsburgh

A Symposium of
THE LEARNING RESEARCH AND DEVELOPMENT CENTER
University of Pittsburgh

ACADEMIC PRESS   New York and London   1971

ACADEMIC PRESS, INC.
111 Fifth Avenue, New York, New York 10003

United Kingdom Edition published by
ACADEMIC PRESS, INC. (LONDON) LTD.
Berkeley Square House, London W1X 6BA

LIBRARY OF CONGRESS CATALOG CARD NUMBER: 78-171212

*This volume is a collection of papers prepared for a sympo-
sium made possible through financial support provided under
a contract with the Personnel and Training Branch, Psychological Sciences Division, Office of Naval Research.*

PRINTED IN THE UNITED STATES OF AMERICA

CONTENTS

Chapter 5

Chapter 6

Chapter 7

Chapter 8

Chapter 9

Chapter 10

PARTICIPANTS

Richard C. Atkinson
Institute for Mathematical Studies in the Social Sciences, Stanford University, Stanford, California

Albert Bandura
Center for Advanced Study in the Behavioral Sciences, Stanford University, Stanford, California

Roger W. Black
Department of Psychology, University of South Carolina, Columbia, South Carolina

A. Charles Catania
Department of Psychology, University College of Arts and Sciences, New York University, Bronx, New York

John B. Carroll
Center for Psychological Studies, Educational Testing Service, Princeton, New Jersey

John W. Donahoe
Department of Psychology, University of Massachusetts, Amherst, Massachusetts

William K. Estes
The Rockefeller University, New York, New York

Harry Fowler
Department of Psychology, University of Pittsburgh, Pittsburgh, Pennsylvania

Robert M. Gagné
Department of Educational Research, Florida State University, Tallahassee, Florida

Jacob L. Gewirtz
National Institute of Mental Health, Bethesda, Maryland

Robert Glaser
Learning Research and Development Center, University of Pittsburgh, Pittsburgh, Pennsylvania

Frank A. Logan
Department of Psychology, University of New Mexico, Albuquerque, New Mexico

David Premack
Department of Psychology, Harvard University, Cambridge, Massachusetts

Lauren B. Resnick
Learning Research and Development Center, University of Pittsburgh, Pittsburgh, Pennsylvania

Todd R. Risley
Bureau of Child Research Laboratories, University of Kansas, Lawrence, Kansas

Robert M. W. Travers
School of Education, Western Michigan University, Kalamazoo, Michigan

James F. Voss
University of Pittsburgh, Pittsburgh, Pennsylvania

Thomas D. Wickens
Institute for Mathematical Studies in the Social Sciences, Stanford University, Stanford, California

Montrose M. Wolf
Bureau of Child Research Laboratories, University of Kansas, Lawrence, Kansas

PREFACE

This book is a result of the fourth in a series of annual conferences on topics in the psychology of learning that are of significance for instructional technology. Each year a topic is selected which is of pervading interest for scientific and technological work. The outstanding men and women in the particular area are brought together to present reviews of theory, research, and application and to ascertain areas of agreement and points of challenge. The objective of these conferences is to report and analyze scientific progress in a field at a time when it is particularly useful in the light of current developments. For this volume, examination of the nature of reinforcement seemed especially relevant because of current theoretical and experimental activities and because of the increasingly wide use of the principles of reinforcement in practical affairs.

The annual conferences have, as has the one on which this book is based, been sponsored by the Personnel and Training Research Programs, Psychological Sciences Division, Office of Naval Research under Contract Nonr-624(18). The conferences are held under the auspices of the Learning Research and Development Center of the University of Pittsburgh, which is one of the research and development centers of the National Center for Educational Research and Development of the Office of Education.

As chairman of the conference and editor of this volume, I am grateful to Karen K. Block, J. Michael O'Malley, and Donald Wildemann for detailed summaries of the conference discussions, to John L. Caruso who prepared the index, and to Jane Rippel and Dianne Predmore for help in preparation of the manuscript. Particular gratitude is due to Mary Louise Marino, research assistant at the Learning Research and Development Center, who acted as editorial associate from initial planning through final product; her suggestions and editorial work were constantly helpful.

Final editing of the book was done while I was a Fellow at the Center for Advanced Study in the Behavioral Sciences, Stanford, California, in the superbly free and intellectual climate that the Center provides.

Robert Glaser

1

INTRODUCTION

ROBERT GLASER

University of Pittsburgh

Background

In any listing of general laws or principles in the science of learning, the principle of reinforcement is a prime entry. Facts and conceptions of reinforcement have pervaded theory, experimentation, and practical application. The general observation is that experimental or natural environmental consequences can increase the probability with which behavior occurs and also can decrease this probability; furthermore, the particular properties of the behavior that is acquired often depend on the details of these environmental consequences. The principle of reinforcement indicates how behavior is shaped and learned through the use of reinforcers — a reinforcer being defined as an event, stimulus, or state of affairs that changes subsequent behavior when it temporally follows an instance of that behavior. Throughout all the various theoretical interpretations of the mechanisms of reinforcement; e.g., drive reduction, sensory feedback, relative response probabilities, and incentive effects, the operational description of reinforcing situations has remained fairly stable: Behavior is acquired and its occurrence regulated as a result of a contingent relationship between the response of an organism and a consequent event.

As a sort of warming up exercise for this volume, we can review some modern history. In the late 1930's and early 1940's there was almost general agreement that the relative strengthening of adequate responses and the associated improvement in performance was attributable to the consequences following adequate and inadequate responses. This generalization was called the empirical law of effect. The supporting experimental studies generally opposed the traditional associationistic view that temporal contiguity of stimulus conditions and response was a sufficient condition for learning.

The law of effect served primarily to name an empirical phenomenon. In investigating the manner of its operation, Thorndike and his co-workers set out to study the specific mechanism of the aftereffect of reinforcement. The vague term "emphasizing effect" was used in relation to whether or not the consequences of a response satisfied or relieved prevailing motivating conditions. Thorndike's notion of a "confirming reaction" that strengthened responses when consequences were given in the form of knowledge of results was presented as an interesting hypothesis to analyze. Extensive investigation was also recommended for the clarification of the definition of reward and punishment because absolutistic conceptions did not seem justified.

In the late 1940's and early 1950's, the theorists who were the proponents of reinforcement as a necessary condition for learning were in the position of defending themselves against the latent learning experimenters who asserted that an organism can learn through processes of perceptual or cognitive organization which depend only on temporal contiguity. Although the cognitive theorists agreed that the law of effect had an important influence on the modification of behavior, they emphasized that the learning of cognitive organization was not satisfactorily explained by the operation of the aftereffects of reinforcement. As this debate was occurring, reinforcement theory was gaining additional power through the numerous investigations and theoretical explanations of secondary reinforcement and generalization gradients, and pursuit of the mechanisms of reinforcement continued. In the 1950 Volume I issue of the *Annual Review of Psychology,* the following was concluded: "It seems unlikely at this time that the reinforcement principle will be abandoned on the basis of any one or several experiments; instead, it appears that attacks on the principle only lead to more fruitful explorations of its complications" (Melton, 1950, p. 20).

It was in this period of the late 1940's and early 1950's that a number of crucial issues grew up around the differences between S-R reinforcement theory and cognitive-field theory. The question of whether the learning process involved a continuous change in the strength of S-R relationships or whether it involved a discontinuous sequence of acts came to be known as the continuity-noncontinuity controversy. Another issue concerned the question of whether the product of the learning process was a specific stimulus-response relationship (response learning) or a cognitive organization or expectancy (a place learning). It was a time for crucial experiments and critical debates. It was a time of contrasts, with Hull and Miller and Dollard on the one hand, and the field-cognition point of view defended by Tolman, on the other. Guthrie was classified with the reinforcement theorists at this time when reinforcement theory was defending itself. Skinner's operant-respondent distinction was generally accepted and seemed important in some accounts of learning and less important to others; it represented either a basic difference in learning processes or a recognition of mere procedural differences. It was concluded as a result of the debates of this period that, depending upon the conditions under which learning occurred, different ways of learning seemed likely to occur; but, the theories and explanations proposed did not predict under what conditions different kinds of learning would occur.

By the beginning of the 1960's, the investigations ranging from Thorndike's work to statistical learning theory implied that learning would not occur unless the consequences of the specific learning act belonged to a general class of "reinforcers." Many characterizations of reinforcers were extant, as were various explanations of reinforcement. Neal Miller (1963) named these explanations: the hedonic hypothesis, the drive-reduction hypothesis, the optimal-level hypothesis, the central confirming response hypothesis, the contiguity hypothesis, the consummatory response hypothesis, the expectancy hypothesis, the motivational feedback hypothesis, and the two-factor hypothesis. Of course, no one explanation or description of reinforcers received general acceptance. But it was pointed out by Estes (1960) that all reinforcers served one or more of the following functions: evocation of a response, termination of a persisting state of affairs, delay of the occurrence of cues for interfering responses, and reduction of needs established by deprivation or experimental instructions. The justifications for treating these many different events and operations as instances of a single class of "reinforcers" were: (1) that they all seemed to have similar effects on response probabality, and (2) that the particular events or operations used as reinforcement made little difference upon subsequent processes such as generalization and transfer, retention, distribution of practice, and discrimination.

At this time there seemed to be some recognition of a dual nature of reinforcement in terms of (a) law of effect interpretations which assumed the direct action of an aftereffect, and (b) explanations in terms of the association and interference processes involved in contiguity theory. A common interpretation was taking shape which was described as follows: "The gist . . . is that new associations, or habits, form simply as a result of the contiguous occurrence of stimulus and response; the function of reward is the motivational one of 'energizing' habits already learned"

(Estes, 1960, p. 758). This distinction between (a) learning by contiguity and (b) performance which could lead to learning was expressed by Arthur Melton in his reaction to hearing about the conference on which this book is based. "As you know," his letter stated, "I am of the opinion that reinforcement, as an independent variable in behavior modification, has its principal, if not only, effects on performance and that learning, in the sense of storage of information about the environment and relations among events in the environment is an automatic concomitant of perception, i.e., a matter simplistically ascribed to 'contiguity.' However, reinforcement does control what is attended to and perceived, and also selects, in the sense of controlling the responses that are emitted in the form of overt behavior" (Melton, personal communication).

As time moved into the 1960's, some new developments that had been brewing became prominent. One of these concerned the relativity of reinforcement which stated the principle that reinforcement can be formulated in terms of the preference values of certain activities, i.e., the probability of occurrence of these activities in an organism's repertoire (see Premack, pp. 187–232). Another development concerned behavior sequences and chaining; in a chain of activities that terminates in a reinforcing event, each response could act as a reinforcer for a previous response. For some investigators, a behavior chain was seen as a very effective vehicle for analyzing conditioned reinforcers (Kelleher and Gollub, 1962). Another development was the increasing investigation in the area referred to as sensory reinforcement (see Fowler, pp. 233–299). A primary reinforcement process was postulated that resulted from the presentation or removal of stimuli of moderate intensities; in general, the proposition was that stimulus change in many modalities functioned in a reinforcing capacity.

At the end of the 1960's, it seemed useful to take stock of things. It was for this purpose that a conference was convened — to see what a group of psychologists would have to say about the facts and theoretical alternatives involved in assessing the role of reinforcement in the experimental-theoretical analysis of learning processes. In June of 1969, with support from the Office of Naval Research, some twenty-five individuals met at the University of Pittsburgh to discuss their experimental findings and theoretical positions. The papers and discussions presented at the conference are the substance of the chapters in this volume.

Foreground

The views presented in this book provide strong evidence that in the past ten years experimentation and theory in learning have significantly influenced the analysis and status of the phenomenon of reinforcement as a fundamental concept in the psychology of learning. Two major developments in psychology that have influenced conceptions of the nature of reinforcement are apparent: (1) the extension of research into new and increasingly complex classes of behavior, and (2) analysis of the constraints and artificialities imposed by the limited range of experimental situations in which reinforcement has been studied. By way of a general characterization of these developments and as a prelude to the details of the specific chapters, this introduction briefly describes eight issues which seem to pervade as general themes and counterpoint. These issues concern the operant-respondent distinction, reinforcement and cognitive processes, reinforcement as a function of task requirements, cognitive versus operational description, learning and performance, social learning phenomena, the relative nature of reinforcers, and applications of reinforcement.

The operant - respondent distinction. The utility of the operant-respondent distinction is directly questioned in the chapter by Catania. These two categories of behavior are seen to have persisted as a dichotomy as a result of differences based on experimental convenience rather than upon the qualitative differences of the behavior involved or upon their theoretical explanation. The functional distinctions that have been demonstrated in order to elaborate on the properties of the two classes of behavior have, in general, not been sustained. The recent work of Neal Miller and his colleagues on the operant conditioning of autonomic responses (1969) further attests to the fallacy of this "ancient view." Behavior studied as respondents, and behavior studied as operants, can be modified by either respondent or operant conditioning procedures. What has maintained the distinction between respondent and operant responses has not been their topographical or physiological properties, but their relationship to the stimulus conditions in a given context. In line with this, Catania suggests that Pavlov chose a limiting case in the selection of unconditioned stimuli that always produced a specified response with a high probability. And Skinner's description of the operant also relied upon the special characteristic of the probability of occurrence of a response in the absence of specifiable eliciting stimuli.

Catania reexamines the operant-respondent distinction in terms of the procedures employed in instrumental and classical conditioning, and the behavior relationships involved in R-R, S-R, R-S, and S-S events. His analysis of the continuities, similarities, and inter-relationships among the operations of elicitation, reinforcement, and stimulus control de-emphasizes the cogency of the classical distinction. The conclusion we come to is that an adequate description of the nature of reinforcement is limited by maintaining the dichotomy between operant and respondent response classes.

Reinforcement and cognitive processes.   With apparent awareness of the fact that the bulk of our knowledge about reinforcement is derived from animal studies in simple task situations and from human experimental contexts in which conditions apparently constrain subjects to employ limited behavioral processes, there is throughout the book the examination of the nature of reinforcement in more complex behavioral phenomena. As Estes points out, the positive results of studies showing that human behavior, like infrahuman behavior, can be modified by reward contingencies, has led to complex problems of interpretation and various opinions about the nature of reinforcement effects in verbal and other human behaviors. Questions arise which suggest that the behavior produced by the manipulation of reinforcement contingencies should be attributed to a combination of cognitive and motivational processes rather than, or in addition to, the more direct strengthening and weakening of conditioned associated connections. One current emphasis in experimentation, primarily by those who interpret human behavior in terms of information-processing concepts, is a strong suggestion of discontinuity in the operation of reinforcement when we move from the simple to higher-order behaviors. On the other hand, a strong countertrend reflected in this volume is not to assume discontinuity and reject the large body of experimental facts about reinforcement, but rather to incorporate this impressive evidence in the context of other behavioral processes. Estes makes the point when he writes that the view that seems best supported by a wide range of evidence is that the mechanisms of reinforcement are basically the same in animal and human learning at all levels of development, but variations in response organization result in different phenotypic manifestations. For lower animals, young children, and retarded individuals, behavior is describable in terms of stimulus-response sequences and consequent rewarding or punishing outcomes. Much mature, adult human behavior is organized into higher-order routines and strategies, and it is these large behavioral organizations whose probabilities are modified by reinforcing contingencies. The nature of the behavior unit is what distinguishes the adult human learner while operation of the principles of reinforcement may be similar for different species and levels of development.

The problem of behavioral units comes into sharp focus with respect to the cognitive and motivational processes assumed in information-processing interpretations where a distinction is made between learning, in the sense of the acquisition of information, and the modification of behavior as the result of consequences. These interpretations assume that human learning (verbal learning specifically) is a matter of information storage and memory processes, and that an aspect of this is the outcomes that occur as a result of task performance. These contingencies, rewards and punishments, do not control learning directly (by direct associative strengthening), but contribute information which modifies the learning process. Reinforcement contingencies provide information about alternative courses of action and influence behavioral strategies. The units of behavior are the ways of processing information, and a major question is whether mechanisms of reinforcement operate similarly for such behavioral units as well as for the more elementary processes usually studied. For example, do these processing strategies function like operants?

Reinforcement as a function of the task requirements. While such variables as delay, stimulus discriminability, reinforcement magnitude, scheduling, and so forth influence the effects of reinforcing events, it also is apparent that reinforcement operates in different ways to result in an increase in response probability. As Bandura points out, the specific form reinforcement takes and the conditions under which it is employed determine the mechanism by which it can effect behavior. For example, in verbal-learning situations, reinforcing stimuli may have their effect through informational value; in behavioral modification programs, where the subjects are informed in advance of the contingencies involved, reinforcement may have its effect through incentive motivational effects.

The operation and effects of reinforcement can be viewed as being derived from more basic aspects of the learning situation. Atkinson and Wickens contend that the processes involved in verbal learning are fundamental in determining the nature of reinforcement. A unified law to explain all reinforcement phenomena is not satisfactory because the effects of reinforcement are often quite varied in appearance and in the manner in which they are produced. Their analysis of memory assumes that the reinforcement process is determined by how the subject uses his memory. In the retrieval of a response, reinforcement provides information which determines where search takes place and the amount of time a subject is willing to spend in searching the memory store. In memory storage and transfer, the kind of feedback obtained from a reinforcing event influences what is stored, and also directs the subject's attention so that more study is given to rewarded items than to others. For the most part, Atkinson and Wickens outline an expectancy interpretation of reinforcement in the tradition set by Tolman. A contingent event sets up an expectancy on the basis of which the subject forms a prediction about stimulus input and correlated information. It is the confirmation of this prediction that determines whether an event is stored and, as a result, dictates the course of learning.

From quite a different point of view — an operant interpretation — Gewirtz points out that the term "reinforcers" has often been used regardless of setting conditions or performance contexts. Events may operate as reinforcers only for particular responses in certain contexts and/or under very special setting conditions. Fowler, as an incentive-motivation theorist, emphasizes the dependent relationship between an event serving as a reinforcer and those antedating or prevailing conditions of stimulation under which the organism performs.

The point to be made is that while different points of view about learning express general agreement about the neglect of contextual and situational aspects upon the operation of reinforcement, there is disagreement on the central role of reinforcement. Gewirtz maintains reinforcement as a propaedeutic process, Atkinson and Wickens give it a subsidiary role in the context of cognitive processes, and Bandura allows reinforcement equal major status with other processes.

Cognitive processes interpretations versus operational description.
As expected, it is apparent in these chapters that the authors are divided in that some are willing to use hypothesized cognitive processes in their theoretical interpretations of reinforcement while others insist that operational description of experimental situations is more scientifically parsimonious and will lead to stronger analyses of the properties of behavior. The latter point of view is most explicit in Gewirtz's discussion of Bandura's chapter and also in the approach taken in Catania's analysis. Catania examines reinforcement in terms of experimental operations, and he indicates that such an analysis keeps preconceptions about the properties of behavior from intruding. His taxonomical dimensions involve only experimental operations, and the question of whether these operations involve different behavioral processes is an empirical one. While Catania states that his classification of behavioral operations is not to be taken as an explanatory theoretical model, the taxonomy does indicate the power of a behavioral analysis of the conditional probabilities among stimuli and responses, devoid of any assumptions about cognitive processes. Premack essentially stays close to operational description, but may fall from grace when he discusses the process whereby organisms make judgments of value which influence response probabilities and the relative reinforcing effects of contingent behaviors. Fowler, in his interpretation of incentive-motivational theory, states that the mediating action of anticipatory attentional responses that are induced by reward afford S-R incentive theory a transition to cognitive theory.

Gewirtz is particularly concerned that explanation of behavior in terms of postulated processes frequently implies a flight from an operational emphasis, as exemplified in the approach of Skinner, and from the explicitness of the empirical law of effect and of operant-conditioning technology. The instrumental or conditioning paradigm has been able to explain certain or complex behaviors for which earlier explanations seemed to require the postulation of special complex processes. Gewirtz asserts that two major conditions of behavior need to be assessed, which if carefully analyzed may keep explanation on an operational, instrumental conditioning basis; these are: (1) prior response and reinforcement history, and (2) the cue relationships and discriminative stimulus control thereby learned as a result of this history which may be present in a new learning situation. Discriminative stimulus control as a basic explanatory mechanism in the description of complex reinforcing events is a feature strongly urged by both Catania and Gewirtz. The position is that analysis in terms of acquired stimulus control should be attempted to explain phenomena before new theories are postulated or modifications are made in the instrumental-conditioning conception.

Learning and performance—direct versus indirect effects of reinforcement. Historically, verbal-learning experiments and most of the work with animals have emphasized the direct strengthening effects of reinforcement. With the analysis of more complex behavior and the breaking down of the rigidities of the standard experimental paradigms, the chapters in this book indicate a shift in emphasis. Interpretations of reinforcement phenomena in terms of indirect effects are becoming more prominent. Direct effects are being seen as a less frequent mechanism in the learning of higher-order behavior in the sense that reinforcement has its principal influence on the control of performance (such as paying attention) which then leads to learning. The issue is whether reinforcing events modify the learning process directly or exert their influence as independent determinants of performance. As Estes points out, the main line of development from law-of-effect theory was the notion that rewarding aftereffects tend to strengthen stimulus-response connections directly and automatically. Skinner and early Hull essentially followed Thorndike in this respect. Later Hull, Spence, and Logan and Wagner still conceived of reward as a determinant of learning but did not assume a unitary conception of associative strength: Response strength depends upon both the frequency of past occurrences, and the frequency with which these S-R occurrences have been followed by reward. S-R frequency per se is subsumed in the conception of habit strength and the frequency of S-R reward occurrences in the concept of incentive motivation, i.e., learning the association and the motivation to practice it. The chapter by Logan summarizes this point of view. For Logan, contiguity is the main mechanism involved in both kinds of associative learning, and rewards function in a way that is called motivational. Motivation, however, is not directly necessary for learning, but does influence performance, i.e., what is practiced and, hence, what is learned. Fowler sees any attempt at drawing conclusions about the nature of reinforcement as essentially a matter of describing incentive motivation.

Along these lines, Estes refers to theoretical schema that he has advanced which make contiguity and reinforcement more equal partners as determinants of learning (Estes, 1969). In general, the learning of stimulus-response and stimulus-outcome relationships proceeds according to association by contiguity. When a stimulus-response sequence eventuates in reward, these two kinds of associations are learned. Upon subsequent occurrences of the event, the stimulus gives rise to an anticipation of the outcome. Experience with different kinds of outcomes establishes different weights for different stimuli which influence response probability. Learning occurs as an interaction of a result of association by contiguity and of the influence of differential reinforcement upon performance.

The indirect effects of reinforcement are clearly seen in Bandura's explanation of the mechanisms of vicarious reinforcement, and these explanatory mechanisms equally apply to the interpretation of the reinforcement of more overt behavior. Depending upon the task and circumstances involved, reinforcing stimuli can serve to: (a) convey and confirm information about the types of responses which obtain reward or avoid punishment, (b) direct attention to discriminated cues which identify situations in which appropriate behavior results in reinforcement, or (c) establish anticipations of response outcomes which result in incentive-motivational effects which facilitate or inhibit behavior. This variety of indirect effects of reinforcement in no way countermands the operation of reinforcing effects in terms of the direct automatic action of aftereffects on stimulus-response occurrences in appropriate situational contexts. The evidence of direct effects is apparent in studies on the physiological mechanisms underlying the phenomena of operant conditioning (Stein, 1969). What appears to be important is that the nature of reinforcement must be interpreted in terms of task factors, situational and context-setting conditions, the characteristics of learning outcomes, and the organism involved.

Social learning — vicarious and self-reinforcement. Until recently, the overwhelming majority of laboratory studies on reinforcement have been carried out in situations where contingencies are provided to the subject by inanimate apparatus and with inanimate objects as reinforcing stimuli. In contrast, in natural settings reinforcement occurs extensively within a social context. The context of what are called "social learning" situations adds some new dimensions to the nature of reinforcement. Bandura's chapter and Gewirtz's followup comments speak to this important aspect. The properties of social learning described by Bandura stem from at least two aspects of human behavior: One is that people continually observe the behavior of others as this behavior is rewarded, ignored, or punished, and this observation influences the subsequent operation and effect of reinforcers on the observers. The second aspect is that individuals regulate their own actions by mechanisms of self-reinforcement, i.e., self-generated anticipatory consequences which allow possible future contingencies to function as current stimuli which influence present behavior. In addition, self-regulation is influenced by the fact that the individual can make self-evaluations of the consequences of his own actions as these consequences are made apparent by reinforcement contingencies.

The phenomenon of vicarious reinforcement extends our conceptions about the nature of reinforcement. Vicarious reinforcement is defined as a change in the behavior of observers as a function of witnessing the reinforcement contingencies accompanying the performance of others. As a result of vicarious reinforcement, individuals (the observers) show facilitation and decrement in behavior as a result of seeing performers (the modelers) of a class of behavior experience rewarding or punishing consequences. In the course of their observation of others, the observers do not perform any overt responses, and the model's outcomes do not have any immediate consequences for the observers. It seems clear that the influence of directly experienced reinforcement administered under social conditions may not be fully understood without considering the possible effects of a history of vicarious reinforcement. Experiments further indicate that the effects of standard variables, such as different schedules of reinforcement, magnitude of reward, and so forth, on vicarious reinforcement are similar to what occurs when reinforcement contingencies are directly administered.

The explanatory mechanisms and theoretical interpretations of vicarious reinforcement are similar to the informational, attention-directing, and incentive functions described for directly administered reinforcement, but some nuances are added. For example, when models exhibit emotional responses as a result of punishing or rewarding experiences, the emotional arousal of observers influences behavioral facilitation or suppression. Reinforcement effects are also influenced by the status of the model being observed. The status of the models in terms of prestige, power, or competence takes on discriminatory value and influences the effect of reinforcement contingencies.

Experiments in social learning have emphasized the fact that behavior is altered and maintained in the absence of directly administered and also directly observed external reinforcement. Individuals exercise control over their actions by self-generated contingencies. Empirical and theoretical work on self-regulatory processes is especially sparse. The little work that has been done focuses on the performance-guiding function of verbal and imaginative stimuli and on whether people can regulate their own behavior through self-produced consequences. Especially relevant in the process of self-reinforcement is the notion that individuals set standards for their behavior and self-administer rewarding or punishing consequences depending upon the extent to which their performances match their self-prescribed demands. Of current research interest is investigation of the conditions under which self-reinforcing responses are acquired and modified, and investigation of the extent to which self-administered consequences serve a reinforcing function in controlling an individual's own behavior. Bandura's chapter examines the functional properties of vicarious and self-reinforcement and the mechanisms through which they influence behavior.

While it is agreed that the empirical facts of vicarious and self-reinforcement point to key processes in understanding the nature of reinforcement in human behavior, the ways in which these processes operate and their theoretical interpretations pose significant areas for debate. Succinctly, the issue here derives from the fact that Bandura postulates cognitive, representational processes which underlie the behavior he describes. Gewirtz, in commenting on Bandura's chapter, is unwilling at this time to postulate "intra-psychic cognitive-act euphemisms." He argues that such "hyphenated-reinforcement" phenomena as vicarious- and self-reinforcement are not anomalous for a reinforcement-learning conception, and that they may be readily explicable in terms of routine conditioning concepts, in particular, extrinsic reinforcement, overt responding, and acquired stimulus control.

The relative versus the absolute nature of reinforcers.   The earlier work of Premack (e.g., 1959, 1965) made prominent one aspect of the relative nature of reinforcement when he showed that reinforcement can be defined by the relation in which a more probable event is made contingent on the occurrence of a less probable event. Access to a more preferred behavior which has a high probability of occurrence can be used to reinforce a less preferred activity which has a lower probability of occurrence. Furthermore, the relative value of such two activities can be changed by alteration of conditions in an individual's history with a consequent change in their effectiveness as reinforcers. In his chapter in this book, Premack now considers the opposite case as a formulation of punishment. Since a transition from a less to a more probable event facilitates responding, a transition from a more to a less probable event may suppress it — so that one and the same event can be predicted to produce both reinforcement and punishment depending upon the probability of the base event relative to that of the contingent event. The general point is made that the special properties of electric shock may be a unique case, as may be food deprivation, and that differentiation between such classes of contingent events may be unnecessary when an underlying common principle is uncovered, such as the relativity relation of preferred activity values. The traditional reference to neutral, positive, and negative stimuli which correspond to neutral stimuli, reinforcers, and punishers may be a misinterpretation of the nature of reinforcement, if reinforcement and punishment only can be dealt with relationally.

The conclusion reached is that reinforcement effects are a function not of the classes of reinforcing or nonreinforcing events, but of their relation, and that reinforcement can be produced with many pairs of values of the probabilities of instrumental and contingent responses. Traditional apparatus and instrumentation, such as the Skinner box, confined investigation to a particular pair of values in a particular order. Furthermore, the traditional way of referring to the reinforcement value of a particular event or stimulus, such as the reinforcing value of food, obscures the fact that reinforcing effectiveness is a function of existing behavioral states *and* the relationships among them. It is these conditions and relationships that must be assessed in order to predict the effectiveness of a potential reinforcer.

Other chapters in this volume substantiate the general conclusion that the extension of research into new categories of behavior and into new experimental paradigms forces the breaking away from the traditional conceptions of what is a reinforcer. Fowler describes the facilitating or suppressing effects that may be obtained from the same contingent event. In sensory reinforcement, it is not stimulus change per se that is reinforcing, but prior conditions of exposure that influence reinforcing effectiveness. The diverse ways in which response contingencies can have their effects; e.g., informational and incentive functions or attention and arousal functions, make it apparent that the situation in which behavior occurs must be characterized before the mechanism of reinforcement can be specified. The principles that hold in making these specifications appear to be increasingly trans-situational, and from this it seems possible to conclude that psychologists are beginning to come into the possession of certain general principles about the nature of reinforcement.

Applications of reinforcement. Thorndike and Skinner after him were impressed with the use and powerful influence of response consequences, reward and punishment, in naturalistic situations and in social institutions. Both sought, on occasion, to extend the implications of their basic laboratory research to meet the complexity of natural and social situations. Other investigators have been less inclined to make such outside contact and extrapolations. Recently, however, largely influenced by Skinner's concern with education and practical affairs, the engineering of what is known about reinforcement contingencies has increased in the form of behavior modification practices and techniques applied to the design of instructional materials, classroom teaching practices, therapeutic techniques, institutional management, and assessment of the effects ot drugs and isolation. This work has had a salutary effect on the redirection of traditional applied practices. It has also served to assess the extent of our knowledge about reinforcement and to test the limits of traditional interpretations and research paradigms.

Indications of this are given by Wolf and Risley, Logan, and Resnick. Wolf and Risley describe the experimental methodology which allows the use and study of reinforcement principles under practical conditions. This methodology forces particular attention to response definition by the observer or practitioner so that the behavior being modified can be reliably observed. Furthermore, it focuses attention on aspects of the environment that are influencing the behavior of the subject and that can be manipulated by the practitioner, e.g., the classroom teacher or therapist.

Logan speculates about the educational implications of his incentive-motivation interpretation. He emphasizes the importance of differential reinforcement as a significant mechanism in education and stresses an awareness of the possible specificity of the effect of reinforcement contingencies; e.g., practicing arithmetic at a slow pace teaches a student to be slow in arithmetic, spelling out loud may mean that a student will make more spelling errors in writing. In distinguishing between drive-motivation and incentive-motivation, Logan speculates that drive-motivation effects contribute little to the variance among students, and that what is most effectively under the teacher's control, and what may provide most of the difference among students, is variation in incentive-motivation effects which are brought about by the arrangement of response contingencies.

Several things are apparent in the applications of reinforcement. With knowledge of the ways in which behavior in practical affairs can be influenced by the arrangement of environmental contingencies, there follows a de-emphasis on theories of internally postulated forces, such as "lack of confidence" or "infantile aggression," which leave the practitioner with minimal influence. And, since environmental rearrangements can effectively provide new possibilities for behavioral change in an individual, increasing responsibility and accountability is placed upon the activities of the change agent. However, as Resnick points out, crucial issues must be addressed before applied research in reinforcement can be expected to have major social impact. One issue relates to the process of maintaining the behavior that has been acquired in special reinforcement programs when the individual returns to the natural community of reinforcers. Systematic analysis of the relationships between "programmed" and "natural" reinforcement settings is required. Another issue relates to the extent to which applications which have been implemented successfully by sophisticated experimenters can be carried out by the average practitioner in the situations in which he operates. These issues are no doubt transient ones. The exciting prospect for application is that limitations of traditional conceptions are being overcome by new investigations about the nature of reinforcement, many of which are discussed in the chapters which follow.

REFERENCES

Estes, W. K. Learning. *Encyclopedia of Educational Research.* (3rd ed.) New York: Macmillan, 1960. Pp. 752–770.

Estes, W. K. Reinforcement in human learning. In J. T. Tapp (Ed.), *Reinforcement and behavior.* New York: Academic Press, 1969. Pp. 63–93.

Kelleher, R. T., and Gollub, L. R. A review of positive conditioned reinforcement. Supplement to *Journal of the Experimental Analysis of Behavior,* 1962, *5,* 543–597.

Melton, A. W. Learning. *Annual Review of Psychology,* 1950, *1,* 9–30.

Miller, N. E. Some reflections on the law of effect produce a new alternative to drive reduction. In M. R. Jones (Ed.), *Nebraska symposium on motivation.* Lincoln: University of Nebraska Press, 1963. Pp. 65–112.

Miller, N. E. Learning of visceral and glandular responses. *Science,* 1969, *163,* 434–445.

Premack, D. Toward empirical behavior laws I: Positive reinforcement. *Psychological Review,* 1959, *66,* 219–233.

Premack, D. Reinforcement theory. In D. Levine (Ed.), *Nebraska symposium on motivation.* Lincoln: University of Nebraska Press, 1965. Pp. 123–180.

Stein, L. Chemistry of purposive behavior. In J. T. Tapp (Ed.), *Reinforcement and behavior.* New York: Academic Press, 1969. Pp. 328–355.

2

REWARD IN HUMAN LEARNING: THEORETICAL ISSUES AND STRATEGIC CHOICE POINTS

W. K. ESTES
The Rockefeller University

When the suggestion was put forward that I discuss alternative theories of reward in human learning at this conference, I cheerfully agreed to the assignment. It falls near the heart of my current interests, and I nonchalantly assumed that I could accomplish it. During the ensuing year, my interest has, if anything, intensified, but my level of aspiration has sunk along a steadily declining curve. The difficulty, in brief, is that a careful search of the contemporary literature turned up nothing that could reasonably be termed a theory of reward in human learning. Theoretical viewpoints, yes. Hypotheses, traditions, dogmas, limited models — but no formulations exhibiting the organization and scope which should characterize a theory.

While it is my dearest wish to see this unhappy state of affairs remedied, I can find no reason to be sanguine. Technological and economic developments have enormously accelerated the volume of research on human learning, and the consequent cascade of data is overloading our capacities for organization and interpretation. This is not to depreciate the quality of current theoretical work; it is in many respects as superior technically to that of earlier periods as is the computer-controlled laboratory to the memory drum. But, in view of these considerations, it now seems to me that the most useful task I can undertake for this conference is to depart from my normal inclination to dig deeply into some particular line of development and, instead, to attempt to clarify my thoughts, and thus perhaps also others' concerning some of the issues which currently fractionate the theoretical surface in human learning. The limited, but possibly realizable, objective will be to point up some of the strategic choice points that appear to lie between us and the goal of a more coherent and functional body of theory.

Range of Empirical Phenomena

In order to bring the task down to manageable proportions, we need first to define at least roughly the range of empirical phenomena to which theories of reward in human learning need currently be addressed. Nearly a half-century ago, when Thorndike initiated the first substantial efforts toward theory construction in this area, the range of relevant data was narrow indeed. His initial problem was simply to give a plausible account of the overwhelming practical importance of rewards and punishments in the control of behavior in everyday life — the original basis for the empirical law of effect. Further, except for Thorndike's own researches (1931), the situation had changed little when the first learning theorists in the modern tradition, Guthrie (1935), Hull (1943), and Skinner (1938), formulated their general theories of learning with only casual reference to the interpretation of reward and punishment in human learning.

Even as recently as the early 1960's, a major review of reward and punishment in human learning (Postman, 1962) was organized largely around the relatively circumscribed line of research growing out of Thorndike's pioneering attempts to analyze the effects of positive and negative aftereffects in simple trial-and-error learning. Early work in this tradition documented in simple laboratory situations the functions of symbolic rewards and punishments (usually simply "right" or "wrong") as distinguished from sheer practice, elucidated the role of "belongingness" and intention to learn, and demonstrated the spread of effect. Later work revolved around the question of whether the effects of rewards in human trial-and-error learning are automatic in the same sense as is generally

assumed to be the case for animal learning. Studies of the role of awareness and of intention to learn were conceived primarily as tests of alternative hypotheses concerning mechanisms involved in the spread of effect.

A major line of research growing out of the Thorndikean tradition,
and influenced strongly by Skinner's systematic ideas, has to do with the
modification of human behavior by operant-conditioning procedures. This
work includes studies of the shaping of behavior of normal children and
adults, of the mentally retarded, of autistic children, and of psychotic
adults by the same general procedures that have been intensively studied
in connection with the control of simple operant responses in rats and
pigeons. By and large, the results of these studies have supported the conclusion that nonverbal behavior of human beings can be modified by
reward contingencies in much the same way as the behavior of animals.
The extension of operant methods to the reinforcement of verbal behavior
in normal children and adults has led to far more complex problems of
interpretation and to a considerable variation of opinion among current
investigators as to whether or not the modifications of verbal behavior so
produced are properly interpreted as a form of conditioning. Nonetheless,
an accumulation of empirical relationships established by this work will
require interpretation in any theory of reward in human learning. Much
the same is true of the substantial literature concerning the role of feedback in the acquisition and maintenance of perceptual and motor skills
(see e.g., Bilodeau, 1966).

In yet another currently active branch of the Thorndikean tradition,
research on choice and decision processes is generating a growing collection of quantitative empirical laws relating choices to the reward values
and probabilities of outcomes in probability learning, social interactions,
and situations involving utilities and risks. Furthest of all from the law-
of-effect tradition, perhaps, is the study of observational learning and
learning from models (Bandura, 1965).

Of special relevance for theory are a number of active lines of experimental work addressed to specific theoretical issues.

1. Incentives, motivation, and recall. Whereas most of the earlier
work by Thorndike and his immediate successors was concerned with the
effects of reward on repetition of responses, interest is currently increasing
in the related problem of an individual's ability to recall his previous
response to a stimulus, as distinguished from his tendency to repeat it.
Studies by Buchwald (1967, 1969) and by Nuttin (1953) and Nuttin
and Greenwald (1968) have been interpreted as indicating that some, at
least, of the commonly observed effects of reward on repetition are indirect, or higher-order phenomena, the more basic process being variation
in memory for previous stimulus-response sequences.

More empirically oriented studies have analyzed the effects of incentives upon recall as a function of the point of administration of the incentives; that is, during learning, during the retention interval, or at the time of testing for recall. A significant interaction between incentive magnitude and retention interval has been observed only when instructions concerning differential incentives were given at the time of stimulus presentation (Weiner, 1966a, b). Further, some related work in progress suggests that the locus of the effects may lie in the process of stimulus coding rather than in the maintenance or retrievability of associations in memory (Medin, 1969).

2. New analyses of delay of reward. In studies of animal learning it has generally been found that effectiveness of reward is inversely related to the delay of reward following the response undergoing acquisition. It has turned out, however, that the relationships in human learning are by no means so simple. Several recent series of researches have clarified somewhat the conditions under which delay of reward does or does not retard acquisition in human learning situations (Atkinson and Wickens, this volume; Brackbill, Bravos, and Starr, 1962; Buchwald, 1967, 1969; Hochman and Lipsitt, 1961; Kintsch and McCoy, 1964).

3. Information and effect. Since the earliest experimental studies of human learning, it has been recognized that, for the adult learner, rewards and punishments serve to an important extent as carriers of information quite independently of any effects they may have as satisfiers or arousers of drives or motives. In classical experiments these two aspects of aftereffects were inextricably confounded, and only recently have substantial experimental efforts been made to separate the functional relationships (Estes, 1967a,b; Farley and Hokanson, 1966; Hillix and Marx, 1960; Humphreys, Allen, and Estes, 1968; Keller, Cole, Burke, and Estes, 1965; Nuttin and Greenwald, 1968).

4. Stimulus weights and selective attention. Several recent studies have begun to clarify the function of rewards in modifying selective attention, and thus in determining the relative weights of different stimuli or stimulus dimensions, as distinguished from any direct strengthening of instrumental responses (Estes, 1966; Nunnally, Duchnowski, and Parker, 1965; Nunnally, Stevens, and Hall, 1965; Witryol, Lowden, and Fagan, 1967).

5. Relativity of reward values and adaptation level. It is often convenient to speak as though the reward value of a stimulus could be characterized by a value on some absolute scale; for example, grams of food in the case of an animal in an operant conditioning experiment or amount of money in the case of a human subject in a multiple-choice situation. However, investigations on both the animal and the human level have begun to make it clear that the prediction of effects of any particular rewarding stimulus must take account of the previous history of the organism with respect to a range of reward values (see, for example, Hilgard and Bower, 1966, pp. 481-487). Studies with human subjects addressed particularly to this point include those of Bevan and Adamson (1960, 1963); Buchwald (1959, 1963, 1966); and Harley (1965a,b).

6. Relation between response times and response probabilities. Traditionally, the data of human learning experiments have been limited to frequencies of correct and incorrect responses. The only major exception until recently was the recording of rates of responding in studies using operant procedures. However, in the analysis of animal learning and conditioning, measures of response time have generally proven more informative than simple frequencies, and some investigators of human learning have begun utilizing latency data. The results impress me as extremely revealing and may well auger an almost revolutionary chance in methods of human learning experimentation. Studies of response latency in relation to reward frequency (Straughan, 1956) and reward magnitude (Keller et al., 1965; Stillings, Allen, and Estes, 1968) not only bear upon qualitative issues but also pose problems of quantitative interpretation which may call for theories of a much higher order of precision and rigor than those that have characterized this area.

General Theoretical Approaches and the Issue of Continuity

Perhaps the broadest issue upon which investigators of reinforcement in human learning differ sharply is the basic question of continuity or discontinuity of theoretical concepts relative to those developed in the context of animal learning and conditioning. Continuity has been assumed, with varying degrees of explicitness, by most investigators associated with Guthrie's contiguity theory, Thorndike's connectionism and its more modern variants, Hull's system, and, perhaps most strongly, by the operant-conditioning school.

Guthrie (1940, 1952) believed that learning in both animals and men was basically a matter of conditioning by contiguity and that at all levels the effects of rewards and punishments could be interpreted on the basis of contiguity principles.

If my reading of Thorndike is correct, he began with a working hypothesis of continuity, but with no firm commitment to it, and directed much of his research toward the goal of determining the extent to which learning under the influence of reward and punishment in human beings is an automatic, almost mechanical, process of strengthening and weakening of associative connections, of the kind he assumed to be operative in trial-and-error learning by animals. On the whole, Thorndike's own researches (1931, 1935) and those of later investigators in his tradition (Postman and Sassenrath, 1961) tended to support the assumption of continuity, and this assumption appears to characterize the approach of such current representatives of the Thorndikean tradition as Postman (1962, 1966).

Hull (1937, 1943) set himself the goal of a single unified behavior theory that could apply at least throughout the range of mammalian behavior. He allowed for the possibility that special principles might be required at the human level, and among his followers, Spence (1960) seemed the most inclined to believe that such principles would be necessary. Miller, however, in his basic research and theorizing and also in his extensive efforts to apply behavior theory to human problems, appears to have worked consistently on the premise of continuity (Dollard and Miller, 1950; Miller, 1959; Miller and Dollard, 1941). In a recent treatment of reward and punishment following what is often termed the "neo-Hullian" approach, Logan and Wagner (1965) take the position that "the same basic principles apply to all organisms that can learn" (p. 8) although special boundary conditions may well differ at the animal and human level. Much the same view has characterized my own theoretical writings (Estes, 1959, 1967a,b), and to a considerable extent most of the investigators working within the general framework of statistical learning theory (Neimark and Estes, 1967).

The theoretical and methodological approaches of current investigators who lean toward discontinuity are even more variegated. Some simply take issue, on specific empirical grounds, with certain assumptions having to do with the automatic action of aftereffects. Thus, Dulany (1962), and Spielberger and his associates (Spielberger, 1962; Spielberger, Bernstein, and Ratliff, 1966) have introduced variations into the classical experiments on operant conditioning of human verbal behavior with a view to analyzing more carefully the role of the subject's awareness of reward contingencies. They conclude that awareness is a critical variable in this type of learning and, thus, that the changes in verbal behavior produced by manipulations of reward should be attributed to a combination of cognitive and motivational processes rather than to any automatic strengthening and weakening of associative connections. In similar vein, Bandura (1965) has conducted numerous studies of the way in which children learn from models and on the basis of these concludes that much human learning is not reducible to conditioning principles.

A more sharply defined theoretical position on the discontinuity side is that associated with the currently active school which seeks to interpret human behavior in terms of information-processing concepts. These approaches range from that of Hunt (1962), who proposes that some of the problems of complex human learning, especially concept formation, can most expeditiously be handled by the development of special theories which are temporarily, at least, autonomous relative to more basic learning and conditioning theories, to that of Miller, Galanter, and Pribram (1960), who argue more strongly against the reducibility of human learning, even in the long term, to associative concepts.

For the most part, however, among experimental investigators of human learning, discontinuity is a tacit rather than an explicit assumption. During the past ten years or so, perhaps the greatest volume of research having to do with reward in human learning has been associated with the area of probability learning and processes of decision and choice in situations involving risk, bets, and gambles. Except perhaps for the approach growing out of statistical-learning theory (Estes, 1964; Suppes and Atkinson, 1960), this work has been guided mainly by concepts of subjective probability and utility deriving from economic theory, game theory, and statistical-decision theory. With the exception of Siegel (1959, 1961) and Suppes (1961), investigators in this last tradition have simply worked toward the development of special theories of human behavior in situations involving payoffs and uncertainties with no attempt to relate these to more general learning theories (e.g., Coombs and Huang, 1969; Coombs and Pruitt, 1961; Edwards, 1962; Luce and Suppes, 1965).

My own views on the continuity issue have shifted somewhat over the years. At one time (Estes, 1950) I assumed that all phenomena of learning, both animal and human, could be interpreted in terms of basic concepts of stimulus-response association by contiguity. Though I can no longer recapture the mood of sanguinity and faith in reductionism of that period, I am still inclined to believe that, up to a point, reason favors the continuity approach. The fact that linguistic and problem-solving behaviors of adult human beings seem superficially to be of a qualitatively different character from anything observable in lower organisms impresses me rather less than the solid and steadily accumulating body of experimental facts showing that various forms of learning in children, and under simplified conditions even in adults, proceed in accord with principles drawn largely from the study of animal learning and conditioning. The behavior of autistic children, schizophrenic adults, and the mentally deficient of all ages has proven amenable to modification by careful application of operant-conditioning methods even in situations where all the other available approaches have failed (Krasner and Ullman, 1965). The major advances recently reported with respect to demonstrating control of visceral processes by reward contingencies in human beings as well as in animals (Miller, 1969) give strong reason to believe that even when the adult human being is at his most sophisticated and cognitive, various of his bodily processes are being modified in accord with basic principles of conditioning.

The view which now seems to be best supported by a wide range of evidence is, in brief, that mechanisms of reward and punishment are basically the same in animal and human learning, and in human learning at all levels of development, but that owing to wide variations in response organization, the phenotypic manifestations may be very different. (By "animals" in this context I am of course referring only to those sub-human species for which substantial data are available demonstrating learning and conditioning processes comparable in major respects to those observed in human beings.) For the lower animals, for very young children, and to some extent for human beings of all ages who are mentally retarded or subject to severe neurological or behavior disorders, behavior from moment to moment is largely describable and predictable in terms of responses to particular stimuli and the rewarding or punishing outcomes of previous stimulus-response sequences.

In more mature human beings, much instrumental behavior and, more especially, a great part of verbal behavior is organized into higher-order routines and is, in many instances, better understood in terms of the operation of rules, principles, strategies, and the like than in terms of successions of responses to particular stimuli. Thus, in many situations, an individual's behavior from moment to moment may be governed by a relatively broad strategy which, once adopted, dictates response sequences, rather than by anticipated consequences of specific actions. In these situations it is the selection of strategies rather than the selection of particular reactions to stimuli which is modified by past experience with rewarding or punishing consequences.

If one who is attempting to describe and predict the behavior of an adult human learner fails to take account of these behavioral organizations, and attempts to construct an account in terms only of individual stimulus-response units, the principles of operation of rewards and punishments may appear to be quite different from those revealed in simpler experiments with animals or immature human learners. Actually, it may be that the principles of operation of these factors are the same in all cases and that the difference lies in the nature of behavioral units whose probabilities are being modified as a result of the experience with various types of outcomes.

Although the importance of higher-order strategies in human problem solving is widely recognized, scarcely a start has been made toward analyzing the way in which these develop as a result of learning experiences. Perhaps most progress to date has been made with respect to accounting for the way in which different strategies or hypotheses are sampled by an individual from the set of alternatives available in a given situation (Levine, 1967; Restle, 1962; Trabasso and Bower, 1968). Except for some unpublished work conducted during the last couple of years in my own laboratory, I know of essentially no work dealing with the specific processes whereby rules or strategies gain and maintain control of responding.

Reward — A Determinant of Learning or Performance?

Orthogonal to the issue of continuity is that of whether reward modifies the learning process directly or exerts its influence as an independent determinant of performance. The former view has generally characterized the main line of development of law-of-effect theory. Thorndike quite uniformly assumed that rewarding aftereffects tend to strengthen stimulus-response connections directly and automatically, though, as is well known, he changed his opinion from time to time as to whether punishments operate similarly. Skinner (1938) and his numerous followers have almost without exception followed Thorndike closely in this respect. Essentially the same is true of the original formulation of Hull's theory (1943). Punishment was not considered explicitly, but reward was taken to be a major determinant of the acquisition of habit strength. In later revisions of Hull's theory (Hull, 1951) and in more recent derivative theories (Spence, 1960; Logan and Wagner, 1965), reward is still conceived to be a determiner of learning, but learning is not subsumed under a single unitary conception of associative strength. The tendency of a stimulus to evoke a response is assumed to depend both upon the frequency of past S-R occurrences and upon the frequency with which these have been followed by reward. The effects of S-R frequency per se are subsumed in the conception of habit strength and the frequency of S-R-reward occurrences in the concept of incentive motivation. In the terminology of human learning, the former aspect might be taken to refer to the learner's ability to remember his previous response to a stimulus and the latter aspect to his motivation to make the response.

Influenced by the growing accumulation of new findings concerning reward by electrical stimulation of the brain, Miller (1963) has tentatively suggested a revision of reinforcement theory which departs even further from Hull's original formulation. According to this new suggestion, reward is still a determiner of learning, but only indirectly in that responses followed closely by reward are in a sense intensified while in progress and thus are more likely to be conditioned to concurrent stimuli by contiguity than other responses which are not so intensified.

A still sharper conceptual distinction, with reward regarded as a determiner of performance on a par with other conditions of drive and motivation, is by no means a new idea. In some of Thorndike's early writings on the law of effect (1931), the idea of a "representational" theory of aftereffects was proposed. According to this idea, it is assumed that the learner, as a result of a series of experiences with rewards or punishments, simply acquires information in a cognitive sense as to the outcomes which have followed various stimulus-response sequences. Then, following the acquisition of such information, the learner modifies his choices among alternative responses on the basis of anticipated consequences. On the basis of various experimental results which seemed to demonstrate direct and automatic action of aftereffects on stimulus-response connections, Thorndike rejected the representational theory. However, essentially the same theory has been taken up and elaborated by Mowrer (1960) and Nuttin (Nuttin, 1953; Nuttin and Greenwald, 1968) the former primarily on the basis of a reinterpretation of secondary reinforcement in animal learning and the latter primarily on the basis of studies of human trial-and-error learning in variants of the Thorndikean situation.

Mowrer, who had earlier supported a classical law-of-effect theory, now proposes that habits develop entirely independently of aftereffects and that the function of rewards and punishments is to attach, by conditioning, positive or negative emotional states (hope or fear, respectively) to rewarded or punished responses. Following such conditioning, an organism upon reexposure to the situation in which learning has occurred, scans its repertory of available responses and tends to avoid those leading to unpleasant emotions and to select those leading to pleasant emotions.

A theoretical schema advanced by Estes (1967a, b) shares the emphasis of Miller (1963) and Mowrer (1960) on the importance of cybernetic relationships between rewards or punishments and performance but differs in the specific type of mechanism proposed. The learning of stimulus-response and stimulus-outcome relationships is assumed to proceed simply according to association by contiguity. However, the evocation of responses by stimuli is assumed to require a summation of input from positive or negative feedback mechanisms with the input from conditioned or discriminative stimuli. The activity of the feedback mechanisms themselves is conditionable just as is any other type of bodily reaction. Thus when a stimulus-response sequence has eventuated in reward, the conditioning process establishes learned associations such that upon a recurrence of the situation the initial stimulus gives rise anticipatorily to the activity of the positive feedback mechanism. The effect of the latter, however, is not to modify the response in progress (as in Mowrer's schema) but to facilitate the occurrences of later responses in the sequence which previously led from the initial stimulus to a rewarding outcome. Thus the result of experience with rewards and punishments is not, so to speak, to establish differential preferences for different responses as in other theories of this family, but rather to establish different weights for different stimuli.

Causes and Consequences of Changing Views of the Law of Effect

The problem of attaining some clear perspective concerning the evolution of the presently most influential conceptions of learning in relation to aftereffects is complicated immeasurably by the fact that such critical terms as "law of effect" and "reinforcement" are used in two senses: empirical generalizations describing the way in which performance is modified by rewards and punishments, and theoretical concepts abstracted from observational data and referring to assumed effects of rewards and punishments upon learning, itself an inferred process rather than a directly observable class of data. Throughout all the perennial theoretical controversies concerning the relation of aftereffects to learning and performance, it has been customary to maintain that the sovereignty of the law of effect as an empirical generalization remains unchallenged. Thus, in so authoritative a source as the most recent edition of *Theories of Learning* (Hilgard and Bower, 1966) it is maintained that the law of effect, or reinforcement, is the most important principle of learning. However, I am by no means convinced that the facts warrant this continued obeisance to the law of effect, even as an empirical principle.

One must note, first of all, that the empirical basis of the law of effect is by no means as broad as is commonly assumed. The law of effect did not arise in psychology as a generalization from experimental results, but rather was bequeathed to us from a centuries-old philosophical tradition. Hedonistic interpretations of behavior in philosophy presumably have their origins in everyday-life observations that both human beings and lower animals are able to modify their actions as a result of experience in order to increase their likelihoods of obtaining rewards and avoiding punishments. However, the frequency with which animals and men in nonlaboratory situations repeat punished actions and fail to repeat rewarded ones is so great that, as a statistical generalization, an empirical law of effect is all but vacuous.

In the laboratory, several decades of intensive research upon simple forms of learning have indeed provided solid evidence for an empirical principle of reinforcement, and this body of data provides the basis for such statements as that of Hilgard and Bower mentioned above. But, it must also be recognized that an extremely limited range of situations gives rise to these data, by far the greatest part coming from intensive study of a very few organisms such as rats, mice, and pigeons, and a very few experimental situations—mazes, operant-conditioning chambers, and discrimination boxes.

The steadily increasing rigor and precision of laboratory experimentation upon learning of a few selected animals in a few standard situations during the past few decades has been paralleled by steady advances in observational studies of the behavior of a broad range of animal species outside of these laboratory situations, particularly by the ethologists and other investigators with training in the traditions of biology (see e.g., Thorpe, 1963). One of the major developments of this latter line of research is a growing body of evidence that in most, if not all, animals the possibilities of modifying behavior by law-of-effect principles are strongly restricted by species-specific behavioral organization. Investigators who choose to place greater weight upon the more biologically oriented studies of animal behavior rather than those of the operant laboratory currently propose interpretations of reinforcement which would make the law of effect a subsidiary factor rather than a major organizing principle (see e.g., Glickman and Schiff, 1967).

In the experimental psychology of human learning, the law of effect has never, in fact, functioned to a major extent in the guidance or interpretation of research. The majority of studies of aftereffects have been designed to ascertain whether a relatively simple and mechanistic conception of reinforcement deriving from research in animal learning could be extended to the human case. These attempts appeared relatively successful when the experiments were conducted almost entirely within certain highly restrictive experimental situations in which the data were limited to frequencies of repetition or nonrepetition of simple responses followed by different kinds of aftereffects, and the learners were given little opportunity to manifest the results of any form of learning which did not fit into the law-of-effect conception.

More recently, a number of investigators interested in uncovering any basic inadequacies of the law of effect have introduced various modifications of the standard experimental procedures, generating a number of experiments in which the results predicted from a classical law-of-effect interpretation have differed sharply from those anticipated if learning, as distinguished from changes in performance, is independent of aftereffects. To a rather striking degree, the results of these experiments have favored the latter interpretation (Buchwald, 1967, 1969; Estes, 1966, 1967b;

Humphreys, Allen, and Estes, 1968; Keller et al.; 1965; Stillings, Allen, and Estes, 1968). I have recently reviewed this class of studies in some detail (Estes, 1967b) and need not repeat the discussion here. The principal conclusion of immediate pertinence is that, for a number of simple experimental situations in which changes in performance during learning are almost exclusively under the control of differential reward contingencies, a number of phenomena can be demonstrated which are most simply interpreted on the assumption that learning proceeds independently of reward values; no aspects of the data appear to demand the contrary assumption.

I hasten to add that I do not mean to imply that these, or indeed any other specific types of experiments, are primarily responsible for the strong shift in the climate of opinion concerning the function of after-affects in human learning. On the contrary, I believe that the shift in outlook is influenced most strongly by rather general theoretical considerations. In an earlier period, when organisms were thought of primarily as homeostatic mechanisms, it was natural to confine attention largely to learning experiments which demonstrated the organism's responsiveness to the rewarding and punishing aftereffects of its actions. During the past ten years or so, many psychologists have been increasingly impressed with the usefulness of analyzing the functioning of organisms as information-processing systems, and thus have been led to emphasize experiments designed to bring out the disparities, often extremely large, between the amount of information stored in memory as a result of a learning experience and the amount which is directly manifest in the changed probabilities or other properties of specific reference responses, e.g., conditioned responses or choices within limited sets of alternatives. Within an information-processing framework it is difficult to imagine how there could fail to be a rather sharp separation between learning, in the sense of the acquisition of information simply as a function of experience, and the modification of behavior as a result of consequences.

Although, inevitably, some investigators of human learning continue to have reservations, it seems fair to say that the majority are presently operating on the assumption that at least for human beings, and perhaps for all the higher organisms, learning is primarily a matter of storing in memory information concerning relationships between events which have occurred contiguously in past experience, and that one aspect of this learning has to do with the relationships between stimulus-response sequences and rewarding or punishing outcomes. The primary function of rewards and punishments is not to control learning directly but rather to enter into the learning process as important classes of events about which information must be stored in order that the learner can later modify his choices among alternative actions in the light of past experience.

Theoretical Decision Points

On the route toward any specific and workable theory of this general type, one can see a number of decision points at which clarification is a prerequisite to progress and which thus provide foci of current research activity. One of the branch points has to do with a major unsettled question concerning the relationship between outcomes and rate of learning. Even though it seems increasingly clear that learning is not basically a matter of differential strengthening of stimulus-response connections in accordance with the reward values of aftereffects, there is considerable evidence that the rate of establishment of associations may, under some circumstances, be influenced by what might be termed the significance of outcomes to the organism. Roughly speaking, learning tends to be more rapid in many situations when it involves events which are very rewarding or very punishing as compared to situations in which all of the constituent events are relatively neutral. This observation has led to the suggestion that reinforcement might be interpreted in terms of arousal, or other activating effects of outcomes on the nervous system (Berlyne, 1967; Landauer, 1969). In the construction of any formal theory of reinforcement it will be necessary to decide whether this relationship represents a basic process or a derivative one.

In the case of human learning studies, differences in the possibility of rehearsal may be responsible for variations in the effects of outcomes on learning and recall. Rehearsal, however instigated, is known to be an important modifer of rate of learning and degree of retention in human learning. Whenever aftereffects are found to modify rate of learning, a possible interpretation is that they do so simply by modifying the likelihood or duration of rehearsal. The hypothesis is attractive on grounds of parsimony and also appears to offer considerable explanatory power for a considerable range of phenomena. Thus, for example, the differences between experiments in which Thorndike and his associates did and did not find positive relationships between reward values and rate of trial-and-error learning (Thorndike, 1931), and the differences between classes of aftereffects which Nuttin (1953) and Nuttin and Greenwald (1968) conceived to generate different degrees of "task tension" and thus indirectly to modify learning rate, have in each case been interpreted by other investigators in terms of the differential possibilities of rehearsal (Estes, 1967b, and Postman, 1966, respectively).

Interpretations of effects of rewards and punishments in terms of the instigation of rehearsal are, however, only stopgaps in a sense, for one must in turn explain why different aftereffects lead to different rehearsal tendencies. A mechanism which might accomplish this is embodied in a feedback model in which differential rewards and punishments are assumed to operate primarily by modifying the relative weights of stimuli or stimulus properties (Estes, 1967b). An individual will, in this conception, differentially rehearse rewarded responses if conditions are such that he is led to attend selectively to the cues which evoke them, or to the representations of these cues in immediate memory.

A still more important decision point has to do with the connection between outcomes and performance. One of the principal attractions of the old-fashioned connectionist's theory is that it bypasses this problem by conceptualizing variations in both learning and performance in terms of variation in strength of stimulus-response connections. Once, however, we come to the belief that learning proceeds independently of motives and incentives, we require a subtheory or model to prescribe the way in which the learning of relations between actions and their consequences leads to modifications in response selection on subsequent occasions.

For the most part, this problem has received little explicit attention from investigators of human learning, and the most widely held assumption, perhaps more often tacit than explicit, is that an individual chooses among alternative actions on rational grounds given his state of information. This view appears to characterize approaches as diverse as those of decision theory, the information-processing approach of Hunt (1962) or Miller, Galanter, and Pribram (1960), and the more limited theories of reward in human learning proposed by Nuttin (1953) and Nuttin and Greenwald (1968), and by Buchwald (1969). It is assumed that the individual attaches differential values or utilities to different possible outcomes of his actions, and that once he perceives which outcomes are likely to follow each of his possible choices in a given situation, he makes his decision so as to maximize the expected value of the outcome.

Although the conception of response selection as a process of rational decision making is descriptive up to a point, I am inclined to believe that it does not provide an adequate basis for the interpretation of response selection within a theory of learning and should be derivable from more primitive assumptions. One difficulty is that in many situations individuals, even mature human beings, do not in fact always make the choices that we should expect on the basis of rational considerations. Consequently, rational decision models continually have to be propped up by the assumption of special kinds of utility (for example utility for novelty, utility for variability). Further, as soon as we go beyond the frequencies of different choices and attempt to account also for such data as response times, it becomes apparent that more attention needs to be given to the specific chain of events whereby anticipated outcomes modify response occurrences.

Not only does a rational decision model lack any means of representing detailed properties of response times, but also the intuitive expectations concerning relations between response times and reward values which are generally taken to follow from such a theory are not always borne out in fact. For example, it is commonly assumed that in any situation involving a choice among alternatives having different utilities, response time should be related to the difficulty of the decision, hence to the difference in value between different alternatives. However in one of the few human learning situations for which substantial response-time data are available, it has been found that response times are related in a simple way, not to the differences in reward values attaching to the two alternatives in the binary-choice situation, but rather to the sum of the values (Keller et al., 1965).

I do not question that human beings can use rational decision procedures, but I am inclined to regard these simply as examples of the types of response strategies that human learners can acquire as a result of specific experience. The tendency to select one response strategy rather than another in a given situation must itself be modified by past experience with rewarding or punishing outcomes. A strategic question which must be fundamental to the further development of theory in this area is that of whether the laws and mechanisms of reinforcement are the same for these higher-order behavioral units as for the more elementary responses studied in most laboratory experiments.

My own current efforts are concentrated on an intensive exploration of the possibility that the same processes are operative at these different levels of behavioral organization. A rule or strategy can be analyzed into a prescription, or instruction, for some sequence of actions and a characterization of the occasion upon which execution of the instruction should be initiated. It seems quite possible that associative relations between mnemonic representations of initiating stimulus situations and the reinforcing outcomes of adopting different rules could be established by the same process as those between stimuli, responses, and reinforcing events in simple trial-and-error learning. If, further, the same type of feedback process mediates the effects of anticipated outcomes upon response selection, it may be possible to account for the relations between response times and choices by the same principles in both simple and complex learning situations.

Rationality would not be assumed as a basic principle in this type of theory, but neither would it necessarily be lost. Rather, we should hope that the occasions on which behavior does and does not conform to rational principles might prove to be derivable from a single basic theory.

REFERENCES

Atkinson, R. C., and Wickens, T. D. Human memory and the concept of reinforcement. This volume, pp. 66–120.

Bandura, A. Vicarious processes: A case of no-trial learning. In L. Berkowitz (Ed.), *Advances in experimental social psychology*. Vol. 2. New York: Academic Press, 1965. Pp. 1–55.

Berlyne, D. E. Arousal and reinforcement. In D. Levine (Ed.), *Nebraska symposium on motivation*. Lincoln: University of Nebraska Press, 1967. Pp. 1–110.

Bevan, W., and Adamson, R. Reinforcers and reinforcement: Their relation to maze performance. *Journal of Experimental Psychology*, 1960, *59*, 226–232.

Bevan, W., and Adamson, R. Internal referents and the concept of reinforcement. In N. F. Washburne (Ed.), *Decisions, values, and groups*. Vol. 2. New York: Pergamon Press, 1963.

Bilodeau, E. H. (Ed.) *Acquisition of skill*. New York: Academic Press, 1966.

Brackbill, Y., Bravos, A., and Starr, R. H. Delay improved relations of a difficult task. *Journal of Comparative and Physiological Psychology*, 1962, *55*, 947–952.

Buchwald, A. M. Experimental alterations in the effectiveness of verbal reinforcement combinations. *Journal of Experimental Psychology*, 1959, *57*, 351–361.

Buchwald, A. M. Variations in the apparent effects of "right" and "wrong" on subsequent behavior. *Journal of Verbal Learning and Verbal Behavior*, 1962, *1*, 71–78

Buchwald, A. M. The effect of some variations in procedure on response repetition following verbal outcomes. *Journal of Verbal Learning and Verbal Behavior*, 1966, *5*, 77–85.

Buchwald, A. M. Effects of immediate vs. delayed outcomes in associative learning. *Journal of Verbal Learning and Verbal Behavior*, 1967, *6*, 317–320.

Buchwald, A. M. Effects of "right" and "wrong" on subsequent behavior: A new interpretation. *Psychological Review*, 1969, *76*, 132–143.

Coombs, C. H., and Huang, L. C. Polynomial psychophysics of risk. In MPP69-1, *Michigan Mathematical Psychology Program*, 1969.

Coombs, C. H., and Pruitt, D. G. Some characteristics of choice behavior in risky situations. *Annals of New York Academy of Science*, 1961, *69*, 784–794.

Dollard, J., and Miller, N. E. *Personality and psychotherapy*. New York: McGraw-Hill, 1950.

Dulaney, D. E., Jr. The place of hypotheses and intentions: An analysis of verbal control in verbal conditioning. In C. W. Eriksen (Ed.), *Behavior and awareness.* Durham, N. C.: Duke University Press, 1962, Pp. 102–129.

Edwards, W. Subjective probabilities inferred from decisions. *Psychological Review*, 1962, *69*, 109–135

Estes, W. K. Toward a statistical theory of learning. *Psychological Review,* 1950, *57*, 94–107.

Estes, W. K. The statistical approach to learning theory. In S. Koch (Ed.), *Psychology: A study of a science.* Vol. 2. New York: McGraw-Hill, 1959. Pp. 380–491.

Estes, W. K. Probability learning. In A. W. Melton (Ed.), *Categories of human learning.* New York: Academic Press, 1964. Pp. 90–128.

Estes, W. K. Transfer of verbal discriminations based on differential reward magnitude. *Journal of Experimental Psychology*, 1966, *72*, 276–283.

Estes, W. K. Outline of a theory of punishment. In B. A. Campbell and R. M. Church (Eds.), *Punishment and aversive behavior.* New York: Appleton-Century-Crofts, 1969. Pp. 57–82. (a)

Estes, W. K. Reinforcement in human learning. In J. Tapp (Ed.), *Reinforcement and behavior.* New York: Academic Press, 1969. Pp. 63–94. (b)

Farley, J. A., and Hokanson, J. E. The effect of informational set on acquisition in verbal conditioning. *Journal of Verbal Learning and Verbal Behavior,* 1966, *5*, 14–17.

Glickman, S. E., and Schiff, B. B. A biological theory of reinforcement. *Psychological Review*, 1967, *74*, 81–109.

Guthrie, E. R. *The psychology of learning.* New York: Harper and Bros., 1935.

Guthrie, E. R. Association and the law of effect. *Psychological Review*, 1940, *47*, 127–148.

Guthrie, E. R. *The psychology of learning.* (Rev. ed.) New York: Harper and Bros., 1952.

Harley, W. F., Jr. The effect of monetary incentive in paired-associate learning using a differential method. *Psychonomic Science*, 1965, *2*, 377–378. (a)

Harley, W. F., Jr. The effect of monetary incentive in paired-associate learning using an absolute method. *Psychonomic Science*, 1965, *3*, 141–142. (b)

Hilgard, E. R., and Bower, G. *Theories of learning.* (3rd ed.) New York: Appleton-Century-Crofts, 1966.

Hillix, W. A., and Marx, M. H. Response strengthening by information and effect in human learning. *Journal of Experimental Psychology,* 1960, *60*, 97–102.

Hochman, C. H., and Lipsitt, L. P. Delay-of-reward gradients in discrimination learning with children for two levels of difficulty. *Journal of Comparative and Physiological Psychology*, 1961, *54*, 24–27.

Hull, C. L. Mind, mechanism, and adaptive behavior. *Psychological Review,* 1937, *44,* 1–32.

Hull, C. L. *Principles of behavior.* New York: Appleton-Century-Crofts, 1943.

Hull, C. L. *Essentials of behavior.* New Haven: Yale University Press, 1951.

Humphreys, M. S., Allen, G. A., and Estes, W. K. Learning of two-choice, differential reward problems with informational constraints on payoff combinations. *Journal of Mathematical Psychology,* 1968, *5,* 260–280.

Hunt, E. B. *Concept learning: An information processing problem.* New York: Wiley, 1962.

Keller, L., Cole, M., Burke, C. J., and Estes, W. K. Reward and information values of trial outcomes in paired-associate learning. *Psychological Monographs,* 1965, *79* (Whole No. 605).

Kintsch, W., and McCoy, D. L. Delay of informative feedback in paired-associate learning. *Journal of Experimental Psychology,* 1964, *68,* 372–375.

Krasner, L., and Ullman, L. P. *Research in behavior modification.* New York: Holt, 1965.

Landauer, T. K. Reinforcement as consolidation. *Psychological Review,* 1969, *76,* 82–96.

Levine, M. The size of the hypothesis set during discrimination learning. *Psychological Review,* 1967, *74,* 428–430.

Logan, F. A., and Wagner, A. R. *Reward and punishment.* Boston: Allyn and Bacon, 1965.

Luce, R. D., and Suppes, P. Preference, utility, and subjective probability. In R. D. Luce, R. R. Bush, and E. Galanter (Eds.), *Handbook of mathematical psychology.* Vol. 3. New York: Wiley, 1965. Pp. 249–410.

Medin, D. L. Effects of incentives assessed by a stimulus reproduction test. Technical Report, Rockefeller University, 1969.

Miller, G. A., Galanter, E., and Pribram, K. H. *Plans and the structure of behavior.* New York: Holt, 1960.

Miller, N. E. Liberalization of basic S-R concepts: Extensions to conflict behavior, motivation and social learning. In S. Koch (Ed.), *Psychology: A Study of a science.* Vol. 2. New York: McGraw-Hill, 1959. Pp. 196–292.

Miller, N. E. Some reflections on the law of effect produce a new alternative to drive reduction. In M. R. Jones (Ed.), *Nebraska symposium on motivation.* Lincoln: University of Nebraska Press, 1963. Pp. 65–112.

Miller, N. E. Learning of visceral and glandular responses. *Science,* 1969, *163,* 434–445.

Miller, N. E., and Dollard, J. *Social learning and imitation.* New Haven: Yale University Press, 1941.

Mowrer, O. W. *Learning theory and behavior.* New York: Wiley, 1960.

Neimark, E. D., and Estes, W. K. *Stimulus sampling theory*. San Francisco: Holden-Day, 1967.

Nunnally, J. C., Duchnowski, A. J., and Parker, R. K. Associations of neutral objects with rewards: Effects on verbal evaluation, reward expectancy, and selective attention. *Journal of Personality and Social Psychology,* 1965, *1*, 274–278.

Nunnally, J. C., Stevens, D. A., and Hall, G. F. Association of neutral objects with reward: Effect on verbal evaluation and eye movements. *Journal of Experimental Child Psychology*, 1965, *2*, 44–57.

Nuttin, J. *Tache, réussite et échec*. Louvain, Belgium: Publications Université de Louvain, 1953.

Nuttin, J., and Greenwald, A. G. *Reward and punishment in human learning*. New York: Academic Press, 1968.

Postman, L. Reward and punishment in human learning. In L. Postman (Ed.), *Psychology in the making*. New York: Knopf, 1962, Pp. 331–401.

Postman, L. Reply to Greenwald. *Psychological Bulletin*, 1966, *65*, 383–388.

Postman, L., and Sassenrath, J. The automatic action of verbal rewards and punishments. *Journal of General Psychology*, 1961, *65*, 109–136.

Restle, F. The selection of strategies in cue learning. *Psychological Review,* 1962, *69*, 329–343.

Siegel, S. Theoretical models of choice and strategy behavior: Stable state behavior in the two-choice uncertain outcome situation. *Psychometrika,* 1959, *24*, 303–316.

Siegel, S. Decision making and learning under varying conditions of reinforcement. *Annals of New York Academy of Science*, 1961, *89*, 766–782.

Skinner, B. F. *Behavior of organisms*. New York: Appleton-Century-Crofts, 1938.

Spielberger, C. D. The role of awareness in verbal conditioning. In C. W. Eriksen (Ed.), *Behavior and awareness*. Durham, N.C.: Duke University Press, 1962. Pp. 73–101.

Spielberger, C. D., Bernstein, I. H., and Ratliff, R. G. Information and incentive value of the reinforcing stimulus in verbal conditioning. *Journal of Experimental Psychology*, 1966, *71*, 26–31.

Spence, K. W. *Behavior theory and learning: Selected papers*. Englewood Cliffs, New Jersey: Prentice-Hall, 1960.

Stillings, N. A., Allen, G. A., and Estes, W. K. Reaction time as a function of noncontingent reward magnitude. *Psychonomic Science,* 1968, *10*, 337–338.

Straughan, J. H. Human escape learning in relation to reinforcement variables and intertrial conditions. *Journal of Experimental Psychology,* 1956, *52*, 1–8.

Suppes, P. Behavioristic foundations of utility. *Econometrics*, 1961, *29*, 186–202.

Suppes, P., and Atkinson, R. C. *Markov learning models for multiperson interactions*. Stanford, California: Stanford University Press, 1960.

Thorndike, E. L. *Human Learning*. New York: Appleton-Century-Crofts, 1931.

Thorndike, E. L. *The psychology of wants, interests, and attitudes*. New York: Appleton-Century-Crofts, 1935.

Thorpe, W. H. *Learning and instinct in animals*. (2nd ed.) London: Methuen, 1963.

Trabasso, T., and Bower, G. H. *Attention in learning theory and research*. New York: Wiley, 1968.

Weiner, B. Effects of motivation on the availability and retrieval of memory traces. *Psychological Bulletin*, 1966, *65*, 24–37. (a)

Weiner, B. Motivation and memory. *Psychological Monographs*, 1966, *80* (Whole No. 626). (b)

Witryol, S. L., Lowden, L. M., and Fagan, J. F. Incentive effects upon attention in children's discrimination learning. *Journal of Experimental Child Psychology*, 1967, *5*, 94–108.

ARE REINFORCEMENT CONCEPTS ABLE TO PROVIDE REINFORCEMENT FOR THEORIZING IN HUMAN LEARNING?

JAMES F. VOSS
University of Pittsburgh

Professor Estes states that his paper has "the limited, but possibly realizable, objective . . . to point up some of the strategic choice points that appear to lie between us and the goal of a more coherent and functional body of theory (p. 17)," and that he arrived at this objective only after "a careful search of the contemporary literature turned up nothing that could reasonably be termed a theory of reward in human learning (p. 16)." Thus, at a conference devoted to hearing variations on the theme of reinforcement, we find that the opening notes echo not a bold statement of the importance of reinforcement theory in human learning, but instead yield a sound of discord. We are told that despite the fact that reinforcement has had a central role in areas such as conditioning and discrimination learning, the topic of human learning somehow has been too stubborn or too elusive to be molded into a set of reinforcement principles. Probably the most notable attempts to accomplish such a feat

37

have been made by Berlyne (1965) and by Mowrer (1960), but even their provocative works fall short of the desired harmony between human learning and reinforcement theory.

Professor Estes begins the major portion of his paper by attempting to delineate the range of empirical phenomena that are especially pertinent to a reinforcement theory. Thorndikean-oriented work with its modern derivative of verbal conditioning is included, as well as the role of feedback mechanisms, and Bandura's work on imitation. Subsequently, Professor Estes addresses himself to six current lines of experimentation which he feels are especially relevant to theoretical issues.

Without discussing each of the six areas in detail, I think that one common characteristic of them should be noted; namely, that each has provided evidence which indicates that reinforcement principles, such as found traditionally in the framework of conditioning, may not account successfully for the respective findings. Such results, of course, either place a limitation upon reinforcement theory or require modification of the theory. Professor Estes, I believe, takes the position that modification and elaboration are desirable; i.e., by suggesting that these six phenomena should be taken into account by theoretical development, Professor Estes implies that reinforcement notions may be applicable.

Moving from his consideration of empirical phenomena, Professor Estes discusses theoretical approaches to the reward issue. Of particular importance, he seems to feel, is the question of continuity of process between man and infrahumans. Behind this concern lies the implicit assumption that if continuity of process exists, then theory which is developed at the animal level should also be appropriate at the human level. Professor Estes cites the views of learning theorists as well as more recent work involving strategy and decision behavior, and concludes by stating that the view he sees as most supported is that reward and punishment processes are the same at all levels, but response organization and phenotypic manifestations may be different. He especially makes this point in the final paragraphs of the section by stating that it may be that human behavior is not reinforced simply in terms of S-R units, but instead the behavioral components on which reinforcement operates may be larger units of organization such as strategies or rules.

Despite Professor Estes' concern regarding the continuity issue, I feel that this question is virtually irrelevant as far as our immediate future is concerned. I find the issue of human-animal continuity philosophically interesting, but scientifically superfluous. The fact is that theoretical development is an empirical question, and whether the same or different basic processes underlie human and infrahuman behavior is a question which will likely receive successively approximating answers in future theoretical developments. The real problem for today is how to develop satisfactory theory in the area of human learning, whether it is based upon reinforcement notions or some other framework, whether it had its origins in animal work, in perception, or in some other source.

The continuity issue, it also should be noted, is two-edged. If, for example, a substantial theory of human learning is developed that is rooted in a perceptual framework, it follows from a continuity position that we should be able to apply the principles of such a theory to animal behavior. Thus, even if one adheres to the continuity position, it does not necessarily follow that a reinforcement framework should be adopted for understanding reward and punishment in human learning; instead, it also would be possible that development of some other view may be fruitful, and even applicable to animal behavior.

Following consideration of the continuity issue, Professor Estes raises the question of whether reward influences learning or performance. The issue is considered in historical form, beginning with Thorndike's notions, proceeding with the Skinnerian, Hullian, and neo-Hullian views, and concluding with feedback models of reward as proposed by Miller, Mowrer, and Estes. I believe the significance of including the learning-performance distinction in a general paper on reinforcement in human behavior does not reside in the important similarities and differences of the various models; instead, the most salient trends presented in Professor Estes' account seem to be: (a) that there is an increasing tendency to consider reward as influencing performance, not learning; and (b) that the learning-performance distinction may be an oversimplification.

In his consideration of the "Causes and Consequences of Changing Views of the Law of Effect," Professor Estes calls into question the generality of the empirical law of effect and submits essentially two arguments against its primary role. The first is that recent animal behavior work has made effect subservient to species-specific behavior; the second is that certain data indicate that rewarding aftereffects influence performance and not learning.

Professor Estes subsequently, and I think quite correctly, attributes the change in view regarding the influence of reward upon performance as related to a Zeitgeist-type shift in the conceptualization of reward on behavior. Specifically, he points out that there has been a change from the homeostatic, drive- or tension-reduction analysis, which suggested that a response is important in relation to its motivational and incentive-related consequences, to an information-processing view which essentially states that learning involves storage of experience, and behavior consists of retrieving certain aspects of stored information. Rewards thus become one aspect of experience and information which subsequently may be utilized upon retrieval. It probably should be added, however, that the information-processing metaphor and approach is yet to be developed to the point where it may be reviewed critically with respect to its treatment of reward factors.

In the final section of his paper, Professor Estes' optimism regarding the potential development of reinforcement theory becomes apparent. He feels, however, that in order for a substantial theoretical account of reward to be developed, certain decision points need clarification. The first has to do with whether rate of learning is influenced by outcomes in a primary or secondary way, i.e., whether the effect of outcomes may not be derivations of other processes such as arousal. The second decision point focuses on whether outcomes may be viewed as providing for increased rehearsal, thus suggesting that differences in learning as a function of outcomes may be due to rehearsal and not to outcomes per se. The third decision point involves ascertaining how, once an aftereffect has occurred, the individual again selects the particular response leading to the aftereffect when confronted with the same situation. With respect to the third problem, I agree completely with Professor Estes in his apparent skepticism of a so-called rationality approach, primarily because of the ubiquitous and vague nature of a utility parameter.

In order to develop a way to treat the problem of a response selectivity, Professor Estes discusses a feedback model, which effectively weights the stimulus and thus provides for differential response selection. The model, as described in general in the present paper and specifically elsewhere, provides a mechanism for handling certain reward phenomena in relation to performance and to indirect learning effects such as the role of rehearsal.

Having discussed Professor Estes' paper in terms of its parts, I now shall consider it as a whole. The first question to which I want to address myself is whether the paper does in fact achieve its stated purpose; namely, to point up some of the strategic choice points that lie between current knowledge and the goal of a theory of human learning which handles reward and punishment. I believe that question should be answered in the affirmative, *provided* that one adopts or agrees with the framework of Professor Estes in his approach to the problem.

The general orientation of Professor Estes' paper is that of traditional S-R theory. Within this framework, he considers a particular range of phenomena for which a reinforcement theory should provide, discusses six empirical phenomena which, as mentioned previously, are difficult for a traditional reinforcement theory to handle, points out relevant problems such as the continuity issue and the learning-performance distinction, and concludes with the outline of a feedback model designed to take into account how aftereffects weight stimuli. Reference is made at one point to an information-processing view, and a general definition of learning is presented in terms of a processing position, but an information approach is not developed beyond this point. Scanning mechanisms are not considered nor are issues of serial versus parallel processing in an organism's selection of a response. There are no distinctions of short- and long-term storage and no mention of executive or even selector mechanisms. As a whole, the paper follows in the reinforcement tradition, raises issues related to this view, and states the problems likely requiring solution in order to obtain a more coherent and complete reinforcement theory of human learning. Within this framework, I believe the paper does fulfill its objective.

The second question I want to raise regarding the paper as a whole is one which Professor Estes implicitly raises, but does not consider: Why did a search of the literature reveal an absence of adequate theoretical development regarding the issues of the paper? I believe that Professor Estes' optimism implies that the reason for the lack of an adequate theory of reinforcement is because one has not yet been forthcoming, and, if we consider certain empirical phenomena, if we look at certain theoretical issues, and if we make certain cogent decisions, then such a theory may be possible to develop. I am afraid that I do not share such optimism, if indeed I am correct that Professor Estes implies it. I think, rather, that there are very real reasons for the absence of a highly developed reinforcement theory of human learning today and it is these reasons I now wish to consider.

The first reason is that at the present state of knowledge, the manipulation of rewards and punishments is extremely difficult because of the subjective nature of such parameters. Thus, although the concept of utility may be quite fruitful to the social sciences, it either has not provided the investigator of human learning with a means of manipulating subjective value or such investigators have not taken advantage of the concept. In any event, the subjective nature of rewards and punishments has, I think, tended to impede research in the area.

Another reason for the lack of a reinforcement theory of human learning is, I feel, that many phenomena of human learning simply do not lend themselves to an analysis in terms of traditional reinforcement concepts. Consider a simple human learning paradigm. A subject is given a list of *n* words and is asked to recall them — single-trial free recall. We find, let us say, that of a list of 16 words, the subject recalls seven. Let us ask: What was reinforced and what was reinforcement? First, was it the subject's overt response that was reinforced? No, because he was provided no feedback or any information regarding his response. Second, perhaps since he was instructed to learn the list, reinforcement consisted of his reading each word as he tried to learn the list. But clearly, his recall is not perfect so that even though, according to this view, he was reinforced by reading and trying to learn each word, all reinforcements did not apparently operate in the same manner. Furthermore, even assuming a finite processing capacity, one may ask why some items are recalled and some are not. The answer that I think most human learning investigators would give is that in all likelihood, the individual learned the items based upon their positions in the list and upon his own verbal habits. Thus, in order to study the problem, the line of attack would be to focus upon effects such as primacy and recency, and to try to relate an individual's verbal structure to the list components. In this relatively simple situation, therefore, it is quite difficult, I think, to develop an analysis based upon response and reinforcement concepts.

The point of importance in the single-trial free recall example is this: Many problems studied by investigators of human learning do not lend themselves to a description of either the response to be reinforced or to the nature of the reinforcement that is involved. Hence, to manipulate reward and punishment parameters, when the response to be reinforced and the reinforcement involved in the learning of the task per se are not readily specified, constitutes an extremely difficult task.

But, where has reward and punishment been studied in human learning? I believe the answer is clear. Such effects have been studied in Thorndikean situations and in areas such as probability learning, motor learning, and verbal conditioning in which *the primary object of study is the output per se.* We find aftereffects studied, virtually by definition, when the response to be rewarded or punished is known. Unfortunately perhaps, such a circumscribed domain does not include many topics involved in the study of human learning in which the primary issues of concern are: (a) How do individuals process and organize input information? and (b) How does input information combine with stored information?

Finally, I wish to conclude this discussion on a note that is less skeptical and even hopeful. As mentioned previously, I think Professor Estes' paper attacks the issue of reinforcement theory in human learning via an S-R approach; the most prevalent alternative today is the information-processing type of view. I believe the secret, if there is one, to the impending marriage of the perceptual-cognitive-input orientation with the reinforcement-output orientation rests upon the need to develop a far more extensive theoretical understanding of response processes. We currently are riding a wave of information processing which I believe has not yet crested; on the other hand, there is evidence that emphasis upon the role of the response is increasing, as in orienting response work; e.g., Maltzman and Raskin (1965) and Sokolov (1963); by Festinger et al. (1967) in their research on efferent sets in visual perception; and by interest shown in motor patterning, as summarized by Adams (1968) and Keele (1968).

To be more specific, from the writing of Sechenov through the chapter by Atkinson and Wickens in this volume (pp. 66–120), some individuals have stressed the importance of knowing how an individual matches input with what is stored, how an individual matches an outcome with an expectancy, and how a mismatch may give rise to thought or some other adjustive reaction. I cannot help but think that, e.g., in the Atkinson and Wickens paper, if information goes from a short-term to a long-term store, it does so by a response process, or perhaps a better name would be an efferent process. Such a process likely regulates and selects the information, just as an organism attends and selects from an environment. When we better understand the nature of these efferent systems, I think we then will be able to provide a more complete account of the action of rewards and punishments. In principle, this view is similar to Guthrie's (1940) comments regarding the importance to learning theory of studying the movements an organism makes in learning to get to the goal box rather than only studying the act of arriving at the goal and being reinforced. The study of efferent processes with respect to human learning, however, is much more complicated because the movements are considerably less accessible. Nevertheless, I feel that processing and storage just do not simply happen, but they are regulated and selected by efferent mechanisms — and these mechanisms quite possibly operate in terms of reinforcement principles.

REFERENCES

Adams, J. A. Response feedback and learning. *Psychological Bulletin*, 1968, *70*, 486–504.

Berlyne, D. E. *Structure and direction in thinking*. New York: Wiley, 1965.

Festinger, L., Ono, H., Burnham, C. A., and Bamber, D. Efference and the conscious experience of perception. *Journal of Experimental Psychology*, 1967, *74*, No. 4 (Whole No. 637).

Guthrie, E. R. Association and the law of effect. *Psychological Review*, 1940, *47*, 127–148.

Keele, S. W. Movement control in skilled motor performance. *Psychological Bulletin*, 1968, *70*, 387–403.

Maltzman, I., and Raskin, D. C. The effects of individual differences in the orienting reflex on conditioning and complex processes. *Journal of Experimental Research in Personality*, 1965, *1*, 1–16.

Mowrer, O. H. *Learning theory and behavior.* New York: Wiley, 1960.

Sokolov, Ye N. *Perception and the conditioned reflex.* New York: Macmillan, 1963.

3

INCENTIVE THEORY, REINFORCEMENT AND EDUCATION

FRANK A. LOGAN
University of New Mexico

The most influential, true reinforcement theory of learning appeared in 1943 as Hull's *Principles of Behavior*. That theory postulated not simply that reinforcement is necessary for learning, but that the amount of learning depends upon the amount of reinforcement. It further hypothesized that reinforcement is occasioned by the reduction of a prevailing drive. Rooted in evolutionary principles, Hull's theory conceptualized the organism as being motivated by drives based on survival needs and learning responses in proportion to the extent to which they led to drive reduction. In reviewing this and other theoretical interpretations of learning, Suence (1951) made a critical distinction intended to sharpen the controversies concerning the nature of reinforcement. It bears repeating: Questions about the empirical law of effect are at a different level of discourse from questions about reinforcement as a theoretical construct. It is easy for a discussion of reinforcement to slip between empirical and theoretical questions.

Reinforcement can be dealt with as a purely empirical principle: Reinforcement is the occurrence of an event after a response, which in turn, leads to an increased probability of that response in the future. Ignoring the fact that this statement does not pertain to classical conditioning, one is left with the problem of identifying reinforcing events. Consistent with the empirical approach is the functional definition: A reinforcer is an event previously found to be reinforcing. The circularity of this approach has long been recognized but is at least mitigated by the further assumption of transituationality (Meehl, 1950). The assumption that an event that can reinforce one response can equally reinforce any response could be (and, indeed, probably is) in error.

There should be no controversy about reinforcement when treated as an empirical topic. We can agree upon the operations performed, the outcomes of those operations, and the terms to be used in describing them. Detailed experimental analysis has led to the discovery of a large number of empirical laws concerning the effects of various schedules and conditions of reinforcement and has raised additional empirical questions for further research. Vigorous and valuable as this empirical approach is, it must be carefully distinguished from the (reductive) theoretical enterprise.

What are the circumstances that affect learning? How do some events gain control over behavior? Attempts to answer these theoretical questions are necessarily bound by other assumptions about what is learned and the role of the various independent variables in determining response tendency. In the present context, reinforcement is a hypothetical construct, the nature and necessity of which depend upon the theoretical framework. To illustrate this point in an historical context, no one has proposed a cognitive theory in which reinforcement is necessary for learning, nor is it readily apparent what the concept would mean in such a theory. Accordingly, the present discussion is meaningful only in the context of one "incentive theory" and for that reason, some review of the essentials of that theory seems appropriate.

The Nature of Incentive Theory

The critical difference between a reinforcement theory and an incentive theory is in the role ascribed to rewards and punishments. According to the former, there is a single learning process, the strength of which depends not only on the number of times the response has occurred in the presence of the stimulus but also on the consequences of that response. In contrast, incentive theory introduces a second process through which the parameters of reward and punishment affect excitatory potential.

Where reinforcement theory assumes that the larger the reward, the better the response is learned, incentive theory assumes that people learn to expect emotionally significant events that have previously followed a response and that this expectation motivates the performance of that response according to the value of the consequent events.

The basic assumptions of incentive theory (Hull, 1952; Spence, 1956; Logan, 1960) can be stated somewhat more formally. First, it is assumed that whenever a response is practiced in a given situation, there will accrue a habit association (sHr) linking that response with that situation. If emotionally significant events follow the response, there will accrue an incentive association (sINr), the strength of which depends on the value of the reward and punishment. It is also assumed that the person's wants, desires, and needs are reflected in drive motivation (D) which impels him to do something. These three processes combine into a resultant excitatory potential (sEr) according to the equation,

$$sEr = sHr (D + sINr).$$

There are, of course, other special assumptions necessary to complete an incentive theory. For example, it is assumed that the stimulus and the response are defined by both their qualitative and quantitative properties, and that sHr and sINr generalize along all of these dimensions. However, these additional assumptions are not unique to incentive theory and are not critical in identifying the role of reinforcement in such a theory.

According to incentive theory, behavior is occurring more or less continuously over time, the person selecting at each instant from among the available responses according to their relative excitatory potentials. The reason for the emphasis on incentive within the theory is that sINr is typically the most critical determinant of choice. In most laboratory, as well as everyday, situations there will have been sufficient practice of the available responses so that the competing habits will be equal at their limit. Drive is nonspecific. Hence, it is predominantly incentive that guides the selection of responses so as to maximize reward and minimize punishment. That is not to say that habit is not important. In some situations, various alternative responses are more or less equally successful and the person is then likely to adopt one or another habitual mode of responding. For that matter, incentive is not even necessary to produce performance once a habit has become firmly established. Nevertheless, incentive typically provides for the greatest selective control over behavior.

What is learned? "Learning" is typically considered to be those associative processes postulated by the theory to result from practice. In that sense, there are two learning processes in the present theory, namely, habit and incentive. Habit is the association of a response with a stimulus so that subsequent occurrences of the stimulus are likely to evoke the response.

Incentive is the association of a stimulus with a response, so that subsequent opportunities to make the response lead to an expectation of the consequent stimulus.

These two learning processes differ by their very nature, habit being akin to the behavioristic S-R association and incentive being akin to the cognitive S-S association. Although both are based on the temporal contiguity of the events being associated, they follow somewhat different laws. Most importantly, habit is a gradual, cumulative process which is relatively permanent and can only be supplanted by a stronger habit; incentive can increase or decrease rapidly as a result of changes in the contingencies.

Incentive theory is strained if forced to fit the traditional dichotomy between learning and motivation since incentive falls within both categories. A more appropriate analysis first distinguishes between associative and nonassociative processes and then, within these, between those processes which are unidirectional and relatively permanent as opposed to more transitory and reversible processes. Such an analysis is shown in Table 3-1, where the entries are illustrative but not exhaustive. This analysis suffers from much the same difficulty as the distinction between learning and motivation, namely, the attempt to dichotomize factors into distinct categories. For example, there are undoubtedly degrees of reversi-

Table 3-1

MATRIX SHOWING THAT INCENTIVE IS BOTH A
LEARNING (ASSOCIATIVE) PROCESS AND A
MOTIVATIONAL (REVERSIBLE) PROCESS

	Associative	*Nonassociative*
Reversible	Incentive	Primary drive
Irreversible	Habit	Surgical destruction

bility. But the tables does not show that there are several dimensions along which hypothetical constructs may vary, and the present effort to maintain continuity with conventional categories gives a somewhat distorted picture of the nature of incentive theory.

Incentive Theory and the Nature of Reinforcement

As a theoretical term, "reinforcement" refers to those operations postulated by a theory to effect learning. Although the basic assumption of incentive theory is that learning results from the temporal contiguity of the events being associated, this does not mean that the concept of reinforcement does not apply. However, since there are assumed to be two learning processes, there are correspondingly two natures of reinforcement.

Habit is the association of a response with a stimulus; to effect this kind of learning, it is necessary that the response be elicited in the presence of the stimulus. Hence, reinforcement of habit obtains when a response is followed by a stimulus which elicits that very response. This is most obvious in the context of classical conditioning, where an unconditioned stimulus provides the reinforcement. But it equally pertains to operant and instrumental situations as well. Any time an organism is induced to make a response, that fact will reinforce the (habit) association of that response with the prevailing stimuli. The more frequently this sequence is practiced, the stronger the habit. For this purpose, it is a matter of indifference as to whether the eliciting stimulus has emotional value or, if so, whether that value be positive or negative.

Incentive is the association of a stimulus with a response; to effect this kind of learning requires that a stimulus with emotional (incentive) value follow the occurrence of a response. Such stimuli are customarily referred to as rewards and punishments, and it is here assumed that these are occasioned by resulting changes in drive. That is to say, events that lead to decreases in drive are positive, events that lead to increases in drive are negative, and the amount of such change determines the value reflected in incentive. If a response has several consequences, these combine to determine net incentive, and if the consequences of a response change, incentive changes appropriately.

Accordingly, the essence of the present theory is the postulation of two learning (associative) processes which differ in a number of ways, including the nature of the events that reinforce them. The process whereby responses become associated with stimuli is called habit, which develops simply as a function of practice. Whether it be a rat running through a maze, a pigeon pecking a key, a child reciting the multiplication tables, or an adult human swinging at a golf ball, whatever behavior occurs becomes associated with the prevailing stimulus situation. The nature of the reinforcement for this learning process is the arrangement of conditions such that the behavior occurs. This can be accomplished by means ranging from presenting a stimulus that already produces the behavior, to giving instructions. In addition to the habit resulting directly from practice, a second associative process will develop if the behavior is followed by an emotionally significant event. The nature of the reinforcement necessary to produce incentive learning is a change in the level of drive motivation. This can be accomplished by means ranging from giving food that reduces hunger, to giving praise that reduces the fear of social disapproval.

Optimal procedures for controlling behavior take both associative processes into account. In the first place, it is important to minimize the occurrence of undesirable responses either by physically preventing their occurrence or insuring immediate correction. Alternatively, mild punishment will produce negative incentive to prevent weak habits from developing strength through practice. But it is not enough to insure that desirable responses occur; incentive for their performance requires that rewards be given. Different conditions and schedules of reward lead to different incentive values and determine the stability and persistence of the response. In sum, incentive theory holds that associations are formed by contiguity, but habit is reinforced by providing for the occurrence of the response and incentive is reinforced by providing emotionally significant events consequent on the response.

Evidence for two learning processes.   An understanding of the roles of the two learning processes is perhaps best gained in situations where they oppose each other and lead to dilemmas for uniprocess theories. There are several such situations that can be mentioned briefly here.

Recently an attempt was made to demonstrate the value of treating punishment symmetrically with reward as producing negative incentive (Logan, 1969). Toward this end, rats were first trained to run in two different alleys, one containing a larger reward than the other, until they were showing not only a consistent preference for the larger-reward alternative when given a choice, but also a faster approach when forced to run in one or the other alley. Then, electric shock punishment was added to the large-reward alternative, at first at a very low intensity. The observation of interest was that, as the intensity of the shock was gradually increased, the rats reached a stage where they were running more slowly to the large-reward (and punished) alternative, but were still choosing it on free trials. Although alternative accounts might be given by other theorists, my interpretation is that the preferred alternative still had a larger net incentive value which determined choice, but the speed of the approach response reflected anticipatory, incompatible habits elicited by the shock.

An early line of research which suggests this theory was conducted by Sheffield (1965). His own particular concern was the anthropomorphism reflected in the concept of "avoidance," and he devised a comparable procedure with appetitive conditioning. In omission training, a CS precedes food, provided the dog does not salivate before the scheduled food delivery. Sheffield found that dogs had great difficulty adjusting to this procedure, continuing to salivate even though it prevented the food from being given. According to the present theory, the difficulty resulted from the fact that the two learning factors were pitted against each other. On the one hand, food elicited salivation leading to a habit to make that response to the CS; on the other hand, food is a reward producing incentive not to respond. The observed behavior reveals the conflict these opposing tendencies produced.

A similar result can be seen in an avoidance paradign. It is well known that avoidance learning is difficult if the required response is incompatible with that elicited by the US, but this difficulty could result simply because of reduced likelihood that the response will ever occur and be reinforced. That this is not the entire difficulty can be seen in the paired avoidance situation. Two rats may be individually trained to make an avoidance response to a high criterion of performance, and then placed together in the situation. What is typically observed (Logan and Boice, 1969) is that their avoidance behavior is decreased or even completely eliminated by this pairing. Following the line of research by Ulrich and Azrin (1962), rats paired in an aversive situation tend to aggress against each other, and this habit interferes with the performance of the avoidance response previously learned on the basis of negative reinforcement.

As a final example, consider the phenomenon of autoshaping: A pigeon may learn to peck a lighted key without special shaping or even intentional reinforcement. One simply turns on the key light a few seconds before lighting the food hopper when it is automatically made available at irregular intervals. The pigeon not only pecks the grain but eventually begins to peck the key when it is lit. To this point, there is perhaps nothing too mysterious; generalization from pecking into the lighted hopper could induce pecking at a lighted key which then, being followed by reward, continues as a kind of superstition. But Williams and Williams (1969) have complicated this description by using a variant of the omission procedure. The program is arranged so that, if the pigeon pecks the key, its light immediately goes out, and the scheduled food delivery does not occur. Now a rat can readily learn not to press a bar if pressing prevents a food delivery, but pigeons have difficulty learning not to peck a lighted key that has the same consequence. The conflict between the two learning processes should be apparent: Although not-pecking is rewarded and hence generates incentive motivation to avoid the key, generalization from the response elicited by the reward produces a habit to peck.

Relation to other learning theories. The theory described here is a mongrel. Its most direct lineage is clearly in the Hull-Spence tradition and it uses terminology devised by Hull (1952) and Spence (1956). However, Hull never fully abandoned his earlier assumption that reward was necessary for learning, and both he and Spence treated incentive quite differently than described here. To them, incentive was a general motivational factor mediated through the stimulus-intensity dynamism properties of the fractional anticipatory goal response-produced stimuli. This distinction is emphasized by the present use of sINr rather than K to symbolize the assumption that incentive is a selective associative process.

The reinforcement assumption with respect to habit will be recognized as related to that of Guthrie (1934) although he assumed that process to be reversible. Incentive is analogous to expectancy in Tolman's (1932) early theories although his distinctions among the types of learning lacked parsimony. There have been a variety of "two-factor" theories (Mowrer, 1947; Skinner, 1938; Spence, 1956), but it should be clear that the present approach does not distinguish between classical and instrumental/operant conditioning, between autonomic and skeletal responses, between respondent and operant responses, or between positive and aversive control. It assumes that, in any situation, there are two potential kinds of reinforcement for two learning processes which subsequently combine to determine performance.

There are also several contemporary theories which, while eschewing the term "incentive," have taken an approach similar to the present one: Cofer and Appley (1964), Miller (1963), Mowrer (1960), Seward (1956), and Sheffield (1966). The core assumption in each is that rewards control behavior through a process which, while necessarily learned, functions more in a manner which would traditionally be called motivational. That is to say, reward does not increase the likelihood of a response by "stamping in" the habit; instead, rewards excite habits that have produced them in the past. These theories disagree as to the nature of a rewarding event, be it drive reduction, the consummatory response, stimulation of a reward center in the brain, or simply a pleasant experience. They disagree as to the precise mechanism through which the effects of rewards are realized. But they agree that the empirical law of effect is a performance principle, the nature of reinforcement being to provide for future selective potentiation of responses.

Incentive Theory and Education

A teacher teaches in the same sense that a cook cooks. The cook himself does not change state; it is the meal that cooks. So, too, it is the student who changes state — he learns. The job of both cook and teacher is to arrange the conditions so that the desired product results. To do so, they need knowledge — artistic lore or scientific theory — to guide their decisions. The requisite knowledge is the body of principles governing the changes in the subject; for example, in the one case, that dough rises in relation to yeast content and temperature; in the other case, that learning depends on motivation and stimulation.

Let us not belabor the analogy. The point is that teachers *do* teach in the sense of arranging the conditions for learning to occur. They are members of a large class of "learning aids" to which also belong textbooks and the various newer media of education. Learning aids attempt to control the stimuli to which the learner is exposed and thereby to determine what learning will occur. Learners also partly control the stimuli to which they are exposed; to this extent, the learner is also his own learning aid.

Most books in educational psychology are like cookbooks in that they attempt to prescribe specific ingredients for teachers' use. However, a theory of educational psychology should provide principles from which one can derive optimal programs and teacher behavior. Such a theory is partly a theory of learning, specialized to the conditions arising in an educational setting. The purpose of this section is to describe several aspects of incentive theory which appear to have implications for a theory of educational psychology.

Learning in the Classroom

People learn about stimuli, about responses, and about rewards. If stimuli occur in temporal sequence, this association is learned. If responses occur in the presence of effective stimuli, including stimuli produced by previous responses, those responses become associated with those stimuli. And if rewards or punishments follow the occurrence of a response, people learn that rewards or punishments are associated with that response. In any situation, stimulus discriminations, response differentiations, and reward/punishment consequences are learned.

The assumption of incentive theory is that such associations are formed on the basis of contiguity of the events in question. Let us illustrate these assertions as revealed in an educational context. First, stimulus associations: If a history teacher somewhat regularly appears in class with torn underarms of her dress, history to the students comes to mean, in part, that image. Second, stimulus-response associations: If a psychology teacher gives a multiple-choice examination, and a student selects an answer, he learns that answer even if it is later proven to be wrong. Finally, response-reward associations: If an English teacher happens to give better grades for longer essays, the student learns to prolong his responses. In each case, the behavior may be perfectly appropriate: The history teacher may be reflecting her inadequate salary, the psychology teacher may be reflecting a penchant for objectivity, and the English teacher may be reflecting an appreciation of literary talent. But the outcomes may be importantly different from those intended!

The stimulus.   The stimulus that gains the greatest control over behavior is that very particular complex of effective energy changes impinging on the person at the moment that learning occurs. This learning generalizes to similar stimuli in proportion to the degree of similarity. Stimuli may acquire increased similarity or distinctiveness by virtue of having associated with them same or different responses respectively. The stimulus complex includes not only specific external events but also their context (spatial and temporal), the relationships among them, and internal cues to prevailing states or past responses. Learning may to some extent be focused on aspects of the stimulus complex to which the person is selectively oriented and attending. Finally, the attractiveness of stimuli satiates over time of exposure.

Let us review some of these assertions in an educational context. If a student studies arithmetic in the same room at the same time each day, he learns to be better at arithmetic in that room at that time. If a student learns aversive reactions to one course in "math," he will also respond aversively to other courses with a similar title or context. And if the stimuli arising in class each day are very much the same, he becomes bored with school.

The response.   The response that is learned best is that very particular pattern of movements, at the particular speed or amplitude made, described dynamically as a moment-by-moment process over time. This learning generalizes to some extent to responses that are similar either qualitatively or quantitatively, the degree of similarity among responses being dependent upon the degree of similarity of the resulting feedback. All responses produce characteristic internal feedback stimuli via channels of proprioception and kinethesis. People feel themselves responding in particular ways and use these cues to differentiate among responses. Some responses also affect the environment so as to produce characteristic external feedback stimuli. People observe the changes in the environment and their relationship to it; these cues also differentiate among responses. It is also possible for different responses to acquire a degree of equivalence on the basis of equivalent treatment by the environment; conversely, similar responses may acquire increased distinctiveness if differentially reinforced. And finally, the attractiveness of responses satiates over time of practice.

In an educational context, we are saying that the student who practices doing arithmetic at a slow, careful pace is learning to be slow in arithmetic. If a student learns to spell out loud, he will make more spelling errors in writing. However, spelling a word aloud, writing the word down, circling the correct spelling on a page, or indicating a choice on an answer sheet are topographically distinctive responses which may acquire some degree of equivalence by virtue of being scored similarly by teachers. And if prolonged practice of the same material is required, the student becomes bored with it.

Motivation. Motivational factors are typically considered to be ones whose effects on behavior can be increased or decreased rapidly. In that sense, there are two motivational factors in the present theory, namely, drive and incentive. Indeed, we have seen that the feature distinguishing incentive theory from reinforcement theory is the assumption that rewards affect performance in a motivational manner. Here it has been assumed that these two aspects of the motivational complex are intimately related, drive reflecting the person's wants and incentive reflecting his expectation of satisfying them.

Hence, if one asks about a student's motivation to learn, the question has two parts. Thus, to say that he is motivated by grades is to say both that he wants to get good grades, perhaps from fear of failure, and that he expects to do so if he studies. To say that he is motivated to please his parents is to say that he wants that outcome and expects it if he does well in school. It should be re-emphasized in this context, however, that the present view is that motivation is not directly necessary for learning. Nevertheless, motivation does importantly affect what is practiced — and hence learned — and thus is an important part of any attempt to control learning in an educational setting.

Extrinsic and Intrinsic Motivation to Learn

Some responses naturally reduce prevailing drives. Eating reduces hunger, drinking reduces thirst, and copulating reduces the sex drive. These drives may, therefore, be thought of as intrinsic sources of motivation for the performance of these consummatory responses. By *intrinsic* is meant that drive reduction is inherently occasioned by the very nature of the response. On the other hand, many responses, including the consummatory ones, may be motivated extrinsically. A thirsty rat will press a bar, a hungry pigeon will peck a key and a sexually aroused human will spend money — all, of course, in the interest of making subsequent consummatory responses. By *extrinsic* is meant that drive reduction, although enabled after a response, does not directly result from the response itself.

This distinction is not always clear cut. For example, the consummatory responses of eating, drinking, and having sexual relations have, as a by-product of the antagonism between the branches of the autonomic nervous system, an implicit effect of reducing anxiety. Similarly, working for water might simultaneously reduce an "activity drive." Nevertheless, we shall reserve as intrinsic motivation those situations where the response uniformly leads to direct drive reduction.

Extrinsic motivation to learn. Any drive will motivate behavior, insure exposure to environmental events, and hence lead to learning. And the reduction of any drive will lead to incentive motivation to repeat that learned response. Frequently, incentive to learn in the classroom is provided by extrinsic sources of motivation. For example, praise by parents and teachers provides for a reduction in the fear of social disapproval and will motivate a child to learn arithmetic. So, too, threats and restrictions on freedom may be imposed to induce a student to expose himself to the material to be learned. Somewhat more positively, money or presents may be earned by a good report card.

There are two problems associated with the use of extrinsic motivation (drive and incentive) to learn. One of these concerns identifying events that are rewarding; the second concerns understanding the principles surrounding their use so as to maximize their effectiveness. The first problem is important not only so that a teacher may know what rewards are available for her use, but also to help avoid misusing unknown rewards. For example, being listened to and paid attention by someone is a powerful reward to most people, presumably because it helps reduce chronic fears of inferiority. This reward can be used to encourage class discussion; it can also be misused since, if the utterance is not desirable, listening to it will reward it.

The theoretical proposition that reward is occasioned by the reduction in a prevailing drive may have limited value in identifying rewards in a classroom. This is because it is often more difficult to identify drives than to identify rewards. A more practical approach is to follow a functional approach: Events that are rewarding are rewarding. That is to say, the teacher can determine by trial what events have rewarding value for a student and then, regardless of what drive that reward is servicing, use it to establish incentive motivation for desired responses.

Concerning the effective use of known rewards, the major impact of incentive theory on education pertains to correlated reinforcement. Conditions of correlated reinforcement are ones in which some dimension of the reward (its amount, delay, quality, or probability) vary systematically with some dimension of the response (its speed, vigor, or rate). The importance of correlated reinforcement results from the interpretation that maximal incentive motivation results from maximal reward, and if this depends on the way the response is made, the learner will come to practice and hence learn that way of responding that is maximally rewarded.

A great deal of research, both in the laboratory and in the classroom, will be needed to refine the techniques of correlated reinforcement. Suppose, for example, that a teacher is given money, toys, or other attractive objects to use as rewards for learning; there is still the question of when most effectively to bestow the rewards. Correlated reinforcement says only that more reward should be given for better performance but it does not say how to arrange that correlation. Specifically, should the condition be lenient so that rewards are given for every response except the very worst ones or should it be stringent, rewarding only the few best responses? Should the condition provide for small increments in reward for small improvements in performance, or should a large change in reward be concentrated to distinguish the better from the worse responses? We do not yet have general principles, much less specific guidelines to advise the teacher.

The one rule we can state confidently is that the correlation in reward must make contact with the individual's performance. That is to say, variations in reward must occur within the range of variation in performance of which the learner is then capable. In effect, the standards should not be absolute but should be relative to the student's current level of proficiency. As a specific illustration, an arithmetic teacher who gives an occasional speed test to encourage fast work and who gives stars to the student who finishes first is not having the desired effect on the majority of the class who never earn a star. Even though some individuals may have performed faster than usual for them, no differential reinforcement occurs to shape their behavior.

The fact that correlated reinforcement encourages the learner to perform in the desired manner is only part of the story; it is further the case that he learns to perform in whatever manner he practices. Hence, unless correlated reinforcement is used to insure that the desired responses are practiced, quite unintentional results may obtain. We earlier suggested that students may learn to do arithmetic slowly, just as we know they learn to read slowly. They may also learn to talk, listen, and think at a particular speed. Indeed, learners even learn to learn under particular conditions (Rogers, 1967). To demonstrate this last assertion, students may be presented with a series of paired-associates lists to learn, with the rate of presentation controlled at different speeds for different learners. Over the series of lists, they learn to learn such lists. But if they are then given a new list to learn at a different rate of presentation, be it slower or faster, they cannot learn as well.

Intrinsic motivation to learn.   There are several concepts that could be used to identify intrinsic sources of motivation for learning. The most familiar of these are the so-called curiosity, exploratory, or manipulatory drives. In keeping with the principle that one learns anything he experiences, a drive such as curiosity would lead an organism to expose himself to novel stimuli and as a result, to learn. The difficulty with these concepts has been that they have appeared to be too vague to incorporate within a more general, formal theory of learning. The necessity to anchor one's hypothetical constructs to both independent and dependent variables is widely recognized but has not been fully realized by those intent upon demonstrating that not all behavior is motivated by hunger, thirst, sex, pain, and fear.

Although there might be much to gain from attempting to build on these earlier concepts, I would like to explore a somewhat different approach, namely, that *there is a primary drive to learn.* At present, I can only speculate about this approach, about explicitly anchoring the learning drive to antecedent conditions and consequent events, and about its implications in conjunction with the other constructs of incentive theory. Hopefully, the following tentative ideas will help stimulate its further development.

The learning drive is a result of deprivation, more like sex than hunger and thirst. That is to say, although physical and mental well-being are probably enhanced by healthy expression of the drive, satisfaction of it is not necessary for individual survival. Furthermore, excessive indulgence is possible but not productive. The consummatory response is learning, or more properly, exposure to situations in which learning can occur. In the presence of a prevailing learning drive, learning is inherently reinforcing; the greater the learning, the greater the reinforcement and hence the greater the incentive motivation to practice those responses that led to learning. In turn, the learning drive increases asymptotically with deprivation of an opportunity to learn (a more specific hypothesis will be proposed shortly).

Sequentially, events run the following course: The deprived person has some level of the learning drive. This drive can be reduced by any form of learning — academic, athletic, social, etc. Historically, the person will have found some situations more productive of learning than others and, insofar as possible, this stronger incentive motivation will lead the motivated person to prefer those situations. Once the learning drive is thus reduced, further efforts based on extrinsic motivation will be largely fruitless.

The concept of a learning drive is to be evaluated principally by its behavioral implications. However, it may help give a better understanding of this concept if it is considered in terms of a widely speculative physiological base. Imagine, then, that learning either requires the availability of certain biochemical substances in the brain and/or involves the production of waste by-products which impede further learning. The strength of the learning drive would then reflect these particular biochemical states of the brain. The necessary substances are produced and/or the waste substances eliminated during times when learning is not occurring; a more radical, but I think probable hypothesis is that these restorative processes occur predominantly during dream sleep. In any event, the drive to learn might profitably be thought of *as if* based on whatever physiological process constitutes learning.

At this point, one might ask the question whether the learning-drive concept can imply the phenomena that have led to notions such as curiosity. I believe the answer is largely affirmative, but I also believe that exploring that question in depth would require a clearer description of the conditions necessary for learning. Important as that goal is, our present purposes are better served simply by mentioning several implications of this idea for education.

First and most important, the belief that one must motivate students to learn, in the sense of *drive* motivation, is in error; people are naturally, intrinsically motivated to learn. Undoubtedly, there are some individual differences in the maximum strength of this drive, but the real task of motivating students is to provide *incentive* motivation. The student is motivated to learn something, somewhere, somehow. If the educational program is one in which his efforts to learn are highly successful, the resulting drive reduction will directly reward those efforts and generate incentive motivation to repeat them in future states of learning-drive motivation. If, however, his efforts are relatively unsuccessful, he will come to prefer contexts other than the classroom in which to learn. The goal, then, is to develop appetites for learning particular materials.

Extrinsic sources of motivation may be useful in this connection. If a student has not discovered that he can learn from a particular program, or if he has discovered that he cannot learn from what appear to be similar programs, then he will not adequately expose himself to the program on the basis of the intrinsic learning drive. In such cases, other inducements may encourage such exposure until the resulting learning experiences generate sufficient incentive to be self-perpetuating.

It also follows that relatively little is to be gained from requiring practice in the absence of any drive to learn. In the classroom, this may be difficult to estimate. But in principle, the time to stop practice for the day is when the student has stopped learning from an effective program. This may provide one basis for the familiar advantage of distributed practice in learning. In this context, it should be noted that other-than-academic learning reduces the learning drive.

There are any number of practical implications involving optimal scheduling of classes and other activities. And if the physiological speculations have any merit, exciting possibilities for the motivation and control of learning will arise. But it would be premature to do more at this time than to offer this concept of a primary drive to learn, imbedded within a more general theory of learning and motivation, as a promising one for discussion and future research.

REFERENCES

Cofer, C. N., and Appley, M. H. *Motivation: Theory and research.* New York: Wiley, 1964.

Guthrie, E. R. Reward and punishment. *Psychological Review,* 1934, *41,* 450–460.

Hull, C. L. *Principles of behavior.* New York: Appleton-Century-Crofts, 1943.

Hull, C. L. *A behavior system.* New Haven: Yale University Press, 1952.

Logan, F. A. Punishment as negative incentive. In B. A. Campbell and R. Church (Eds.), *Punishment and aversive control.* New York: Appleton-Century-Crofts, 1969. Pp. 43–54.

Logan, F. A., and Boice, R. Aggressive behaviors of paired rodents in an avoidance context. *Behavior,* 1969, *34,* 161–183.

Meehl, P. E. On the circularity of the law of effect. *Psychological Bulletin,* 1950, *47,* 52–75.

Miller, N. E. Some reflections on the law of effect produce a new alternative to drive reduction. In M. R. Jones (Ed.), *Nebraska Symposium on Motivation.* Lincoln: University of Nebraska Press, 1963. Pp. 65–112.

Mowrer, O. H. On the dual nature of learning — A reinterpretation of "conditioning" and "problem solving." *Harvard Educational Review,* 1947, *17,* 102–148.

Mowrer, O. H. *Learning theory and behavior.* New York: Wiley, 1960.

Rogers, J. G. Input and output speed components of learning-to-learn. Unpublished doctoral dissertation, University of New Mexico, 1967.

Seward, J. P. Drive, incentive and reinforcement. *Psychological Review*, 1956, *63*, 195–203.

Sheffield, F. D. Relation between classical conditioning and instrumental learning. In W. F. Prokasy (Ed.), *Classical conditioning: A symposium*. New York: Appleton-Century-Crofts, 1965.

Sheffield, F. D. A drive-induction theory of reinforcement. In R. N. Haber (Ed.), *Current research in motivation*. New York: Holt, 1966. Pp. 98–121.

Skinner, B. F. *Behavior of organisms*. New York: Appleton-Century-Crofts, 1938.

Spence, K. W. Theoretical interpretations of learning. In S. S. Stevens (Ed.), *Handbook of experimental psychology*. New York: Wiley, 1951. Pp. 690–711.

Spence, K. W. *Behavior theory and conditioning*. New Haven: Yale University Press, 1956.

Tolman, E. C. *Purposive behavior in animals and men*. New York: Appleton-Century-Crofts, 1932.

Ulrich, R., and Azrin, N. H. Reflexive fighting in response to aversive stimulation. *Journal of Experimental Analysis of Behavior*, 1962, *5*, 511–521.

Williams, D. R., and Williams, H. Auto maintenance in the pigeon: Sustained pecking despite contingent nonreinforcement. *Journal of Experimental Analysis of Behavior*, 1969, *12*, 511–520.

SOME PROBLEMS WITH INCENTIVE MOTIVATION TO LEARN

ROGER W. BLACK
University of South Carolina

Professor Logan has sought to provide a tentative analysis of the roles of motivation in the classroom learning situation. He notes that most textbooks concerned with this problem (i.e., with educational psychology) tend to be of the "cookbook" variety; that is, they describe specific teaching procedures to be used in particular situations without providing any general principles from which these recommended procedures can be derived or by which they can be justified. One of Professor Logan's purposes was to demonstrate the possibility of deriving recommendations regarding classroom procedures as implications of a much more general theory of learning.

Professor Logan assumes that the classroom learning situation involves at least two classes of factors; learning per se and motivation (drive and incentive motivation). Learning occurs solely as the result of the contiguity between events; drive impels the subject to act and become exposed to contiguous events; and, incentive motivation results from reinforcement (drive reduction) and reflects subject's expectations with respect to the reward or punishment contingencies associated with particular responses. Within this context the basic question becomes: What provides the motivation and reinforcement for learning in the classroom?

There are, of course, a variety of potential sources of such motivation and reward: achievement motivation, praise or reproof from teachers and parents, competition with peers, and so forth. Logan refers to these as forms of extrinsic motivation in that the responses (e.g., studying, learning) do not themselves reduce drive but do enable subsequent drive reduction. Some responses, on the other hand, are viewed as "naturally" or "inherently" reducing the prevailing drive. These are frequently consummatory responses (such as eating in the case of hunger) and are described as "intrinsically motivated." Logan assumes that learning falls into this latter class. There is a primary "drive to learn," learning reduces this drive, and the responses which led to such learning are thus reinforced.

The view that there is something in the process of learning which is inherently reinforcing seems quite plausible to me. I wonder, however, if it is necessary to postulate a "drive to learn" in order to account for this apparent reinforcement effect. If one adopts the view that incentive motivation to learn is an important determinant of classroom performance and that such incentive motivation depends upon drive reduction, then the importance of finding a drive which learning reduces is obvious. There seem to be, however, considerable data which suggest that drive reduction may not be a necessary condition for the occurrence of reinforcement or the establishment of incentive motivation. For example, there are a variety of experimental results which seem quite consistent with the view that the evocation of a consummatory response, even in the absence of any discernible drive reduction, is a sufficient condition for reinforcement or the development of incentive motivation. If this is the case, then it is at least possible that the reinforcement inherent in learning results from the occurrence of intrinsically reinforcing responses rather than the reduction of a special "drive to learn."

The preceding comments do not differ radically from those stated by Professor Logan. Indeed, he specifically refers to learning as a "consummatory response" which is inherently reinforcing. Thus, the only difference regards the matter of whether it is necessary to postulate a special "drive to learn," the reduction of which constitutes the reinforcement. It is true, of course, that if no "drive to learn" is postulated, other motivational conditions under which learning occurs must be specified. It is possible that such motivation may result entirely from "extrinsic sources."

A final question in this connection regards the specification of the "consummatory response" involved in learning which possesses inherent reinforcement properties. The statement that "the consummatory response is learning, or more properly, exposure to situations in which learning can occur (p. 58)," seems to somewhat strain the usual definitions of a response. It is, no doubt, perfectly reasonable to refer to learning as a "response" in a neurological sense, but behaviorally it usually refers to some sort of change in the association between a stimulus and response or between two or more stimuli, and so forth. Similarly, "exposure to situations in which learning can occur (p. 58)" would seem more conventionally described as a stimulus event rather than a response event. This is not to suggest that one or both of these elements of the learning process might not be source of reinforcement for that process; rather, it suggests that neither element resembles "consummatory responses" as the term is generally used.

There is one possible candidate for the equivalent or analogue of a "consummatory response" in the learning process which can be mentioned in a most tentative and preliminary manner. When events are experienced under appropriate circumstances they are apparently "encoded" or "stored" in some manner, i.e., they are learned. In Professor Logan's view, with which I concur, such learning proceeds on the basis of contiguity. Subsequently, appropriate circumstances may lead the *subject* to "retrieve" the information which he has learned, e.g., to recall a name or to make an instrumental response. It seems possible that the act of retrieving or recalling an association constitutes the analogue of a "consummatory response" in learning; each time it is recalled, it is inherently reinforced by the very act of recall. Some of the findings from studies of short-term memory seem consistent with this assumption. Thus, if following the presentation of a verbal stimulus, little or no opportunity for retrieval or rehearsal is permitted, very little learning and/or retention is observed.

Turning to another matter, Professor Logan describes a number of implications of his analysis with respect to classroom teaching. I find his discussion of these implications to be interesting and illuminating, especially his pointing out the desirability of correlated reinforcement in the classroom. Thus, high levels of performance should be associated with "large" or "good" reinforcements, while low levels of performance should be associated with "small" or "poorer" reinforcements. In this manner, the student is encouraged to maximize performance in order to maximize reward. It is not clear whether Logan would consider knowledge of results as a form of reinforcement in the classroom learning. If one does, however, then it is clear that correlated reinforcement is employed in most educational settings — i.e., test scores and grades, and the like, are, hopefully, correlated with level of performance. It is intriguing to speculate as to the effect of making test scores and test performance non-correlated by assigning nominal scores to students in a random manner. Presumably, since the student would not be able to maximize reinforcement in this situation, his performance would show less improvement and be poorer than that of students trained with correlated reinforcement. As Logan notes, a great deal of research needs to be done before attempting to formulate general principles to serve as guidelines for the teacher.

Another important implication of Professor Logan's analysis regards the details of what it is that the student is learning. He notes that if learning is reinforcing and reinforces practice, then *how* the student performs *what* he has learned will depend upon how he practices it. If he practices a task slowly, he will perform it slowly. If this is true, then the particular techniques of instruction adopted by an individual teacher would be expected to significantly affect his students' performance. Thus, one source of differences between the effectiveness of different teachers might lie in their choice of details of the teaching methods that are not usually standardized or even specified.

Professor Logan assumes that individual differences in "drive to learn" are not of great importance — at least in comparison with differences in incentive motivation. I found this somewhat puzzling since it seems obvious that people do differ greatly in what appears to be "drive to learn." If I understand him correctly, his explanation is that students in educational programs in which their efforts at learning have been highly successful will be highly motivated to study or practice in those programs. Students who have not been successful will not be motivated to work in those programs but may be in some different situations. This does not seem to account for the fact that wide individual differences exist even among students in the same program. Such differences are, of course, often attributed to differences in ability to learn (e.g., intelligence). A theory of classroom learning will almost certainly have to take such differences into account.

In summary, Professor Logan has sought to apply his general theoretical approach to learning and motivation to some problems of educational psychology. He concerns himself primarily with the problem of motivation to learn and concludes that there is a primary "drive to learn" which serves as the basis for the establishment of incentive motivation to learn. He also describes several implications of his approach, although he points out that a great deal of research must be carried out before these implications can genuinely be evaluated. Perhaps of greatest importance, however, is that Professor Logan has rather convincingly demonstrated the possibility of applying principles generated in simple laboratory situations to the analysis of much more complex behavior occurring outside of the laboratory.

4

HUMAN MEMORY AND THE CONCEPT OF REINFORCEMENT[1]

RICHARD C. ATKINSON and THOMAS D. WICKENS[2]

Stanford University

The purpose of this paper is to offer a theory about the role of reinforcement in human learning and to evaluate the theory against data from several different types of experiments. It should be emphasized that this analysis is restricted to human learning. Our discussion of reinforcement will be based on a more general theory of memory (Atkinson and Shiffrin, 1968a) that has been derived primarily from results of verbal-learning experiments. The remarks that we shall make about reinforcement have not been applied outside of this context, and accordingly we

[1]Preparation of this paper was supported by the National Aeronautics and Space Administration, Grant NGR-05-020-036, and by a fellowship from the National Institutes of Health to the second author. The authors would like to thank several of their co-workers who carried out experiments reported here; each will be acknowledged at the appropriate point in the paper. Thanks are also due to William Cook, Geoffrey Loftus, and John Schnorr for a critical reading of an earlier draft of this paper.

[2]Now at the University of California, Los Angeles.

are unwilling at this time to extrapolate the analysis to animal learning.

In his discussion of the law of effect, Thorndike (1931) proposed two alternative views regarding the nature of reinforcement. One view, which he favored, assumed that the action of a reinforcement produced a direct and automatic strengthening of stimulus-response associations. The other view, which Thorndike considered and rejected, postulated that reinforcement did not affect learning per se, but rather determined the choice of a response once the subject recalled the relevant events that had occurred on preceding trials of the experiment. These two alternative views have been maintained in the literature since that time, and much research has been done in an attempt to determine which is the true state of affairs (for an excellent review of this research see Postman, 1962). This distinction may be useful in a general way to categorize theories of reinforcement, but it is becoming increasingly clear that the set of theories qualifying in each category is so large and variegated that it is not possible to formulate experimental tests which meaningfully differentiate between them. With this reservation in mind, it still seems worth noting that we regard our discussion of reinforcement as most closely allied to the second of the two views. Thus our analysis is in general accord with the theorizing of Tolman (1932) and with the more recent analyses offered by Estes (1969) and by Buchwald (1969).

Our discussion of learning and memory is in terms of information-processing concepts (Broadbent, 1963; Simon and Newell, 1964). Accordingly, we view the processes involved in learning as an exchange and transfer of information between a number of memory storage units. The nature of these transfers and the properties of the storage units will be specified in some detail, but we offer no speculations about their inner structure or possible physiological representations. In our view, learning involves the transfer of information generated by sources both external and internal to the organism into some form of memory store that can hold it until it is needed later. Reinforcement is a modulation of this information flow. A reinforcing event, in this sense, serves two functions: first, to set in motion the processes that cause the transfer to take place, and second, to select what information is to be transferred. When the study of some item occurs in an experiment, information associated with it is coded and transferred to the subject's memory. In order to produce a response at a later point in time, this information must be retrieved by a process which involves a more or less active search of memory. Thus, the operations involved in a typical learning situation can be divided into two classes, one associated with storage and the other with retrieval of information from memory. In many experiments this distinction is reflected in the study and test phases of a trial. The distinction between storage and retrieval is fundamental to the system and is reflected in our analysis of reinforcement.

Reinforcement manipulations that affect the storage process are the ones most commonly studied. Indeed, typically when the term reinforcement is used, it refers to operations that cause information about events which have taken place (including, perhaps, the reinforcing event itself) to be stored. To understand how transfer is effected, it is necessary to realize that a reinforcing event plays two separate and distinct roles in determining the storage of information: an informational role and an attentional role.

The first concerns the knowledge that is provided by giving feedback to the subject about whether or not his response to a particular stimulus was correct. When a subject is told that his response was, for example, correct, this provides the information that he must store to assure correct performance on subsequent trials. The quality of this feedback can be varied in a number of ways, most obviously by varying the amount of information provided to the subject after an error. The use of a correction procedure, in which the subject is told the response that should have been made after an error, makes more information available than does a partial correction or a noncorrection procedure in which the correct response is not completely specified (Bower, 1962; Keller, Cole, Burke, and Estes, 1965; Millward, 1964). The quality of information provided by the feedback also can be manipulated by introducing a delay between the subject's response and this feedback. Under these conditions, some information about the situation may be lost or confused, so that the feedback information, when presented, is of less value.

The attentional component of reinforcement in the storage process is closely related to conventional ideas of reward. Reinforcement, in this sense, acts to direct the subject's attention to one aspect of the situation and not to others. Thus, when a reward is associated with certain items presented for learning and not with others, more study may be given to the rewarded items and consequently they may be learned more rapidly (Harley, 1965a). Indeed, we postulate that this is the principal role of incentives when presented at the time of study: to cause the subject to attend to certain items or aspects of the situation more intensely than to others.

The storage aspects of reinforcement have received a good deal of study. The same cannot be said about the role of reinforcement in the retrieval of information and the production of a response. Again, we believe that these effects can take at least two forms. On the one hand, when the payoff value associated with a particular item is presented at the time of study, it may become part of the information complex placed in memory and may even determine where in memory it is stored. If this is the case, storage for an item with a high payoff value, for example, will be different in some way from storage of an item with low payoff. Knowledge given at the time of test regarding the payoff value assigned to the item, therefore, can aid the subject by indicating where in memory to look and hence cause him to set up a more effective search. The other effect that reinforcement may have on retrieval is to dictate the effort and time the subject is willing to spend in searching memory. It often happens that the information necessary to produce a response may be available in memory, but for various reasons cannot be recovered without an extended search. Presumably, when items are presented for test which have been assigned high payoff values, the subject will engage in a more extensive search and hence will be more likely to retrieve the appropriate information. Unfortunately, these two effects are largely speculative and have not been carefully documented experimentally. We have, however, undertaken some preliminary studies, which will be described later, on reinforcement effects during retrieval.

The main body of this paper is divided into two sections. The first develops the theoretical system, and the second deals with applications of the theory to a number of experimental situations. The theoretical section begins with a fairly extensive discussion of the structure of human memory. Although this discussion will not explicitly consider the question of reinforcement, the nature of the reinforcing process is so much determined by how the subject uses his memory that it cannot be analyzed without first considering these more basic processes. As we have noted above, the action of reinforcement may be thought of, in part, as an attentional process. Accordingly, the second step in our analysis specifies more exactly the ways in which attention acts within the framework of the theory. This consideration brings us in turn to a discussion of reinforcement.

In the second section the theory is applied to a number of experiments involving the manipulation of reinforcement variables. The first of these demonstrates the workings of the memory system when items are given varying numbers of reinforcements under different presentation sched-. ules. This example will also illustrate a number of the complexities that can plague an analysis of reinforcement: in particular, the ways in which the short- and long-term properties of memory can lead to apparently contradictory effects. The second application examines delay of reinforcement and illustrates how this variable can have many different effects depending on the precise conditions of learning. The role of feedback in learning will be examined in another way as part of a third experiment, using a concept-identification paradigm. One of the primary purposes of this discussion is to demonstrate that the actual responses made by a subject frequently fail to provide an adequate indicator of the reinforcing processes involved. The experiment will also show how superficially similar reinforcements can have markedly different effects, depending upon the strategy used by the subject. Finally, the last set of experiments considers the ways in which reward magnitude can lead to selective study of certain items and, in turn, affect both the storage and retrieval of information.

Before starting our discussion, a warning should be added. We view reinforcement as a complex process and one which is derived from other, more fundamental aspects of the learning situation. Because of this fact, the effects of reinforcement are often quite varied, both in their appearance and in the manner by which they are produced. Our discussion, therefore, may well prove unsatisfactory to someone who is looking for a single, unified law to explain all reinforcement phenomena. Such a law, we feel, does not exist.

Theoretical System

The memory system. Although the theory on which our discussion of reinforcement will be based has been described in other papers (Atkinson and Shiffrin, 1965, 1968a,b; Shiffrin and Atkinson, 1969), a brief review will provide a starting point for the work to be presented. This discussion will not present the theory in its full detail. In particular, no attempt will be made to consider all of the possible variants of the memory system, nor will explicit mathematical predictions of the theory be derived. For these matters, and for a description of the evidence which supports this formulation, the reader is referred to the previously cited theoretical papers and to reports of related experimental work (Atkinson, 1969; Atkinson, Brelsford, and Shiffrin, 1967; Brelsford and Atkinson, 1968; Brelsford, Shiffrin, and Atkinson, 1968; Freund, Loftus, and Atkinson, 1969; Phillips, Shiffrin, and Atkinson, 1967; Rundus, 1970; Rundus and Atkinson, 1970; Shiffrin, 1968; Thomson, 1967).

In what follows, the memory system will be assumed to be divided into three components: a sensory register (SR) which receives information from the sense organs; a short-term store (STS) which may temporarily hold information that has been passed to it, either from the SR or from the third component of the system, the long-term store (LTS). The LTS represents permanent memory, and it is only here that information[3]

---

[3]In this paper the term "information" is used to refer to codes, mnemonics, images, or other material that the subject places in memory and that can help him to generate a response; we will not use the term in its formal information-theoretic sense.

may be retained for an extended period of time. All three of these stores are capable of retaining information received from any of the sense modalities. Since the experiments that will be discussed in this paper have used verbal material exclusively, no attempt will be made to consider memory other than of a linguistic nature. This restriction does not represent a limitation of the theory, since the system can accommodate other sorts of material (see Atkinson and Shiffrin, 1968a, for a more complete discussion).

At the outset, it is important to make a distinction between two aspects of the proposed memory system. On the one hand, there are certain fixed structural features of the system that are invariant and cannot be modified by the subject. On the other hand, the operation of the system is determined by a set of control processes that may change from one point in time to another. Thus, for example, information that is transferred from the SR to LTS must pass through STS since the functional connections between the three states are structural aspects of the system. The way in which STS is used to make this transfer, however, is a control process selected by the subject that can be quite different in nature from one task to the next. In one task the subject may use STS to rehearse several items simultaneously in order to maintain them over a short retention interval, whereas in another task each item may be studied and coded individually in an attempt to form a mental image for longterm storage. We shall return to an example in which different uses of STS are illustrated after a brief description of the components and control processes of the system.

The interconnections between the three stores are illustrated in Fig. 4-1. New information can enter the system only via the SR. In order to be retained, it must be passed from there to STS. It is in this store that most processing of information takes place. The STS, therefore, receives input not only from the SR but also from LTS. Information may be transferred from LTS to STS, for example, during recall, during the formation of associations while coding an item, or during the comparisons of one event with the memory of another. Finally, information which is to be permanently stored in LTS is "copied" into it from STS. Notice that the transfer of information from one store to another is a nondestructive process; that is, the information in the original store is not lost as a result of a transfer per se.

In the case of visual input[4], the information entered into the SR usually takes the form of a fairly complete image of the observed scene which will decay in a matter of a few hundred milliseconds. The control processes at this level are concerned primarily with the selection of ma-

---

[4]The properties of the SR are best known for visual input; for some information on other modalities, however, see Crowder and Morton, 1969; Hill and Bliss, 1968.

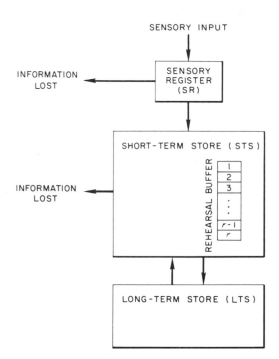

FIGURE 4-1. Structure of the memory system.

terial for transfer to STS. Much more information is present in the SR than it is possible to transfer to STS. For example, partial report studies of visual memory (Sperling, 1960) show that subjects are able to recall correctly one line of a tachistoscopically presented 3×4 array of letters if they are instructed which line to remember immediately after presentation. If the recall instruction is delayed by more than a tenth of a second, the number of letters that are correctly recalled drops sharply, indicating that information originally present in the SR was lost before it could be transferred to STS.

Information entered in STS will also decay, but at a slower rate than in the SR. The measurement of this decay is complicated by the fact that the subject is able to retain information in STS almost indefinitely by rehearsal. Experiments (e.g., Peterson and Peterson, 1959) which attempt to prevent rehearsal have generally indicated that, without rehearsal, information in STS decays with a half-life on the order of ten to fifteen seconds, the exact rate being highly dependent on the interpolated activity (Spring, 1968).

Control processes associated with STS may be grouped into three classes. The first of these classes is associated with the search for information in STS and its retrieval. There is evidence that the storage of information in STS is structured, hence that the use of a particular search strategy may lead to more or less rapid recovery of certain aspects of the data (Murdock, 1967; Sternberg, 1966). These search processes do not play an important role in experiments of the type that we shall be considering in this paper, so will not concern us further.

The second class of control processes in STS is far more important in the typical learning experiment. Processes of this type involve the rehearsal of items in STS in order to circumvent their decay. As long as information is rehearsed in STS it is preserved, but it begins to decay as soon as rehearsal ceases. In order to formalize this rehearsal process, it is assumed that the subject sets up a buffer in STS that can hold a fixed number, r, of items (see Fig. 4-1). This buffer is not a structural feature of the system, but is set up by the subject when required. The size of this buffer, when it exists, will depend both on the nature of the material that is being rehearsed and on the learning strategy that the subject is currently employing. It is not necessary that every item which enters STS be incorporated into the rehearsal buffer. The decision as to whether an item is to be entered into the buffer is another control process and depends on, among other things, the nature of the item and on the current contents of the buffer. Since the buffer is of fixed capacity, when an item is entered another must be deleted. The probability that a particular item in the buffer is forced out depends on such factors as the age of the item, the ease with which it can be rehearsed, and so forth (Brelsford and Atkinson, 1968). Once an item has been deleted from the buffer it undergoes rapid decay in STS.

The third important class of STS control processes are those associated with the transfer of information to LTS. In general, whenever information is in STS, some of it will be transferred to LTS. What is transferred, however, may vary greatly, both in the quantity and the quality of the resultant representation in LTS. If the major portion of the subject's effort is devoted to rehearsal in STS, relatively little information will be transferred to LTS, whereas if he attempts to develop appropriate ways of organizing and encoding the material, a great deal may be transferred. For example, in the learning of paired-associates, long-term performance is greatly improved if the subject searches for some word or phrase that will mediate between the stimulus and the response rather than simply rehearsing the item (Montague, Adams, and Kiess, 1966). Of course, the reduced rate of transfer to LTS as the result of the generation of a rehearsal buffer is frequently offset by the greater length of time which the information will reside in STS and hence be available for transfer to LTS. The size of the buffer can also affect the rate at which information is transferred in another way. All of the items in STS at any one time are, in a sense, competing for transfer to LTS. Thus, when the buffer is large, the amount of information transferred to LTS about each item is proportionally smaller.

In the view of this theory, information that is stored in LTS is not subject to decay. Information, once stored, remains in LTS indefinitely. This does not imply, however, that this information will always be immediately available for recall. It is essential here to distinguish between the storage of information in LTS and its retrieval. Information which has been stored at one time may fail to be retrieved at a later time either because the strategy which the subject employed to locate the information is inadequate, or because later learning may have resulted in the storage of additional information that was sufficiently similar to that stored about the item in question as to render the original information, when recovered, insufficient for the generation of a correct response. In general, the control processes which are associated with LTS are involved with storage and with the determination of appropriate search routines. These will not be important in the discussion of reinforcement to follow, so the reader is again referred to the papers by Atkinson and Shiffrin (1968a,b) and Shiffrin and Atkinson (1969).

In the remainder of this section, an unpublished study run by Geoffrey Loftus at Stanford University will be described. We have three reasons for presenting this experiment. First, it will illustrate the continuous paired-associate task that has been used in much of the experimental work to be considered later in this paper. Second, it will extend our discussion of the memory system, in particular indicating how it can be given an explicit quantitative formulation. Finally, the experiment will provide an illustration of the way in which control processes in STS are affected by the nature of the task.

In this experiment, subjects were required to keep track of a randomly changing response paired with each of nine different stimuli. To be more specific, the task proceeded as follows: At the start of the experiment each of the nine stimuli (which were the digits 1 through 9) was paired with a randomly selected letter from the alphabet. After these initial presentations the experiment proper began. At the start of each trial a randomly chosen stimulus was presented to the subject, and he was required to make a response indicating which letter had last been paired with it. As soon as the response had been made, the same stimulus was presented for study paired with a new response chosen at random from the twenty-five letters not just paired with the stimulus. The subject had been instructed to forget the old stimulus-response pairing and to remember only the new one. After a brief study period this pair disappeared and the next trial was started. In this manner three hundred trials could be presented during a session lasting about an hour.

The motivation for Loftus' experiment was to examine how the type of test employed to measure retention would affect the strategy used by the subject to store information. In particular, strategies were to be examined when the subject knew that he was to be tested using a recognition procedure, when he knew that a recall procedure was to be used, and when he had no information about the type of test. There were, thus, three experimental conditions, only one of which was used during a single session: (1) Items were tested by a recognition procedure; that is, at test a stimulus was presented along with a letter that was either the correct response or another randomly chosen from the remainder of the alphabet. The subject made his choice by striking either a key marked "YES" or a key marked "NO" to indicate whether or not he thought that the letter was indeed the one last paired with the stimulus. This condition will be referred to as the *recognition* condition. (2) Items were tested by a recall procedure; that is, a stimulus was presented alone for test and the subject was instructed to strike a key indicating which of the twenty-six letters of the alphabet he thought was correct. This condition will be referred to as the *recall* condition. (3) On each trial the choice of whether to use a recognition or a recall test was made randomly with equal probability. The data from this *mixed* condition must, therefore, be analyzed in two parts, according to which type of retention test was used. Unlike the other two conditions, when subjects were serving in the mixed condition, they were unable to tell at the time of study how that item would be tested.

Eight college students served in this experiment, each running for a total of sixteen daily sessions. In each session one of the three conditions was used. In order to allow subjects to become familiar with the apparatus and with the nature of the test procedures, the first session was run in the mixed condition and the data collected were excluded from analysis. During the remainder of the experiment each subject served in each condition for a total of five sessions. To avoid warmup effects during the later sessions, the first twenty-five trials of each session were also eliminated. The resulting data consists of 1,375 trials for each condition and each subject. The experiment was controlled by a modified PDP-1 computer which was operated on a time-sharing basis to drive eight KSR-33 teletypes, one for each of the subjects. These teletypes were used to present the material and to receive responses. The output from each teletype was masked so that only a single line of typed material was visible to the subject. This allowed control of the duration of the exposure and prevented the subject from looking back to the results of earlier trials.

Since the stimulus that was presented on a trial was chosen randomly, the number of trials that intervened between the study of a particular stimulus-response pair and its subsequent test was given by a geometric distribution with parameter equal to the reciprocal of the number of stimuli, in this case $1/9$. The data which were collected, therefore, can be summarized by plotting the proportion of correct responses as a function of the number of trials that intervened between study and test. We shall refer to the number of intervening trials as the *lag* of the test for that item. In Fig. 4-2 the proportion of correct responses at a given lag is plotted for each of the conditions. There are over one thousand observations at lag zero for the recall and recognition groups and about half that many for the two curves from the mixed condition. The number of observations falls with increasing lag according to the geometric distribution mentioned above; thus there were only about two hundred observations for each condition by lag 14. Beyond this lag, therefore, the lag curves begin to show considerable instability and have not been plotted. The recognition data

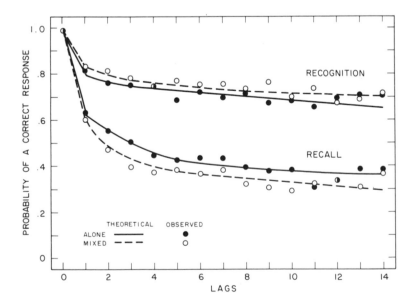

FIGURE 4-2. Probability of a correct response as a function of the lag between study and test for different retention-test conditions.

may be separated into two subsets, depending upon whether the pair presented to the subject for identification was actually correct or incorrect. In Fig. 4-3 lag curves reflecting this distinction are plotted: The upper curves show the probability of a hit (i.e., of a correct identification of a true pair) while the lower curves show the false alarms (i.e., the incorrect designation of a false pair as correct). These two functions were used in the analysis of the recognition data rather than the probability of a correct response.

The lag curves of Figs. 4-2 and 4-3 show a consistent difference between the mixed condition and the two homogeneous conditions. When serving in the recall condition, subjects were able to perform better than in the mixed condition. On the other hand, a greater proportion of the items were correctly recognized in the mixed condition than in the recognition condition. This result is also apparent in the proportion of hits and, to a lesser extent, of false alarms.

In order to interpret these results in terms of the memory system previously discussed, the assumptions of the theory must be given in a more explicit form (for a more detailed discussion of these assumptions and their implications, see Freund, Loftus, and Atkinson, 1969). The first step

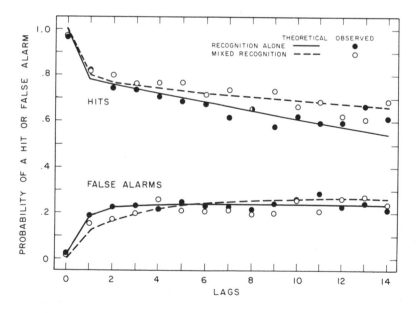

FIGURE 4-3. Probability of a hit and false alarm as a function of the lag between study and test.

is to clarify the conditions under which a new stimulus-response pair will enter a rehearsal buffer in STS. Whenever a stimulus is presented for study, there is a possibility that it will already be in the buffer, although the response that is paired with it will now be incorrect. If this happens, it is assumed that the new pairing invariably replaces the old pairing in the buffer. In the case where the stimulus that is presented for study is not represented in the buffer, we assume that entry is not assured, but takes place with probability α. The value of the parameter α is not known in advance and will need to be estimated from the data. If the new item enters the buffer, another item must be removed so that the buffer size remains constant at r items. As mentioned above, the choice of which item to delete from the buffer depends on many factors, but for this analysis it is sufficient to assume that it is random, with each item having the same probability of being knocked out.

The second set of assumptions that are required to make explicit predictions from the theory involves the transfer of information from STS to LTS. Since every item that is presented enters STS (although it does not necessarily enter the buffer), there will be some minimum amount of information about it transferred to LTS. This quantity of information will be denoted by Θ'. If the item is also included in the buffer, it will reside in STS for a longer period of time, and hence more information about it will be transferred. In particular, it will be assumed that for each trial that passes, an additional amount of information, Θ, will be transferred.[5] Thus, for an item which enters the buffer and resides in it for j trials, the amount of information in LTS will be $\Theta' + j\,\Theta$. For simplicity we identify the two transfer parameters Θ' and Θ so that the information transferred will be $(j + 1)\,\Theta$.

Information once stored in LTS is postulated to remain there indefinitely. Nevertheless, with the passage of time, other information may also be transferred to LTS which makes the original information less easy to

---

[5]The model that is represented by this assumption may be contrasted with a "single pulse" model in which rehearsal in STS does not induce additional information to be transferred to LTS, that is, in which $\Theta = 0$ but $\Theta' > 0$ (Atkinson, Brelsford, and Shiffrin, 1967, Appendix). Evidence for the continual transfer assumption that we have used is provided by a free-recall experiment run by Dewey Rundus at Stanford University (Rundus and Atkinson, 1969). In learning the list of items to be recalled, subjects were instructed to rehearse out loud as the study list was being presented by the experimenter. This rehearsal was tape-recorded, and the set under rehearsal after the presentation of each new item could be precisely determined. Under these conditions the probability of correctly recalling an item when tested was a sharply increasing function of the number of times that it was in the rehearsal buffer: Items that were in the buffer for a single time period were correctly recalled only 12 per cent of the time, while items that were rehearsed for nine or more times were almost always given correctly.

retrieve or which renders it ambiguous once retrieved. To quantify this decrement we assume that *retrievable* information decreases by a proportion $1 - \tau$ for every trial which passes after the item has left STS $(0 < \tau \leq 1)$.[6] In summary, the amount of information which will be retrievable from LTS for an item that remained in the buffer for j trials and was tested at a lag of i trials $(i \geq j)$ is $(j + 1) \Theta \tau^{i-j}$.

The final class of assumptions specifies the relationship between information in LTS and the production of an appropriate response. There are three cases to consider here, depending on the disposition of the item in STS. The first of these is the case where the test is at a lag of zero. It is assumed here that the correct response is always available in STS regardless of whether the item was entered into the rehearsal buffer or not. No error is made. Similarly, when the lag is greater than zero but the item has been entered into the buffer and is still resident in it, a correct response will be made with probability one. Only in the third case, when the item is not in STS and must be retrieved from LTS, is an error possible. The probability that a correct response is produced here will depend upon the amount of information transferred to LTS. There are a number of ways in which this correspondence can be made; in the analysis of the experiment considered here, a postulate based on signal-detection theory was used. This equated the sensitivity parameter, d', with the amount of retrievable information, i.e.,

$$d'_{ij} = (j + 1) \Theta \tau^{i-j}.$$

For the recall data, this value can be converted to the probability of an incorrect response (Elliot, 1964) which we shall denote by η_{ij}. For the recognition data, the results must be analyzed in terms of hits and false alarms, requiring the introduction of a bias parameter, c, associated with the subject's tendency to respond "YES."

---

[6]In a more precise model of memory the decay of information in STS would be represented by the same sort of exponential process that we have used here to describe the deterioration of information in LTS. This loss of information would be through actual decay, however, rather than through problems of retrieval that have been postulated for LTS. Formally, parameters Θ'' and τ'' would be required, the first representing the amount of information available in STS at the time when an item is knocked out of the buffer, the second representing the rate of decay of this information in STS. The amount of information retrievable from both STS and LTS would, therefore, be $(\Theta' + j\Theta) \tau^{i-j} + \Theta''\tau''^{i-j}$. The original amount of information in STS would be greater than that in LTS ($\Theta'' > \Theta$ or Θ'), but its rate of decay would be more rapid ($\tau'' > \tau$) so that the short-term contribution would become negligible while the contribution of LTS was still large. For the purposes of the analysis at hand, however, we can assume that information in LTS becomes unavailable so much more slowly than in STS, that the short-term decay factors may be ignored without changing the quality of the predictions.

The final step in the analysis involves the calculation of the actual probabilities of correct or error responses. From the assumptions about the probability that an item enters the buffer and that it is later forced out, we can calculate the probability that an item resides in the buffer for exactly j trials given that it is tested at a lag greater than j. This probability will be denoted as β_j. Since errors may occur only when the item is not in the buffer (i.e., only when it has resided in the buffer for a number of trials less than the lag), the net probability of an error is equal to the probability that an item remains in the buffer j trials multiplied by the probability of an error given this number of trials in the buffer, these terms summed over values of j less than or equal to i. Hence, the probability of an error at lag i is

$$P(E_i) = \sum_{j=0}^{i} \beta_j \eta_{ij},$$

where the case of $j = 0$ is used to indicate that the item did not enter the buffer. The derivation of the hit and false-alarm functions follow very much the same pattern.

The predictions of the theory, therefore, depend on the integer-valued parameter r and on the four real-valued parameters α, Θ, τ, and c. In order to estimate these parameters, a minimum chi-square procedure was used. For the recall condition, the observed frequencies of correct responses and of errors were compared to their predicted values with a standard Pearson chi-square. Because the probabilities of correct responses are not independent at different lags, the result of this calculation is not assured of being distributed as a true chi-square. Nevertheless, it should be approximately correct and in any case should be nearly monotone in goodness of fit. The set of parameters that minimize the chi-square will, therefore, be a good estimate of the true parameter values. In order to evaluate approximately how well a particular parameter set fits the data, the resultant "chi-square" can be compared with a true chi-square distribution. For this comparison, each of the fourteen points on the lag curve will contribute a single degree of freedom to the chi-square. Subtracting one degree of freedom for each of the four parameters estimated (performance in the recall conditions does not depend upon c) the total number of degrees of freedom is $14 - 4 = 10$. In the case of the recognition condition, the data consist of two functions, the hits and the false alarms. By fitting both of these functions simultaneously, the number of degrees of freedom in the initial sum is doubled. Since in this case five parameters are to be estimated, a total of $2 \times 14 - 5 = 23$ degrees of freedom are available. Finally, for the mixed condition, minimization must be carried out simultaneously over the hits and false alarms for the recognition data and the number of correct responses for the recall data. There are, then, thirty-seven degrees of freedom in this chi-square.

TABLE 4-1

ESTIMATES OF MODEL PARAMETERS FOR PAIRED-ASSOCIATE ITEMS TESTED BY A RECOGNITION, A RECALL, OR A MIXED PROCEDURE

| | *Experimental condition* | | |
	Recognition	*Mixed*	*Recall*
r	1	2	3
α	0.79	0.73	0.53
Θ	0.79	0.52	0.30
τ	0.95	0.97	0.99
c	0.71	0.62	*
χ^2	22.3	29.3	11.3
df	23	37	10

*The paramenter c was not required for this group.

The results of these estimations are shown in Table 4-1. It is first worth noting that the chi-squares are roughly on the same order as the number of degrees of freedom, and so in every case the fit is satisfactory. However, because the assumptions of the Pearson chi-square are not satisfied here, a comparison of the relative goodness of fit between the groups may not be made.

The values taken by the five parameters indicate the nature of the differences between conditions. The changes in all of the parameters are monotonic across the three conditions, with the mixed condition showing estimated parameters between those of the two unmixed conditions. The parameter c is not too useful here since it was estimated for only two of the conditions and since it does not differ much between them. The parameter that changes most dramatically is the size of the buffer, r. This parameter is estimated at 1 for the recognition condition, at 2 for the mixed condition, and at 3 for the recall condition. At the same time the probability that a new item enters the buffer, α, drops from 0.79 in the recognition condition to 0.53 in the recall condition. This difference in parameters implies that in the recognition condition subjects enter most items into the buffer, but hold them there for little more than a single trial, whereas in the recall condition almost half of the items fail to enter the buffer at all, although when they do enter, they tend to stay for a fairly long time. The mean number of trials that an item stays in the buffer, given that it is entered, is r/α, which is 1.3 trials for the recognition condition and 5.7 trials for the recall condition. At the same time, the amount of information about each item that is transferred into LTS on each trial, indicated by the value of Θ, is much larger for the recognition condition than for the recall condition.

These results may be interpreted as characterizing two alternative strategies that the subject can adopt to deal with the two testing procedures. When the recognition test is used, the quality of the information required to produce a correct response is fairly low. It would, for example, frequently be sufficient to code the response letter E simply as an early letter in the alphabet or as a vowel. In this condition the parameter estimates suggest that the subject chose to concentrate on each item when it was presented and to transfer as much information about it as possible to LTS. Although the quality of this representation was probably poor and became largely unavailable at long lags ($\tau = 0.95$, but, e.g., $\tau^8 = 0.66$), it was frequently sufficient to determine a correct response. On the other hand, the recall condition required much more complete information. Apparently, in this condition the subjects tried to maintain some items in STS for a longer time, at the expense of other items. A strategy similar to that used for the recognition condition apparently transferred so little information to LTS as to be unable to support recall. The strategy employed, therefore, seems to be to use STS as much as possible for information storage (remember that more short lags are present than longer lags), even though this allowed information about each item to accumulate in LTS only slowly ($\Theta = 0.30$ compared to 0.79 for the recognition group). In order to do this, some incoming items had to be skipped almost entirely. In the mixed condition, subjects apparently were forced into an intermediate strategy, retaining items in STS for longer than they had in the recognition condition, but not for as long as in the recall condition. It is interesting to note that fewer errors were made on the recognition task in the mixed condition than in the recognition condition. Apparently, the strategy selected for the mixed condition actually was better on recognition tests than the strategy selected when the recognition task only was present. It seems that subjects do not always choose the set of control processes which produce the best performance.[7]

---

[7]The interpretation given to the above experiment is based in part on the parameter estimates presented in Table 4-1. It should be noted that the interpretation also depends on a detailed analysis of the sequential properties of the data that have not been described here. The reason is that such analyses are complex and require a lengthy description; further, analyses of this sort will be considered later in treating a similar experiment (pp 88–97).

Attention. It is difficult to consider the concept of reinforcement without at least attempting to relate it to attention.[8] The extent to which a particular event modifies a subject's later behavior is influenced by the attention he gives to that event as much as by any reward or punishment associated with it. Accordingly, before reinforcement is considered, we shall examine the ways in which attentional variables can be incorporated into the framework of our memory system. We assume that attentional variables affect this system in three different ways, associated with the input of information into the SR, STS, and LTS. In the next section, when considering reinforcement, our interpretation of it will be very similar to the third of these attentional processes: that associated with entry of information to LTS.

The first place where attention can affect information transfer is at the very outset, by selecting information for entry into the SR. The processes which determine this selection are, in general, gross behavioral ones, primarily involving the orientation of the subject toward sources of stimulation so that the appropriate sense organs are stimulated. Once the sense organs have been activated, however, we assume that the incident information will be transferred to the SR.

The attentional processes involved in the transfer of this information to STS are more complex. This transfer results in a great reduction in the amount of information that is processed, since only information of importance to the subject is entered into STS. Such information may roughly be grouped into three classes which we associate with three different types of transfer control processes. The first class of information transferred to STS relates directly to the task with which the subject is currently involved. Thus, for example, in reading this text, one more or less automatically transfers information about the next words into STS (note, however, that the eye-movements involved in scanning the page are an attentional process of the first type). To account for this transfer, it will be assumed that the presence of information of a particular sort in STS will induce transfer of any similar information in the SR to take place. It is immaterial whether the control processes involved here are thought of as comparing the contents of the SR to STS, or as reaching out from STS and tracking a particular part of the SR. In any case, these control processes allow the system to track activity in the environment as long as information about it is maintained in STS. The second class of information transferred requires a somewhat more elaborate set of control processes. It is postulated that all information entered into the SR is rapidly analyzed

---

[8]See Guthrie (1959) for an interesting discussion of this point.

and, as part of this analysis, a reference is made to LTS. At this stage, the primary result of this reference is the retrieval of a quantity, the *pertinence* associated with the information (Norman, 1968). For the purposes of this discussion, the pertinence may be thought of as a scalar quantity, with the property that information which has a high pertinence is likely to be selected for transfer to STS and information which has a low pertinence is likely to be allowed to decay without attention. The value that is taken by the pertinence function will depend on many different variables. The recency of a reference to the information in LTS and the frequency with which the information has been referenced, for example, are two such variables. The reference to LTS and the transfer to STS take place only after the information in the SR has been analyzed at a fairly high level. If anything is entered into STS as a result of these attentional processes, it will be far more complicated than a sensory image and will include some of the information recovered from LTS, for example, its context and several associations to it. The last class of information which may be transferred from the SR to STS concerns sudden changes in the environment. It is postulated that whenever there is a sharp discontinuity in the contents of the SR that is not correlated with an observing response or other subject-induced activity, there is a tendency for the new material in the SR to be transferred to STS. It is worth noting that these three classes of processes are competing with each other for the limited processing capacity available in STS, as well as with information that is being transferred from LTS and information that is being maintained in STS. What actually will be entered depends on the relative demands of all these sources of input, rather than on the magnitude of any one request.

The third place where attention influences the transfer of information is in the link between STS and LTS. It is clear that we remember a great deal about some aspects of the environment and very little about others, even when we have "attended" to all of them. In interpreting such effects it is not necessary to add anything to the collection of control processes that have already been introduced. In the previous section we noted that the transfer to LTS was influenced by any of a number of control processes acting on STS. The number of items in STS, the formation of a rehearsal buffer, or the retrieval of information from LTS to form mnemonics are examples of these processes. We shall not dwell on these attentional processes here, since they will be discussed in the next section.

The concept of reinforcement.   In the preceding two sections a theory of memory and attention has been outlined that we believe can account for most of the results from simple verbal-learning experiments. In this section an attempt will be made to discuss reinforcement in the framework of this system. We do not think that a single formulation can explain the variety of reinforcement effects that have been demonstrated with human subjects. Rather, it appears that the major determinants of learning are the memory and attention processes, and that the concept of reinforcement may best be understood in terms of their action. In several of the applications to be discussed in the second part of this report, results will be presented where the reinforcement effects appear at first glance to be quite complicated. When these effects are analyzed in terms of the theory, however, their basis will be seen to be relatively simple. The memory and attentional processes available to the subject provide bounds, often quite strict, that limit the set of control processes that can be used, and thereby constrain the action of reinforcement.

In many ways our interpretation of reinforcement is quite similar to the ideas of attention that were discussed in the preceding section. Transfer of information to LTS takes place only while that information is resident in STS. Thus, if learning is to take place, the appropriate information must be maintained in STS for some period of time. As indicated before, however, STS is a system of limited capacity, and many potential sources of information are competing for access to it. At the same time that an item is being studied for later recall, processing space in STS is also demanded by incoming stimuli and by other items already in STS. The extent to which information about the item is successfully processed depends on the limitations imposed by the task and on the strategy selected by the subject.

The data collected in an experiment may appear to be unduly complicated for another reason. The system of memory has two distinct ways in which information about an item may be stored. An improvement in performance as a result of a study trial may be brought about either because information is temporarily maintained in STS or because it is permanently stored in LTS. The relative importance of these two stores will depend on many factors, such as the nature of the task, the presence or absence of competing stimulation, and the length of time between study and test. The operation of reinforcement will have an effect on both of these processes; that is, feedback or payoff may lead the subject both to retain information in STS and to try to transfer it efficiently to LTS. Although the term reinforcement typically is used to refer to processes that have an effect on the permanent storage of information, in many experiments these long-term effects can become confused with those due to STS. The long-term and short-term effects may be very different from each other. In the next section, for example, we shall consider an experiment in which the effects of a series of similar stimuli on the storage of information in LTS agree with predictions from classical interference theory, whereas the effect on the contents of STS is exactly the opposite. The overall behavior is, of course, a mixture of long- and short-term effects and thus, at first analysis, appears to show inconsistencies. In short, we do not feel that it is possible to study reinforcement variables without first making a careful analysis of the role of the two types of memory in the learning situation.

There are actually at least three sets of control processes by which information can be maintained in memory for later use. If the information is to be used immediately and then can be discarded, the subject may choose to simply maintain as much of it as possible in STS via rehearsal without any attempt to transfer it to LTS. With such a strategy the subject will be highly accurate at short lags, but performance will drop rapidly to chance thereafter. The second type of strategy also involves maintenance of information in STS via rehearsal, but this time in lesser quantity so that an attempt can be made to transfer it to LTS. Again, performance will be good at short lags, but now items tested at long delays will not experience as large a drop in performance. Finally, the subject may attempt to code the information and store it in LTS as it comes along without maintaining it in STS for any length of time. This set of control processes usually involves the retrieval of information from LTS to help generate a more robust image for permanent storage, usually by forming associations or by the use of mnemonic devices. The choice of which of these control processes to use is usually not freely available to the subject. The nature of the material that is presented frequently restricts the possibilities or even dictates exactly the method that must be used. The dynamics of the information processing that goes on in the three cases is different, however, and so the effect of an external manipulation will depend on the particular control processes that are used. In a later section on reinforcement magnitude, a case will be seen where a seemingly minor change in the stimuli led to a change in study procedure, which in turn resulted in vastly different reinforcement effects. An analysis of the information-transfer aspects of the situation is necessary before the role of reinforcement can be understood.

In spite of the restrictions that have been set forth in the previous paragraph, we shall now consider a general description of the reinforcement process. This formulation should not be thought of as an exact statement of the action of reinforcement, but as an outline which is frequently modified in its specifics. This description is, basically, an expectancy interpretation of reinforcement, and as such is in the tradition of the ideas set forth by Tolman (1932) and by Brunswik (Tolman and Brunswik, 1935). Essentially, it consists of two components: first, the formation of a prediction (and possibly the production of a response) based on the stimulus input and on correlated information retrieved from memory, and second, the comparison of this prediction with subsequent events. It is the result of this comparison that determines whether information about the episode will or will not be transferred to LTS.

As noted in the section on attention, the transfer of information about an external event to STS involves more than simply a transfer from the SR to STS. In particular, a reference to LTS is required in order to generate a pertinence measure, and some of the recovered information will be entered into STS along with information from the SR. This information, along with other information that may be retrieved later from LTS, is used by the subject to select a response if one is necessary. In addition, this information allows the subject to generate an expectation or prediction about the events that will follow the stimulus. Any response that is required is based on this prediction, but the prediction usually is more elaborate than may be inferred from the observable response. When the outcome event in question occurs, it is compared with this prediction. The extent to which the outcome fails to agree with the prediction determines the degree and nature of the study the item receives. Usually, large discrepancies between the prediction and the outcome dispose the subject to apply control processes that maintain the relevant information in STS and induce the transfer of information to LTS. The information which is transferred is primarily associated with those components of the prediction that were most deviant from the actual outcome. The result is to reduce the disparity between the outcome and information now stored in LTS, so that if the same stimulus and outcome were to be presented again, the discrepancy would be smaller than the original one.[9]

This special analysis simplifies considerably the factors that are involved in causing information to be maintained in STS. It is important to realize that STS is a system of limited capacity and that many potential sources of information are competing for access to it. At the same time that a comparison between a prediction and an outcome indicates a discrepancy, the processing capabilities of STS will also be demanded by external inputs and by other information that is already resident in STS. Whether the item in question will actually receive sufficient processing in STS to have an effect on later performance will depend upon the task in progress, the nature of the competing items, and any control processes

---

[9]The above hypothesis is similar to several other theories that have been proposed. The notion that the condition under which learning takes place involves a discrepancy between a prediction and an outcome is quite close to the expectancy hypothesis developed by Kamin (1969) and by Rescorla (1969). In the restriction of the stored information to that necessary to eliminate an observed discrepancy, our theory is similar to the discrimination net models of Feigenbaum and Simon (Feigenbaum, 1963) and Hintzman (1968). In this respect it also bears a resemblance to dissonance theory (Festinger, 1957; Lawrence and Festinger, 1962).

which may predispose the system to treat information of one type and not of another. This dynamic aspect of short-term processing is responsible for many of the effects of reinforcement, and we shall return to it in several of the applications that will be considered in the remainder of this paper.

Experimental Results

In this section the results of a number of experiments are considered in order to help clarify the role of the various stores and control processes and illustrate how reinforcement variables (e.g., the magnitude of reinforcement, the schedule of reinforcement, or the delay of its presentation) may be interpreted. In the original reports where these experiments were first described, they were given some form of quantitative analysis in terms of the theory. The details of these analyses can be found in the reference articles, so our discussion will be of a more qualitative nature. We hope that this simplification will allow us to consider the problems of reinforcement without becoming involved in questions of mathematical notation and proof.

Number of reinforcements and their presentation schedule. The first experiment is a fairly direct application of the theory to paired-associate learning (see Brelsford, Shiffrin, and Atkinson, 1968, for a more complete treatment). It illustrates the way in which a series of reinforcements can act to build up the strength of a representation in LTS through the successive storage of information. Basically, the same continuous paired-associate task that has already been described in connection with the Loftus experiment is employed, although with several modifications. A new set of eight stimuli (random two-digit numbers) were chosen at the start of each session and were used throughout the session. As in the Loftus experiment, the responses were letters of the alphabet. Each trial of the experiment began with the presentation of a stimulus to which the subject had been instructed to respond with the most recently paired letter. This stimulus was chosen randomly from the set of eight stimuli, so the lags between study and test were again distributed geometrically with parameter $1/8$. Following his response, the subject was given three seconds to study the stimulus paired with a response. This ended the trial. Unlike the Loftus experiment, the study phase of the trial did not always involve pairing a new response with the stimulus. A stimulus-response pair might be given one, two, three, or four reinforcements, the probabilities of these frequencies being 0.3, 0.2, 0.4, and 0.1 respectively. Thus, a stimulus selected for two reinforcements would be studied with the same response following the first test, but after the second test a new response would be introduced. This procedure continued for 220 trials per session. Each subject was run for at least ten sessions.

As in the previous experiment, the principal finding can be expressed in the form of lag curves (Fig. 4-4). Separate curves are presented showing the probability of a correct response, depending upon the number of prior reinforcements. Hence, there is a lag curve for stimulus-response pairs tested after one, two, and three reinforcements. By the nature of the presentation schedule, the number of observations at each point declines with increasing lag, and also with increasing number of reinforcements. Since at the time a subject was tested on an item, he had no way of knowing whether that item would be studied again, the first test of every item could be used in plotting the lag curve for one reinforcement. Similarly 70 per cent of the items received two or more reinforcements and therefore contributed to the second lag curve. Only in the case of the fourth reinforcements (which occurred for only 10 per cent of the items) were the frequencies too small to permit stable curves to be plotted. The three curves in Fig. 4-4 show a resemblance in form to the lag curves

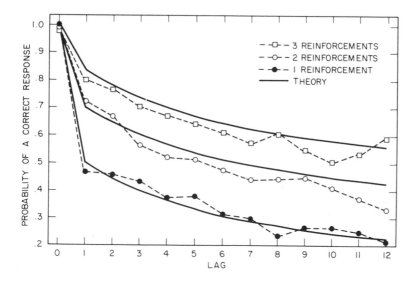

FIGURE 4-4. Observed and predicted probabilities of a correct response as a function of lag for items tested following their first, second, or third reinforcement.

obtained in Loftus' experiment. In particular, the curve for one reinforcement is quite similar to the comparable curve for the Loftus recall
group. The curves in Fig. 4-4 also indicate that the proportion of errors
at a given lag decreased as more reinforcements were given.

In order to account for the effects of multiple reinforcements, only a
few minor changes need be made in the model used to analyze Loftus'
data. As before, it is assumed that if a stimulus is presented for study
paired with a new response and the stimulus is one of the r-items currently in the rehearsal buffer, then the subject will simply replace the old
response with the new one. Otherwise, no change is made in the contents
of the buffer. The case of an item which is not in the buffer at the time
of presentation is somewhat more complicated.[10] Whenever the stimulus
for such an item is presented for test, the subject must retrieve information from LTS in order to make a response. Again we assume that the
amount of available information can be represented as a d'-measure for
that item. On the basis of this information, the subject generates a response, in this case his prediction about the outcome of the trial. Accordingly, we postulate that whenever the response is correct (indicating a
good correspondence between the prediction and the outcome), the item
will not receive additional study and hence will not be placed in the buffer.
Whenever the correspondence is small (an error is made), the item will
enter the buffer with probability α. The probability of failing to enter the
buffer, $1 - \alpha$, represents the combined effects of the many sources of competition in STS that may take precedence over entry of an item; for example, the presence of a naturally compatible stimulus-response pair or
of an easily rehearsable combination of items in the buffer. Once the item
has entered the buffer, however, we assume that transfer to LTS takes
place in the same manner as discussed before: For every trial in the buffer
an amount of information Θ is transferred to LTS. Every trial in which the
item is absent from STS results in a proportion $1 - \tau$ of the information
in LTS becoming unavailable for recovery and response production. Like
the recall condition in the previous experiment, the predictions of the
theory depend on the four parameters: r, α, Θ, and τ. To make these estimations, the same type of pseudo-chi-square procedure employed in the
Loftus study was used here, this time simultaneously on all three lag
curves and also on the double lag curves presented in Fig. 4-5. From this

---

[10]The analysis used here is not quite identical to that used by Brelsford et al.
(1968, p. 6), the principal change being in the mathematical form of the response-
generation postulate. The quantitative predictions of the two formulations are virtually identical; the one that is presented here is more in line with our current
thinking regarding reinforcement. In the version of the theory used by Brelsford
et. al., the parameters have slightly different meanings, and hence their values cannot be directly compared with those estimated for the Loftus experiment.

minimization, a set of parameters was found which generated the predicted curves shown in Figs. 4-4 and 4-5 and in the subsequent figures. The estimated buffer size was $r = 3$.

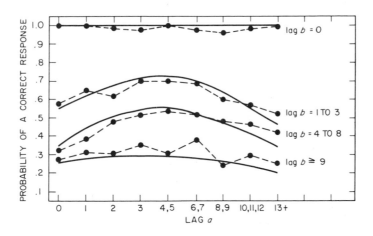

FIGURE 4-5. Observed and predicted probabilities of a correct response as a function of the spacing between the first and second reinforcement (lag a) and the lag between the second reinforcement and the final test (lag b).

The lag curves of Fig. 4-4 give a good idea of the general rate of learning, but they are not the best way to look at the effects of reinforcement. These effects are better examined by looking at sequential properties of the data; that is, at the effects of one reinforcement on a later one. Accordingly, in the next few paragraphs we consider a number of different summaries of the data, and show how they are predicted by the theory.

The first set of results to be examined relates the lag between the first study and test of an item to the performance on the second test. In particular, the presentation of an item with two or more reinforcements can be represented as follows:

Some test and first study on new item	lag a	First test and second study	lag b	Second test and some study

This describes a new pair that is studied, then first tested at lag a, is studied again, and next tested at lag b. We wish to look at the way in which results of the second test depend on lag *a*, with lag *b* held roughly constant. Plots of this relation are shown in Fig. 4-5. For lag $b > 0$ these curves are bow-shaped, with fewer correct responses when lag *a* is either small or large. As would be expected from the curves in Fig. 4-4, more errors are made when lag *b* is large than when it is small. It is relatively easy to see how these curves are predicted by the model. For small values of lag *a*, little information will be transferred to LTS during the interval between trials, so the primary effect of the first reinforcement is to increase the likelihood that the pair is in STS when the second reinforcement occurs. This will slightly increase the probability of a correct response, particularly at short lag *b*. For somewhat longer values of lag *a*, this effect is coupled with the transfer of a considerable amount of information into LTS before the second study. Thus a facilitative effect of the first reinforcement is expected even when the item has been deleted from the buffer before the second test. Finally, when lag *a* is very large, the item will almost certainly have departed from the buffer and much of the information that had been deposited in LTS will have become unavailable (in this experiment the estimate of τ was 0.82, so the retrievable information in LTS had a half-life of only about three trials).

In the preceding paragraph the effect of the lag between the first and second reinforcement of a stimulus-response pair was examined. In this paragraph we shall again consider the effects of the lag between two successive reinforcements involving the same stimulus; however, in this case the two presentations represent the last occurrence of one pairing and the first occurrence of a new pairing:

Some test and final study of an item	lag *a*	Final test and first study of new item	lag *b*	First test of new item and some study

Here, a stimulus-response pair is given its last study and tested at lag *a*. A new response is then paired with the stimulus and is given its first test at lag *b*. The predictions for this case are somewhat surprising and are worth examining closely. If the item is not in the buffer at the end of lag *a*, it should have no effect on whether the new pairing is studied or not. If the previous stimulus-response pair is in the buffer, however, it should have a facilitative effect on the new learning, since the new item is now guaranteed to enter the buffer. In this case, the probability of a correct response on the new item should be relatively large. Unfortunately, the presence of the pair in the rehearsal buffer is not an observable event, but it is probabilistically related to the occurrence of an error and to lag *a*.

In particular, if an error was made on the final test of the old item, we know that it was not in the buffer, and therefore predict that the probability of a correct response on the new item, when tested later, will be independent of lag *a*. When a correct response is made on the old item, it may be in the buffer, and furthermore, it is more likely to be in the buffer if lag *a* is small. In this case, small values of lag *a* should be associated with fairly large probabilities of a correct response, and these probabilities should fall with increasing lag *a*. Note that this prediction is quite different from what would be predicted by interference theory, since it associates good performance on a transfer task with good performance on original learning.

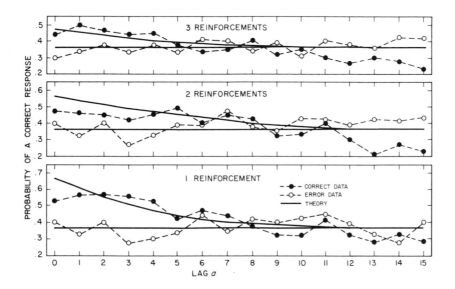

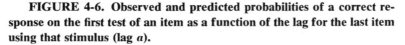

FIGURE 4-6. Observed and predicted probabilities of a correct response on the first test of an item as a function of the lag for the last item using that stimulus (lag *a*).

This prediction, however, seems to be well supported by the data as indicated by the functions plotted in Fig. 4-6. In this figure, unlike Fig. 4-5, the results have been averaged over all values of lag *b*. Three sets of curves have been plotted, depending upon whether the item given on trial *n + a + 1* received its first, second, or third test. It is interesting to note that the magnitude of the difference between the correct and the error data declines as the number of prior reinforcements increases. This may be attributed to the fact that the facilitation is purely a result of study in STS, and that this study takes place only when the subject's prediction based on LTS information is incorrect. When several reinforcements have been given, there is a greater likelihood that the item will be correctly recovered from LTS, and hence that no rehearsal in STS will take place. Accordingly, the proportion of correct responses that occur because the item was maintained in STS decreases, and with it the size of the facilitation effect. It should also be noted that the probability of a correct response to the new item, conditional on a correct response to the old one, appears to fall systematically below the prediction when a long lag intervenes between the two study trials. This effect, which is exactly the opposite of the one observed at short lags, is evidence for the activity of more conventional interference processes in LTS. Items that are correctly recalled at long lags are likely to have been recovered from a good representation in LTS. Apparently this strong trace interferes with the establishment of a new trace based on the same stimulus. Additional evidence for these interference effects will be presented in Fig. 4-8.

The last two results to be considered involve the effects of a sequence of similar or dissimilar stimuli and provide further evidence for some of our postulates about study effects in STS. Consider a series of consecutive trials all involving the same stimulus, but in which the response paired with the stimulus on the final study trial is different from that on the immediately preceding trial. The theory predicts that the longer the string of presentations, the more likely it is that the final item when eventually tested will be correctly recalled. This is so because the probability that a pair containing the stimulus is in the rehearsal buffer increases with the sequence of zero-lag presentations. On each successive trial of this sequence, a pair containing the stimulus may be entered into the buffer if it is not already there, and if there are no competing items to force it out. The resulting effect is shown in Fig. 4-7. In this figure the probability of correctly recalling the last item of a series of trials all involving the same stimulus (averaged over all test lags) is plotted as a function of the length of the series. As expected, this is an increasing function, and falls quite close to the predicted function. Note that again this effect is quite the opposite of predictions from a traditional interference theory. Such a theory would predict that the repeated presentations would interfere proactively with the new pair and that this would decrease the probability of responding correctly to the transfer item. It is important to realize that these effects are the result of activity in STS and say nothing about the nature of interference in LTS. Indeed, the long-term effects appear to be the opposite of the short-term effects. Figure 4-8 shows the probability that, on the first trial of a new item, the response that had been correct

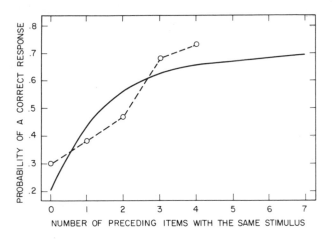

FIGURE 4-7. Observed and predicted probabilities of a correct response as a function of the number of consecutive preceding items using the same stimulus.

on the previous occurrence of the stimulus is given instead of the current correct response. The probability of these intrusion errors is plotted as a function of the lag at which the new item is tested (the three curves depend on the number of times that the previous pairing had been reinforced). Intrusion errors were more frequent when the previous item had been given several reinforcements than when it had received only a single reinforcement. The fact that the response is actually an error indicates

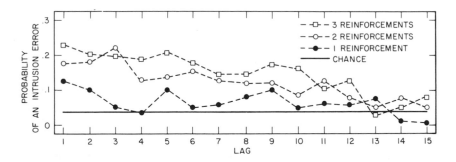

FIGURE 4-8. Probability that the correct response for the preceding item using a given stimulus will be made as an intrusion error to the present item.

that the item was not in the buffer at the time of test, hence that this more typical proactive effect is associated with long-term storage.

A series of consecutive trials using the same stimulus, as indicated in the preceding paragraph, tends to cause that stimulus to be entered into the rehearsal buffer, but will not create any further disruption of other items in the buffer. On the other hand, a series of items with different stimuli produces maximum disruption, since each of them will have some probability of being entered into the buffer. This effect is illustrated by the way that the items which intervene between study and test of a given item affect the probability of a correct response. In particular, suppose that the test of an item following its kth study occurs at lag x. The case where all of the x intervening items involve the same stimulus and the case where they involve all different stimuli will be examined, with the prediction that the all-same condition will produce better performance than the all-different condition. For each of the three values of k, this prediction is supported (Fig. 4-9).

This experiment has illustrated the way in which the theory can be applied to show increases in LTS strength as a result of a series of reinforcements. It has also shown a simple way in which the correspondence

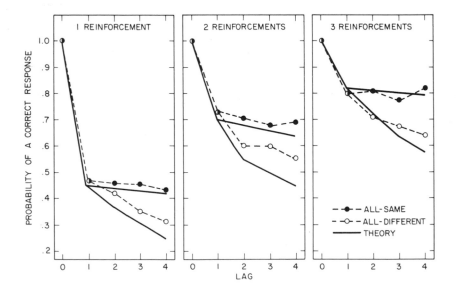

FIGURE 4-9. Observed and predicted probabilities of a correct response as a function of lag for the cases where the intervening stimuli are all identical or are all different.

between the subject's prediction and the outcome of a trial can determine rehearsal patterns. Finally, by considering the sequential properties presented in the last five figures, evidence has been given which supports our particular two-process formulation of memory.

Delay of reinforcement. The second experiment to be considered examines one of the most confusing issues in the area of human reinforcement: that of its delay. It appears that a delay in the feedback of information about a response can have many different effects. Some studies (Greenspoon and Foreman, 1956; Saltzman, 1951) have indicated that a delay will impair learning, others show no effect (Bilodeau and Ryan, 1960; Bourne, 1966; Hochman and Lipsitt, 1961), and still others appear to show a facilitative effect of delay (Buchwald, 1967, 1969; Kintsch and McCoy, 1964). We shall attempt to show that any of these effects can be accommodated by our analysis and shall discuss an experiment (Atkinson, 1969) in which all of these effects were obtained as the result of several fairly simple manipulations.

The basis of this experiment was a continuous paired-associate task similar to the one just described. The stimuli were randomly generated consonant trigrams and were paired with single-digit responses (digits 2 through 9). Every stimulus-response pair received between three and seven reinforcements, with each pair being equally likely to receive any number of reinforcements within this range. A stimulus was used only once during the course of the experiment; that is, a stimulus trigram would receive several study and test trials with a particular response number, and then would never be used again. The major difference between the presentation schedule in this experiment and those discussed earlier concerned the lag structure. Sixteen different stimuli were active at any time. The stimulus that was presented, however, was not chosen at random from this set, but only from the six stimuli that had not been presented on the previous ten trials. Thus, the minimum possible test lag was ten and the mean lag was fifteen items.

The manipulation in this experiment involved assigning each stimulus-response pair to one of fourteen conditions. This assignment was made randomly for each pair, but was the same for all reinforcements of that pair. All conditions were run simultaneously; that is, the set of items that were active at any time included ones assigned to many different conditions. The fourteen conditions resulted from combinations of three independent variables affecting reinforcement: (1) The first of these variables was the delay itself. The presentation of the stimulus was terminated by the response, then the feedback (reinforcement) appeared, either immediately or following a delay of three, six, or twelve seconds. (2) During this delay, the subject was either allowed to do as he pleased or was instructed to count backwards from a randomly selected three-digit number. These conditions will be referred to as the *no-count* and the *count* conditions. (3) The feedback consisted either of the correct digit response presented alone or of both the stimulus trigram and the correct response. These conditions will be referred to as the *feedback-only* and the *stimulus-plus-feedback* conditions. In either case the duration of the reinforcement was four seconds. When the delay is zero, the count and no-count conditions are the same, hence only fourteen conditions are possible, instead of the $4 \times 2 \times 2 = 16$ conditions which might be expected.

The primary dependent variable considered in the experiment was the proportion of correct responses averaged over trials 2 through 7 (the initial trial, of course, was a random guess and has not been included in the average). In Fig. 4-10 this proportion is plotted as a function of the delay for the various reinforcement conditions. This figure shows all three of the trends which were mentioned above: the count, feedback-only condition shows a drop in the mean proportion correct as a function of delay;

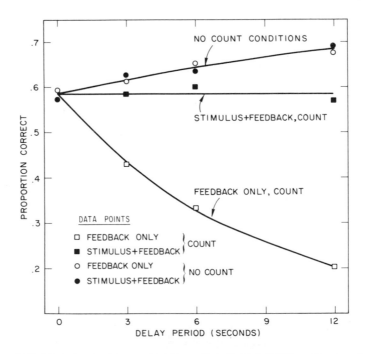

FIGURE 4-10. Observed and predicted probabilities of correct responses as a function of delay for two types of feedback and two types of delay activity.

the count, stimulus-plus-feedback condition shows no effect of delay; while both of the no-count conditions show an improvement with delay.

In interpreting the effects of reinforcement delay here, it is important to realize that the roles of rehearsal and of LTS are quite different in this task than they were in the two previous experiments. The presentation schedule was constructed so that there was always a substantial lag between successive appearances of an item. Because of this it was not practical for the subject to use a rehearsal buffer to maintain information until a response was required — too many of the items which intervened between study and test would have had to be ignored altogether. Instead, subjects were forced to rely primarily on LTS as a source of information storage. In such a case, subjects usually do not form a rehearsal buffer, but instead try to code each item as it is presented, and then turn their attention to the next item when it appears. The use of unique and relatively unfamiliar stimuli for each pair also increased the likelihood that this coding scheme was used.

The results of the count conditions are now fairly simple to interpret. The counting procedure had the effect of preventing rehearsal of information in STS; in particular, the subject could not readily remember the stimulus that was presented throughout the course of the delay period. Thus, in the feedback-only condition, the subject would frequently be unable to remember the stimulus by the time feedback was presented and would, therefore, be unable to associate the stimulus-response pair. In such a case, the probability of a correct response would drop toward chance as the likelihood increased that the stimulus could not be remembered; that is, as the delay interval increased. In the stimulus-plus-feedback condition, forgetting the stimulus during the delay period should have no effect since both members of the pair would always be available at the time of study. The counting task would, however, prevent any other processing from occurring during this interval, so the delay would be expected to have no effect at all.

In the no-count conditions the subject should have no problem in retaining the stimulus in STS during the delay interval; consequently, there should be no differences between the stimulus-plus-feedback and the feedback-only conditions. In fact, the delay interval can be spent in processing information in such a way as to make later LTS storage easier and more efficient. There are several ways in which this can be done; for example, the subject may engage in some sort of pre-processing of the stimulus, such as generating images or mnemonic codes which will aid in efficient storage once feedback is provided. Furthermore, after several reinforcements have been presented, the subject may be able to recover the response from LTS and recognize it as the correct one before the feedback is presented. He can then use the delay interval to further study the item. Either of these two processes can generate the increasing delay function that was observed.

Atkinson (1969) has described the amount of information which was transmitted to LTS by each reinforcement by an increasing exponential function for the no-count conditions and by a decreasing exponential function for the count conditions. These functions have been used to generate the predictions shown in Fig. 4-10. Although the sort of sequential investigations illustrated by Figs. 4-6 through 4-9 have not been made, the overall accuracy of these predictions support the interpretation.

The above analysis was able to accommodate effects that at first appeared to be inconsistent into a fairly simple framework by focusing attention on the informative value of the reinforcement, rather than treating it as a simple event. A similar, if not identical, analysis, we feel, will be able to reconcile the discrepant results that have been found for the effects of delay of reinforcement by other workers. It is experimental results of this sort that make a particularly strong case for our contention that factors involved in learning and memory are fundamental in determining the phenomena of reinforcement rather than the other way around.

Concept identification. In the following section, the theory will be applied to a concept-identification paradigm in which the effects of reinforcing events are quite different from those that have been discussed so far. The concept-identification task requires the subject to observe a series of stimuli and to classify them, one by one, into a fixed set of categories. Following each response, the subject is told the correct classification of the stimulus, and it is this feedback that gives rise to learning. The concept-identification procedure differs from the paired-associate procedure in that the classification depends systematically on some property (or properties) of the stimuli. This means that once the subject has solved the problem and has learned the rule by which stimuli are classified, he will be able to classify a novel stimulus correctly. There are, of course, an infinitely large number of possible stimulus properties and rules that can be used to partition the stimuli. In the experiment to be discussed below, we shall treat only a very few of these possibilities, those where the stimuli are composed of orthogonal binary dimensions and where the classification rule depends on only one of these dimensions. The procedure for the experiment that will be discussed (for a complete treatment see Wickens, 1969) will show these restrictions more clearly.

Subjects were seated before a teletype keyboard and saw stimuli projected on a screen in front of them. These stimuli were pictures which were constructed to vary along twelve different dimensions. Each of these dimensions, or attributes, of the pictures could take on either of two different values, only one value in each picture. One set of stimuli, for example, consisted of line drawings of houses in which the dimensions were represented by one or two windows, by a chimney on the left or on the right, and by ten other distinctions. From the twelve attributes a total of $2^{12} = 4,096$ distinct stimuli could be constructed. The rules used to determine the correct classifications were based on exactly one of these attributes; all stimuli for which that attribute took one value falling into one of two categories, all stimuli for which it took the other value falling into the other category. As each stimulus was presented, the subject indicated his choice of category by pressing the zero or the one key on the keyboard and was informed of the correct alternative by indicator lights mounted above the keyboard. A series of such trials was presented to the subject, the series continuing without interruption for the duration of a session. Whenever the subject had correctly identified the relevant attribute, as indicated by a string of twelve consecutive correct responses, he was signaled that the current problem was complete and was immediately started on a new problem, using a rule based on one of the eleven attributes that had not just been used. Subjects were run for two hours per day for five days. The number of problems solved by a subject during the experiment ranged from 53 to 115. During the first 25 problems or so, subjects showed improvement. After this point, however, the number of trials to solution remained approximately constant. The analysis to be discussed below is based on this stable, asymptotic data only.

The analysis that will be made of concept-identification is based upon the general idea of hypothesis testing (Bower and Trabasso, 1964; Restle, 1962). We assume that the subject solves concept problems by formulating hypotheses about the rule that determines the classification, then observing the sequence of classified stimuli to see whether the hypothesized rule is supported or not. A rule which is consistent with the true classification will enable the subject to respond correctly and thereby to solve the problem, whereas a rule that is inconsistent will cause errors to be made. When an inconsistency appears, the subject will abandon the rule under test and select a new one. It is apparent that this sort of solution is composed of two different processes: the selection of rules and their test. This dichotomy will represent an important part of our analysis of the role of reinforcement in concept identification.

We assume that initially there is a set of hypotheses which the subject considers to be potential solutions to the problem and which he wishes to test. The size of this pool depends on the nature of the task and on the subject's familiarity with it. In his first attempt to solve a concept-identification problem, a subject may have a large set of hypotheses which he views as possible, many of which hypotheses are quite complicated and cannot be the true solution to the problem. In the case of the experiment mentioned above, in which considerable practice was given and the subject was adapted to the task, the set of hypotheses may reasonably be identified with the set of attributes of the stimuli. In the following discussion, we shall speak of sampling *attributes*, indicating the specific nature of this experiment. One may, however, think of this as sampling from a pool of much more general hypotheses.

When solving a concept-identification problem, it is assumed that the subject starts by choosing a sample of r attributes from the total set and maintains them in STS by rehearsal. The matching of the values taken by these attributes to the two response alternatives is assumed to show local consistency (Gregg and Simon, 1967); that is, the assignment is made in such a way as to be consistent with the outcome of the last trial that has taken place. By comparing this assignment to the values that these attributes take in a new stimulus, the subject makes several predictions regarding the outcome of the new trial. Each of these predictions is based on one attribute in the sample: If the value of this attribute is the same as the value it took in the previous stimulus, then the same classification is predicted; if the value is different, then the classification is predicted to change. If more than two attributes are sampled, it is possible that the set of predictions may have internal inconsistencies, since each attribute may be varied independently of the others. The subject's classification response is generated from these predictions in some manner or other. The actual method of generation is not crucial to our analysis: He may choose a prediction at random, may select the response indicated by the largest number of predictions, or may use any of several other strategies.

The outcome of the trial provides confirmation of some of these predictions and disconfirmation of others, implying that those attributes on which incorrect predictions were based are no longer tenable candidates for the solution. Accordingly, these attributes are dropped from the rehearsal buffer. On the following trials, this process is continued, either until the buffer is emptied or until the problem is solved, in the sense that only one attribute is being considered and this is the correct one. If the buffer is emptied, the subject is forced to draw a new sample of attributes for testing. Here, for the first time, LTS becomes important. While the first set of attributes was being tested, information about them was being transferred to LTS. Now, when resampling is taking place, this information in LTS may allow the subject to avoid resampling those attributes which have already been tested and rejected. Resampling of an attribute that has already been tested may take place, but only when information about that attribute cannot be recovered from LTS, either because only a small amount of information was originally transferred or because of a failure of the search process. As more and more samples are drawn, there will be a greater and greater likelihood that the correct attribute will be selected and the problem solved.

The formulation of concept-identification learning given here is similar to a number of those that have been discussed in the literature, although it is not identical to any of them. In addition to the reference mentioned above, Trabasso and Bower have presented models in which questions of the delay of resampling (Trabasso and Bower, 1966) and the size of the test sample (Trabasso and Bower, 1968) have been discussed, while Gregg and Simon (1967) have considered a series of models which make a number of different assumptions about the selection of new hypotheses for test. All of these models, however, are different from our model in one critical respect, for they assume that the occurrence of an incorrect response causes the whole sample to be eliminated and redrawn. In contrast to this assumption, our theory makes a clear distinction between the effects of information feedback and the effects of reward. The important variable in determining what learning takes place is not whether the overt response was correct or in error, but rather the way in which the various predictions about the attributes were confirmed or disconfirmed. Since the subject can make a response that is not consistent with some of his predictions, it is possible for these predictions to be disconfirmed, and therefore rejected, at the same time that the response is correct. Only in the case where the buffer size is one (i.e., only a single attribute is under test) will the reward and information feedback aspects of the reinforcement be equivalent.

The fact that resampling does not take place on every error is central to our analysis of the role of reinforcement in this situation. It is relatively easy to demonstrate that this cannot occur as frequently as do errors. If resampling is postulated to take place after every error, the rate of learning for problems based on a particular attribute is independent of the value of r and can be represented by the probability that no more errors follow a given error; that is, by the probability that the correct attribute is both selected for rehearsal and is used as the basis for response generation. This solution probability can be estimated from the number of errors required to solve the problem. If m_i is the mean number of errors to solve problems based on the ith attribute,, then the solution probability for that attribute, c_i, can be estimated as follows (Restle, 1962):

$$c_i = \frac{1}{m_i + 1} \, .$$

The c_i's should form a probability distribution over the set of attributes. Using data from repeated problems for a typical subject, Wickens (1969) was able to determine c_i for all twelve attributes in the stimulus. These estimates summed to 1.8, which was significantly larger than the maximum value of 1.0 that would be permitted for a true probability distribution. The conclusion must be that the subject was learning more rapidly than could be accounted for by a process that depended only on whether the response was correct or not. Subjects must have used rehearsal buffers with sizes that were greater than one and must have depended on outcome information to adjust the contents of STS.

In his treatment of the data from this experiment, Wickens used a somewhat simplified version of the LTS postulate put forward in the preceding paragraphs; indeed, he did not separate his analysis into short- and long-term components as we have done. He assumed that all items contained in a particular sample were unavailable to the next   samples, where   = 0, 1, 2, . . . , and that this value of   was constant for all attributes.[11] Using these assumptions, he was able to derive the distribution of the trial of last error and of the total number of errors, parametrized by combinations of r and   . Figure 4-11 presents predictions for the mean trial of last error and compares them with the observed mean trial of last error for each of the forty-five subjects who served in the

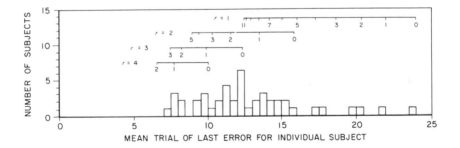

FIGURE 4-11. Frequency distribution of the mean trial of last error for individual subjects on a simple 12-dimensional concept-identification problem. Upper axes show theoretical predictions for four buffer sizes ($r = 1, 2, 3, 4$) and an appropriate range of delays in sampling replacement.

---

[11]The model that we have proposed above would predict that items from the same sample could remain unavailable for different lengths of time, and that these periods should depend upon the number of trials that the attributes resided in the rehearsal buffer.

experiment. The observed means are plotted as a histogram at the bottom of the figure, while the predictions are plotted along four short axes; a separate axis for $r = 1, 2, 3,$ or 4. Points along these axes indicate values of θ. For example, there were three subjects whose mean trial of last error over all problems fell between 9.5 and 10.0. Mean trials of last error in this range are predicted by strategies in which $r = 4$ and $\theta = 0$, in which $r = 3$ and $\theta = 1$, or, to reasonable accuracy, in which $r = 2$ and $\theta = 4$. None of the strategies with $r = 1$ would be satisfactory for these subjects since, even with perfect long-term retention ($\theta = 11$), a mean trial of last error smaller than about 12 would be extremely unlikely. It is apparent from Fig. 4-11 that there is a very large spread in the observed data and that no single set of parameters can adequately account for all of the subjects. It is clear, however, that subjects with low values for the mean trial of last error were using strategies which required an r of at least 3 or 4 and which made significant use of LTS. The presence of these subjects who used rehearsal buffers of larger than a single attribute is again evidence for our contention that it is the confirmation of predictions about the attributes rather than the reward of a response that dictates the course of learning.

Magnitude of reward. The amount of reward associated with a correct response or the punishment associated with an error are variables that have not received a great deal of systematic consideration in human learning. In general, the studies that have examined amount of reinforcement have varied the degree of information feedback made available to the subject after his response (e.g., Keller, Cole, Burke, and Estes, 1965) or the amount of time that he is given to study the item (e.g., Keller, Thomson, Tweedy, and Atkinson, 1967). When reward magnitude has been considered, however, the extent of its effects seem to depend upon whether reward conditions have been compared between or within subjects. Several experiments by Harley (1965a,b) illustrate this clearly. He ran subjects in a paired-associate experiment using an anticipation procedure to learn CVC pairs. Incentive was provided for some pairs by telling the subject that he would receive twenty-five cents for each one that he correctly anticipated on a later trial. In one experiment (1965b), Harley tested for the effects of this reward in an absolute manner by comparing two groups of subjects: One group received twenty-five cents for every correct anticipation, whereas the other group received no rewards at all. The rate of learning for these two groups was virtually identical (see Fig. 4-12). When both reward values were used simultaneously with the same subject, half of the pairs receiving a reward and half not, the rewarded items were correct significantly more often (Harley, 1965a). As Fig. 4-12

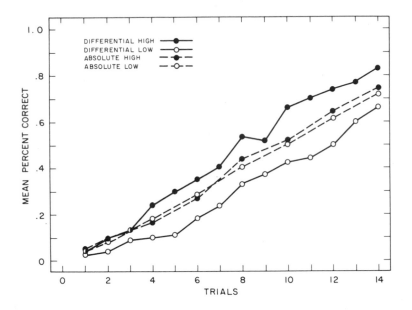

FIGURE 4-12. Learning curves for high- and low-rewarded paired-associate items tested with both reward values present at the same time differential procedure) or with values presented alone (absolute procedure). Data is replotted from 4-second groups in Harley 1965a, b).

indicates, this effect appears to take the form of an improvement in performance on the rewarded items and a decrement in performance on the unrewarded items when compared to either of the absolute groups. This interpretation is placed in some doubt by a later experiment (Harley, 1968) which suggests that the reward effect should be attributed primarily to poorer performance on the low-incentive items rather than to an improvement on the high-incentive items. In any case, these experiments indicate that the relative reward was the important variable, not the absolute magnitude of the reward.

In the system of reinforcement considered here, the reward associated with an item can influence performance only by altering the way in which information about the item is processed in STS. With this view, it is relatively easy to see why absolute rewards may not be important. The subject in a typical verbal-learning experiment is usually motivated to perform well, even in the absence of monetary incentive. The way in which information is processed in STS will be determined primarily by the nature of the test material and by the structure of the experiment. A difference in the absolute reward level will not make very much change in this scheme. When items with different reward values are presented, however, they may receive different treatments within the same general scheme. In particular, for tasks in which a rehearsal buffer is set up, the effects of differential rewards will be reflected in the relative probabilities of entering an item into the buffer or of deleting it once entered. Thus, high-reward items would be more likely to receive study than low-reward items, and so would be learned better. When only a single level of reinforcement is present, however, all items are equally likely to receive study, regardless of the level of reinforcement. The overall rate of learning in either case will be determined by the nature of the material to be learned and will not depend on the reward.

We have said that the effects of reward are determined by differences in the processing of high- and low-value items in STS. If this is the case, the nature of the reward effect should be influenced by the presence or absence of a rehearsal buffer. When a buffer is used, differential processing of high- and low-value items can occur easily, since high-point items may be entered into the buffer with a higher probability than low-point items, while low-point items (if recalled as such) may be more likely to be deleted from the buffer. On the other hand, if a coding strategy (similar to the one induced in the delay of reinforcement study) is used, each item will be studied as it is presented and there will be relatively little opportunity for an effect of reward magnitude to appear. Fortunately it is possible to predispose the subject to use either a rehearsal or a coding strategy by a fairly simple experimental manipulation. This effect has been demonstrated clearly in an experiment by Atkinson, Brelsford, and Shiffrin (1967) using two groups of subjects in a continuous paired-associate task in which number-letter pairs were given single reinforcements. In one group a fixed set of stimuli was used, pairing new responses with each stimulus throughout the course of a session. In the second group each stimulus was used only for a single pair, then retired (these two presentation procedures will be discussed more fully in the next paragraph). For the first group, clearly separate lag curves were obtained by varying the number of pairs that the subject was required to keep track of at any point in time; for the second group there was no effect of this manipulation on the lag curves. This difference is readily explained by assuming that subjects in the first group set up a rehearsal buffer, while subjects in the second group attempted to code each item during the interval before the presentation of the next pair.[12]

An experiment which looks at reward effects while manipulating the stimuli in this way has been conducted by Kirk Gibson at Stanford University. The paradigm of this experiment was, in general, similar to those that we have already analyzed. Subjects were seated at teletypes and were presented with a series of pairs to be learned. The stimuli were CVC trigrams and the responses were the letters of the alphabet. Each pair received only a single study and a single test. Two groups of subjects were run: In the *fixed-stimulus* condition a set of nine stimuli were selected at random at the start of each session and were used throughout that session. After each test in this condition, the same stimulus was presented for study paired with a new response. The second group of subjects was run in a *variable-stimulus* condition. In this condition, the item just tested was permanently discarded and a new stimulus-response pair was presented during the study phase of the trial. As in the fixed group, however, the subject was trying to keep track of only nine stimulus-response pairs at any given point in time. The same random presentation schedule employed in most of the other experiments was used, so that the test lags were distributed geometrically beginning with lag zero.

The second aspect of the experiment concerned the reward values assigned to the pairs. As each new item was presented for study, a value of either 11, 22, or 99 points was randomly assigned to it (i.e., each of these three values was equally likely to appear). The values were assigned independently for each item; in particular, a stimulus in the fixed group could receive different reward values when paired with different responses. The subject was told that if he correctly recalled an item, its points would be credited to his score for the session. At the time of test, the subject was not shown the point value associated with the item. Indeed, subjects were given no immediate feedback on their accumulation of points, although at the start of each session they were informed what percentage of the total possible points had been obtained during the previous session. The subjects were paid for participation in the experiment in proportion to this percentage.

The results of this experiment are shown in the form of lag curves in Figs. 4-13 and 4-14. For the fixed-stimulus group (Fig. 4-13) there was

---

[12]In their original paper Atkinson et al. (1967, p. 295) interpreted the difference in the two conditions by assuming that, for the second group, items were maintained in the buffer even after they had been tested. In light of later evidence, it now appears that this explanation is unrealistic and that the results may be more reasonably explained, as we have done, by the failure to form a buffer.

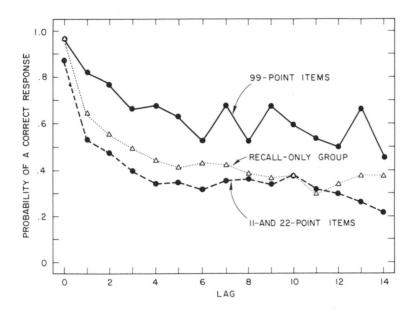

**FIGURE 4-13. Probability of a correct response as a function of lag
for items receiving different amounts of reward. The stimuli were a fixed
set of trigrams.**

a marked difference between performance on the 99-point items and on
the other two types of items, although there was not a statistically significant difference between the 22- and the 11-point items. In contrast to
these results there were no differences among the payoff conditions for the
variable-stimulus procedure (Fig. 4-14). Apparently, varying the stimuli
was sufficient to eliminate the basis for any reward effect.

The results of this experiment are in accord with our view of learning
and reward. As indicated by subject reports at the conclusion of the experiment, the variable-stimulus pairs (a unique stimulus trigram and response
letter) were fairly easy to code on an item-by-item basis. For this material,
however, the subject experienced difficulty if he tried to maintain several
items simultaneously in STS via rehearsal. Since it was much easier for the
subject to code the items than to maintain a rehearsal buffer, he tended to
study each item when it was presented and then turn his attention to the
next item. Using this strategy, every item will be studied and the point

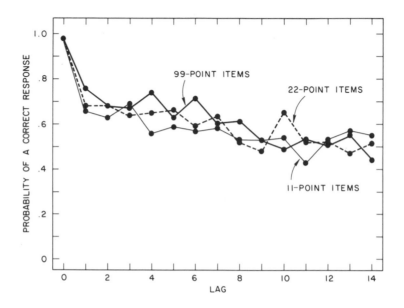

**FIGURE 4-14. Probability of a correct response as a function of lag
for items receiving different amounts of reward. A unique stimulus trigram was used for each item.**

values will not play an important role in the amount of information transferred to LTS. Consequently, little or no effect of reward value should be
observed, as indeed was the case for the variable-stimulus procedure.

On the other hand, for the fixed-stimulus procedure, the set of stimuli
quickly became very familiar, and subjects reported that it was easy to set
up a rehearsal buffer of three to five items. Coding, however, was much
more difficult for this procedure, since it is almost impossible to generate
noncompeting codes for the same trigram paired with many different letters during the course of a session. For this group, then, several items will
be maintained in STS at any given time, and it will be easy to give preferential study to an item in the buffer by ignoring another item just presented. Similarly, a high-point item will almost always be entered into the
buffer at the expense of some item that is already there. Thus the reward values will determine which items are studied and for how long they
are maintained. Accordingly, a reward effect is predicted for the fixed-
stimulus procedure, as was observed.

We do not want to argue from these results that a reinforcement effect cannot be obtained using the variable-stimulus procedure. If sufficiently large rewards are offered for correct responses to certain items, then there is no doubt that they will receive additional study, probably both by rehearsal and by coding. The point that we feel is important here is that with the particular payoff levels used in the study, a marked difference in reinforcing effects appeared between the fixed- and variable-stimulus procedures, two procedures which in a logical sense place identical demands on a subject. Although both procedures require the subject to keep track of the same number of stimulus-response pairs at any given point in time, the particular nature of the stimulus material caused different methods of study to be used, and in turn made reinforcement effects evident in one case and not in the other. This is another example where a given reinforcing operation can lead to markedly different effects depending on the particular information-processing requirements of the learning task.

One interesting feature of the experiment is the high accuracy of recall obtained for the variable-stimulus condition. Although there was no effect of the reward, the overall proportion of correct responses is approximately at the same level as the 99-point items for the fixed-stimulus group. This presumably reflects the fact that stimulus-response pairs in the variable-stimulus condition are less subject to interference from other pairs than in the fixed-stimulus condition. Further studies are currently in progress to investigate the exact form of the STS structure that is set up for the two conditions.

It is not possible to make a direct comparison of rewarded and unrewarded performance within this study. Some sort of comparison can be made, however, between another of Gibson's groups and a group from the experiment by Loftus reported in the first part of this paper. The group in question used a fixed-stimulus procedure, but with the digits 1 through 9 as stimuli instead of trigrams. This procedure is exactly the same as the recall-alone condition of the Loftus study, except for the presence of rewards. If these rewards are neglected, performance in the two experiments is almost exactly the same; if the three reward values are combined, the mean lag curve is indistinguishable from that observed by Loftus. The unrewarded responses of the recall-alone condition fall roughly between the items which had been given high and low incentives (see Fig. 4-15). In this figure the 11- and the 22-point items have been combined, hence each data point in this curve includes approximately twice the number of observations as the corresponding point in the high-reward curve (this means that the average of the two curves does not lie midway between them; in fact it falls almost exactly on the curve for the recall-alone group). While hardly conclusive, this comparison again suggests that the

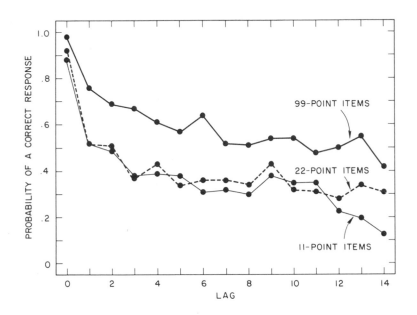

FIGURE 4-15. Probability of a correct response as a function of lag for items receiving different amounts of reward. The stimuli were a fixed set of numbers. The recall-alone condition, which received no reward, has been replotted from Fig. 4-2.

99-point items have been given additional study at the expense of the low-point items.

Effects of reinforcement on retrieval. Throughout this paper, a distinction has been made between storage and retrieval processes in learning. As noted in the introduction, this distinction is also relevant to an analysis of reinforcement. The applications considered so far have been primarily concerned with how reinforcement influences the study of items, hence the storage of information. The reason for not turning sooner to retrieval aspects of reinforcement is that there are few experiments dealing specifically with this topic (Wasserman, Weiner, and Houston, 1968; Weiner, 1966).

   In an attempt to remedy this state of affairs, we have initiated some experiments in which the reward associated with paired-associates has been manipulated both at the time the item is first studied and later at test.

None of these experiments is yet complete, but we want to present some pilot data from an experiment by Geoffrey Loftus which illustrate some effects of interest. This experiment employed a continuous memory task that was almost identical to the fixed-stimulus procedure described in the section on reward magnitude. The stimuli were the digits from 1 to 9, and the responses were letters of the alphabet. Each new stimulus-response item was assigned a value of either 11, 22, or 99 points. When an item was presented for study, however, its point value was not always displayed. For about half of the items, no information about the reward was given at this time; the subject was instructed that the items for which no point values appeared had, nevertheless, been assigned one of the three values at random by the computer controlling the experiment, and that these values would count in his total score for the session. Similarly, when the items were tested, their reward value might or might not be displayed. Again, the reward value was presented on about half of the tests. The presentation of the reward value at test was independent of whether the reward had been presented during study; thus the subjects might receive information about the rewards assigned to a particular item at the time of study, at the time of test, at both times, or at neither time. If a reward value was presented at study and test, then the same value appeared both times.

Some preliminary results from this study are presented in Fig. 4-16. The graph gives the proportion of items correctly recalled, averaged over all test lags, as a function of the presentation schedule and reward value. The mean latencies of correct and error responses are also shown. As in Gibson's experiment, there was very little difference between the 11- and 22-point items, so these have been grouped together as low-value items. The two points on the left of the graph are for the conditions in which the subject was informed during study that he was being shown a high (i.e., 99) point item. One of the observations (HH) shows the results when the reward information was also presented at test, the other (H-) when it was not. Similarly, the three middle points (-H, – –, -L) are associated with conditions in which no reward was presented at the time of study, while the two right-most points (L-, LL) give results for items studied with a low-point value (11 or 22). Although all test lags have been combined in this figure, the general form of the results appears to be the same at both short and long lags.

The major effects in Fig. 16 are due to the reward values displayed during study. Items that were assigned 99 points at study had a higher probability of being recalled than items for which no reward value was assigned. These items were, in turn, better remembered than the low-point items. The explanation that we offered for Gibson's data in the previous section is consistent with these findings if items with an unspecified reward

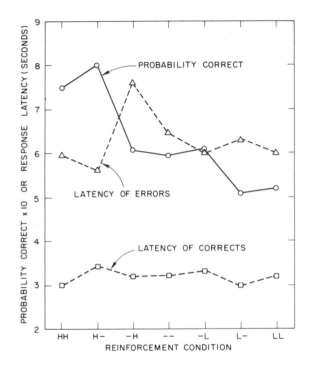

FIGURE 4-16. Probability of a correct response and latency of correct and error responses as a function of reward information given at study and test. The first letter in the condition label designates reward at study, the second designates reward at test; H indicates 99-point reward, L indicates 11- or 22-point reward, — indicates that no reward information was given.

are assumed to receive a level of study intermediate between that given to high- and low-point items.

   In the introduction, two ways were mentioned by which reinforcement could aid retrieval. The first of these suggested that the reward value associated with an item might act as a cue to facilitate the retrieval of information from LTS. These preliminary data provide little support for this hypothesis, for there is no indication that items for which the reward value was presented on both study and test are better recovered than those that received reward only at the time of study. This result indicates that in this experiment the reward had negligible cue value. The second potential effect of reward on retrieval receives more support; namely, that a subject would be willing to spend more time in attempting to retrieve items that had been assigned a high value than items that had been assigned low values. This effect is quite clearly shown in the latency of incorrect responses, particularly for the conditions in which the reward value had not been identified during study (i.e., conditions -H, – –, and -L). The latency of errors shows the same effect for the two conditions where point values were presented during study, although not to as marked an extent. Curiously, this effect is totally lacking in both the latency and probability of a correct response. These results suggest that either the subject was able to retrieve an item without much difficulty (with a latency of about three seconds), or else no recovery was possible. When an item could not be recovered, the additional search time spent on items with large reward values was not of much help. There was no limit on the time that was available to make a response, so the failure to retrieve cannot be attributed to a premature termination of the trial.

These results must be regarded with some caution. The amount of data represented is not great, and it is likely that the specific characteristics of the task are not optimum for demonstrating retrieval effects. The fixed-number procedure that was used is one which almost invariably leads the subject to set up a rehearsal buffer. Indeed, several of the subjects reported being able to successfully set up a nine-item buffer by visualizing the responses arrayed in a 3 × 3 matrix! The process of retrieving items from the buffer is a fairly simple one and invariably will lead to a correct response. Items that are recovered in this manner will not contribute to any effects of reinforcement on the recovery of the item. We would expect that more substantial effects will be observed in a task in which the subject is forced to put greater reliance on LTS. Nevertheless, an effect of reinforcement on retrieval time was clearly evident in this study, showing, as expected, an incentive effect. This effect would not be predicted from a theory that assigned to reinforcement only the role of strengthening connections; it is, however, consistent with the view that reinforcement acts to direct attention and to control information flow. [13]

Conclusion

In this paper we have attempted to present a theoretical framework within which to view the phenomena of reinforcement. Basically, the

---

[13] A replication of this experiment (Loftus and Wickens, 1970), using a slightly modified procedure, demonstrated effects of study and test cueing of incentive on both the probability of a correct response and on response latency. These results are in agreement with the analysis presented here.

framework involves an account of learning and attention in terms of the storage of information in memory and its subsequent retrieval. Reinforcement is the modulation of this information flow as it influences both storage and retrieval processes. It is our belief that a given reinforcing operation can have many different and often seemingly contradictory effects depending on the particular study and test procedures that are used. In order to illustrate some of these effects, the theory was applied to results from several different experimental paradigms. These applications, we hope, have demonstrated the general principles by which the transfer of information in memory is controlled and shaped by reinforcement.

It is unfortunate that our discussion of reinforcement cannot be summed up in the form of a set of simple statements. Statements of this type, such as that of the law of effect, do not provide a consistent and unambiguous explanation of the range of reinforcement phenomena that have been observed. If the effects of reinforcement are analyzed in the context of an information-processing theory of the type outlined in this paper, we believe that they will appear relatively orderly and consistent.

REFERENCES

Atkinson, R. C. Information delay in human learning. *Journal of Verbal Learning and Verbal Behavior,* 1969, *8,* 507–511.

Atkinson, R. C., Brelsford, J. W., Jr., and Shiffrin, R. M. Multiprocess models for memory with applications to a continuous presentation task. *Journal of Mathematical Psychology,* 1967, *4,* 277–300.

Atkinson, R. C., and Shiffrin, R. M. Mathematical models for memory and learning. Technical Report 79, Institute for Mathematical Studies in the Social Sciences, Stanford University, Stanford, California, 1965. (To be published in D. P. Kimble (Ed.), *Proceedings of the third conference on learning, remembering and forgetting.* New York: New York Academy of Sciences.)

Atkinson, R. C., and Shiffrin, R. M. Human memory: A proposed system and its control processes. In K. W. Spence and J. T. Spence (Eds.), *The psychology of learning and motivation: Advances in research and theory.* Vol. 2. New York: Academic Press, 1968. Pp. 89–195. (a)

Atkinson, R. C., and Shiffrin, R. M. Some speculations on storage and retrieval processes in long-term memory. Technical Report 127, Institute for Mathematical Studies in the Social Sciences, Stanford University, Stanford, California, 1968. (b)

Bilodeau, E. A., and Ryan, F. J. A test for interaction of delay of knowledge of results and two types of interpolated activity. *Journal of Experimental Psychology*, 1960, *59*, 414–419.

Bourne, L. E. Information feedback: Comments on Professor I. McD. Bilodeau's paper. In E. A. Bilodeau (Ed.), *Acquisition of skill*. New York: Academic Press, 1966. Pp. 297–313.

Bower, G. H. An association model for response and training variables in paired-associate learning. *Psychological Review*, 1962, *69*, 34–53.

Bower, G. H., and Trabasso, T. R. Concept identification. In R. C. Atkinson (Ed.), *Studies in mathematical psychology*. Stanford, Calif.: Stanford University Press, 1964. Pp. 32–94.

Brelsford, J. W., Jr., and Atkinson, R. C. Short-term memory as a function of rehearsal procedures. *Journal of Verbal Learning and Verbal Behavior*, 1968, *7*, 730–736.

Brelsford, J. W., Jr., Shiffrin, R. M., and Atkinson, R. C. Multiple reinforcement effects in short-term memory. *British Journal of Mathematical and Statistical Psychology*, 1968, *21*, 1–19.

Broadbent, D. E. Flow of information within the organism. *Journal of Verbal Learning and Verbal Behavior*, 1963, *4*, 34–39.

Buchwald, A. M. Effects of immediate vs. delayed outcomes in associative learning. *Journal of Verbal Learning and Verbal Behavior*, 1967, *6*, 317–320.

Buchwald, A. M. Effects of "right" and "wrong" on subsequent behavior: A new interpretation. *Psychological Review*, 1969, *76*, 132–143.

Crowder, R. G., and Morton, J. Precategorical acoustic storage (PAS). *Perception and Psychophysics*, 1969, *5*, 365–373.

Elliot, P. B. Tables of d'. In Swets, J. A. (Ed.), *Signal detection and recognition in human observers: Contemporary readings*. New York: Wiley, 1964. Pp. 651–684.

Estes, W. K. Reinforcement in human learning. In J. Tapp (Ed.), *Reinforcement and behavior*. New York: Academic Press, 1969. Pp. 63–94.

Feigenbaum, E. A. The simulation of verbal learning behavior. In E. A. Feigenbaum and J. Feldman (Eds.), *Computers and thought*. New York: McGraw-Hill, 1963. Pp. 297–309.

Festinger, L. *A theory of cognitive dissonance*. Evanston, Ill.: Row Peterson, 1957.

Freund, R. D., Loftus, G. R., and Atkinson, R. C. Applications of multiprocess models for memory to continuous recognition tasks. *Journal of Mathematical Psychology*, 1969, *6*, 576–594.

Greenspoon, J., and Foreman, S. Effect of delay of knowledge of results on learning a motor task. *Journal of Experimental Psychology*, 1956, *51*, 226–228.

Gregg, L. W., and Simon, H. A. Process models and stochastic theories of simple concept formation. *Journal of Mathematical Psychology*, 1967, *4*, 246–276.

Guthrie, E. R. Association of contiguity. In S. Koch (Ed.), *Psychology: A study of a science*. Vol. 2. New York: McGraw-Hill, 1959. Pp. 158–195.

Harley, W. F., Jr. The effect of monetary incentive in paired-associate learning using a differential method. *Psychonomic Science*, 1965, *2*, 377–378. (a)

Harley, W. F., Jr. The effect of monetary incentive in paired-associate learning using an absolute method. *Psychonomic Science*, 1965, *3*, 141–142. (b)

Harley, W. F., Jr. Delay of incentive cues in paired-associate learning and its effect on organizing responses. *Journal of Verbal Learning and Verbal Behavior*, 1968, *7*, 924–929.

Hill, J. W., and Bliss, J. C. Modeling a tactile sensory register. *Perception and Psychophysics*, 1968, *4*, 91–101.

Hintzman, D. L. Explorations with a discrimination net model for paired-associate learning. *Journal of Mathematical Psychology*, 1968, *5*, 123–162.

Hochman, C. H., and Lipsitt, L. P. Delay-of-reward gradients in discrimination learning with children for two levels of difficulty. *Journal of Comparative and Physiological Psychology*, 1961, *54*, 24–27.

Kamin, L. J. Predictability, surprise, attention and conditioning. In B. A. Campbell and R. M. Church (Eds.), *Punishment and aversive behavior*. New York: Appleton-Century-Crofts, 1969. Pp. 279–296.

Keller, L., Cole, M., Burke, C. J., and Estes, W. K. Reward and information values of trial outcomes in paired-associate learning. *Psychological Monographs*, 1965, *79* (Whole No. 605).

Keller, L., Thomson, W. J., Tweedy, J. R., and Atkinson, R. C. Effects of reinforcement intervals in paired-associate learning. *Journal of Experimental Psychology*, 1967, *73*, 268–277.

Kintsch, W., and McCoy, D. F. Delay of information feedback in paired-associate learning. *Journal of Experimental Psychology*, 1964, *68*, 372–375.

Lawrence, D. H., and Festinger, L. *Deterrents and reinforcement: The psychology of insufficient reward*. Stanford, California: Stanford University Press, 1962.

Loftus, G. R., and Wickens, T. D. The effect of incentive on storage and retrieval processes. *Journal of Experimental Psychology*, 1970, *85*, 141–147.

Millward, R. B. An all-or-none model for noncorrection routines with elimination of incorrect responses. *Journal of Mathematical Psychology*, 1964, *1*, 392–404.

Montague, W. E., Adams, J. A., and Kiess, H. O. Forgetting and natural language mediation. *Journal of Experimental Psychology*, 1966, *72*, 829–833.

Murdock, B. B., Jr. Recent developments in short-term memory. *British Journal of Psychology*, 1967, *58*, 421–433.

Norman, D. A. Toward a theory of memory and attention. *Psychological Review*, 1968, *75*, 522–536.

Peterson, L. R., and Peterson, M. J. Short-term retention of individual verbal items. *Journal of Experimental Psychology*, 1959, *58*, 193–198.

Phillips, J. L., Shiffrin, R. M., and Atkinson, R. C. The effects of list length on short-term memory. *Journal of Verbal Learning and Verbal Behavior*, 1967, *6*, 303–311.

Postman, L. Rewards and punishments in human learning. In L. Postman (Ed.), *Psychology in the making*. New York: Knopf, 1962. Pp. 331–401.

Rescorla, R. A. Conditioned inhibition of fear. In W. K. Honig and N. J. Mackintosh (Eds.), *Fundamental issues in associative learning*. Halifax: Dalhousie University Press, 1969. Pp. 65–89.

Restle, F. The selection of strategies in cue learning. *Psychological Review*, 1962, *69*, 329–343.

Rundus, D. Paired-associate recall following a distractor task: Initial and second choice performance. *Journal of Mathematical Psychology*, 1970, *7*, 362–370.

Rundus, D., and Atkinson, R. C. Rehearsal processes in free recall: A procedure for direct observation. *Journal of Verbal Learning and Verbal Behavior*, 1970, *9*, 99–105.

Saltzman, I. J. Delay of reward and human verbal learning. *Journal of Experimental Psychology*, 1951, *41*, 437–439.

Shiffrin, R. M. Search and retrieval processes in long-term memory. Technical Report 137, Institute for Mathematical Studies in the Social Sciences, Stanford University, Stanford, California, 1968.

Shiffrin, R. M., and Atkinson, R. C. Storage and retrieval processes in long-term memory. *Psychological Review*, 1969, *76*, 179–193.

Simon, H. A., and Newell, A. Information processing in computer and man. *American Scientist*, 1964, *52*, 281–300.

Sperling, G. The information available in brief visual presentations. *Psychological Monographs*, 1960, *74* (Whole No. 498).

Spring, C. Decay and interference theories of short-term forgetting. *Psychonomic Science*, 1968, *12*, 373–374.

Sternberg, S. High-speed scanning in human memory. *Science*, 1966, *153*, 652–654.

Thomson, W. J. Recall of paired-associate items as a function of interpolated pairs of different types. *Psychonomic Science*, 1967, *9*, 629–630.

Thorndike, E. L. *Human learning.* New York: Appleton-Century-Crofts, 1931.

Tolman, E. C. *Purposive behavior in animals and men.* New York: Appleton-Century-Crofts, 1932.

Tolman, E. C., and Brunswik, E. The organism and the causal texture of the environment. *Psychological Review*, 1935, *42*, 43–77.

Trabasso, T. R., and Bower, G. H. Presolution shifts in concept identification: A test of the sampling with replacement axiom in all-or-none models. *Journal of Mathematical Psychology*, 1966, *3*, 163–173.

Trabasso, T. R., and Bower, G. H. *Attention in learning: Theory and research.* New York: Wiley, 1968.

Wasserman, E. A., Weiner, B., and Houston, J. P. Another failure for motivation to enhance trace retrieval. *Psychological Reports*, 1968, *22*, 1007–1008.

Weiner, B. Motivation and memory. *Psychological Monographs*, 1966, *80* (Whole No. 626).

Wickens, T. D. Attribute elimination strategies for concept identification with practiced subjects. Technical Report 3, Laboratory of Human Learning, Brown University, Providence, R. I., 1969.

5

CATCHING UP WITH COMMON SENSE OR TWO SIDES OF A GENERALIZATION: REINFORCEMENT AND PUNISHMENT[1]

DAVID PREMACK

University of California, Santa Barbara

In this paper I have two objectives: to clarify some old statements about reinforcement and to make some new statements about punishment. Since I will treat punishment as the exact opposite of reinforcement, the need to return to the old cannot be a complete loss for the new. Earlier (Premack, 1965) I presented a summary of the reinforcement position which I still think to be a good statement, but since it did not allay all mis-understanding I shall attempt a different version here. Although both

[1] Preparation of this paper was supported in part by NIH Grant USPHS MH 15616.

versions describe the same position, there is reason to believe that this one will be better understood. One advantage of this restatement is that it will show how vastly more sympathetic is common sense to this view than to that of traditional psychology. The distance from common sense back to traditional psychology is, however, far greater than the distance forward to this position.

Value and Motivational Laws

I make the following assumptions in dealing with motivational phenomena:

1. Organisms order the discriminable events of their world on a scale of value.
2. The value that an organism assigns to a stimulus can be measured by the probability that the organism will respond to the stimulus. The probability can be estimated from the duration for which the organism responds. Durations can be compared over all possible stimulus and response dimensions under constraints which reduce to the requirement that either the rate-time functions for the several responses be comparable, or the probabilities compared be momentary rather than average.
3. Value is a unitary dimension.
4. Motivational phenomena — reinforcement, punishment, contrast, arousal — all result from a common state of affairs: a difference in value. In the rest of this section I will expand on each of these assumptions, in each case with an eye to coping with misunderstandings brought on by former presentations.

Universality of value.   If only to counteract the misimpressions of traditional psychology, it seems advisable to emphasize that species assign value to all the events of their environment. The reference to neutral stimuli, and positive and negative stimuli, has been so unqualified that even if it is recognized that these terms refer to positions on a continuum, it is time to re-emphasize the continuum. What stands forth is not continuity but the notion of categories with fixed membership. We are told that all species approach some stimuli, withdraw from others, and for the remaining majority, do neither; also that these correspond to reinforcers, punishers, and neutral stimuli respectively. Both assumptions are false. First, the environment is not divisible in the manner indicated, and second, when a defensible division is shown, it does not correspond to the aforementioned concepts. I will expand on those problems; however, even here we may note that although the environmental division can be made on a nonrelational basis, reinforcement and punishment cannot be dealt with except relationally, and logically it is impossible to establish a correspondence between relational and nonrelational predicates.

But the point I want to make can be illustrated more simply. Some years ago, Walter Kintsch and I did experiments in which we asked college students to sort chromatic stimuli on the basis of either standard judgments about color or their preference for the stimuli. Earlier I had required students to indicate which weight they preferred in an otherwise standard weight-judgment experiment. The results from both experiments showed two things: first, that value judgments can be made for stimuli which we sometimes suppose to be immune to such judgments; second, that the amount of information transmitted — the number of categories in which the stimuli were successfully sorted — was only slightly less for the preferential than for the judgmental mode. Though a bit silly, these (actually tedious) experiments re-established the obvious: Value is a scale that can accept all stimuli, and people can make close value judgments about stones and color swatches on the basis of very little practice.

Another set of experiments converges on a similar point from a different direction. One of four Cebus monkeys tested on a set of five indestructible manipulanda proved to have virtually no preferences (Premack, 1963). The absence of preference raises the question: What is peculiar, the monkey or the manipulanda? If we change the manipulanda, would the monkey show preference, or would we have rather to change the monkey in order to observe preferences? Consider two extremes. Some organisms will show preference for *any* set of items; for other organisms there is *no* set of items for which they will show preference. We did not have either other monkeys or other indestructible manipulanda, so we carried the question to children and dime-store items, both of which are in good supply.

Marilyn Benson, in pursuing her master's thesis, assembled a set of deliberately inconsequential trinkets, erasers, tiny dolls, paper clips, into two five-item sets, and then gave paired comparisons over both sets. In each case the child was asked to say which item in the pair he liked better. In addition, the child was given the same items one at a time and allowed to play with each one for two minutes. Every ten seconds Benson judged whether or not the child was in physical contact with the item. The two procedures, paired comparisons and duration of response, were administered in counterbalanced order to thirty-six children. In addition to finding a product-moment correlation of about 0.8 between the two measures, the outcome most immediately relevant here is this: Almost all children showed consistent preferences (despite the deliberately junky nature of *all* the items in the sets). Consistency of preference could be seen by plotting frequency of choice per item against rank order of item. If a child showed a steep curve for this plot on set A, he showed an equally steep plot for set B. Moreover, when the most preferred items of sets A and B were combined, and the procedures repeated, the preference curve for the new set A-B was indistinguishable from the curves for A and B. Only three or four children resembled the monkey whose lack of preference gave rise to the experiment. These children showed little preference on set A, equally little on B, and the same for the recombined set A-B. They had a "bad reputation" in the class and were considered "backward" by the teacher.

These data are compatible with the hypothesis that normal organisms will show preference for *any* set of (nonidentical) items, the degree of preference being determined not only by the items but also by the individual. Sensing, stating, even inventing preference is something organisms do. But this first assumption, it should be clear, is not likely to tremble for lack of proof. It stands barely on the threshold of verificational concern, heavily in the shadow of the context of discovery. It is offered both as an antidote to standard motivation theory, and as an introduction to the more propositional assumptions to follow.

Value and response probability.   The notion of value will be as helpful as our ability to obtain an untroubled measure of it. This is close to saying that the measure could be substituted for the concept, or that the concept is expendable where the measure is successful. This is the operational bias under which I prefer to operate and would do so now but for a desire to communicate more broadly. Unfortunately, neither operationism nor any other form of pure descriptivism communicates well, which is ironical since they are extolled on grounds of clarity. But operationism is a source of lucidity only *after* communication has already taken place on a more intuitive level, i.e., it can do a great cleanup job but is relatively poor at making contact.

The basic test procedure is to provide the subject with a stimulus and to record its contacts with it. The procedure must guarantee two conditions. First, the subject must apply the stimulus to itself, and second, the consequences of the application must be intrinsic, not extrinsic. Extrinsic can be distinguished from intrinsic by treating certain behaviors, e.g., run, drink, eat, as primitives. When the occurrence of one primitive makes possible the occurrence of another, the second represents the extrinsic consequences of the first. A response is said to occur on the basis of its intrinsic consequence only when its occurrence does not make possible the occurrence of another primitive. There is no constraint on the type of behavior; e.g., if subjects apply unconditioned stimuli to themselves, the behavior can be elicited — self-elicited — but it can also belong to a category in which the response is less determinately affected by a stimulus (see Catania, this volume, pp. 196–217).

I have been accused of ignoring the stimulus; in fact, all the response probabilities we have measured have involved explicit stimulus operations, e.g., pellets, sucrose solutions, pinball machines, manipulanda, activity wheels, etc. On the other hand, this reliance on stimuli is entirely practical. We need to be able to duplicate in the contingency situation the response probability measured in the base condition, and there is no easier way to do this than to present the same stimulus in both situations.

Yet the stimulus is but one of several determinants of response probability — and it is a mistake to treat it as a cause while assigning a lesser role to the other determinants (e.g., deprivation). Consider that the usual way in which we assess the value a subject assigns to, say, a sucrose solution, is to first stabilize the subject on a deprivation condition and then repeatedly offer the sucrose. The value so determined is subsequently translated into a reinforcement value by making the sucrose solution contingent upon a base event. The sucrose solution appears to be the cause of drinking, more than the deprivation condition. Being imposed by the experimenter, deprivation obtains at all times, whereas contact with the sucrose, which is in the subject's hands, obtains only at those times the subject chooses. But a hypothetical experiment, which is a reversal of the customary one, will show that the deprivation condition is equally a cause of drinking. In the hypothetical experiment, sucrose tubes obtain at all points in the test space, even as the deprivation condition previously obtained at all points, but only by touching a particular one of the tubes with its mouth does the subject enter a deprivation condition (and thus drink). This value of drinking, too, can be translated into one of reinforcement by making not sucrose but the deprivation condition contingent upon a base response. The fact that this experiment could actually be done these days with brain stimulation is a technicality, the fundamental point being that response probability has many determinants. To treat the stimulus as special — a cause where the other determinants are merely contributive — is to mistake engineering for something deeper. Still, it may be no more than sound perceptual theory to assign greater weight to determinants with sharp onset-offset characteristics. In principle, however, all response determinants could be given the same pulse shape. Our understanding of behavior will be improved when not only the stimulus but all response determinants are used as contingent events.

Recent work shows that rats will press for deprivation or its neural equivalent quite as they press for food. When a rat is hungry but lacks food, it responds for food. This traditional experiment, it is now clear, is but half the story, a half which is misleading in suggesting the view that organisms respond "to reduce drives." The other half of the experiment, done only recently (Mendelson and Chorover, 1965), shows that when the rat has food but lacks (the neural equivalent of) hunger, it presses for hunger (or the neural equivalent). In brief, eating depends on two conditions, food and hunger. When the rat has either of the two conditions, it will respond for the one that it does not have.

Furthermore, eating is but one form of a more general process that might be called stimulus contact and which may include self-fistula feeding as well as feeding by mouth. It would be of interest to repeat Mendelson's clever experiment when it is not food that is available to the rat but a gastric-injection device. Perhaps self-fistula feeding may also depend upon hunger and a food source; when the rat has one but not the other, it may in this case, too, respond for the missing condition. Organisms apparently seek stimulus contact, not the "reduction of drives"; we must leave open the question of the loci at which the contact may be effective.

Probably the most common misinterpretation of this position is that I treat the response as the cause of reinforcement value. There are five points that apply here, all of them small, though sizable in combination.

1. Even the most resolute cognition theorist cannot reasonably demean the response since it affords the only direct way of calibrating the value the subject assigns to a stimulus.

2. The contribution to value of responding per se could not be extracted without experiments of a kind which I have never done and have no intention of doing. There will be cases in which the response factor will loom large and other cases in which it will not. In tennis or volleyball, for example, the activity per se will be an important source of value, whereas, conceivably, injected sucrose may be no less reinforcing than the ingested version. Is it safe to confess that I have little interest in these essentially physiological matters?

3. It should be clear that in talking about response probability I could not have in mind anything comparable to the view that response magnitude or vigor is a predictor variable. If vigor or magnitude are assigned more than metaphorical meaning, then we should be surprised by even the most common reinforcement outcomes, e.g., by the fact that licking can reinforce running. Licking is a very small movement, whereas running involves the whole body. If it is objected that there was never any intention to apply these measures across responses, but only to compare one vigor of, say, licking with another such, then once again it should

be clear that this proposal does not bear on mine; it was my intention from the beginning to make comparisons across responses, since only in this way can we fully predict what will reinforce what.

4. Even though it is desirable to take the position that a response is a means of calibrating the value a subject sets on a stimulus, and that the precise contribution which the response factors make to value is a matter for research, we should not swing so far in the other direction as to return to the traditional stimulus error. For example, tradition talks about the reinforcement value of food. But food has no value; we must talk about the value of food when it can be smelled (but not seen), seen (but not smelled), both seen and smelled, eaten, etc. It is part of the advantage of response language to avoid this kind of error automatically.

5. Are there stimuli which cannot be calibrated directly since they lack an associated response? And, if so, how shall we handle them? (We might just kick them under the table since the number and diversity of those on top of the table are entirely sufficient for a respectable test of any law.) I shall leave open the question of whether in the intact organism there are any such stimuli; certainly there are in the surgical preparation, e.g., fistula feeding. Does the reinforcement value of stimuli which cannot be directly calibrated differ in any important way from those which can be directly calibrated? Value can be assessed indirectly by appealing to a scale based upon the stimuli that can be directly calibrated. Using the test (or "indirect") stimulus as a contingent event, we ask which of the responses associated with the scaled stimuli will the test stimulus reinforce. All properties established for the directly calibrated stimuli (e.g., transitivity, nonreflexivity) must hold equally for the indirect cases. Almost certainly, the difference between stimuli for which there are and are not clearly associated responses will prove to be trivial; we will not require different laws for such stimuli, only different procedures for assessing their value.

Value is a unitary variable.   Outside the laboratory, organisms do not spend much time comparing 32 per cent sucrose with 16 per cent, or 12 foot-candles with 16 foot-candles, and so forth. Insead, they routinely compare cases which, far from being confined to a common stimulus scale, are of a kind which would make a psychophysicist shudder, e.g., dancing with a redhead versus eating Florida lobster, sailing a boat versus staying home and watching television, and the like. Comparisons of this general kind must be commonplace or the motivational laws to which we will turn in a moment would be quite different. However, we know painfully little about the processes by which organisms make these comparisons. What we can talk about instead are the procedures which an experimenter can carry out that will permit him to make predictions about the subject's behavior. This is a step in the right direction if only because a first guess about the subject's process is that he uses measures like those that work for the experimenter; this especially would seem to be a reasonable conjecture when the subject and experimenter are products of the same evolutionary history.

Suppose we assume that organisms use a general measure in making value judgments, and then pursue this measure on the basis of blind empiricism. I would think such a program to be greatly encouraged by the demonstration that reinforcement is reversible. We know that running will reinforce drinking under some circumstances, quite as drinking will reinforce running under other circumstances (Premack, 1962). Therefore it must be an *experiential* factor, not any intrinsic characteristics of running or drinking, that determines what will reinforce what. But if the rat can reliably discriminate this factor why should the experimenter be unable to find it or something correlated with it?

All responses, no matter how different their form, have in common the fact of extension in time. Further, given that certain standard assumptions are met, response probability can be estimated from response duration. Nevertheless, although responses are commensurable with respect to time, there is a reluctance to compare them on that basis. Why? The answer would seem to involve differences in duration of different response units, along with a would-be hedonic factor which does not always seem to be well correlated with time. Sex of course is the outstanding example. On the other hand, would we be less reluctant to use the measure if all responses had the same duration? There is a way in which to normalize response duration.

The total period for which a stimulus is available to a subject can be partitioned into small units of time, each one equal to the minimum duration of the response in question. In drinking, for example, possible response time would be divided by units equal to 1/7 second, the approximate duration of a lick; in eating, by 1/5 second, the approximate duration of a chew; in face-grooming, by 1/5 second, etc.[2] For each such unit a digital decision would be made as to whether or not the subject contacted the stimulus. The measure would then consist of the ratio: actual

---

[2] Personal communication from John Rugh.

contacts/possible contacts. If the distribution of contacts within the time period is random, the ratio estimates the average probability of responding for the time period. The partitioning of possible response time by units proportional to the duration of specific responses is what I had in mind in an early discussion which argued that a minimum unit (spu: smallest possible unit) could be found for each behavior (Premack, 1959). Fortunately, before attempting to carry out this proposal, I realized that these minimum durations, if such there be, are not needed in order to estimate response probability.

Making digital decisions about responding over a normalized time grid affords a crude approximation of a measure which a clock gives more accurately. That is, finally it became clear that counting up the little positive units is equivalent to what a clock does better, and that the simple ratio, actual response time/possible response time, is an equivalent, in fact more accurate, estimate of response probability for the time periods in question.

There are several constraints that need to be observed in the use of response probabilities to predict reinforcement values. In one way or another they refer back to the fact that responding is not constant over time. Because responding changes over time, *average* response probabilities may badly misrepresent momentary response probabilities. The observance of a simple rule would seem to safeguard most of the difficulties: Do not rely upon average response probabilities, unless you know that the duration-time curves for the responses being compared are approximately comparable.

Consider, for example, the curves shown in Figs. 5-1 and 5-2. The curves in Fig. 5-1 show the average frequency with which a monkey operated each of four manipulanda (Premack, 1963). They show the typical decrement over time, and are among the relatively few sets in which the curves are more or less congruent. Which is to say, the rank order among the curves is nearly constant over time so that the average probabilities properly represent the momentary probabilities. The set in Fig. 5-2, showing the average duration for which three groups of rats turned activity wheels and drank each of two sucrose solutions, is more typical in lack of congruence of the curves (Hundt, 1964).

Whenever the rate-time curves for two responses intersect within a session — a condition more common than may be appreciated (e.g., Premack, 1962) — we fail to exploit a test opportunity in saying simply that the response with the greater average probability will reinforce the one with the lower average probability. If the test is done properly, the initially more probable response will reinforce the other response "early" in the session, but later in the session the contingency can be reversed,

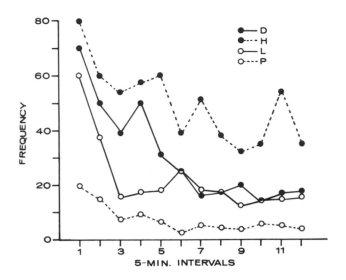

FIGURE 5-1. Frequency of manipulation by a Cebus monkey of each of four individually presented manipulanda, showing approximately equal habituation rates (after Premack, 1963).

and the initially less probable but currently more probable response will do the reinforcing (Bauermeister, 1969). In other words, it is possible to reverse the reinforcement relation on a within-session basis — by exploiting reversals in momentary response probabilities caused by differences in habituation rates — and not only on the relatively crude between-session basis on which it was first done (Premack, 1963).

It is important that the parameter values used in the reinforcement session — contingent time and interstimulus interval, which can themselves affect response probability (e.g., Premack, 1965) — are also employed in the session used to measure the response probabilities. For example, if the reinforcement session is to use a VI 60-second schedule with a contingent time of five seconds, then exactly these temporal parameters should be used in the measurement of the response probabilities. The opportunities to run or drink should be made available, independent of a response requirement, once a minute on the average, each time for five seconds. The subject's utilization of these opportunities over the course

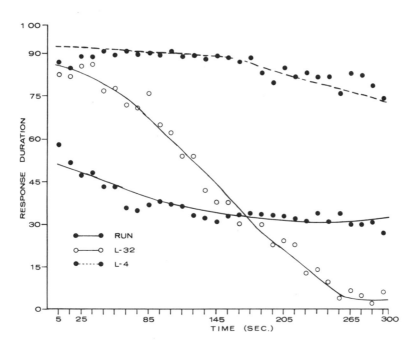

FIGURE 5-2. Duration of drinking 32 per cent and 4 per cent sucrose and running in an activity wheel over time by three groups of rats showing unequal habituation rates (after (Hundt, 1964).

of the session will permit estimates of its momentary probabilities of running and drinking. When these events are subsequently made contingent upon the bar-press, and the increment to the bar-press is plotted as a function of the previously determined probabilities of running and drinking, not only will the function be proportional to these probabilities, it will tend to be linear (Greeno, 1968; Hundt, 1964).

Another difficulty which can ensue through the indiscriminate use of average response probabilities is shown in the curves contrasted in Fig. 5-3. Response A depicted in the curve on the right attains an extremely high probability at relatively long intervals, whereas response B shown on the left attains half that probability but at half the interval. The *average* probabilities of the two responses are thus equal; however their momentary reinforcement values will not be equal. At T_x the reinforcement value of response A is $K \times 0$, that of response B, $K \times .5$; whereas at T_y, the reinforcement value of A is $K \times 1$, while that of response B is half that value. Response A is intended to afford at least a heuristic account of

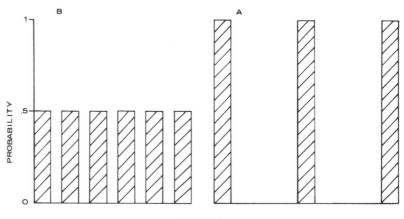

FIGURE 5-3. Hypothetical curves (see text for explanation).

copulation, an explanation of the seeming incompatibility between the great appeal of this behavior and its limited duration.

Motivation and relativity. All motivational laws can be stated as a relation between two or more values; they differ in the operational context in which the values are brought together. Thus, the difference between reinforcement and behavior contrast or between contrast and arousal is in the way a procedure operates upon the value relations. In reinforcement, access to the more-valued object is contingent upon prior responding to the less-valued object. In behavior contrast, a reduction in the availability of one high-valued event leads to increased instrumental responding to a second high-valued event, which may or may not be the same as the first (e.g., extinction of the opportunity to run produced an increase in bar-pressing to drink [Premack, 1969]). There is no contingency between responding less in the first case and more in the second, and for this procedural reason we distinguish contrast from reinforcement, yet both are intimately linked to differences in value and would not take place without such differences.

Changes in arousal also appear to be expressible as value functions. Observation of two white Pekin ducks in a backyard which these domestic birds shared with some wild children showed the ducks to have a set of ambient behaviors with fairly stable base rates. These behaviors included grooming, foraging, scanning of the sky, and preflight movements. Suppose we introduce a container of water, too small to permit swimming but big enough to allow dunking. The bird dunks several times; then we note a marked increase in the rates of grooming, foraging — all the ambient behaviors. The value of water-in-a-medium-container (of dunking) is greater than that of the stimuli associated with the ambient behaviors. The introduction of a stimulus or response opportunity whose value is greater than that of the obtaining stimuli leads to an increase in the ambient behaviors. Since this is procedurally different from both contrast and reinforcement, we give it a special name, but it too is a case of response facilitation arising from a difference in value.

Tradition has sought to distinguish drive stimuli, both positive and negative, from other stimuli, and to use these distinctions to explain reinforcement and punishment. It is possible to show, first, that the usual basis for the distinctions will not work, and second, that when workable bases are shown they are completely wanting in the desired explanatory function. For example, following Skinner's (1938) suggestion, hunger and thirst were defined as a positive functional relation between hours of deprivation for x and amount of responding to x when x was subsequently restored. But although the operationism here is impeccable, the proposed functional relation fails to segregate out from stimuli generally a special class which common sense supposes to have motivational properties of unusual interest. For example, if we apply this test to a lever — a prototypic example of a neutral or nondrive stimulus, since it is the prime instrumental event — we find no less a positive relation than we find when the same test is applied to food. That is, lever-pressing is an increasing function of hours of lever deprivation so-to-speak (Premack and Bahwell, 1959; Premack and Collier, 1963). And indeed, until shown otherwise, we have no reason to doubt that *every* stimulus to which a species responds will instance Skinner's drive definition.

But this does not do justice to common sense which I think is correct in wanting to set certain stimuli aside as being more interesting motivationally than others. Although Skinner's proposal will not oblige common sense, other definitions will. For example, we can add to Skinner's proposal what amounts to a consecutiveness requirement and get the desired separation. To obtain the function in the case of a lever we must give a number of consecutive tests at a particular value before moving to a new value; otherwise the function washes out, i.e., the animal responds as much after only three hours of "deprivation" as after forty-eight. For instance, the monkey mentioned earlier was tested seven times at each value of lever deprivation before being shifted to a different value.

Subsequently, this same experiment was repeated with groups of rats which were given the opportunity to press a bar that turned on a light. All groups were given 40 sessions, 8 at each of 5 intersession intervals ranging from 3 to 48 hours. Rats that received all 8 tests at an intersession interval before being rotated to a new interval showed strong interval effects: They made more and, to some extent, longer presses at 48-hour intervals than at 24, more at 24 than at 12, and so forth. Rats tested only 4 times before being rotated showed weak interval effects, and those tested only once before being rotated showed none; they responded as much after 3 hours rest as after 48 (interestingly, the average overall level of responding was the same for all groups). Thus, the drive function is found in nonrecurrent behaviors ("neutral class") only with repeated consecutive measures at each interval. This restriction does not appear to apply to recurrent behaviors. In the case of food, for example, the subject can be rotated through all values of deprivation with no consecutive tests at any value and still show clear deprivation or interval effects. Accordingly, there is the suggestion that in the neutral class, but not in the motivationally interesting one, consecutiveness is a boundary condition for the drive function.

But the separation can be made on an even simpler basis. Put the stimulus in home cage and ask whether or not the subject responds to it indefinitely. In some cases the asymptotic response level is greater than zero, and in some cases it is not. For example, rats eat food, drink water, and turn activity wheels indefinitely, the amount chastened only by senility; but a lever or light-contingent lever installed in home cage is ultimately ignored. Collier and I (1963) called these cases recurrent and nonrecurrent, which is sticking pretty close to the facts; simple as the distinction is, the classes that result overlap closely with what common sense has in mind when it proposes to set some cases aside as being of unusual motivational interest.

Unfortunately, however, there is no correspondence between these classes and what is punishing, reinforcing, or neither. You may object to my distinctions and wish to propose your own. Entirely reasonable. My only contention is that as long as you concur with common sense that there are some motivationally interesting cases, no matter what basis you may propose for getting at them, it will not coincide with or illuminate reinforcement (or punishment) any more than the basis proposed here.

Consider that we have separated two classes of stimuli, on whatever basis you choose, amounting to those that are and those that are not motivationally interesting. The "positive" or interesting class will include such things as eating, drinking, and so forth; the "neutral" class such things as pressing a lever, looking at the sky, rubbing a piece of velvet, and so forth. The standard procedure for doing reinforcement is to make responding to a member of the first class contingent upon responding to a member of the second class. That is the standard way and, if it were the only way, the drive division of the environment would correspond to and even perhaps explain the reinforcement division. But, in fact, in terms of these two classes there is not one but four ways of producing reinforcement.

First, both the instrumental and contingent members could be taken from the positive class as, for example, when dessert is made contingent upon eating string beans, or in the laboratory analogue, 32 per cent sucrose (in a food-deprived rat) is made contingent upon drinking 8 per cent sucrose. Although the relational character of reinforcement should already be apparent, a theory which resists this perspective and wants to hold that only positive drive stimuli can produce reinforcement, could still do so. However, even at this point there should be some head scratching. What is the class of events that can be reinforced? These examples show that, as common sense knew but traditional psychology overlooked, the events subject to reinforcement are not restricted to responses associated with neutral stimuli. Goal responses are subject to reinforcement.

More serious trouble arrives with the next case in which both the instrumental and contingent events are taken from the neutral class. Here, in a desperate attempt to produce revelatory illumination at a single stroke, I once successfully reinforced (horizontal) lever-pressing with (vertical) lever-pressing (Premack, 1963). But the scene lighted by the data showed few faces and none with expressions indicative of deep understanding.

Finally, one can return to the opening case, positive contingent upon neutral, and reverse it, thereby completing the four possibilities. Reinforcement can be produced in four ways, two within class and two between classes, and, so far as I can see, the relation that determines what will reinforce what is the same in all four cases. Which is to say, after stimuli are divided into positive and neutral classes, on whatever basis one chooses, it is no more possible to predict what will reinforce what than before the division was made.

I am sometimes told that traditional psychology was well aware of all this, as common sense certainly is, and demonstrated as much by emphasizing the variable efficacy of food. The potency of food was always referred to a deprivation schedule and was emphasized to be conditional upon that schedule. With food contingent upon the bar-press, the increased efficacy of food produced by food deprivation would be shown by an increased rate of bar-pressing. But this is not the relativity I am talking about, and indeed the use of the word for this purpose is gratuitous since the efficacy of every psychological event is conditional upon a history of prior operations. The increased probability of eating produced by food deprivation translates into a two-fold increase in reinforcement efficacy. First, the one that tradition observed, the increased magnitude of instrumental responding, but second, one that tradition did not see, an increase in the number of responses that eating will reinforce (along with a complementary reduction in the number of responses that will reinforce eating).

A further point can be extracted from this relation. Reinforcement can be produced with many pairs of values, where the values refer to the probability of the instrumental and contingent responses respectively, e.g., .2–.4, .3–.6, .1–.9. and so forth. But tradition produced all of its reinforcement with essentially one pair of values, i.e., 0–1, the bar-press having little or no value and eating in the starved rat having a probability of close to one. There is no reason to suppose that every property which holds for the 0–1 case will hold for all other cases, yet tradition has based all of what it supposes to be general properties of reinforcement upon the one case. This is a slight inductive base from which to reach for the universal properties of reinforcement.

The 0-1 case is, of course, the experimental mapping of the traditional view that is found explicitly in Skinner (1938): There is a class of events that is reinforcing, a class that is not, and all of the former are trans-situational (i.e., any member of the former will reinforce any member of the latter). Interestingly, this view is essentially built into the Skinner box. The box offers the key peck or bar press on the one hand, and eating or drinking on the other. The former will almost always have an independent probability or base level less than that of the latter. Eating and drinking can be reduced, of course, but if they are, the bar press or key peck will tend to fall to a still lower level, so that in all circumstances in which reinforcement is possible at all, members of the one class will have a higher base level than members of the other class. The consequence of this artificial state of affairs is to make it appear as though eating and drinking were special, capable of reinforcing other responses but incapable of being reinforced themselves. Conversely, the same artificiality imputes special properties to the bar press and key peck: These responses are capable of being reinforced but are not themselves capable of reinforcing other responses. This is a false representation of the motivational space of any species with which I am familiar, and is the sense in which the situation is artificial. In fact, organisms are capable of a complete reversal in the independent probabilities of a number of pairs of responses, and this reversal is interesting because it can provide an exceptionally direct and simple disconfirmation of the absolute theory of reinforcement. Is the relation between Skinner's theory and apparatus coincidental? That is, does the Skinner box (or any other apparatus for that matter) succeeed in being a neutral test space, a kind of theoretically-uncommitted area for carrying out a descriptive behaviorism? On the contrary, if all experiments were confined to this apparatus, it would be impossible to disconfirm the absolute theory of reinforcement despite the fact that the theory is false.

Reinforcement and Punishment: Two Sides of a Generalization

I have dealt with reinforcement as the outcome of a relation in which a more probable or preferred event is made contingent upon a less probable one. Two co-workers, Weisman and Hundt, each in his own way has proposed treating the opposite proposition as a formulation of punishment. That is, since a transition from a less to a more probable event facilitates responding, a transition from a more to a less probable event may suppress it.

A direct and simple way of testing this possibility is to return to old cases, used earlier to produce reinforcement, reverse them (so as to make the more probable lead to the less probable event), and see if they yield suppression rather than facilitation. The outcome of several such studies will be reported, along with a discussion of the question, "But is that really punishment?" Classification is an interesting if puzzling matter, and an opportunity to look at that puzzle should not be missed.

Consider that one established in rats a probability of running intermediate between two probabilities of drinking. For example, a thirsty rat will be more likely to drink than run, whereas a rat with an unrestricted water supply will be more likely to run than drink. D_1 is a probability of drinking less than R_1 which is a probability of running less than D_2 which is another probability of drinking, i.e., $P_{D_2} > P_{R_1} > P_{D_1}$. The contingency if D_1 then R_1 should result in reinforcement, an increase in drinking, since running is more probable than drinking. But the contingency if D_2 then R_1 should result in punishment, a decrement in drinking, since running is less probable than drinking. This pair of contingencies affords a clear test of the hypothesis. One and the same event is predicted to produce both reinforcement and punishment, depending only upon the probability of the base event relative to that of the contingent event.

A provision is needed in this experiment, however, which was not needed for reinforcement alone. Since punishment involves a transition from a more- to a less-preferred event, fulfillment of the instrumental requirement will afford the animal access to a stimulus to which it is less likely to respond than to the stimulus of the instrumental response. Unless the subject is forced to respond to the contingent stimulus, it will simply continue instrumental responding, and the contingency will not be realized. In the case of reinforcement there is no such problem since the contingent event is more probable than the instrumental one. Thus, in punishment the subject needs to be forced to respond to the contingent event, whereas in reinforcement it needs merely to be presented with the opportunity for response. This distinction between being forced and allowed to respond corresponds to two kinds of contingencies which we might call direct and indirect.

In the indirect contingency, fulfillment of the instrumental requirement presents the subject with a stimulus, an opportunity to respond, whereas in the direct contingency, it places the subject into contact with the stimulus, into a state of responding. Until recently, the direct case had been restricted to punishment, the indirect to reinforcement; but with the advent of brain stimulation and the use of self-forced running, the direct contingency has been extended to reinforcement.

The importance of this distinction, at this point, is to establish that the predicted punishment or reinforcement results not from differences in the form of the contingency, but strictly from the difference in the probability relations. Fortunately, it is easy to control for this factor. Although punishment is possible with only one form of the contingency, reinforcement is possible with both forms. Thus, if in both cases we force the animal into a state of running, yet produce reinforcement in one case and punishment in the other, the difference in outcome could not be attributed to the form of the contingency.

The apparatus used in most of the experiments reported here was a modified Wahman activity wheel equipped with a brake, one or two retractable drinkometers, and, on some occasions, a retractable bar, as shown in the sketch in Fig. 5-4. The brake and all the retractable devices are controlled by compressed air. The kind of running used to accommodate the special requirements of punishment is a form of self-forced running (Hundt and Premack, 1963; Kavanau, 1963). The wheel is not

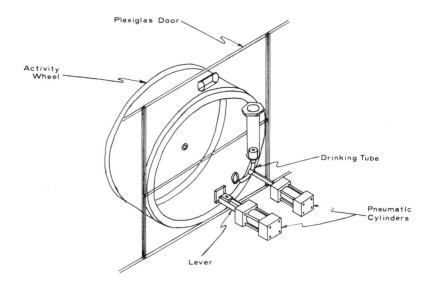

FIGURE 5-4. A sketch of the run-drink apparatus (see text for explanation).

free to turn but is attached to a variable-speed motor. When the motor is turned on, the wheel rotates and the rat is forced to run. Any of several responses can be used to turn on the motor, including bar pressing, drinking, or a still different mode which resembles the rat's natural way of initiating and stopping running. Photocells are located along the circumference of the wheel, to the right and left of center line. When the rat moves a short distance up the wheel, as it does in initiating free running, it interrupts the beam and starts the motor; conversely, when it falls slightly behind the movement of the wheel and is carried back a short distance, it interrupts the opposite beam and stops the motor. Unless otherwise stated, the bar-press was used to activate the motor in the experiments reported here.

The duration of drinking was measured by an electronic clock that operated continuously as long as it received at least four pulses per second from the drinkometer. Free running was defined by direct observation as a rotation producing a current of at least 19 milliamperes on a tachometer attached to the wheel. At lesser currents, the characteristic topography of running was not observed (see Premack and Schaeffer, 1962, for a description of running in the rat). For each second of running (which maintained the criterion current), one pulse was fed into the programming circuit, and ratio schedules were defined on this basis. In addition, an electronic clock operated continuously whenever the criterion current was produced. In free running, most rats turned the wheel about one rotation per second; in forced running, they turned the wheel at approximately half this speed.

In a first experiment on this matter, four female albino rats, about 120 days old, Sprague-Dawley strain, were used in a crossover design (Weisman and Premack, 1966). Two were first maintained on free food and water, then on free food and 23-hour water deprivation; the other two received the same maintenance conditions in the reverse order. There were three main steps in the experiment: a base condition establishing the preferences for running and drinking, a contingency between the two behaviors, and a return to base. The experiment was repeated after the maintenance conditions were reversed. The rats were given daily 15-minute sessions in which the drinkometer was present continuously and each bar-press turned the motor on for a 5-second period. The base data in the first panel of Fig. 5-5 show that drinking was preferred to running when water was restricted, but that running was preferred to drinking otherwise. In the second step, the bar was retracted and running was made contingent upon drinking, i.e., following a predetermined number of licks, the motor was turned on and the wheel rotated for a 5-second period. Consider first the case in which drinking was more probable than

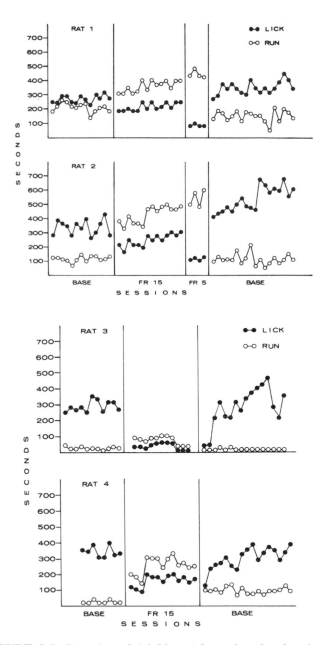

FIGURE 5-5. Duration of drinking and running showing the base level of each behavior, the suppression of drinking by running, and the subsequent return to base (after Weisman and Premack, 1966).

running so that suppression of drinking or punishment was predicted. Further, since order proved to have no effect, consider the punishment case for the two rats which received this contingency as their first experience (E-1, E-2), and for the two which were reinforced before being punished (E-3, E-4).

In all cases, the contingency produced an immediate suppression in drinking. The suppression was substantial and lasting in two rats (E-1, E-3), but was largely overcome during the course of contingency sessions in the two other rats. The recovery of baseline responding over contingency sessions has been reported in classical punishment studies when the electric shock was mild (Azrin and Holz, 1966). It is no coincidence that the two rats showing lasting suppression have a lower probability of running than the two that recovered. Even in the rats that recovered, however, a notably sharper decrement was produced in the next step by lowering the fixed ratio from fifteen licks to five. An increase in running may be seen to have accompanied the change in FR, but it was small compared with the greatly increased suppression in drinking. The lack of a simple proportionality between the increase in running and decrease in drinking suggests that suppression was not produced through the simple mechanical interference of running.

In the last step of the design the contingency was terminated and the base condition was restored. The results are shown in the last panels of Fig. 5. Drinking not only recovered its baseline but went on to attain values in excess of baseline. Interestingly, running also recovered its baseline, this despite the fact the rat had been forced to run both at times and in amounts not of its own choosing. In this case at least, the prior use of an event as a punisher did not deny its possible subsequent use as a reinforcer. Indeed, the crossover part of the design, which is presented for two of the rats, shows that, following the restoration of water and a reversal in the preferences for running and drinking, the same contingency then produced reinforcement, facilitation of drinking.

Figure 5-6 presents data for the two rats which were first tested in the punishment case and then in the reinforcement case. The first panel shows that with unrestricted water, running was preferred to drinking. The second panel shows that the contingency which previously suppressed drinking now facilitated it. In the last step, with the base condition reinstated, both drinking and running tended to recover baseline values; neither showed any rebound effect such as was seen at a comparable stage in the punishment procedure. In brief, the same contingent event which previously suppressed drinking now facilitated it. Thus, the outcome cannot be ascribed to the intrinsic properties of running but only to the relation between running and the response upon which it was contingent.

The two subsequent experiments add to the determinacy of the punishment outcome. First, in one experiment (Weisman and Premack, 1966), three older rats, in all of which the probability of running was close to zero, were subjected to the same contingency. The suppression of drinking was nearly 100 per cent and essentially permanent. For these animals, being forced to run and to endure electric shock are more nearly comparable. Both are states which the animal has little probablity of entering, i.e., of applying to itself. But the depressed running in these older rats would have made them unsuitable for the previous experiment. To show that the same event can both punish and reinforce demands that the event have an independent probability greater than zero.

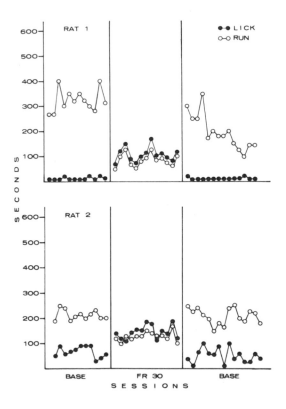

FIGURE 5-6. Duration of drinking and running showing the base level of each behavior, the reinforcement of drinking by running, and the subsequent return to base (after Weisman and Premack, 1966).

A recent experiment (Terhune and Premack, 1970) examined the proportionality between the probability of not-running and the punishment effect of being forced to run. In the base condition, the rat was given the opportunity to drink for 10 seconds every 40 seconds on the average; in addition, it was forced to run every 40 seconds on the average and could turn the wheel off with a lever-press. Two kinds of data were provided by the base condition. First, the frequency with which the opportunity to drink was exploited (at least five licks), and second, distributions showing the probability that the rat would turn the motor off at $t + n$ seconds, given that it was turned on at exactly t. In the second phase of the study, various durations of forced-running were made contingent upon drinking. The drinking tube was presented for 10-second periods by the same VI 40-second schedule as before, but the lever was removed and the motor was no longer turned on by its schedule. Instead, each time the subject made five licks it was forced to run for a predetermined duration. Four different

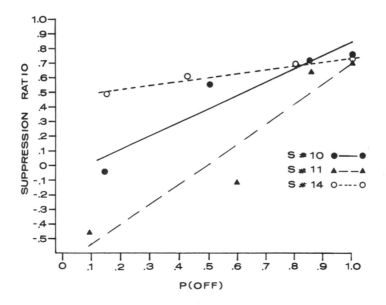

FIGURE 5-7. The suppression of drinking as a function of the probability of not-running; each curve is for an individual rat (after Terhune and Premack, 1970.

fixed durations of forced-running were used with each subject, not the same four, but durations determined by the P(off)-distribution for the subject. In each case the durations used corresponded to P(off)-values of approximately 0.1, 0.5, 0.8, and 1.0. The four rats being thirsty, the probability of drinking was greater than that of running; the contingency should, therefore, suppress drinking, as shown by the previous experiments. What was not known was the functional relation between the magnitude of suppression and the probability of not-running. A clear answer to that question is given in Fig. 5-7 where per cent suppression $(1 - \dfrac{\text{contingency drinking}}{\text{base drinking}})$ is plotted as a function of the probability of not-running. Although slope differs from subject to subject, the relation tends to be linear.

It is of interest to compare this punishment function with a reinforcement function recently reported by Langford, Benson, and Weisman (1969). These writers first measured the probability of operant-level drinking as a function of hours of water deprivation, and then, using the same deprivation values, made drinking contingent upon bar-pressing. In Fig. 5-8, the probability of drink-contingent bar-pressing is plotted as a function of the previously determined probability of drinking. Like the punishment function, this function tends to be linear with slope varying from subject to subject. In Fig. 5-9, the probability of drinking is plotted as a function of water deprivation. The function is nonlinear and, moreover, it could be given a number of other forms merely by appropriate changes in the deprivation procedures. For example, when the drinking interval is regularly 24 hours, the subject will drink more at that time than at intervals both greater and less than 24 hours. Changes in the deprivation function should not, however, affect the relation between the probability of drinking and bar-pressing for the opportunity to drink. That is, the linear relation shown in Fig. 5-8 is not special to the deprivation procedures of that experiment, but should hold for all deprivation procedures, whatever shape the deprivation function may take.

The reinforcement function shows that facilitation is a linear function of the probability that the subject will perform the contingent event; the punishment function that suppression is a linear function of the probability that the subject will not perform the contingent event. The constant of proportionality differs from subject to subject. Terhune and I are now determining both the reinforcement and punishment function in the same subjects. Will the constant of proportionality for the two functions be the same for a given individual? That may be an excessive demand on parsimony. It would be an adequate simplification if the rank order of the slopes for the two functions were the same from subject to subject.

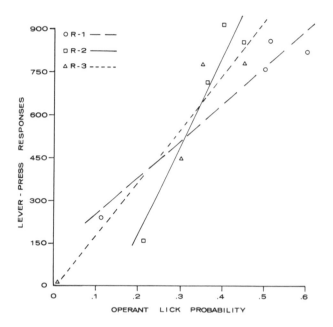

FIGURE 5-8. The probability of drink-contingent bar pressing as a function of the probability of drinking (after Langford, Benson, and Weisman, 1969).

Is this really punishment? In answering that question keep in mind that the alternatives are not "yes" or "no," but rather, this is "a new member of an *old class*," or this is "a member of a *new class*." The latter, of course, is the radical option so that the evidence for its adoption must be stronger than that for the conservative option. There is a tendency to misunderstand the options which are presented by "new phenomena" — a tendency reflected in the common remark, ". . . that's interesting, but it's not so and so." However "interesting" is not a category. Replicable outcomes cannot be lift in limbo, denied membership in one class without some other class being provided for them.

There are four molar properties in which the present results accord with those produced by electric shock and none I know of in which tests showed a failure of concordance. First, the suppression is immediate, occurring at a maximum value from the onset of the contingency. Second, in

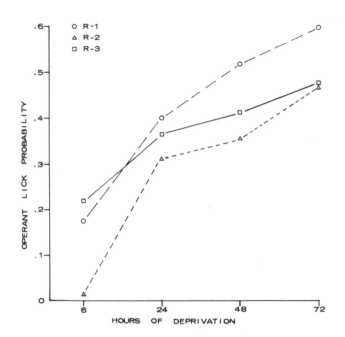

FIGURE 5-9. The probability of drinking as a function of hours of water deprivation (after Langford, Benson, and Weisman, 1969).

some cases, the suppression is overcome wholly or in part during the course of the contingency sessions. Third, there is an order effect such that suppression is greater if the first of the several values experienced is one that maximizes suppression. For example, in the preceding experiment, two of the rats were tested on ascending probabilities of not-responding and two on descending probabilities. Suppression was greater in those tested on descending values, even as it is in rats tested on descending values of voltage. Fourth, when the contingency is disrupted, the instrumental event often overshoots its former baseline (see Azrin and Holz, 1966).

It will be instructive to place the suppression produced in this manner into direct opposition with suppression produced by electric shock and then ask the subject to choose between them. Consider an experiment in which drinking is suppressed on one tube by 40 per cent with a procedure of the present kind, and on a second tube by an equal amount through a contingency with electric shock. If, when presented with both tubes, the subject were to choose equally between them, this would be a gratifying comment on the simplicity of the world. But I would reject an equality of this kind as a necessary condition for regarding both suppressions as belonging to the same class. That is too severe a demand; electric shock may entail special properties that are not entirely reflected in suppression but which may nonetheless influence choice. Indeed, experiments of this kind might be one way of extracting the possibly special properties of electric shock.

The laboratory environment can be divided into stimuli with which species both initiate and terminate contact, and those with which they only terminate. Tradition has produced punishment only with the latter. There is a parallel with negative reinforcement. By definition, a negative reinforcer is one that is effective by removal whereas a positive reinforcer is one that is effective by presentation. An anthropologist looking at psychological lab practice could readily note that a vast specialization has taken place; there are experts in food on the one hand, and in electric shock on the other. But this use of two different classes of stimuli to produce these effects is both unnecessary and misleading. All stimuli which species work to turn on they will also work to turn off. Somewhat unfortunately, this fact first came to light in the context of brain stimulation (e.g., Bower and Miller, 1958), creating the impression that the property was unique to brain stimulation. In fact, it would appear to apply to all stimuli for which species initiate contact. Thus, Hundt and I (1963) showed that running could serve as both a positive and negative reinforcer, with rats barpressing above base level to start running and then drinking above base level to subsequently stop running. No surprise to common sense but strangely at odds with traditional psychology which, prior to brain stimulation, had never produced positive and negative reinforcement with the same event. Always two classes, and always the assumption of fixed membership. The question that now remains is whether suppression produced by stimuli which species both apply and terminate is inherently different from suppression produced by stimuli which species terminate but do not apply. The conservative conclusion, as I indicated above, is that they are largely the same thing, though the latter may have additional and special properties.

Complementary relations between reinforcement and punishment. There are some striking complementary relations between reinforcement and punishment that this procedure makes clear in a way that traditional procedures do not. The relations are revealed by obtaining baselines on *both* of the responses that are subsequently paired in the contingency.

Notice that reinforcement involves not one change but two: an increase in the instrumental event (the defining outcome), but also a *decrement* in the *contingent response* which has gone unobserved or in any case does not enter standard discussions of reinforcement (see Figs. 5-5 and 5-6). That is, in the case in which running contingent upon drinking facilitated drinking, the duration of running in the contigency was notably *less* than in the base condition. Indeed, there is reason to believe that this decrement is a necessary condition for reinforcement — that without it instrumental responding does not increase (Premack, 1965). However, the decrement may not represent a necessary condition additional to that of the probability relations as much as a way of realizing those relations. If the contingency suppresses the contingent response, giving it a rate of occurrence below its base rate, when the opportunity for the contingent response does arise, the probability of its occurrence should be especially high (higher than if there had been no suppression). In brief, any contingency which suppresses the contingent response will indirectly maximize its momentary probability of occurrence.

Notice now the strong parallel in punishment where, too, there is not one change but two: a decrease in the instrumental event (the defining outcome), but also an *increase* in the *contingent response*. That is, when running contingent upon drinking suppressed drinking, the duration of running in the contingency was notably *greater* than in the base condition. Thus, in the present examples, the facilitation or reinforcement of drinking was accompanied by a decrement in running, whereas the suppression or punishment of drinking was accompanied by an increment in running. Operationally, reinforcement is produced by denying the subject the opportunity to occupy a state as long as it would choose to, whereas punishment is produced by forcing the subject to occupy a state longer than it would choose to. Neither outcome depends upon the intrinsic character of the state; we have seen the same state (running) produce both outcomes.

Summary

All motivational phenomena are generated by preference — by the differences in value which normal subjects characteristically assign to the events in their environment. Value can be measured directly by the probability that the subject will respond to the events in question, making it possible to state all motivational functions in terms of response probabilities. The two functions we considered here, reinforcement and punishment, can be stated as follows. If a more probable response is made contingent upon a less probable one, the result will be facilitation — an increase in the base event. If a less probable response is made contingent upon a more probable one, the result will be suppression — a decrement in the base event. Reinforcement and punishment are therefore opposite sides of the same operation; the conditions which make one possible also make the other possible. Finally, there is the suggestion that both the reinforcement and punishment functions are linear. The facilitation ratio appears to be a linear function of the probability that the subject will perform the contingent event; the suppression ratio, a linear function of the probability that the subject will not perform the contingent event.

REFERENCES

Azrin, N. H., and Holz, W. C. Punishment. In W. K. Honig (Ed.), *Operant behavior: Areas of research and application.* New York: Appleton-Century-Crofts, 1966. Pp. 380–447.

Bauermeister, J. J. Positive reinforcement: Further tests of the Premack theory. Unpublished doctoral dissertation, Florida State University, 1969.

Bower, G. H., and Miller, N. E. Rewarding and punishing effects from stimulating the same place in a rat's brain. *Journal of Comparative and Physiological Psychology*, 1958, *51*, 669–674.

Greeno, J. G. *Elementary theoretical psychology.* Reading, Mass.: Addison-Wesley, 1968.

Hundt, A. G. Instrumental response rate and reinforcement density. Unpublished doctoral dissertation, University of Missouri, 1964.

Hundt, A. G., and Premack, D. Running as both a positive and negative reinforcer. *Science*, 1963, *142*, 1087–1088.

Kavanau, J. L. Compulsory regime and control of environment in animal behavior. I. Wheel running. *Behaviour*, 1963, *20*, 251–281.

Langford, A., Benson, L., and Weisman, R. G. Operant drinking behavior and the prediction of instrumental performance. *Psychonomic Science*, 1969, *16*, no. 3.

Mendelson, J., and Chorover, S. Lateral hypothalmic stimulation in satiated rats: T-maze learning for food. *Science*, 149 (whole no. 3683), 559–561.

Premack, D. Toward empirical behavioral laws: I. Positive reinforcement. *Psychological Review*, 1959, *66*, 219–233.

Premack, D. Reversibility of the reinforcement relation. *Science*, 1962, *136*, 255–257.

Premack, D. Rate differential reinforcement in monkey manipulation. *Journal of Experimental Analysis of Behavior*, 1963, *6*, 81–89.

Premack, D. Reinforcement theory. In D. Levine (Ed.), *Nebraska symposium on motivation*. Lincoln: University of Nebraska Press, 1965. Pp. 123–180.

Premack, D. On some boundary conditions of contrast. In J. Tapp (Ed.), *Reinforcement and behavior*. New York: Academic Press, 1969, Pp. 120–145.

Premack, D., and Bahwell, R. Operant-level lever pressing by a monkey as a function of inter-test interval. *Journal of Experimental Analysis of Behavior*, 1959, 2, 127–131.

Premack, D., and Collier, G. Analysis of nonreinforcement variables affecting response probability. *Psychological Monographs*, 1962, *76*, No. 5 (Whole No.), 524.

Premack, D., and Schaeffer, R. W. Distributional properties of operant-level locomotion in the rat. *Journal of Experimental Analysis of Behavior*, 1962, *5*, 89–95.

Skinner, B. F. *The behavior of organisms*. New York: Appleton-Century-Crofts, 1938.

Terhune, J., and Premack, D. On the proportionality between the probability of not-running and the punishment effect on being forced to run. *Learning and Motivation*, 1970, *1*, 141–147.

Weisman, R. G., and Premack, D. Reinforcement and punishment produced by the same response depending upon the probability relation between the instrumental and contingent responses. Paper read at Psychonomic Society Meeting, St. Louis, 1966.

6

IMPLICATIONS OF SENSORY REINFORCEMENT[1]

HARRY FOWLER

University of Pittsburgh

As the topics to this and other recent books (e.g., Tapp, 1969b) readily attest, a major focus of the past decade has been on the specification of new forms and conceptualizations of reinforcement, and of approaches to understanding its nature. My concern in this area has been primarily with curiosity and exploratory phenomena or, with reference to its stimulus aspects, novelty and stimulus-change rewards, or more broadly, sensory reinforcement. When viewed together with those recent developments that bear on the motivational and perceptual impact of a stimulus per se, the phenomenon of sensory reinforcement seems to offer several broad implications regarding the nature of reinforcement; in particular, the factors that constitute reinforcement and the mechanisms or processes by which it operates so as to facilitate performance. (It should be obvious

[1] Preparation of this article and the research that is described were supported in part by Grant HD-00910 from the National Institutes of Health, U.S. Public Health Service. The author gratefully acknowledges the assistance of the following individuals in conducting the reported experiments: Ray L. DeMarco, Jeffrey Epstein, Joel Harper, Kristin Hoeveler, Barry Krickstone, Stephen Lewis, Donald M. Lubin, Jon B. Messer, Christiana Narr, Michael C. Tennebaum, and Ronald L. Williams.

that my usage of the term "reinforcement" is in the Thorndikean sense of "strengthening" preceding behaviors, as opposed to the Pavlovian notion of eliciting consistent reactions, although the two are certainly theoretically related.)

My purpose in this paper is to point up the developments relating to sensory reinforcement and, in discussing their implications, to interpret reinforcement phenomena in terms of general motivational and perceptual processes. Specifically, I have attempted to accomplish this aim as follows: first, by describing briefly the early course of development of "curiosity" research and the major theoretical issues which this research engendered; second, by evaluating my own theoretical position (Fowler, 1967) within this framework and on the basis of recently collected data on sensory (light-onset) reinforcement that have led me to alter and liberalize the position rather considerably; and third, by relating these current data and their reinterpretation to associated developments within the field, hopefully with the result of summarizing the major facets of the reinforcement process.

History and Significance of "Curiosity" Research

The renewal of interest in curiosity and exploratory phenomena in the early and mid-1950's was significant in several respects but primarily in highlighting a simple S-R relationship: Stimuli that were novel, in the sense of providing a change or a discrepancy in the animal's prevailing stimulation, elicited consistent reactions that were classifiable as orientation, approach, investigation (e.g., sniffing), manipulation, and the like. The basis for this S-R relationship, which had earlier been described by Pavlov (1927) as an "investigatory reflex," was now quite broad, encompassing a variety of experimental settings and response measures. Rats, for example, showed increased and ordered sequences of locomotor activity in novel as opposed to familiar mazes (e.g., Montgomery, 1951, 1952); similarly, they approached and entered that arm of a T- or Y-maze which had been changed in brightness from a prior exposure (e.g., Kivy, Earl, and Walker, 1956), and even when both arms were of the same brightness at the time of choice (Dember, 1956; Fowler, 1958); and, they spent more time sniffing and coming into contact with novel rather than familiar objects and configurations (e.g., Berlyne, 1950, 1955; Berlyne and Slater, 1957). Chimpanzees performed comparably, exhibiting increased responsiveness in novel and complex, as opposed to simple, situations (Welker, 1956a, b), and monkeys showed considerable manipulatory behavior with complex latch and puzzle devices (e.g., Harlow, 1953; Harlow, Blazek, and McClearn, 1956).

Initial interpretations of this investigatory or response-to-change phenomenon were based on an assortment of drive-motivational constructs including Berlyne's (1950) "curiosity drive," Harlow's (1953) "manipulation motive" and "visual-exploration drive," and Montgomery's (1953) "exploratory drive." Of these, Berlyne's (1950) account of a "curiosity" drive was representative: Confronted with a novel stimulus object, the animal engaged in a "drive-stimulus-producing response" (called *curiosity*) which aroused investigatory responses that were directed to the curiosity-producing stimuli. With this formulation, as well as with others of the drive genre, novel or complex stimuli thus provided an operational referent for the animal's curiosity and, as presumed motivational stimuli, they were accorded both cue (directing) and drive-producing (i.e., energizing) properties.

Novelty as a reinforcer. The research which ensued in the mid- and late 1950's and extended to the early 1960's was equally important in highlighting still another relationship: Novel stimuli presented in a contingent relationship to specific behaviors had the effect of facilitating these behaviors. The empirical basis for this reinforcement effect was comparably broad. For example, rats learned to press a bar and/or to run in a shuttle box so as to gain entry into a novel compartment (e.g., Myers and Miller, 1954; Zimbardo and Miller, 1958); and, in a discrimination context, they learned to select that arm of a T-maze which provided the opportunity to explore a complex checkerboard maze (e.g., Montgomery, 1954; Montgomery and Segall, 1955). Similarly, monkeys learned to push a panel in order to view the stimulus variation that was provided outside of their walled cages by moving electric trains, other caged monkeys, and so forth (e.g., Butler, 1954, 1957a); and, both rodents and primates learned to press a lever for any of a variety of so-called sensory reinforcers including light onset (or offset), different visual patterns, noises, and the like (see Fowler, 1965; Kish, 1966). These and similar observations indicated clearly that novel stimuli, which via the earlier curiosity studies had been shown to elicit exploratory reactions of approach, investigation, and so forth, would also reinforce any of a variety of responses that produced these stimuli. Thus, taken together with their previously ascribed cue and motivating functions, novel stimuli were now accorded a reinforcing function. Such a development was significant, indeed, for it generated a series of perplexing theoretical issues.

The first major problem was that confronting contemporary motivational theory. Given that novel stimuli were both reinforcing and drive-producing, the fact that animals learned to respond for novelty indicated that sensory reinforcement effects were associated with an *increase* in drive and not with its reduction or termination. It seemed evident, therefore, that this phenomenon could not be reconciled with classical drive theory and its correlative hypothesis of reinforcement through drive reduction. What was needed apparently was a conceptualization in which reinforcement depended upon both increases and decreases in drive, a formulation which would designate reinforcement not only on the basis of a decrease in intense stimulation, as with the animal's escape or avoidance of aversive stimuli, but also on the basis of the "increased" stimulation that the animal gained as a result of performing responses that produced novel stimuli and the like. Herein, a basis was laid for theories which would stress that the animal's performance was subject to *optimal levels* of stimulation and arousal: Both increases and decreases in stimulation could be reinforcing (or motivating, for that matter) depending upon the animal's initial level of stimulation and arousal (Fiske and Maddi, 1961; Hebb, 1955; Leuba, 1955). Unfortunately, these new theoretical formulations had their own shortcomings which posed the second set of problems.

To account for the facilitation (or suppression) of performance resulting from a response-contingent event, reference was made within the arousal formulation to the organism's initial level of stimulation and the extent to which the response-contingent event generated stimulation more closely approximating an optimal level of arousal. Accordingly, meaningful prediction of different performance outcomes could only be accomplished via the a priori specification of what constituted an optimal level of arousal for the organism at different points in time, and under different conditions of stimulation. Such specification was clearly wanting, however, and thus an accounting of behavior was dependent upon the post hoc assumption of the animal initially having "too much" or "too little" stimulation and arousal, as the data might dictate (see Fowler, 1965).

A second, if not more critical, problem related to the manner in which arousal (or activation) was to be interpreted as a motivational construct. As a concept which would replace drive, and yet maintain the latter's motivational (i.e., energizing) character, arousal was equated with drive as an "energizer," as an "energizing mechanism," or as "the intensive dimension of behavior" (cf. Fiske and Maddi, 1961; Hebb, 1955; Malmo, 1958, 1959). Thus, with reference to the motivation of behaviors that were instrumental to novel stimuli and the like, and were reinforced by these stimuli presumably because they provided for *increased* stimulation and arousal (i.e., more closely approximated an optimal level), it followed from the arousal formulation, as stated, that such instrumental behaviors were highly motivated (i.e., energized and aroused) only when the "intensifying-energizing" aspect of behavior (viz., arousal) was minimal or absent! Indeed, only with the receipt of novelty and thus increased stimulation was the organism theoretically subject to the "intensifying-energizing" effect of increased arousal. The same problem had earlier been posed for the curiosity or exploratory-drive interpretation. Operationally dependent on novel stimuli, such a drive could not account for those instrumental behaviors by which the organism gained the novel stimuli, because these drive-producing stimuli were present only as a consequence of the organism's response, and thus only after the organism had made the response was the drive supposed to be motivating (see Brown, 1961).

Comparison with other reinforcers. The problem associated with the ascription of drive- or arousal-producing properties to sensory reinforcers was apparent in still another way. Given their functional properties, novel stimuli could only be viewed as unique among classes of reinforcing events. In comparison, positive reinforcers, like food and water, were ascribed both cue and reinforcing properties, but it certainly was not generally held that food, for example, was a drive-producing event. (However, see Sheffield, 1966a, b). On the other hand, so-called "negative" reinforcers, like electric shock, bright lights, and loud noises, were accorded both cue and drive properties, but no one viewed response-contingent shock as a reinforcer — at least not in the sense of strengthening responses that led to the shock.[2] In the case of sensory reinforcers, however, the early work on curiosity behaviors cast novel stimuli and the like in a mold which accorded them all three properties; functionally, they appeared to serve as drive, cue, and reinforcing events. Thus, a major issue underlying the development of theories of sensory reinforcement lay in the manner in which sensory reinforcers were to be related to other classes of reinforcing events. Were novel stimuli comparable to appetitive stimuli, or to aversive stimuli, or to both?

Actually, a resolution to this problem seemed straightforward. There was no question empirically that novel stimuli could serve as cues by which investigatory behaviors were elicited and directed. This was established early with the observation that animals selectively responded to changed or novel-stimulus alternatives and could even accomplish this feat when the characteristics of the stimulus alternatives (e.g., brightness) were identical at the time of choice (see Dember, 1956). Similarly, there

---

[2] This comparison may also point up the misnomer involved in referring to aversive stimuli, like shock, as negative reinforcers. Insofar as the functional property of a reinforcer is to facilitate prior behavior, negative reinforcement has appropriate reference to the facilitation produced by the removal or termination of an aversive event, with its counterpart in positive reinforcement referring to the presentation of a preferred event (see Campbell and Church, 1969, p. 518 f.).

was no question about the reinforcing property of novel or changed stimuli, as the phenomenon of sensory reinforcement did in fact attest, and even under stringent test arrangements (see Berlyne, 1969). What *was* suspect, however, was the drive-motivational (i.e., energizing) property that had early been ascribed to novel events in an effort to account for the occurrence of responses of orienting, approaching, sniffing, manipulating, etc., that were directed to or elicited by the novel or changed-stimulus events. When one acknowledged, however, that these behaviors attested only to the cue or US (i.e., directing and eliciting) properties of novel stimuli, and further that these behaviors were not different in function from those unconditioned reactions of chewing, salivating, or ingesting a food object (i.e., in permitting the organism to react to, experience, or "consume" the eliciting stimulus), it seemed evident that sensory reinforcers were of the same mold as appetitive reinforcers. Like appetitive events, then, novel or changed-stimulus events apparently were not to be cast as drive-producing events. But herein lay an additional problem: If novel stimuli were not motivating in the specific sense of energizing that class of investigatory behaviors appropriate to them, what was the source of motivation by which the organism was, in fact, aroused or driven to engage in these investigatory reactions, or even those instrumental responses by which the novel events were produced? Again, the answer seemed to follow directly from the comparison with positive and negative reinforcers.

In the appetitive case, the reinforcing effect of food depended upon an antedating condition of deprivation; similarly, in the aversive case, the reinforcement provided by the termination of a stimulus like shock was dependent upon an antedating condition entailing the presentation of the aversive stimulus. Thus, in both cases, specific antedating conditions set the occasion for reinforcement and, in both cases, these antedating conditions of deprivation or of intense stimulation were accorded drive-motivational properties. Regarding sensory reinforcement effects, this comparison suggested that the reinforcing efficacy of novel or changed stimuli should also depend on specific antedating conditions, and further, that such conditions, in view of the apparent functional parallel between appetitive and sensory reinforcers, would relate to the deprivation of novelty or of stimulus variation (Fowler, 1963, 1965). Logically, deprivation of novelty would prevail with the organism's exposure to familiar and unchanging stimuli, and thus, operationally, it would relate to the *duration* and *constancy* of the stimuli confronting the organism prior to or during its instrumental response for novelty reward and/or its investigatory response to the novel stimulus itself. Given this interpretation, the motivational problems raised by the earlier theoretical formulations seemed conveniently resolved: With sufficient exposure to a simple or even complex set of stimuli, the organism would become satiated (i.e., "bored") with these stimuli and thus it would be motivated to respond both *instrumentally for* stimulus variation and *directly to* novel objects that were introduced into its immediate environment. As such, stimuli that were familiar to the organism by way of its exposure to them could tentatively be cast as having both cue and drive properties, whereas novel stimuli were to be accorded their empirically established functions of serving both as a cue which would elicit and direct behavior and as a reinforcer which would facilitate instrumental responding.

By designating familiar and unchanging stimuli as operational referents for an exploratory drive, the proposed formulation (Fowler, 1965, 1967) offered one additional consequence. With sensory and appetitive reinforcers cast in a common mold wherein both depended upon antedating conditions of deprivation (of either novelty or of food), sensory reinforcers were subject to extant interpretations of the nature of appetitive reinforcement. That is to say, theories such as Hull's (1952) and Spence's (1956), which had been formally elaborated in the context of instrumental appetitive conditioning, were now fully applicable in construct designation (and correlative mechanisms of operation) to performances based on sensory rewards. According to Spence (1956), for example, the effect of food reward on instrumental performance was mediated by the anticipatory occurrence of consummatory or "goal" reactions (R_g's) to the food object. More specifically, through classical conditioning (and also stimulus generalization), fractional components of R_g would occur in the context of those cues (i.e., CS's) which antedated the US of food and were associated with the instrumental response. Accordingly, this fractional anticipatory consummatory response and its associated "feedback" stimulus (i.e., $r_g - s_g$) would be contiguous with the instrumental response and could exert an intensifying influence on its performance — as through CS-intensity or summation effects (i.e., the addition of s_g to prevailing cues) and/or conflict-frustration effects (i.e., the "blocking" of a full r_g due to the absence of food during instrumental responding). Essentially, then, appetitive rewards were conceptualized as *incentives;* that is, response-contingent events which, via the organism's anticipation of them, exerted a *motivating* (i.e., intensifying) effect on instrumental performance.

Spence's (1956) incentive-motivational interpretation of appetitive rewards could easily be applied to the action of novel or changed stimuli serving as sensory reinforcers. That is to say, responses of orienting, approaching, sniffing, manipulating, and so forth, which were elicited by these stimuli, could be viewed as a class of investigatory responses by which the organism reacted to, experienced — in effect, "consumed" — the novel or changed-stimulus event. Hence, following Pavlov's (1927) conceptualization of the investigatory reaction as a UR to a "neutral" stimulus (in this case, novelty or a change in stimulation), the same conditioning basis existed by which fractional components of these investigatory responses could become anticipatory and, via their associated feedback stimuli (i.e., s_g), could exert an incentive-motivational effect on on instrumental responding. Given this interpretation, the proposed reformulation of exploratory motivation (Fowler, 1965, 1967) did not, in fact, vitiate the motivational function that had been accorded novel stimuli in the earlier theoretical formulations; rather, it recast this influence (and function) as part of a broader drive-incentive formulation wherein novel stimuli, although disassociated from a drive-motivational effect, were treated formally as incentives. From the standpoint of this interpretation, "curiosity" was no longer a drive-stimulus-producing response elicited by novel stimuli; instead, it was an *incentive-mediating* response (viz., r_g) that related to the organism's *anticipation* of novelty reward. Totally viewed, this drive-incentive formulation argued that the motivation underlying instrumental performance depended both upon the organism's satiation or boredom with familiar stimuli and upon its curiosity (anticipation) of the change in stimulation that would prevail contingent upon its instrumental response.

Assessment and reinterpretation of a drive-incentive formulation.
The proposed interpretation was convenient not only from the standpoint of resolving the problems posed by the earlier formulations, but also because it served as a highly specific, circumscribed, and thus easily tested model that had developed from work on instrumental appetitive conditioning. For example, by designating in the case of sensory reinforcement drive (D) and incentive-motivational (K) constructs comparable to those posited in the context of appetitive reinforcement, comparable effects and functional relationships between the constructs could be expected with manipulation of the specified D and K variables. Thus, variation in the organism's length of exposure to a homogeneous set of stimuli (as an operational expression of the organism's familiarity with these stimuli) would be expected to produce variations in D, as reflected by different performance levels associated with the organism's response for changed or novel stimuli. Similarly, manipulation of the magnitude of the change in stimulation (i.e., the degree of relative novelty) contingent upon a response would be expected to yield comparable K produced variations in performance, and when taken together with the noted D manipulation, provide an evaluative basis for assaying the drive-motivational function

of familiar stimuli; that is, both as "energizing" stimuli and as the basis for reinforcement. Assessment, of course, could also be extended to the interaction of the D and K factors, and to the effects of associated reinforcement parameters such as the delay, pattern, and schedule of novelty reward. Herein, a basis existed for studying a potential inhibitory process, as had been designated in the context of instrumental appetitive conditioning (see Spence, 1956).

Exposure and change as D and K variables. To some extent, the operations designated as underlying the satiation (D) and curiosity (K) constructs had already been investigated when the formulation was initally elaborated (Fowler, 1965) and, in general, the findings of these studies were in substantial agreement with the interpretation. For example, studies by Butler (1957b) and Fox (1962) showed that operant response rates by monkeys for general visual incentives or for light-onset reinforcement in particular were progressively heightened with increasing hours of deprivation of the visual incentives. Similarly, rates of responding by both monkeys and rats were higher with varied and complex visual incentives (e.g., Barnes and Baron, 1961; Butler and Woolpy, 1963) and with increasing extents or amounts of change in response-contingent light stimulation (McCall, 1965). However, these and other studies bearing on the proposed D and K constructs had been restricted in the case of the drive operation to assaying relatively lengthy periods of confinement (as opposed to immediate or short-term exposure), and none of the studies had been directed to the functional relationship of the exposure and change variables, or to their proposed status as motivational factors. Given these concerns, a program of research was undertaken in which the condition of exposure imposed upon the animal prior to its instrumental response and the subsequent condition of a change in stimulation made contingent upon that response were structured, respectively, as the start and goal conditions of a straight-alley apparatus. Thus, the research focused on the acquisition of a simple running response when the only imposed variables were regulated and sequential exposure to the discernible features of the test apparatus.

The research initially conducted (Fowler, 1967) consisted of four independent experiments, utilizing the same general training procedure: The subjects, albino rats, were individually transported from their home cages to a start compartment which was a uniform brightness (e.g., black) as effected by painted wall inserts. Then, after a specified length of exposure (e.g., 1, 3, or 7 minutes) to the start-compartment brightness, the subject was permitted to run and be exposed to a change in brightness (e.g., to white) at the goal, where it was also detained for a specified period (typically 1 minute) prior to being removed and returned to its home cage. It is important to note that both the alley and the far wall of the goal were the same brightness as the start compartment so that the subject's receipt of a change in brightness was *contingent* upon its entry into the goal, that is, upon its viewing of the side and rear walls of the goal including the back of the guillotine goal-box door.

In the first and second experiments, length of exposure to the start-compartment brightness and magnitude of brightness-change at the goal (e.g., black to white, gray, or black) were factorially manipulated along with length of exposure to the goal brightness. This latter variable was included so as to assess the possible satiation (i.e., drive-producing or "punishing") effects of overexposure to the goal brightness. In the third experiment, start-exposure time and magnitude of goal-brightness change were again factorially manipulated as in the prior studies, but following acquisition training, subgroups of each of two exposure and change conditions were shifted to one or the other of both of these conditions so as to assess whether performance differences among the conditions reflected associative (i.e., prior training) or motivational (i.e., current training, "momentary") effects. The fourth study also manipulated start-exposure time, but with goal-brightness change held constant and instead, both rearing and maintenance (home-cage) brightness varied. Thus, this last study assessed the effect of exposure (satiation) to similar or different rearing-maintenance brightnesses in relation to the brightnesses of the start and goal conditions.

The results of these initial four experiments were generally consistent in showing that the runway response was indeed reinforced by a simple change in brightness at the goal, that the acquired response was maintained without diminution over extended training (150 trials or more) — except under a no-change (e.g., black start to black goal) extinction condition — and that such performance related positively to both length of exposure to the start brightness and magnitude of brightness-change at the goal. Performance effects were, moreover, amplified by exposure to maintenance (home-cage) brightnesses that were similar to the start brightness (or conversely, different from the goal brightness) and were reduced by extended exposure to the changed brightness at the goal. Hence, the data indicated that increased time of exposure to the homogeneous stimulus conditions that antedated the running response either proximally (in the start box) or distally (in the home cage) progressively facilitated the response; contrarily, extended exposure to the changed-stimulus condition postdating the response progressively weakened the response analogous to a punishment effect.

Regarding these findings, the results of Experiment 3 were particularly important in showing that alterations in start-exposure time and goal-brightness change led to rapid and appropriate shifts in performance, pointing up the motivational (as opposed to associative) nature of the exposure and change variable. Taken together with the other results, these findings indicated that antedating conditions of exposure and subsequent conditions of change contingent upon the response could serve within the context of sensory reinforcement as empirical referents for the operation of both drive and incentive-motivational processes (Fowler, 1967). Given exposure to one set of stimulus conditions, the animal was apparently motivated via drive effects and, with the opportunity to perform a response that would lead to a changed-stimulus condition, it was also motivated via incentive effects to respond specifically for that change.

Extensions to light-onset reinforcement: General effects. These initial results were quite promising, but there remained the need for additional assessment as, for example, regarding the functional relationship of the D and K factors. Although the obtained data were consonant with the findings on appetitive reinforcement, showing an interaction of the D and K variables, assessment of this interaction in the present research had been limited to manipulations of high and low (near-0) values of D and K. Of theoretical significance was the fact that in instrumental appetitive conditioning, manipulations of *moderate* and high values of D and K generally produced an additive (i.e., noninteractive) relationship between the variables (see Black, 1965). Comparable assessment could be performed within the context of brightness-change reinforcement, but it required a better scaling of change values than was provided by the wall plates that had been used to effect the start and goal brightnesses.

A second and more important consideration related to the decremental effect obtained with extended exposure to brightness change at the goal. This outcome suggested the operation of an inhibitory process and called for the study of such potentially related factors as a delay of reward, partial and intermittent schedules of reward, and the like. But, again, these types of manipulations (e.g., a delay of reward) could not be readily accomplished with the wall plates that had been used to effect a change in brightness at the goal. For these reasons, and others to be noted, a followup program of research was initiated employing light-onset reinforcement. Although equally concerned with D and K manipulations, this research focused on the relationship between reinforcement and inhibition processes, as assessed by manipulations of the parameters of light onset, specifically, its intensity, duration, delay, pattern, and schedule of occurrence both within and across training trials.

In this subsequent and as yet unpublished work, the same subjects, general procedure, and apparatus were utilized with the exception that, in place of wall inserts, the entire runway was painted a uniform black. To effect light onset at the goal, the far wall of the goal was replaced with a frosted Plexiglas plate that was illuminated from behind by two 10-watt bulbs connected to a Powerstat. Also, as had been the case in the earlier research (Fowler, 1967), ambient overhead illumination was employed so as to regulate general lighting conditions within the start and alley sections of the runway at approximately .01–.06 foot-candles (near darkness to dim illumination). Finally, in addition to start and run-speed measures, the present research employed goal speeds; that is, reciprocal transformations of the time from the subject's interruption of an infrared photobeam at the end of the alley to its contact with a sheet-metal plate located on the floor in front of the frosted light panel of the goal. Inclusion of this goal-speed measure and, relatedly, use of light onset at the goal were specifically for the purpose of assessing a K interpretation of sensory-reinforcement effects. Because this interpretation holds that magnitude-of-reinforcement effects depend on the strength of the subject's consummatory or "goal" reaction (R_g) to reward, an attempt was made to evaluate the goal component of the runway response as a "consummatory" reaction to change, specifically, by assessing the extent to which a discrete change in stimulation, such as light onset, would elicit and maintain simple approach.

Although the results of this program of research have not yet been fully processed, the major findings can be sufficiently elaborated to point up significant parallels between sensory and appetitive reinforcement, and thus the implications which these parallels offer for understanding the nature of reinforcement. Regarding general effects, the findings of the present program of research were similar to those of the initial research showing that speed of running increased as a consequence of light onset at the goal (and conversely, decreased without light onset at the goal); that the acquired response was maintained without diminution over the course of extended light-onset training (180 trials); and further, that performance was positively related to both start-exposure time (4 vs. 8 minutes) and magnitude of light-onset reinforcement at the goal. In the present research, reinforcement-magnitude effects were positively related to both the intensity of the light (.00–.36 millilamberts) and, within limits, its duration (0–60 seconds); however, as with the earlier findings, performance was found to be degraded by an extended duration of light at the goal (i.e., 120 vs. 60 seconds).

In addition to confirming the findings of the initial studies, the present research showed that performance based on light-onset reward was subject to a decremental effect of increasing delay of reward (0–20 seconds) and, as with appetitive reinforcement, was comparably influenced by the trial-schedule of light-onset reward (25, 50, 75, or 100 per cent): Not only did partial light-onset reward protract extinction, and moreso the smaller the percentage of rewarded trials, but in addition, terminal acquisition performance was found to be an inverted-U function of reward schedule. That is to say, at the end of acquisition training, the 50- and 75-per cent groups showed somewhat better performance than the 100-per cent group and all three performed considerably better than the 25-per cent group (cf. Goodrich, 1959). Thus, as expected, both the delay and partial-reward extinction data suggested the operation of an inhibitory process analogous to that posited for performances based on appetitive reward (see Spence, 1956). In addition, the partial-reward acquisition data indicated that the "frustration" interpretation developed by Amsel (1962, 1967) for performances relating to the scheduling of appetitive rewards was equally applicable to performances based on light-onset reward.

Parameters of light-onset reinforcement: Interaction effects. By demonstrating these parallels between sensory and appetitive reinforcement, the findings of the present research, as well as those of the earlier research, suggest that both reinforcement systems are subject to the same principles and mechanisms of operation. For this reason, certain interaction effects occurring in the present research are of considerable signficance regarding the interpretation of sensory reinforcement and thus of appetitive reinforcement as well.

Intensity. In the initial experiment, which was concerned with the basic D and K manipulations necessary for demonstrating the prior effects relating to start-exposure time and magnitude of light onset (change) at the goal, a reinforcement effect was obtained with light onset relative to no light onset, but performance was not differentially related to the magnitude of light onset as affected by different intensities of the light (.01–.36 millilamberts). Furthermore, unlike that in the prior research, performance in this initial study was not positively related, but rather inversely related to start-exposure time (4 vs. 8 minutes). In fact, the poorer performance of subjects receiving longer exposure to the start condition was augmented by higher light intensities, so that for these subjects, performance was an inverted-U function of intensity (in contrast to an exponential function for the short start-exposure subjects). These results were virtually the opposite of what had been found in the earlier research (Fowler, 1967), for they indicated that performance was not facilitated (i.e., reinforced) by longer start exposure and greater change in illumination at the goal, but instead that it was suppressed (i.e., punished).

Fortunately, this initial study had employed goal speeds to assess the subject's reaction directly to the light and, although these speeds co-varied with run speeds at the end of training, they also showed an inverted-U relationship to light-onset intensity at the very start of training. Hence, the goal-speed data indicated that the higher light-onset intensities were relatively aversive and thus, contingent upon the running response, they would be expected to be punishing. Taken in conjunction with the run-speed data, the findings now suggested that such aversiveness was augmented by longer exposure to the near-dark (less than .01 foot-candle) start condition, comparable to the effect of dark adaptation on perceived brightness.

Antedating exposure.   To assess the potential punishment-reinforcement relationship between different light-onset intensities and general lighting conditions within the start and alley segments of the apparatus, the second study employed the same light-onset intensities as had been used in the first study, but increased ambient overhead lighting (within the start and alley segments) to a condition of dim illumination (specifically, .06 foot-candle). (Although maintaining the same physical values of light onset as a reinforcing stimulus, this alteration had the effect of reducing the magnitude of the change in illumination at the goal relative to the start brightness; otherwise, the procedure and design were virtually the same.) Under these conditions, goal speeds at the start of training were now not differentially related to light intensity, therefore indicating the absence of any differential aversion to these intensities. Over the course of training, however, goal speeds again co-varied with run speeds, but now both measures showed a positive relationship to light-onset intensity; and now also both measures were positively related to start-exposure time (4 vs. 8 minutes) with the result that performance was a joint, positive function of both start-exposure time and light-onset intensity. Thus, these data duplicated the findings of the initial program of research, demonstrating exposure and change manipualtions to be positive determinants of performance. Taken in conjunction with the results of the first study, however, the present findings were of significance regarding the nature of light-onset both as a punisher and as a reinforcer, for they indicated that even a relatively weak intensity of light was neither a reinforcer nor a punisher except as it related to the subject's antedating condition of exposure. Evidently, what was important in determining an outcome was not simply light-onset intensity, or the length of the subject's prior exposure, but the type of antedating exposure that the subject had received, and thus the way in which this type of exposure could affect its reaction to light at the goal.

Theoretically, the manner in which the subject's antedating exposure can influence its reaction to light is also of significance regarding the relationship of the proposed D (exposure) and K (light-onset) variables. With moderate and high values of both start-exposure time and light-onset intensity, the results of the second study showed no interaction effect, indicative of an additive relationship between the D and K variables. However, with low (near-0) values of light-onset intensity, there was a convergence of the start-exposure functions indicating an interaction. These data are consistent with those generally reported in the context of appetitive (food) reinforcement (see Black, 1965) and, collectively, they pose a problem regarding the theoretical combination of D and K. Indeed, depending on selected values, the obtained functional relationship suggests that their theoretical combination can be either multiplicative (cf. Hull, 1952) or additive (cf. Spence, 1956). Attempting to resolve this dilemma, Black (1965) has argued following Spence's additive rule that the deprivation operation can be viewed as a determinent of D and also as a contributing factor to K. The basis for the inclusion of the D operation as a parameter of K is that D, as a general energizer, should influence any and all responses, including the consummatory reaction (R_g) and its fractional antedating component (r_g) — reactions which underlie the action of K. Unfortunately, a logical difficulty with this resolution, as pointed out by Logan (1968), is that D would have a double weighting in determining the level of instrumental performance; that is, both as a direct energizer of the instrumental response and as an indirect energizer via R_g and the K mechanism ($r_g - s_g$).

Apart from a combination rule for D and K, and the problems associated with it (see Dyal, 1967; Evans, 1967), the implication of the present findings is that it would be better to treat D operations like deprivation or exposure not as the basis for a general energizing factor, but simply as parameters of K; that is, as conditions which potentiate or "set" the action of K. More specifically, exposure to an antedating stimulus condition may, through the subject's adaptation or habituation to this condition, set the occasion for and thereby regulate the strength of the reaction (R_g) to the change in the stimulation provided by light onset of a particular intensity. In effect, this interpretation dispenses entirely with D and posits that K, as operating through R_g and its anticipatory response mechanism ($r_g - s_g$), is determined not only by the extent of the physical disparity between a particular light-onset intensity and the subject's antedating condition of exposure, but also by the kind and length of its antedating exposure. Within this framework, facilitating and suppressing effects of the same physical stimulus are thus reconcilable on the basis of the characteristics of the subject's antedating exposure; that is, the extent to which this exposure may set the occasion for too abrupt or too intensive a change in stimulation and thereby promote an aversive reaction to it.

Delay. The foregoing interpretation of the effects of *"D"* manipulations is also relevant to the outcome of that experiment which assessed the effect of a delay of light-onset reward. In this study, as in the prior-noted ones, moderate and high values of both start-exposure time and light-onset intensity produced an additive relationship (i.e., no interaction) with immediate light-onset reward. However, with delays of light-onset reward extending to 20 seconds, performance levels both decreased progressively and tended to converge, indicating an interaction of the delay variable with both start-exposure time and light-onset intensity. This outcome would seem opposed to any interpretation in which the inhibitory (I) effects of delayed reward are viewed as operating independently of the values of D and K as, for example, in Spence's (1956) formulation of effective reaction potential: $E = H(D + K) - I$. And, although the findings are perhaps reconcilable with a competing-response interpretation stressing differential reinforcement of competing responses with longer delays of reward, the data would appear to be more readily assimilated by assuming simply that a delay of reward, like the D operation, affects K. That is to say, with the reward delayed, the subject's reaction (R_g) to light onset will also be delayed, providing a delayed (and therefore weaker) conditioning basis for r_g as a mediator of K. Given this interpretation, in which delay of reward is cast as an additional parameter of K, what is important is not simply the vigor of the subject's reaction (R_g) to light, as regulated both by exposure and by change, but *when* this reaction occurs relative to the instrumental response and the contextual or apparatus cues with which this response is associated.

Duration. A similar extension of the defining parameters of K is called for by the results obtained on the effect of light-onset duration. Like the initial research (Fowler, 1967), the present research showed a moderate decrement in performance with an extended duration of light onset at the goal (120 vs. 60 seconds), suggesting that both the intensity and duration of light onset may combine to produce an effectively more intense and thus somewhat aversive stimulus. Apart from this suppression effect of extended light-onset duration, the present data also showed that performance was positively related to durations of light onset ranging from 0 to 60 seconds. Hence, these data indicate that, relative to specific exposure conditions, how long the subject is in contact with (i.e., reacts to and "consumes") the light is an important determinant of the reinforcement effect, and further that the magnitude of this effect (or of punishment) is conjointly determined by the intensity and the duration of light stimulation.[3] Taken together with the results of the prior studies, then, these find-

---

[3] In view of the combined reinforcing and punishing effects of light onset observed in the present research it is of interest that the suppressing effects of a punishing stimulus like shock are also conjointly determined by the shock's intensity and duration, i.e., in promoting an effectively more aversive stimulus (see Church, Raymond, and Beauchamp, 1967).

ings argue that the reinforcing effect of light onset may be theoretically viewed as operating through the subject's reaction (R_g) to the light; that is to say, relative to specific exposure or "setting" conditions, sensory reinforcement (K) is regulated not only by the vigor or rate of R_g (as determined by both the length of the subject's antedating exposure and the intensity of the light), but also by the length of R_g and when it occurs relative to the instrumental response and the contextual cues with which this response is associated.

Pattern. The import of the present interpretation regarding the parameters of response-contingent light stimulation (e.g., duration and delay) as joint determinants of K is illustrated nicely in an experiment which investigated the effect of different "patterns" of light-onset reward. In this study, different groups of subjects received fixed on-off cycles of light of 60, 30, 15 or 7.5 seconds that were continuously presented throughout a goal period of 120 seconds. That is, subjects of the 60-second group received immediate light-onset reward for 60 seconds, followed by light offset for 60 seconds, for a total goal time of 120 seconds; subjects of the 30-second group received immediate light-onset reward for 30 seconds, followed by light offset for 30 seconds, with these on-off periods recycled for a total of 120 seconds; and similarly for subjects of the 15- and 7.5-second groups. Although equating both total light received and total time spent in the goal, these fixed on-off cycles of light effectively manipulated the within-trial frequency of light onset at the goal, and thus the number of changes in light stimulation contingent upon the subject's instrumental response. The results of this study showed that performance levels at the end of training, although generally high for all groups, were positively related to the length of the on-off cycle, or conversely, were *inversely* related to the number of light-produced changes.

Given an interpretation of sensory reinforcement which posits that stimulus change is rewarding, how is one to account for these results? The answer derives from the offered interpretation of the determinants of K and from an analogy based on the effects of differential magnitudes and delays of food reward (see Logan, 1965, 1968). Specifically, if one considers the number of light presentations to represent units of reward (cf., amounts of food) that vary in magnitude as determined by the duration of the light cycle, then it becomes apparent that the 60-second subjects received and were permitted to "consume" all of their light reward at once, whereas the 30-second subjects received one-half of this amount immediately and the remainder at a 30-second delay; for the 15- and 7.5-second subjects, respectively, one-fourth and one-eighth of the total amount of light reward was presented immediately and the remainder in comparable units at successive 15- and 7.5-second delays. So viewed, these data indicate that performance was a combined function of differential durations (magnitudes) and delays of light-onset reward and they argue, therefore, that both duration and delay of light onset are joint determinants of K. That these variables also interact with the subject's antedating condition of exposure in determining K is indicated by the fact that, in the present study, longer start-exposure time (8 vs. 4 minutes) had the effect of progressively augmenting performance differences in favor of the longer-cycle groups.

Schedule. That the subject's antedating condition of exposure is appropriately cast as a parameter of K is further indicated by the data obtained on the effect of partial schedules of light-onset reward. As previously noted for this research, performance at the end of acquisition training was an inverted-U function of the percentage of light-onset reward; that is, 50- and 75-per cent reward groups were somewhat superior to a 100-per cent group, and all three were considerably superior to a 25-per cent group. Comparably, in this context, longer start-exposure time had the effect of progressively augmenting performance differences in favor of the higher-reward groups. Emphasis has already been given to the proposed relationship of the subject's antedating condition of exposure to light-onset reward, so that the facilitating effect of longer start-exposure time is not surprising in the case of continuous reward. The same outcome, however, is expected with partial schedules of reward but now indirectly as a result of a presumed frustration reaction analogous to that posited by Amsel (1962, 1967) for partial schedules of food reward.

According to Amsel, partial reward causes the subject to make a frustrative reaction (R_f) to nonreward at the goal because, with the subject's occasioning of at least some reward, it is prevented (i.e., "blocked") from completing anticipatory consummatory reactions. With the occurrence of R_f and its associated feedback stimulus, S_f (to which overt "searching" movements may occur), a basis exists for the anticipatory occurrence of R_f - S_f; that is, r_f - s_f analogous to r_g - s_g. Because of the possible competing (i.e., "searching") responses associated with s_f, however, instrumental performance may be initially disrupted; but with additional training, these competing responses should be eliminated as a consequence of a within-chain delay of reward contingent on running without "searching" (no delay) and running with "searching" (delay). When this occurs, s_f can then become associated with the instrumental response and thus s_f can intensify it in a manner analogous to the effect of anticipatory reward stimulation (s_g). The same frustration interpretation can of course be applied to the present sensory-reinforcement data and consonant with this interpretation, longer start-exposure time should amplify the "positive" (i.e., facilitating) effect of high partial (e.g., 50- and 75-per cent) reward schedules because, as a K factor, longer antedating exposure will produce a larger reaction (R_g) to light onset and hence, from the frustration analysis, it will also produce a larger R_f to the blocking of r_g with the occasioning of nonreward. With low schedules of reward (e.g., 25 per cent), such an effect would be degraded, however, because of the poor conditioning basis for r_g and consequently for r_f as well.

Similar effects of start-exposure time in relation to reward schedules are also expected with extinction. As noted, rate of extinction was faster with larger percentages of reward and, associated with this outcome, longer start-exposure time amplified extinction rates under the higher-reward schedules, that is, produced progressively more rapid extinction with increasing percentages of reward. As in the case of food reward, the general outcome of faster extinction with larger percentages of light-onset reward can be attributed to the occurrence of a frustrative reaction and associated competing ("searching") responses for continuously rewarded subjects as compared with partial subjects that have learned to run in the context of anticipatory frustrative cues (i.e., s_f). However, with the re-emergence during extinction of competing responses for the partial subjects as well (i.e., as a result of the continued absence of reward and thus the lack of any differential delay of reward for running with and without these competing responses), partial subjects should also show an extinction effect and at a rate that is progressively more rapid with larger percentages of acquisition reward; that is, due to the larger R_f and thus stronger competing reaction elicited. Following the previous interpretation of start-exposure time as a reinforcement variable which can influence the strength of r_g - s_g, and thus indirectly the strength of r_f - s_f, the magnitude of associated competing responses in extinction should be amplified by longer start-exposure time. But with such frustration effects dependent upon the frequency or schedule of reward during acquisition training, the amplifying effect of longer start-exposure time on rate of extinction should, as observed, be increasingly greater with higher schedules of acquisition reward.

These data, then, like the other findings described, are amenable to the interpretation that the subject's antedating condition of exposure can be cast as a parameter of K rather than as the operational basis for a general energizing construct, D. Taken collectively, the findings would seem to offer several broad implications regarding the nature of reinforcement, especially when viewed in relation to the developments that have occurred bearing on the motivational and perceptual impact of a stimulus per se.

General Implications for Reinforcement Theory

In the initial section of this paper, relating to the history and significance of "curiosity" research, it was suggested that the problems raised by the early theoretical formulations could be resolved by applying classical theory, in particular, Spence's (1956) *D-K* formulation, to the interpretation of sensory-reinforcement effects. Apart from the data reviewed in the previous section bearing on the specifics of this interpretation, as an adaptation of classical theory, the formulation is particularly interesting from the standpoint of its incorporation of stimulus change as a basis for reward. This becomes especially clear when it is considered that the stimulus-change hypothesis originated with those stimulus theories of reward (cf. Kimble, 1961) that developed in response to the seemingly anomalous effects of rewards such as sweet-tasting substances, exploration, sex, and the like. For this reason, it behooves us to examine the nature of stimulus-change reward and then to assess the *D-K* interpretation originally suggested by the comparison of sensory and appetitive reinforcers. In this manner, we may be in a position to relate both stimulus-change (sensory) and appetitive reinforcement to those motivational and perceptual constructs bearing on arousal, attention, and information reinforcement, hopefully with the result of providing a general overview of the nature of reinforcement and the mechanisms or processes by which it operates.

The relativity of sensory reinforcement. Because the term stimulus change refers to the discrepancy produced by a particular event or condition that is made directly available to the organism or contingent upon a specific response, emphasis has generally been given to the direction and the extent of the change; that is, whether the change represents an increase or a decrease in stimulation and by how much. The consideration, however, that not all sensory events could qualify as reinforcers, as seemed evident in the case of very bright lights, loud noises, electric shock, and so forth, led many investigators to designate stimulus-change rewards as "mild" or "moderate" changes; accordingly, the response-contingent events that produced these changes were comparably referred to as mild or moderate forms or intensities of stimulation.

This constraint on stimulus-change reward is unfortunate because it places undue emphasis on particular kinds or intensities of stimulation as reinforcing and obscures the fact that variations in the magnitude of reinforcement or, indeed, the type of outcome itself (i.e., reinforcement or punishment), can often be obtained with the *same* response-contingent event. When this fact is acknowledged, it becomes quite clear that stimulus change per se (specifically, the extent of the difference between an initial event or condition, A, and a subsequent event or condition, B) is not reinforcing; rather, it is the manner in which the new or novel event B, is received and experienced by the subject relative to its antedating experience with or exposure to A.[4] Consonant with this interpretation, the results of the described research showed that the reinforcing effect of a particular light-onset intensity was conjointly determined by the length of the subject's exposure to an antedating condition of dim illumination and by the parameters of the light itself. In particular, the duration, pattern, and delay data indicated that the reinforcing effect of light onset was not simply a matter of the extent of the change in stimulation, as determined by the intensity of light onset and the subject's antedating exposure, but was equally a matter of how long and when the light was experienced in relation to the subject's antedating exposure.

The relativity of sensory reinforcement becomes even more apparent when consideration is given to the effects of the kind and length of exposure imposed upon the subject prior to its receipt of stimulus change. Thus, the initially described studies showed that the *same* moderate intensity of response-contingent light stimulation had either a facilitating or a suppressing effect depending upon the brightness of the subject's antedating condition and its length of exposure to it: With a setting condition of dim illumination (.06 foot-candle), longer exposure augmented the facilitating effect on performance of a light-onset intensity of .36 millilamberts; however, with an antedating exposure approximating darkness (less than .01 foot-candle), longer exposure induced a suppression of performance with the same light-onset intensity. Thus, these data indicate that a particular stimulus, like light onset of a moderate intensity, is neither a reinforcer nor a punisher except as it is perceived, reacted to, and experienced relative to the setting condition imposed upon the subject. It is noteworthy that such a relationship is not limited to response-contingent events entailing "mild" stimuli such as weak intensities of light, but also prevails with the use of aversive stimuli like shock. Applied to a response made in the absence of any "special" setting condition, shock generally has a suppressing effect and therefore it qualifies as a punisher; however, when the antedating condition to which the subject has been exposed simulates a condition of sensory deprivation, response-contingent shock can facilitate performance and therefore it qualifies as a reinforcer (e.g., Harrington and Linder, 1962; Harrington and Kohler, 1966).

The implication of these considerations regarding sensory reinforcers (or punishers) like light and shock is simply that our designation of a

---

[4] The specific basis for this argument is that neither event A nor B, nor the discrepancy between them, can exist without specifiable parameters (e.g., durations) to both A and B; thus, the effect of a transition from A to B cannot be meaningfully described in terms of the discrepancy or the extent of the discrepancy, but must have reference to the parameters of B relative to those of A.

particular event as a reinforcer — and relatedly our attempt to understand the nature of reinforcement — cannot be based on a functional definition of the action of that event within a selected context. What is determined by a functional definition to be a reinforcer in one context may not be in another and in some cases, as noted, it can even be a punisher despite the fact that the parameters of the stimulus *itself* are identical from one situation to another. (As noted, the same holds true in the case of punishing stimuli like shock but for additional reasons as well; see Fowler, 1971.) It would seem, then, by way of this dismissal of a functional definition of reinforcement, that we are committed to identifying the potential action of a stimulus trans-situationally, that is, independently of the particular reinforcement (or punishment) effect obtained in a selected context. Most directly, a trans-situational assessment can be accomplished by determining the adient or abient properties of a stimulus, specifically, by assessing whether the stimulus is selected and approached, as opposed to avoided or escaped from. Significantly, then, these considerations suggest that the problem of designating both reinforcers and punishers can be reduced to an assessment of preferences and aversions. Indeed, an implicit feature of this approach is that, for a stimulus to be preferred, it must be preferred relative to some "base" or comparison condition with which the organism is confronted, or to which it has been exposed. Consequently, the designation of preferences and aversions is also appropriate to the relative nature of both reinforcers and punishers. (An added implication of this approach is that the use of a preferred stimulus as a reinforcer requires not only that the stimulus be response-contingent, but also that the response provide a transition from the base or comparison condition relative to which the reinforcing stimulus was established as preferred.)

It is noteworthy that similar considerations regarding the relativity of both reinforcement and punishment have been put forth by Premack (1965, 1969; this volume, pp. 121–150). However, Premack's emphasis has been on the relation of response preferences, as expressed by free operant rates, rather than on stimulus relations. In the context of sensory reinforcement, free operant rates have been specifically employed by Lockhard (1963) to determine the preferences of rats for different intensities of illumination within their maintenance environments; in turn, these "maintenance" preferences have been used to explain the efficacy of different light-onset intensities as sensory reinforcers; that is, as events that will facilitate instrumental responding because they produce preferred conditions. This preference-theory approach is certainly consonant with the proposed specification of reinforcers (or punishers) in terms of established preferences, and thus it is unfortunate that it has been viewed as generating an alternative, if not opposed, theoretical orientation to that provided by stimulus-change theory (see Lockhard, 1966; McCall, 1966; also Tapp, 1969a). According to the present interpretation of stimulus change as the relation of a novel or changed-stimulus condition to an antedating one, change or novelty can be designated as a stimulus condition which is preferred relative to the "familiar" antedating condition to which the subject has been exposed and thus, to that extent, has habituated. In effect, this interpretation posits that stimulus-change rewards represent "short-term" preferences which can modify or override "long-term" preferences such as are characteristic of the species (Lockhard, 1962), its rearing-maintenance conditions (Lockhard, 1963), and the like.

As a consequence of the emphasis given to the role of antedating conditions of exposure, the foregoing considerations should point up a convergence not only of stimulus-change and preference theory, but of adaptation-level theory as well (see Helson, 1966; also Bevan and Adamson, 1960). Furthermore, the congruence of these ideas, particularly as they are conjoined by the assessment of preferences, may also be related to incentive theory, for an expression of preferences (or aversions) is a matter of designating the extent to which a response-contingent stimulus can incite the animal to action by "pulling" and attracting it (or "pushing" and repelling it) and thus serving as an incentive. So viewed, it would seem that an understanding of the nature of reinforcement can be reduced to a matter of understanding (a) preferences and aversions and the factors, both long-term and momentary, that govern them, and (b) the principles and mechanisms or processes that are associated with their action as incentives.

Theoretical relation to appetitive reinforcement. Many investigators consider the reinforcing properties of sensory events, such as light onset, to be different from those of appetitive events, such as food and water. For example, based on the operant response rates of rats which show that the rewarding effect of light onset is both transitory and weak, Tapp and Simpson (1966) have argued that light onset functions in the control of behavior in a manner that is different from appetitive reinforcers. Specifically, they suggest that response-contingent changes produced by light onset serve to elicit and temporarily maintain, to the extent of their novelty, continued responding of an exploratory nature; in contrast, the strength and durability of responding produced by appetitive reinforcement may reflect a dependency on the state of the organism and on specific response consequences such as a reduction in drive.

Contrasting with the transitory effect of sensory reinforcement reported by Tapp and Simpson (1966), which incidentally is characteristic of studies employing operant procedures (see Kish, 1966), the results of the present program of research showed that the effect of sensory (light-onset) reinforcement was most durable: With a discrete-trial procedure in which the relation of the subject's exposure or setting condition to light onset at the goal was maintained for each trial-response, instrumental responding was promoted to a high level and itself was maintained without loss or diminution over extended training (180 trials). This difference in outcome in comparison with operant procedures should pose little puzzlement. Given the subject's "short-term" preference for light onset, as regulated by its antedating condition of exposure, frequent and repeated occasions of light — as are obtainable with the free-responding procedure — should relegate light to the status of a background or setting stimulus with the result that any discrepancy produced by subsequent light onset is essentially nil. It would seem, then, that we may dispense with the transitory nature of sensory reinforcement as a significant consideration and treat instead its theoretical relation to appetitive reinforcement, in particular, the principles and mechanisms of operation that are germane to both.

With regard to the problems posed by the early interpretations of "curiosity" rewards, it was argued that a resolution of these problems was made apparent by a comparison based on appetitive rewards (and classical interpretations thereof), and that indeed such a comparison and its suggested resolution required the positing of comparable theoretical constructs in the case of sensory reinforcement. Thus, analogous to the D and K operations specified for performances based on appetitive reinforcement (e.g., Spence, 1956), performances relating to sensory reinforcement were similarly described as influenced by both the degree of the organism's "deprivation" of change (operationally expressed as the length and constancy of the stimuli confronting the organism prior to its receipt of novelty) and the extent or magnitude of the change (novelty) contingent upon its response. As reviewed earlier, this conceptualization was found to be in general agreement with the existing data on deprivation (exposure) and change manipulations (see also Fowler, 1965) and was equally supported by initial research (Fowler, 1967) designed to assess the motivational character of the proposed D- and K-constructs. However, as noted with the current program of research on light-onset reinforcement, further assessment of this position has indicated that, whereas the K construct is entirely consonant with the findings obtained, the D construct can be dispensed with. In particular, the reversibility of the reinforcement-punishment effect of light onset as determined by the kind and length of the subject's antedating exposure, and the interaction of its exposure with the parameters of light onset as a determinant of the reinforcement effect, call for an interpretation in which the subject's antedating condition of exposure is cast, not as the operation for an independent motivational construct, D, but simply as a parameter of K. That is to say, prior exposure can be viewed as a setting condition which effectively deprives the organism of change by habituating it to existing stimuli; consequently, through habituation, such exposure can lower the organism's threshold for change and can thus influence the manner in and the extent to which the organism will react to or experience the changed-stimulus condition. Taken in conjunction with this *potential* action of the organism's setting condition, the parameters of the changed stimulus itself (i.e., its intensity, duration, delay, and pattern) may then regulate how vigorously, how long, and when the reaction occurs relative to the instrumental response producing the change.

Considered in relation to the preceding comments on the relativity of sensory reinforcement, that is, the dependency of the reinforcing action of a particular event on the subject's antedating condition of exposure, such setting or exposure conditions must be viewed as parameters of reinforcement because, without them, sensory reinforcement cannot be expressed. This dependent relationship between a particular event as a reinforcer and the subject's antedating or setting condition holds true not only in the case of sensory events like light onset (or shock, as noted), but also in the case of appetitive events. Furthermore, such a relationship can be demonstrated with regard to the action of an appetitive event both as a US for consummatory reactions and as a reinforcer for instrumental acts. For example, in the context of classical appetitive conditioning, DeBold, Miller, and Jensen (1965) have shown convincingly that water as a US for tongue-licking will not be effective either in establishing a CR or in maintaining the UR when experimental conditions are employed ensuring that the organism is completely satiated (i.e., literally infused with water by a fistula leading into the mouth) and therefore is operating under 0 drive. These results, of course, parallel those early ones reported by Pavlov regarding the ineffectiveness of food as a reinforcer (US) for animals that had recently been fed (Pavlov, 1927, p. 31 f.). Accordingly, appetitive events do not in themselves elicit consummatory acts, but only when they are accompanied by the appropriate setting ("drive") condition.

The complementary side to this picture of the action of appetitive "drives" is that, when they do operate, they readily facilitate both consummatory and instrumental acts; however, comparable to their setting function for consummatory responses (i.e., in enabling a particular event like food or water to serve as a functional US), their effect on instrumental responses is not through the direct facilitation (energization) of these responses, but rather indirectly through the action of the reinforcer. Bindra (1968) has reviewed the evidence bearing on this issue and has argued effectively as follows: Drive manipulations critically regulate the likelihood and strength of consummatory responses and thus, through this influence, they establish the efficacy of particular events as reinforcers for instrumental acts. Consequently, if the action of D is solely through the reinforcer (i.e., through K), as the consummatory-response data would indicate, then D would not be required for the *performance* of an instrumental response but only for its reinforcement. This interpretation is supported directly by the results of an experiment (Mendelson, 1966) which showed that *sated* rats would perform both rapidly and correctly in a T-maze when "drive" stimulation (effected by intercranial electrical stimulation of the lateral hypothalmic feeding area) was present *only* in conjunction with food in one of the goal boxes. Although such performances were initially produced by administering the drive stimulus throughout the apparatus (thus attesting to the selective reinforcing effect of food and eating while being stimulated in one goal box, as opposed to just being stimulated in the other goal box), performance was both slowed down and reduced to a chance level of choice when drive stimulation was eliminated from the food-baited goal but retained in the rest of the apparatus.

These results illustrate the dependent relationship of appetitive reinforcers, and thus they parallel those of the described research on light-onset reinforcement; taken together, the findings suggest that "drive" manipulations (i.e., deprivation, exposure, habituation, and the like) set the conditions under which an event, appetitive or sensory, will function both as a US to elicit "consummatory" reactions, and as a reward to facilitate instrumental responding. Insofar as this interpretation treats the drive operation as a parameter of K and thus effectively eliminates reference to an independent construct, D, some comment should be addressed to the relevance of the criteria by which D, as an independent motivational construct, has previously been assessed. Typically, evidence for the operation of D is based on its ascribed functions of serving as a cue, as an energizer, and as the basis for reinforcement — as through the reduction of D. In the context of instrumental conditioning, assessment of these drive functions has thus been related to a determination of whether a particular response can be associated with and regulated in strength by the drive manipulation, and of course reinforced by the appropriate drive-reducing event. Unfortunately, it has generally gone unacknowledged that these criteria are precisely those by which an incentive-motivational effect is to be assessed. That is to say, via the r_g - s_g mechanism, incentives are thought to provide anticipatory cues for selective or specific responding, to excite or intensify the response and thereby to facilitate its occurrence. Indeed, the facilitation of such selective acts must occur because theoretically the action of K is not simply a basis for reinforcement; rather, its action *is* reinforcement.

These considerations lead us, then, to a conceptualization of reinforcement and, by way of the reversibility of the reinforcement relationship, of punishment as well, as incentive-motivational phenomena: to borrow Mowrer's (1960) terms, the "hoped for" or "feared" anticipation of events that are either preferred or averted relative to the setting condition under which the animal is operating. Such an emphasis on the incentive and how it is perceived and reacted to by the organism thus frees us from an emphasis on the motivational prerequisite of deprivation (i.e., the designated *absences* of specific events, objects, and conditions); rather, it provides a focus on the manner in which a particular state is approached and entered (or avoided and escaped from) relative to that base state under which the organism is performing.

Reinforcement, arousal, and incentive motivation. In treating sensory reinforcement as an incentive-motivational phenomenon and, relatedly, in pointing up its theoretical relation to appetitive reinforcement, certain questions are to be entertained regarding the principles and mechanisms of operation of the sensory-reinforcement effect. For example, what is the consummatory or goal reaction (R_g) that is produced by the novel or changed-stimulus condition serving as a sensory reinforcer? Heretofore, reference has been made to the animal reacting to, experiencing — in effect, "consuming" — the changed-stimulus condition, but can we specify a consummatory reaction analogous to salivating, chewing movements, tongue-licking, etc., as in the appetitive case. Similarly, what is the basis for the "excitement" (motivation) and relatedly, the intensification of the instrumental response that is presumably mediated by the anticipatory occurrence of such consummatory reactions? (And, when is this excitement or stimulation sufficient to be aversive, effecting a suppression of the instrumental response?) These and similar questions become especially relevant in view of our dismissal of D as an energizing mechanism, not only for instrumental responses, but for consummatory reactions as well. Nonetheless, the dismissal of D itself offers a resolution because, with its demise, we are committed to readdressing those interpretations based on the related concepts of activation and arousal.

As noted earlier, the concept of arousal (or activation) was introduced in an effort to relieve drive theory (and its correlative hypothesis of drive reduction) of the embarrassments associated with sensory-reinforcement effects, specifically, the increases in stimulation that were apparent with rewards like exploration, manipulation, sex, and so forth. Thus, the interpretation was advanced that the organism responded so as to maintain an optimal level of stimulation and arousal: Not only would it respond to rid itself of intense stimulation, but also so as to gain and maintain a moderate level of stimulation. However, as a concept that was designed to replace D and yet maintain its motivational character, arousal was identified with D as an "energizer," as an "energizing mechanism," and as the "intensive dimension of behavior" (cf. Berlyne, 1960; Fiske and Maddi, 1961; Lindsley, 1957; Malmo, 1959). This conceptualization of arousal was particularly unfortunate because it posed the problem, previously noted, that the organism was *highly* motivated (i.e., aroused) under *low* arousal as, for example, when it engaged in responses that were instrumental to reinforcing events (e.g., novelty, sex, and so forth) that produced heightened arousal. The equating of arousal with D was also unfortunate because the two concepts were fundamentally different. The basic assumption underlying D theory, as early elaborated (e.g., Moss, 1924; Richter, 1922, 1927), was that the organism was a *passive* creature: Certain drive-producing events had to prevail to energize the animal, to get it going, and when terminated or reduced, the animal would then cease responding, or begin responding subject to the influences of other drive-producing events. Contrasting with this picture, the arousal conception essentially posited an *active* organism: one that did not need to be driven into action, but was active and learning in the absence of specific drive states (cf. Hebb, 1949, 1955; Malmo, 1959; Nissen, 1954). Thus, the "aroused" organism was one for which specific events served only to amplify or modulate its vigilance and ongoing level of activity and thereby to cue specific responses which would promote an optimal level of stimulus impact.

With the dismissal of D as an independent motivational construct in the present formulation, the conceptualization of an "active" organism again prevails; however, within this framework, arousal takes on a specific relation to K, particularly as both concepts bear on the manner in which the organism's behavior will be both cued and intensified. More specifically, by identifying arousal with K, the present interpretation essentially follows a drive-*induction* hypothesis (see Sheffield, 1966a,b; also Glickman and Schiff, 1967) and posits that rewarding events, functioning as US's, are arousal ("drive") inducing.[5] The basis for the proposed relationship between arousal and K is actually quite varied and rests not simply on the similarity of their ascribed functions, but equally so on observations of the aroused state of the organism when it is confronted with reinforcing events. For example, in the context of classical appetitive conditioning, it has long been noted that the organism is in an excited-agitated state just prior to and during its receipt of food (see Zener, 1937).

---

[5] It is interesting in this respect that the rewarding effects of brain stimulation, findings originally viewed as evidence for reinforcement without the induction of drive, have recently been cast into an incentive-motivational framework (see Trowill, Pankseff, and Gandelman, 1969).

Bearing more directly on arousal as a neurophysiological reaction, similar observations have been offered with regard to the organism's receipt of novel or changed stimuli. In particular, the work by Berlyne (e.g., Berlyne, Craw, Salapatek, and Lewis, 1963; Berlyne and Lewis, 1963; Berlyne and McDonnell, 1965) has shown a positive relationship between the imposition of "collative" variables (e.g., novelty, change, complexity, and so forth) and such indices of arousal as EEG frequency and GSR amplitude (see also Furedy, 1968; Grim and White, 1965). Indeed, from an extensive review of the literature covering brain physiology, psychopharmacology, animal learning, and human verbal learning, Berlyne (1967) has drawn the general conclusion that those features of stimuli which have reward value also affect indices of arousal, and further that moderate increases in arousal are rewarding, whereas larger increases are aversive (i.e., punishing).

The findings, as reviewed recently by Berlyne (1967) and by others (e.g., Bindra, 1968; Routtenberg, 1968) would seem clear, then, in pointing to arousal as a neurophysiological reaction; that is, as a *central* response process, that is associated with both reinforcement and punishment. Hence, considered with respect to a K interpretation of the action of sensory reinforcers, the fact that moderate increases in arousal accompany the organism's receipt of novel or changed-stimulus events indicates that arousal is appropriately viewed as a *central* component of the organism's consummatory response to change — heretofore given reference solely in terms of such peripheral reactions as orienting toward, attending to, or perceptually "consuming" the change. From the standpoint of this interpretation, then, the designation of specific consummatory responses (R_g's) to novel or changed stimuli becomes an irrelevant issue, for the absence of specifiable peripheral reactions does not vitiate the K interpretation; rather it places the locus of the consummatory reaction at a central level of observation and/or conceptualization. Comparably, the burden of isolating peripheral r_g's as mediators of the incentive-motivational effect is eliminated, for the interpretation of arousal as a UR elicited by reward implies that, comparable to the anticipatory occurrence of any peripheral UR's (i.e., via their classical conditioning to the cues which antedate the reward), so similarly should the arousal reaction become anticipatory to excite the organism and thereby regulate its instrumental performance. In short, these considerations argue that the anticipatory occurrence of consummatory reactions (R_g's) to reward may comprise peripheral (e.g., orienting) and/or central [arousal] components, the latter representing a neurophysiological counterpart to K (Fowler, 1967).

Tied in this manner to incentive motivation, arousal also has obvious relation to the effects of *"D"* manipulations. Viewed as parameters of

K, D manipulations, such as deprivation, exposure, and the like, should show a positive relation to arousal, but *only* when the organism is in the presence of the reward or those cues that have been associated with the reward and the responses that it elicits. That is to say, analogous to their effect in potentiating any peripheral R_g's, *D* manipulations should also potentiate an arousal reaction to the reward and to the cues associated with the reward. Data bearing on this issue have, for the most part, been limited to the use of heart rate as an index of arousal in water-deprived rats; nonetheless, these data show an amazing consistency with theoretical expectations. When animals are at rest in a nonexperimental situation as, for example, their home cages or a restraining compartment, heart rate bears no relationship to increasing hours of water deprivation or, at most, it is depressed; on the other hand, when the same animals are permitted to bar-press for water and to drink (i.e., when the consummatory response and its fractional anticipatory component are theoretically operative), heart rate shows an almost direct relationship to hours of water deprivation (e.g., Bélanger and Feldman, 1962; Ducharme, 1966b; Eisman, 1966; Goldstein, Stern, and Rothenberg, 1966; Hahn, Stern, and McDonald, 1962; O'Kelley, Hatton, Tucker, and Westall, 1965). Indeed, this effect can also be produced by the external cues that have been associated with water reward, despite the fact that overt consummatory and instrumental responses (and the latter's feedback cues which should act as part of the CS complex controlling anticipatory arousal) are absent (e.g., Ducharme, 1966a; Goldstein et al., 1966; Snapper, Schoenfeld, Ferraro, and Locke, 1965). These data would indicate, then, that not only are increases in arousal induced by reward such as water for the deprived animal, but importantly, such reactions are conditionable to the stimuli associated with reward, and therefore their control of performance is both cued and specific.

An important final aspect of the present interpretation of arousal as a counterpart to incentive motivation is in the relation of arousal to the type of performance outcome obtained. In the research previously noted (e.g., Bélanger and Feldman, 1962), rate of bar-pressing for water reward was also found to be an inverted-U function of hours of water deprivation (and thus level of arousal as indicated by heart rate), an outcome typically cited in reference to the posited "optimal" level of arousal required for efficient performance. This consideration notwithstanding, the implication of the present interpretation is that with arousal viewed as a neurophysiological reaction, the *stimulus aspect* of which should be representative of an intensity dimension, the intensity consequence of high arousal itself can be sufficient to produce an aversive state and thereby generate a suppression of performance. In this fashion, anticipatory arousal as a mediator of *K* can be related to both positive (reinforcement) and negative (punishment) outcomes depending upon the level of arousal induced by the particular response-contingent event. Such a relationship seems apparent in the case of both sensory (light-onset) and appetitive (water) rewards, as noted, and is consistent with the general conclusion drawn by Berlyne (1967, 1969) that moderate increases in arousal are reinforcing whereas larger increases are punishing. (In this regard, it is especially noteworthy that an analysis of the effects of response-contingent aversive stimuli, like shock, indicates that such events, when acting as *punishing stimuli*, are distinguishable from "neutral" and rewarding stimuli only on the basis of the intensive aspect of the stimulation that they provide; see Fowler, 1971.)

Reinforcement and attention: A transition to cognitive theory. Together with those developments bearing on the motivational impact of a stimulus, that is, regarding its arousal value, there has also occurred an accumulation of work on the "perceptual" impact of a stimulus, in particular, the process by which the animal may become aware of and/or attend to selected aspects of its environment. In large part, research concerned with such an attentional process has centered on discrimination learning and therein follows historically from Spence's (1940, 1952) conceptualization of a "receptor-orienting" act. Although quite varied, present interpretations of attention are distinguishable on the basis of the functional position of the discriminative stimulus which serves as an end point for so-called "prereception" models and as the beginning point for alternative or "postreception" interpretations (see Fowler and Siegel, 1971). That is to say, prereception models treat attention as a process operating prior to the associative learning of the instrumental response and the discriminative stimuli; herein, behaviors such as "orienting" (e.g., Sokolov, 1963), "observing" (e.g., Atkinson, 1951; Zeaman and House, 1963), "sampling" (e.g., Polidora and Fletcher, 1964) and "analyzing" (e.g., Lovejoy, 1968; Sutherland, 1964) are emphasized and are accorded the specific function of ensuring that the cues which signal a particular outcome like reward are received by the organism's sensory-perceptual apparatus. In contrast, postreception models interpret attention as a process that is an actual part of associative learning; specifically, these models are concerned with attention as that process by which the discriminative stimuli, *once received*, are perceptually organized, interpreted, or coded into new stimulus compounds to which (as coded or organized) the instrumental response leading to reward can be readily attached (e.g., Egeth, 1967; Lawrence, 1963; Treisman, 1969).

Both of these interpretations of attention represent significant extensions of discrimination learning theory. Indeed, through their analysis of the manner in which particular stimulus events, serving as discriminative stimuli, are received and organized by the animal, the attentional process is provided a specific relation to learning, either as a precursor to or as an actual part of it. Nonetheless, through similar considerations bearing on the manner in which the same stimulus events can function as rewards, as in the context of sensory reinforcement, the process of attention is tied not only to learning, but to reinforcement as well. Such a conceptualization finds several bases of departure within the literature on attention, but may be related directly to the prereception analysis. For example, by way of the role accorded behaviors such as orienting, observing, and the like, prereception interpretations of attention are essentially concerned with exploratory responses to change; that is, those investigatory behaviors (such as orienting, observing, and the like,) and the "collative" variables (i.e., novelty, change, complexity — in effect, the discernible properties of stimuli) that control these behaviors. So viewed, the fact that collative variables such as novelty and change can function as rewards indicates that a major component of the organism's reactions to these rewards, if not all rewards (cf. Sokolov, 1963), is one of actively investigating and thus of attending to them.

The generality of this position is supported by the same extensive body of literature relating the reward value of stimuli to indices of arousal; in particular, these findings (see Berlyne, 1967) indicate that the properties of stimuli that are associated with reward will, in one way or another, also affect components of the orientation reaction. Accordingly, the action of rewards in eliciting a class of consummatory responses (R_g's) can be expanded so as to include not only specific peripheral reactions (e.g., salivating, tongue-licking, etc.) and central (arousal) components, but also those specific and general reactions of attending. Furthermore, like arousal, attention need not be limited to specific peripheral reactions of orienting toward or observing the reward (for example, as reflected by eye movements), but may relate as well to the induction of a central process that enables the organism to become generally aware of and attentive to the rewarding event. Viewed in this fashion, attention becomes an integral part of the reinforcement process, for the action of reward in eliciting a general reaction of increased attention and awareness suggests that the organism can be equally attentive to (i.e., "aware of") the response that produced the reward and the stimulus context in which this response occurred (see Kagan, 1967). At first glance, this interpretation seems to imply the operation of short-term memory or of traces of the instrumental response and its associated cues; that is, so that the response and its cues will be contiguous with the reward and thus subject to the attending response produced by the reward. However, this need not be the case.

Conceived of as a reaction to reward, that is, as a UR elicited by the rewarding stimulus, attention should be subject to the same laws of conditioning as any UR, inclusive of specific orienting reactions and general arousal reactions. Thus, like these reactions, attention as a central response process should operate anticipatorily, becoming conditioned to those cues that antedate the reward and that are associated with the instrumental response. Although reference is herein made to attention as a central response process, it is noteworthy that the Russian conditioning literature has long shown an anticipatory-response effect for specific orienting responses. For example, when one neutral stimulus consistently precedes another, the first will come to elicit orienting responses appropriate to the second (e.g., Narbutovich and Podkopaev, 1936). It is of further interest that components of the orienting reaction to the conditioned stimulus itself become larger, stronger, and quicker than to the same stimulus as a "neutral" event (see Lynn, 1966).

These considerations hold particular significance for S-R theory, for they indicate that the organism can be directly in contact with the reward-antedating cues and engaged in the instrumental response, while making attentional responses that have been induced by the reward. Construed in the sense of an alerting or vigilance process, and operating anticipatorily, attention may thus serve the function of making the organism aware of the situational cues or the discriminative stimuli and the response to these cues that will produce the reward — while at the same time enabling the organism to be aware of the reward itself. Thus, S-R theory is afforded a transition to cognitive theory: The organism can "know (be attentive to and aware of) what leads to what" but not simply in the sense of developing S-S associations; rather for the S-R theorist, this can be conceptualized as a mediating-response process based on the conditioning of attentional responses that are reward-produced. So considered, the nature of reward and its mechanism of operation as an incentive (i.e., through mediating-response processes) may be expanded to include not only peripheral consummatory reactions such as tongue-licking, salivating, and the like, but also those central reactions of both increased arousal ("excitement") and attention ("vigilance"). The juxtaposition of these two processes is particularly noteworthy, for prior to its recent formal inception, attention as an alerting or vigilance process was explicitly subsumed under the rubric of arousal (see Hebb, 1955).

Curiosity and information reinforcement. It will be recalled from the initial section of this paper that the positing of an incentive-motivational process for sensory reinforcement led to the reinterpretation of "curiosity" as a mediating-response mechanism, that is, as opposed to its former conception as a drive (cf. Berlyne, 1950, 1971). The foregoing considerations regarding mediating-response mechanisms lead us finally to consider the nature of curiosity as a mediating-response concept, and relatedly the significance which this conceptualization holds for seemingly broader concepts within the literature.

Regarding the nature of mediating responses, it was argued in the previous section that such responses constitute classically conditioned anticipatory reactions to reward ranging from specific peripheral reactions, such as orientation, to the more general central response processes of increased attention and arousal (awareness and excitement). In the specific context of novelty or stimulus-change reward, these same reactions apply and thus they constitute *curiosity*; that is, the anticipatory occurrence of orientation, attention, and arousal as induced by the novel or changed-stimulus condition that is made contingent upon a specific response. At first glance, this interpretation might seem consonant with the motivational and perceptual nature of curiosity, as introspectively conceived, but it poses a significant problem, for although anticipatory reactions of increased attention and arousal can be viewed as general response processes operating at a central level, they are nonetheless object or condition specific. That is to say, in acquiring these reactions, the organism will have had contact with the novel object or the changed-stimulus condition and, on this basis, it will have learned to anticipate that object or condition *in particular*. Hence, as conceptualized, curiosity is a learned anticipatory reaction based on the organism's reaction to specific and recurrent stimulus events. In effect, the animal "knows" exactly what it is going to get.

This interpretation is clearly at odds with any introspective conceptualization of curiosity, for if, through learning, the organism knows what it is going to receive, how can it possibly be curious about it? To be sure, it can anticipate the event that is contingent upon its response, but in what sense will it be curious about the event — simply that it is going to occur? In this case, curiosity would not be unique to novelty or stimulus-change rewards but would be common to any and all response-contingent events ranging from those that are rewarding to those that are punishing. This may well be the case, but the point to be gained is that, with the *same relatively* novel event (like light onset) repeatedly contingent upon a response, absolutely no information is gained — at least not in the theoretical sense of this term (cf. Shannon and Weaver, 1949) — for there is really no uncertainty about it. Indeed, for this "specific" type of curiosity to operate (i.e., be *learned* as an anticipatory reaction), the same relatively novel event must occur repeatedly — or at least once — and thus its anticipated recurrence qualifies as a redundancy, despite any preference that the organism may have for the object relative to whatever exposure or setting condition under which it is operating. This argument would seem most reasonable, but to the extent that curiosity as an anticipatory reaction is learned, we may expect other bases of learning to influence its development and, accordingly, its nature. One such additional basis becomes apparent when we consider the variety of experiences constituting the organism's life style.

In contrast to the laboratory organism, the animal in its natural setting, even the human organism in its civilized and structured environment, is not subject to regulated, invariant experiences of one and the same kind. It is not run in the same apparatus and it is not confronted with an identical task at the same moment from day to day — rather, it is involved in many and varied experiences and, when confronted with redundant or repetitive events, it can alter these events almost "at will." However, like the laboratory animal with its regulated experiences, the unrestricted organism can be expected to anticipate (i.e., learn) a specific outcome contingent on its behavior in a particular situation or in a selected context, and thus, with reference to its many and varied situational experiences, it can, with each of these situations, be expected to acquire an object- or condition-specific anticipatory reaction. Consequently, for the mature organism with its "established" and yet varied existence and for the developing organism with its increasing array of varied stimulation, there exists or develops a *set* of situations in which the organism can *learn* to anticipate a change in stimulation generally. That is to say, despite the fact that a response-contingent change can be specific to the response and its particular situation, there exists across situations a communality in that the organism can always expect some alteration of its stimulus input simply as a consequence of responding. Hence, there exists a learning-set basis by which the organism can become *generally* curious, learning to anticipate a change in stimulation contingent upon its behavior in a new context where it has not previously responded and therefore cannot know the specific consequence of its behavior. Herein, the organism responds in the face of uncertainty (cf. entropy) for whatever the specific change may be, or for variation in the sequence of its response-contingent events; in effect, it responds for information that is either subjective or objective in nature. This, then, constitutes the full sense of the term curiosity, and so conceived, not introspectively, but on the basis of a learning-set principle, it provides the means by which information reinforcement can be derived as a corollary of curiosity (incentive-motivational) theory.

There are a number of implications of this interpretation, particularly as it is based on the presumption that curiosity, in its general form, is a learning-set phenomenon. For example, to the extent that general curiosity, as conceived, is the basis for information reinforcement, we may expect that information reinforcement will be related to the phylogenetic level of the organism, especially as this variable underlies learning-set formation. Thus, we may anticipate that information reinforcement will occur minimally for the rodent, moreso for infrahuman primates, and certainly for the human adult. Secondly, for the human organism, we may expect that information reinforcement will be related to ontogenetic level, occurring minimally, if at all, with the newborn or infant, but progressively so with the developing child. Thirdly, for the developing child, we may expect that "enriched" environments providing a wide array of experiences (opportunities for stimulus change) will foster a high level of general curiosity and therefore a greater amount of "information seeking," that is, responses that are aimed at information reward. Finally, with curiosity in its general form being dependent upon learning, we may expect that the acquired level of information seeking will be critically regulated by subsequent occasions and magnitudes of information reward. For example, given that the human organism has developed a high level of information seeking (i.e., has acquired a high general curiosity and thus high K), subsequent yields of low information should be "frustrating" or inhibiting by virtue of negative (incentive) contrast, and should lead, therefore, to performances aimed at the same if not higher yields of information than that to which the organism has become accustomed (specifically, has learned to anticipate).

As formulated, the present interpretation thus deduces the major premise of the Dember and Earl (1957) theory of curiosity: The organism will seek to maintain its own (acquired) level of complexity, and consequently occasions of lesser complexity (i.e., less change or stimulus variation) will prove unrewarding. In this respect, too, the position offers a reinterpretation of adult human curiosity as conceptualized by Berlyne (1971): Confronted with ambiguous figures (e.g., slides of moderately blurred objects), the human adult will learn to respond selectively so as to obtain a clear picture of the blurred object rather than a clear picture of a different object. Interpreting this phenomenon as the basis for a curiosity drive, Berlyne appropriately argues that moderate ambiguity can be motivating by way of the uncertainty that it produces; however, this need not be in the sense of a curiosity drive. Rather, in the face of uncertainty, the human organism may anticipate information contingent upon its behavior, and thus it has the incentive to perform selectively.

Summary and Conclusions

Based on the implications of sensory reinforcement and related "curiosity" concepts, the foregoing discussion has centered about a variety of issues inclusive of the relativity of reinforcement, the potentiating action of drive or "setting" conditions, the role of both arousal and attention as central-mediating processes, and the relation of these processes to complex forms of reinforcement, such as information reinforcement. Although diverse, all of these topic-issues have been subjected to an interpretation based on incentive-motivational theory. Consequently, from the stand-point of this treatment and interpretation, any attempt at drawing conclusions about the nature of reinforcement (or of punishment) is essentially a matter of describing incentive motivation. So viewed, two principal considerations are to be posed: (1) the nature of incentives; i.e., the events which constitute incentives, in either positive or negative form, and (2) the motivational action of incentives; i.e., the manner in which these events operate so as to facilitate or suppress performance.

Regarding the first of these considerations, it was argued on the basis of findings illustrating the relativity of sensory (light-onset) reinforcement, in particular, a reversibility of the reinforcement-punishment effect of the same response-contingent event, that such events cannot be identified as punishing or reinforcing on the basis of a functional definition of their action in a particular situation; consequently, some attempt must be made at identifying their properties trans-situationally, as through the assessment of preferences. Thus, it was proposed that the designation of incentives, in either positive or negative form, could be related to the designation of preferences (and aversions) and the factors, both long-term and momentary, that govern them. Relatedly, it was noted that the relativity of reinforcement implicated, in accord with the empirical findings on both sensory and appetitive reinforcers, a dependent relationship between the event serving as a reinforcer and those antedating or "setting" conditions of stimulation under which the organism performs. For this reason, as well as others, "drive" manipulations entailing deprivation, habituation, and the like, are not to be interpreted as the basis for an independent motivational construct (D), but rather as parameters of incentive (K); that is, as conditions which potentiate or set the occasion for a particular event being preferred (or averted) and thus serving as an incentive. Within this framework, then, all stimuli are incentives, more or less, and all have a specific weighting or valence relative to those antedating or "comparison" conditions of stimulation under which the organism operates.

Regarding the second issue, namely, the motivational action of incentives, it was argued after incentive theory that such action occurs primarily through the classical conditioning of consummatory reactions that are produced by the incentive and which, upon being conditioned to the cues that antedate the incentive, may influence and regulate the strength of instrumental responding. Such consummatory responses, however, are not limited to specific peripheral reactions such as orientation, salivation, tongue-licking, and the like; findings relating to sensory and appetitive reinforcement indicate that these reward-induced reactions will also include central reactions of both increased arousal and attention. Consequently, with these central response processes operating anticipatorily, i.e., being conditioned to the reward-antedating cues, the organism is provided with the "excitement" (arousal) by which its instrumental response can be intensified and the "awareness" (attention) by which it can focus on the reward while engaged in the response that produces the reward. The significance of these developments for incentive theory lies in two related considerations: First, through its role in mediating incentive effects, arousal as a former "drive" concept is made consonant with the present interpretation of drive operations as parameters of K; i.e., as conditions which potentiate the action of incentives in eliciting both peripheral reactions and central response processes. Secondly, through the mediating action of anticipatory attentional responses that are induced by the reward, S-R incentive theory is afforded a transition to cognitive theory: The organism can "know" (learn to be attentive and aware) not only of the reward, but of the cues and responses that will produce the reward.

These considerations bearing on the role of central mediating processes suggest, in turn, that there are various ways in which the organism can anticipate specific or general outcomes contingent on its behavior and thereby mediate the effect of these outcomes. For example, with reference to the organism's contact with a variety of situations, all of which are productive of response-contingent changes in stimulation, it was argued that a learning-set basis exists by which the organism becomes generally curious, learning to anticipate stimulus variation contingent upon its behavior in a situation where it has not previously responded and therefore cannot know the specific outcome. Accordingly, curiosity can be viewed as the basis for information reinforcement which, in turn, deriving from a learning-set principle, should relate to the phylogenetic level of the organism. With this consideration pointing up the possible relation between phylogeny and "kinds" of reinforcement, it becomes apparent that the human organism, with its diversified response capabilities, may anticipate specific or general outcomes in any of a variety of ways, as through the "retrieval" of information from memory (see Atkinson and Wickens, this volume, pp. 66–120) or through "imitative" and "self-reinforcement" (see Bandura, this volume, pp. 228–278). All of these processes are forms of anticipation which mediate preferred or nonpreferred outcomes, and thus they reflect the action of incentives in either facilitating or suppressing performance.

REFERENCES

Amsel, A. Frustrative non-reward in partial reinforcement and discrimination learning: Some recent history and a theoretical extension. *Psychological Review*, 1962, *69*, 306–328.

Amsel, A. Partial reinforcement effects on vigor and persistence. In K. W. Spence and J. T. Spence (Eds.), *The psychology of learning and motivation*. Vol. 1. New York: Academic Press, 1967. Pp. 1–65.

Atkinson, R. C. The observing response in discrimination learning. *Journal of Experimental Psychology*, 1951, *62*, 253–262.

Barnes, G. W., and Baron, A. Stimulus complexity and sensory reinforcement. *Journal of Comparative and Physiological Psychology*, 1961, *54*, 466–469.

Bélanger, D., and Feldman, S. M. Effects of water deprivation upon heart rate and instrumental activity in the rat. *Journal of Comparative and Physiological Psychology*, 1962, *55*, 220–225.

Berlyne, D. E. Novelty and curiosity as determinants of exploratory behavior. *British Journal of Psychology*, 1950, *41*, 68–80.

Berlyne, D. E. The arousal and satiation of perceptual curiosity in the rat. *Journal of Comparative and Physiological Psychology*, 1955, *48*, 238–246.

Berlyne, D. E. *Conflict, arousal, and curiosity*. New York: McGraw-Hill, 1960.

Berlyne, D. E. Arousal and reinforcement. In D. Levine (Ed.), *Nebraska symposium on motivation*. Lincoln: University of Nebraska Press, 1967. Pp. 1–110.

Berlyne, D. E. The reward-value of indifferent stimulation. In J. T. Tapp (Ed.), *Reinforcement and behavior*. New York: Academic Press, 1969. Pp. 179–214.

Berlyne, D. E., Incertitude et curiosité. *Psychologie Francaise*, 1970, in press.

Berlyne, D. E., Craw, M. A., Salapatek, P. H., and Lewis, J. L. Novelty, complexity, incongruity, extrinsic motivation and the GSR. *Journal of Experimental Psychology*, 1963, *66*, 560–567.

Berlyne, D. E., and Lewis, J. L. Effects of heightened arousal on human exploratory behavior. *Canadian Journal of Psychology*, 1963, *17*, 398–411.

Berlyne, D. E., and McDonnell, P. Effects of stimulus complexity and incongruity on duration of EEG desynchronization. *Electroencephalography and Clinical Neurophysiology*, 1965, *18*, 156–161.

Berlyne, D. E., and Slater, J. Perceptual curiosity, exploratory behavior and maze learning. *Journal of Comparative and Physiological Psychology*, 1957, *50*, 228–232.

Bevan, W., and Adamson, R. Reinforcers and reinforcement: Their relation to maze performance. *Journal of Experimental Psychology*, 1960, *59*, 226–232.

Bindra, D. Neuropsychological interpretation of general activity and instrumental behavior. *Psychological Review*, 1968, *75*, 1–22.

Black, R. W. On the combination of drive and incentive motivation. *Psychological Review*, 1965, *72*, 310–317.

Brown, J. S. *The motivation of behavior*. New York: McGraw-Hill, 1961.

Butler, R. A. Incentive conditions which influence visual exploration. *Journal of Experimental Psychology*, 1954, *48*, 19–23.

Butler, R. A. Discrimination learning by rhesus monkeys to auditory incentives. *Journal of Comparative and Physiological Psychology*, 1957, *50*, 239–241. (a)

Butler, R. A. The effect of deprivation of visual incentives on visual exploration motivation in monkeys. *Journal of Comparative and Physiological Psychology*, 1957, *50*, 177–179. (b)

Butler, R. A., and Woolpy, J. H. Visual attention in the rhesus monkey. *Journal of Comparative and Physiological Psychology*, 1963, *56*, 324–328.

Campbell, B. A., and Church, R. M. (Eds.) *Punishment and aversive behavior*. New York: Appleton-Century-Crofts, 1969.

Church, R. M., Raymond, G. A., and Beauchamp, R. D. Response suppression as a function of intensity and delay of a punishment. *Journal of Comparative and Physiological Psychology*, 1967, *63*, 39–44.

DeBold, R. C., Miller, N. E., and Jensen, D. D. Effect of strength of drive determined by a new technique for appetitive classical conditioning of rats. *Journal of Comparative and Physiological Psychology*, 1965, *59*, 102–108.

Dember, W. N. Response by the rat to environmental change. *Journal of Comparative and Physiological Psychology*, 1956, *49*, 93–95.

Dember, W. N., and Earl, R. W. Analysis of exploratory, manipulatory, and curiosity behaviors. *Psychological Review*, 1957, *64*, 91–96.

Ducharme, R. Effect of internal and external cues on the heart rate of the rat. *Canadian Journal of Psychology*, 1966, *20*, 97–104. (a)

Ducharme, R. Activité physique et déactivation: Baisse du rhythme cardiaque an cours de l'activité instrumentale. *Canadian Journal of Psychology*, 1966, *20*, 445–454. (b)

Dyal, J. A. On the combination of drive and incentive motivation: A critical comment. *Psychological Reports*, 1967, *20*, 543–550.

Egeth, H. Selective attention. *Psychological Bulletin*, 1967, *67*, 41–57.

Eisman, E. Effects of deprivation and consummatory activity on heart rate. *Journal of Comparative and Physiological Psychology*, 1966, *62*, 71–75.

Evans, S. Failure of the interaction paradigm as a test of Hull vs. Spence. *Psychological Reports*, 1967, *20*, 551–554.

Fiske, D. W., and Maddi, S. R. A conceptual framework. In D. W. Fiske and S. R. Maddi (Eds.), *Functions of varied experience*. Homewood, Ill.: Dorsey, 1961, Pp. 11–56.

Fowler, H. Response to environmental change: A positive replication. *Psychological Reports*, 1958, *4*, 506.

Fowler, H. Exploratory motivation and animal handling: The effect on runway performance of start-box exposure time. *Journal of Comparative and Physiological Psychology*, 1963, *56*, 866–871.

Fowler, H. *Curiosity and exploratory behavior*. New York: Macmillan, 1965.

Fowler, H. Satiation and curiosity: Constructs for a drive and incentive-motivational theory of exploration. In K. W. Spence and J. T. Spence (Eds.), *The psychology of learning and motivation*. Vol. 1. New York: Academic Press, 1967. Pp. 157–227.

Fowler, H. Suppression and facilitation by response-contingent shock. In F. R. Brush (Ed.), *Aversive conditioning and learning*. New York: Academic Press, 1971. Pp. 537–604.

Fowler, H., and Siegel, A. W. Attention. In *The encyclopedia of education*. (Volume on educational psychology, edited by L. J. Cronbach.) New York: Macmillan, 1971.

Fox, S. S. Self-maintained sensory input and sensory deprivation in monkeys. *Journal of Comparative and Physiological Psychology*, 1962, *55*, 438–444.

Furedy, J. J. Novelty and the measurement of the GSR. *Journal of Experimental Psychology*, 1968, *76*, 501–503.

Glickman, S. E., and Schiff, B. B. A biological theory of reinforcement. *Psychological Review*, 1967, *74*, 81–109.

Goldstein, R., Stern, J. A., and Rothenberg, S. J. Effect of water deprivation and cues associated with water on the heart rate of the rate. *Physiology and Behavior*, 1966, *1*, 199–203.

Goodrich, K. P. Performance in different segments of an instrumental response chain as a function of reinforcement schedule. *Journal of Experimental Psychology*, 1959, *57*, 57–63.

Grim, P. F., and White, S. H. Effects of stimulus change upon the GSR and reaction time. *Journal of Experimental Psychology*, 1965, *69*, 276–281.

Hahn, W. W., Stern, J. A., and McDonald, D. G. Effects of water deprivation and bar pressing activity on heart rate of the male albino rat. *Journal of Comparative and Physiological Psychology*, 1962, *55*, 786–790.

Harlow, H. F. Motivation as a factor in the acquisition of new responses. In *Current theory and research in motivation*. Lincoln: University of Nebraska Press, 1953. Pp. 24–49.

Harlow, H. F., Blazek, N. C., and McClearn, G. E. Manipulatory motivation in the infant rhesus monkey. *Journal of Comparative and Physiological Psychology*, 1956, *49*, 444–448.

Harrington, G. M., and Kohler, G. R. Sensory deprivation and sensory reinforcement with shock. *Psychological Reports*, 1966, *18*, 803–808.

Harrington, G. M., and Linder, W. K. A positive reinforcing effect of electrical stimulation. *Journal of Comparative and Physiological Psychology*, 1962, *55*, 1014–1015.

Hebb, D. O. *The organization of behavior*. New York: Wiley, 1949.

Hebb, D. O. Drives and the C. N. S. (conceptual nervous system). *Psychological Review*, 1955, *62*, 243–254.

Helson, H. Some problems in motivation from the point of view of the theory of adaptation level. In D. Levine (Ed.), *Nebraska symposium on motivation*. Lincoln: University of Nebraska Press, 1966. Pp. 137–182.

Hull, C. L. *A behavior system*. New Haven: Yale University Press, 1952.

Kagan, J. On the need for relativism. *American Psychologist*, 1967, *22*, 131–142.

Kimble, G. A. *Hilgard and Marquis' conditioning and learning*. (2nd ed.) New York: Appleton-Century-Crofts, 1961.

Kish, G. B. Studies of sensory reinforcement. In W. K. Honig (Ed.), *Operant behavior*. New York: Appleton-Century-Crofts, 1966. Pp. 109–115.

Kivy, P. N., Earl, R. W., and Walker, E. L. Stimulus context and satiation. *Journal of Comparative and Physiological Psychology*, 1956, *49*, 90–92.

Lawrence, D. H. The nature of a stimulus: Some relationships between learning and perception. In S. Koch (Ed.), *Psychology: A study of science*. Vol. 5. New York: McGraw-Hill, 1963. Pp. 179–212.

Leuba, C. Toward some integration of learning theories: The concept of optimal stimulation. *Psychological Reports*, 1955, *1*, 27–33.

Lindsley, D. B. Psychophysiology and motivation. In M. R. Jones (Ed.), *Nebraska symposium on motivation*. Lincoln: University of Nebraska Press, 1957.

Lockhard, R. B. Some effects of maintenance luminance and strain differences upon self-exposure to light by rats. *Journal of Comparative and Physiological Psychology*, 1962, *55*, 1118–1123.

Lockhard, R. B. Some effects of light upon behavior of rodents. *Psychological Bulletin*, 1963, *60*, 509–529.

Lockhard, R. B. Several tests of stimulus-change and preference theory in relation to light-controlled behavior in rats. *Journal of Comparative and Physiological Psychology*, 1966, *62*, 415–426.

Logan, F. A. Decision making by rats: Delay versus amount of reward. *Journal of Comparative and Physiological Psychology*, 1965, *59*, 1–12.

Logan, F. A. Incentive theory and change in reward. In K. W. Spence and J. T. Spence (Eds.), *The psychology of learning and motivation*. Vol 2. New York: Academic Press, 1968. Pp. 1–30.

Lovejoy, E. *Attention in discrimination learning*. San Francisco: Holden-Day, 1968.

Lynn, R. *Attention, arousal and the orientation reaction*. Elmsford, N.Y.: Pergamon Publishing Co., Maxwell House, 1966.

Malmo, R. B. Measurement of drive: An unsolved problem in psychology. In M. R. Jones (Ed.), *Nebraska symposium on motivation*. Lincoln: University of Nebraska Press, 1958. Pp. 229–265.

Malmo, R. B. Activation: A neuropsychological dimension. *Psychological Review*, 1959, *66*, 367–386.

McCall, R. B. Stimulus change in light contingent bar pressing. *Journal of Comparative and Physiological Psychology*, 1965, *59*, 258–262.

McCall, R. B. Initial-consequent-change surface in light contingent bar pressing. *Journal of Comparative and Physiological Psychology*, 1966, *62*, 35–42.

Mendelson, J. The role of hunger in T-maze learning for food by rats. *Journal of Comparative and Physiological Psychology*, 1966, *62*, 341–353.

Montgomery, K. C. The relationship between exploratory behavior and spontaneous alternation in the white rat. *Journal of Comparative and Physiological Psychology*, 1951, *44*, 582–589.

Montgomery, K. C. Exploratory behavior and its relation to spontaneous alternation in a series of maze exposures. *Journal of Comparative and Physiological Psychology*, 1952, *45*, 50–57.

Montgomery, K. C. Exploratory behavior as a function of "similarity" of stimulus situations. *Journal of Comparative and Physiological Psychology*, 1953, *46*, 129–133.

Montgomery, K. C. The role of exploratory drive in learning. *Journal of Comparative and Physiological Psychology*, 1954, *47*, 60–64.

Montgomery, K. C., and Segall, M. Discrimination learning based upon the exploratory drive. *Journal of Comparative and Physiological Psychology*, 1955, *48*, 225–228.

Moss, F. A. Study of animal drives. *Journal of Experimental Psychology*, 1924, 7, 165–185.

Mowrer, O. H. *Learning theory and behavior.* New York: Wiley, 1960.

Myers, A. K., and Miller, N. E. Failure to find a learned drive based on hunger; evidence for learning motivated by "exploration." *Journal of Comparative and Physiological Psychology*, 1954, 47, 428–436.

Narbutovich, I. O., and Podkopaev, N. A. The conditioned reflex as an association. *Trudy Instituta Fiziolocii Imeni I. P. Pavlova*, 1936, 6, 5–25.

Nissen, H. W. The nature of the drive as innate determinant of behavioral organization. In M. R. Jones (Ed.), *Nebraska symposium on motivation.* Lincoln: University of Nebraska Press, 1954, Pp. 281–321.

O'Kelly, L. L., Hatton, G. I., Tucker, L., and Westall, D. Water regulation in the rat: Heart rate as a function of hydration, anesthesia, and association with reinforcement. *Journal of Comparative and Physiological Psychology*, 1965, 59, 159–165.

Pavlov, I. P. *Conditioned reflexes.* London: Oxford University Press, 1927.

Polidora, V. J., and Fletcher, H. J. An analysis of the importance of S-R spatial contiguity for proficient primate discrimination performance. *Journal of Comparative and Physiological Psychology*, 1964, 57, 224–230.

Premack, D. Reinforcement theory. In D. Levine (Ed.), *Nebraska symposium on motivation.* Lincoln: University of Nebraska Press, 1965. Pp. 123–188.

Premack, D. On some boundary conditions of contrast. In J. T. Tapp (Ed.), *Reinforcement and behavior.* New York: Academic Press, 1969. Pp. 120–145.

Richter, C. P. A behavioristic study of the activity of the rat. *Comparative Psychology Monograph*, 1922, 1, No. 2.

Richter, C. P. Animal behavior and internal drives. *Quarterly Review of Biology*, 1927, 2, 307–343.

Routtenberg, A. The two arousal hypothesis: Reticular formulation and limbic system. *Psychological Review*, 1968, 75, 51–80.

Shannon, C. E., and Weaver, W. *The mathematical theory of communication.* Urbana: University of Illinois Press, 1949.

Sheffield, F. D. A drive-induction theory of reinforcement. In R. N. Haber (Ed.), *Current research in motivation.* New York: Holt, 1966. Pp. 98–111. (a)

Sheffield, F. D. New evidence on the drive-induction theory of reinforcement. In R. N. Haber (Ed.), *Current research in motivation.* New York: Holt, 1966, Pp. 111–121. (b)

Snapper, A. G., Schoenfeld, W. N., Ferraro, D., and Locke, B. Cardiac rate of the rat under a DRL and a noncontingent temporal schedule of reinforcement. *Psychological Reports*, 1965, 17, 543–552.

Sokolov, E. N. *Perception and the conditioned reflex.* New York: Macmillan, 1963.

Spence, K. W. Continuous vs. noncontinuous interpretations of discrimination learning. *Psychological Review*, 1940, *47*, 271–288.

Spence, K. W. The nature of the response in discrimination learning. *Psychological Review*, 1952, *59*, 89–93.

Spence, K. W. Behavior theory and conditioning. New Haven: Yale University Press, 1956.

Sutherland, N. S. The learning of discriminations by animals. *Endeavour*, 1964, *23*, 148–152.

Tapp, J. T. Current status and future directions. In J. T. Tapp (Ed.), *Reinforcement and behavior.* New York: Academic Press, 1969. Pp. 387–416 (a)

Tapp, J. T. (Ed.), *Reinforcement and behavior.* New York: Academic Press, 1969. (b)

Tapp, J. T., and Simpson, L. L. Motivational and response factors as determinants of the reinforcing value of light onset. *Journal of Comparative and Physiological Psychology*, 1966, *62*, 143–146.

Treisman, A. M. Strategies and models of selective attention. *Psychological Review*, 1969, *76*, 282–299.

Trowill, J. A., Pankseff, J., and Gandelman, R. An incentive model of rewarding brain stimulation. *Psychological Review*, 1969, *76*, 264–281.

Welker, W. I. Some determinants of play and exploration in chimpanzees. *Journal of Comparative and Physiological Psychology*, 1956, *49*, 84–89. (a)

Welker, W. I. Variability of play and exploratory behavior in chimpanzees. *Journal of Comparative and Physiological Psychology*, 1956, *49*, 181–185. (b)

Zeaman, D., and House, B. J. The role of attention in retardate discrimination learning. In N. R. Ellis (Ed.), *Handbook of mental deficiency: Psychological theory and research.* New York: McGraw-Hill, 1963. Pp. 159–223.

Zener, K. The significance of behavior accompanying conditioned salivary secretion for theories of the conditioned response. *American Journal of Psychology*, 1937, *50*, 384–403.

Zimbardo, P. G., and Miller, N. E. Facilitation of exploration by hunger in rats. *Journal of Comparative and Physiological Psychology*, 1958, *51*, 43–46.

7

ELICITATION, REINFORCEMENT, AND STIMULUS CONTROL[1]

A. CHARLES CATANIA
New York University

The classic distinction between operants and respondents, as separate types of behavior that are amenable to different types of conditioning, has persistently resisted reduction. Although many attempts to reduce either type to a special case of the other have treated them as behaviorally compatible, the types have remained operationally distinct. The present account will deal with this operational distinction by treating operant and respondent conditioning as special cases within a broader context of procedures.

The paradigms are familiar. In the respondent or Pavlovian case, two stimuli are presented in succession: the conditioned stimulus or CS, and

[1] The preparation of this manuscript was supported in part by NIH Grant MH-13613 to New York University. A special debt is owing to W. N. Schoenfeld, whose influence is perhaps best noted by referring to the analysis of reinforcement schedules in terms of procedural continua (Schoenfeld, Cumming, and Hearst, 1956), and to an editorial on the distinction between operant and respondent behavior (Schoenfeld, 1966).

the unconditioned stimulus or US. If the US produces a characteristic response, the CS may also come to produce a response and this response, if not identical to that produced by the US, has as least some resemblance or relationship to it. In the operant or Thorndikean case, on the other hand, a response is not elicited, but when it occurs it is followed by some consequence, the reinforcer. The frequency of the response typically increases after this operation.

These two simple operations have been described as S-S and R-S procedures. Though they have been closely related in their historical development (e.g., as when Skinner indicated an eliciting stimulus in his early treatments of operants, in the notation s-R-S, even though the stimulus was unidentified), the operational distinction has remained the fundamental basis for dichotomization. But the dichotomization also has been bolstered by other considerations. One of these was the assumption that the two types of behavior and conditioning were correlated respectively with autonomic and somatic effector systems. Two directions of research have called this basis for the distinction into question: one demonstrating the control of autonomic responses by operant procedures, and the other demonstrating the control of somatic responses by respondent procedures. Of the many instances of operant control of autonomic responses, the work of N. E. Miller and his associates (e.g., Miller and Carmona, 1967), has provided the most dramatic and unequivocal cases. Instances of respondent control of somatic responses are suggested in ethological research and in the work of J. Konorski and his associates (e.g., Wyrwicka, 1967), but perhaps the most explicit demonstration has been the auto-shaping of the pigeon's key-peck by Brown and Jenkins (1968).

Elaborations of the properties of behavior that distinguish operants and respondents and their amenability to conditioning have taken a variety of forms, and often have been supplemented by the demonstration of functional differences in the two types of conditioning. Of these, only the comparison of the ineffectiveness of partial reinforcement in respondent procedures and its powerful control in operant procedures has maintained a prominent status. Other distinctions that purport to be functional, such as those between laws of contiguity and laws of effect or between stimulus-stimulus learning and stimulus-response learning, are in themselves derived from the dichotomization that they were marshalled to defend and therefore may be of questionable value.

But where the historical view displayed behavior in terms of dichotomizations, the current view may profit by attending to the continuities of behavior. Salivation can be elicited by specifiable stimuli, and under such circumstances may be modified by respondent conditioning; but salivation also occurs spontaneously, and when it does so it may be brought under operant control. Pecking occurs spontaneously, and can be brought under operant control; but pecking also can be elicited, and under such circumstances may be modified by respondent conditioning. For any given combination of stimulus and response, the probability of elicitation can be specified, and this relationship can be located along a continuum defined in terms of the effect of a stimulus on the probability of a response. The reflex, the relationship in which this change in probability is close to 1.0, is only one extreme on such a continuum. The other extreme is the case in which a stimulus reduces the probability of a response (e.g., as in Pavlov's external inhibition). Between these extremes is the case in which the available stimuli do not affect the probability of a response, when we speak of the response as an operant. But whether a given response is an operant or respondent then depends not on its topographical or physiological properties, but rather on its relationship to the stimuli presented within a given experimental context.

The dichotomization of behavior into operants and respondents has obscured this continuity for a number of reasons. Most important, perhaps, was that Pavlov's studies necessarily involved unconditioned stimuli that produced a specified response with a high probability. Pavlov probably would not have gotten far if he had selected stimuli and responses such that the unconditioned stimulus produced the response only with a probability of 0.05 or 0.10 or even 0.25, because it would then have been exceedingly difficult to assess changes in the probability of the response to the conditioned stimulus. Thus, the reliable relationship characterized as a reflex was essential if the initial analyses of the effects of stimulus combinations on behavior were to be effective; the study of respondent conditioning might not have been able to proceed at all with unconditioned stimuli that had unreliable eliciting effects. What therefore must have begun at least in part as a matter of experimental expedience became a matter of theoretical import. The rationale also received historical support, in Sherrington's (1906) and Sechenov's (1863, as reprinted in Sechenov, 1965) treatment of the reflex as a physiological unit rather than as a behavioral relationship. Skinner's (1931) elaboration of the behavioral status of the reflex as a correlation between stimuli and responses came too late to affect the implicit incorporation of such a treatment into much of subsequent learning theory. Pavlov's salivary preparations might have been taken as prototypes that showed forth clearly certain relationships among stimulus combinations and behavior, but some of the incidental features of these prototypical cases were carried with them into later accounts of conditioning.

The salience of reliable elicitation in this limiting case had another consequence as well: To the extent that the relationships of concern were elicitation relationships, attention was restricted to responding in the presence of various eliciting stimuli, both CS's and US's. Responding at other times was of lesser interest. Pavlov took note of such responding (e.g., Pavlov, 1927, Lectures II and III), and it has been investigated (e.g., by Zener and McCurdy, 1939). But in comparison with the elicited responding, spontaneous responding has received only passing experimental attention in theoretical accounts of respondent behavior, perhaps even in part because those who are interested in the variables that affect spontaneous or emitted behavior must necessarily be concerned with a different kind of experiment.

Behavior can be dealt with not only in terms of the probability relationships between stimuli and their elicited responses, but also in terms of the probability relationships between responses and their stimulus consequences. The latter relationships are the concern of operant procedures, the historical development and theoretical treatment of which involved factors that formally parallel some of those in the respondent case. For example, the analysis of operant behavior was for some time restricted to the limiting case in which responses produced a particular stimulus only with a probability of 1.0, just as respondent treatments began with reflex relationships in which the probability of elicitation was essentially 1.0. The shift to the more general operant procedures involving intermittency or probabilities less than 1.0, as in the considerable body of research on schedules of reinforcement, is relatively recent.

The characterization of the operant, too, was at least to some extent a matter of experimental expedience. The analysis of operant procedures could proceed most effectively with responses that had some substantial probability of occurrence in the absence of specifiable eliciting stimuli because only in such cases could the effects of response consequences on subsequent responding be assessed independently of the elicitation of responses by stimuli. It was this kind of consideration, at least in part, that was the basis for Skinner's 1935–1937 debate with Konorski and Miller (1937). One of Konorski and Miller's procedures involved the elicitation of leg-flexions by shock to a dog's leg, and the subsequent reinforcement of the flexion by food presentations. The behavior generated by such a procedure is more difficult to analyze than that generated by the reinforcement of responses without specifiable eliciting stimuli, if only because the combined effects of two distinct experimental operations must be assessed. But one other consequence of this experimental rationale was the concentration of attention on the responding that occurred in the absence of the reinforcing stimuli. Within such an experimental context, the relationship of the spontaneous or emitted responses to those elicited by the reinforcing stimuli was of little interest until recent developments in ethology, in the applied work of the Brelands (1961), and, most explicitly, in Premack's (1959) analysis of reinforcement.

These considerations summate to suggest that the distinction between respondent and operant conditioning must be examined once again. Attempts to reduce either type of conditioning to a special case of the other seem to have lost momentum. Operant conditioning has been treated as a consequence of respondent-conditioning processes in which the interoceptive or proprioceptive concomitants of behavior acquire the properties of conditioned stimuli; respondent conditioning has been treated as a consequence of operant-conditioning processes that operate because reliable successions of events and consistencies of behavior within a restricted experimental environment can generate stereotyped performance, such as in the development of an experimental superstition. But, as Kendon Smith (1954) has argued, such reductions cannot bring the matter to rest because unobserved events can always be appealed to and it may follow that such accounts are, in principle, impossible of empirical test. Thus, the only way to deal adequately with the relationship between S-S and R-S procedures may be to place them both within the context of a more exhaustive account of behavioral relationships.

The account thus far suggests that a precondition for undertaking such a task must be the avoidance of the prejudices and preconceptions that traditional respondent and operant approaches have generated. On its own terms, eschewing a reductionist account, the analysis of behavior is concerned with only two types of events: environmental events called stimuli, and behavioral events called responses. The major emphasis in what follows will be procedural, so that these events can be taken as defined in terms of experimental operations and measurements, with stimuli and responses specified as classes of events respectively controlled and observed by the experimenter. Such an account is admittedly naive, and it avoids the issue of specifying criteria for behavioral units, either in terms of lawfulness or of logic. Thus, the account may not permit statements to be made about the behavioral consequences of any specific procedure. But it will necessarily adhere closely to what is done and what is seen, and may therefore serve the heuristic function of keeping preconceptions about the properties of behavior from intruding into it.

Behavior is fundamentally a series of events in time, a continuous stream involving stimuli and responses. Whatever else might be involved in the analysis of behavior, it must be concerned at some point with the specification of the probabilities of transition among the various events in the stream. Responses may be followed by responses; by observing the organization and probability relationships among responses when stimuli do not intervene, the experimenter may be able to classify responses into larger units and to describe their structures and their hierarchial properties. Stimuli may be followed by responses; by observing these probability relationships, the experimenter can define the control of behavior by environment in the elicitation relationship and can thereby take control over behavior by the manipulation of relevant stimuli. Responses may be followed by stimuli; by establishing probability relationships between behavior and the environment, the experimenter can examine the ways in which behavior can be controlled by its consequences. Stimuli may be followed by stimuli; by stating probability relationships among stimuli, the experimenter can characterize and manipulate certain properties of the environment. Taken together, these four probability relationships exhaust the possible two-term contingencies among environmental and behavioral events. Because neither stimuli nor responses are of any interest in isolation, a convenient and perhaps essential starting point for analysis is given by these four simple relationships: response-response or R-R; stimulus-response or S-R; response-stimulus or R-S; and stimulus-stimulus or S-S.

The R-R relationship is one in which a particular sequence of responses is observed in the absence of intervening stimuli. A given R-R sequence may be generated experimentally by relating specific responses to prior eliciting stimuli or to subsequent consequences, but such cases are irrelevant to the present purposes because any such sequences can be dealt with only by taking into account the other relationships that have been enumerated. Concern with the R-R relationship is therefore fundamental to the problem of response units, because dependencies among responses that vary together in the absence of intervening stimuli may indicate something about the structure of behavior. The analysis of the properties of behavior that can be dealt with independently of the stimulus conditions under which the behavior is generated (e.g., as in a psychophysiologist's concern with rapidly emitted and topographically complex sequences such as a musician's arpeggio [Lashley, 1951] or in a linguist's concern with the formal structure of language [Chomsky, 1963]) must restrict itself to R-R relationships. Such analyses may have empirical consequences by demonstrating that response classes having certain structural properties might be easier to modify by specified experimental procedures than other response classes having different structural properties. In addition, the study of R-R relationships may reveal the hierarchical properties of behavior and thereby bear on the consequences of the experimental operations that are superimposed on behavior, as in Hull's (1943) concern with the habit-family hierarchy and Premack's (1959) treatment of the relative probabilities of responses in predicting the effectiveness of reinforcers. But beyond restricting the classes of responses upon which certain procedures may be effective, such analyses do not limit the classification of the types of experimental procedures that are available to the experimenter.

The S-R relationship is also one in terms of which we may characterize the properties of behavior. We have already suggested that the traditional reflex is only an extreme instance in this type of relationship, and it is therefore appropriate to outline the properties of this relationship more explicitly. Consider a situation in which behavior is sampled at specified times, such as successive five-second intervals, and in which the probability or relative frequency of a particular response is separately determined in those five-second intervals that immediately follow the presentation of a given stimulus and those five-second intervals that do not follow a stimulus presentation. The probabilities can be represented graphically as in Fig. 7-1. (The similarity to coordinates for plotting receiver-operating characteristics in signal detection will be immediately evident. Speculations are possible on the relationship between elicited responses and spontaneous activity, such as that they may follow iso-sensitivity contours [e.g., Green and Swets, 1966], but no attempt will be made to elaborate on such possibilities here.)

Several regions have been distinguished in Fig. 7-1. In region A, the probability of a response is high after stimulus presentations, and is relatively low in the absence of such presentations. Those S-R relationships that fit in this region have traditionally been called reflexes. Region B also includes relationships in which the probability of a response is raised by the presentation of a stimulus, but within this region the increase in prob-

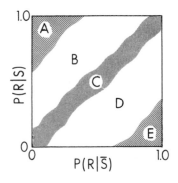

FIGURE 7-1. The stimulus-response continuum. The reflex relationship is represented by region A and the operant relationship by region C. $P(R/S)$ — probability of a response given a stimulus; $P(R/S)$ — probability of a response given no stimulus.

ability is substantially less than 1.0. Many examples can be cited, perhaps the simplest of which is that in which the intensity of the eliciting stimulus of a reflex is reduced toward threshold values. This by no means exhausts the available cases, however. Region B also includes the types of relationships sometimes observed in the ethological analysis of fixed action patterns, in which the measures in terms of which data are ordinarily presented consist of relative frequencies or probabilities of response in the presence of various stimuli (releasers). The figure actually encompasses the full range of ethological relationships, in that the highly reliable production of a fixed action pattern by a releaser may be represented in region A, the occasional production of a fixed action pattern by a releaser that usually produces a different fixed action pattern (displacement activity) may be represented in region B, and the occurrence of the fixed action pattern in the absence of a releaser (vacuum activity) may be represented in region C. Region C, however, also represents another class of relationships, i.e., those in which the probability of a response is not affected by a specifiable eliciting stimulus within the experimental situation. Such a response is said to be emitted, and region C therefore represents the S-R relationship appropriate to the analysis of operant behavior. Regions D and E complete the possible relationships, and represent those cases in which the presentation of a specified stimulus reduces the probability of a response (e.g., as in classical reflex inhibition, or as in appeasement activities in ethological courtship patterns, when stimuli provided by one organism may reduce the probability of aggressive responses by a potential mate).

It is important to emphasize that, just as the reflex must be characterized as a relationship between stimuli and responses and cannot be dealt with in terms of either stimuli or responses in isolation, so also the coordinates in Fig. 7-1 represent S-R relationships rather than the properties of any particular stimuli or any particular responses. Thus, no response can be represented by a specific point or region in the figure, because the response cannot be located without reference to the stimulus in terms of which the S-R relationship is described. For example, salivation, when it is produced by food as in the familiar salivary reflex, may be represented in region A, but salivation produced by water in the mouth may be represented in region C, and the effect of electric shock or a sudden loud noise on salivation may be represented in regions D or E. More generally, any given stimulus may change the probabilities of a variety of different responses, but these changes in probability are likely to be different for each of the responses; inversely, for any given response its probability is likely to be modified in different ways by different stimuli. The regions in Fig. 7-1 are shown as somewhat distinct, but they actually blend into one another. We have inherited various dichotomizations of behavior, but they may not be consistent with the continuities emphasized in Fig. 7-1.

Whatever an experimenter does to study the S-R relationships in Fig. 7-1, his experimental operations must involve only the presentation of stimuli. The figure suggests that he must look not only at the response as it is produced by stimuli, but also as it occurs between stimulus presentations. As will be elaborated later, some of the crucial properties of elicitation for the analysis of other behavioral processes may rest with its effects on the responding that subsequently occurs in the absence of the eliciting stimulus.

The two remaining classes of relationships, response-stimulus and stimulus-stimulus, both represent experimental operations, or properties of the environment, rather than properties of behavior. In the R-S relationship, the dependency of stimuli on responses can be represented in much the same way as that of responses on stimuli, i.e., in terms of stimulus probability given either a response or no response. These coordinates are shown in Fig. 7-2 (similar coordinates have been suggested by Seligman, Maier, and Solomon [in press], as the "instrumental-training space"). Once again, regions of the coordinate system correspond to various traditional categories in the analysis of behavior. For example, if stimulus probability is low in the absence of responding but becomes high whenever a response occurs, as in region A of Fig. 7-2, the response may be said to produce the stimulus; the relationship is typically described as

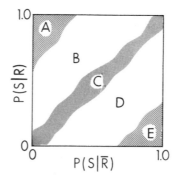

FIGURE 7-2. The response-stimulus continuum. The reinforcement or punishment relationship is represented by region A, the respondent or response-independent relationship by region C, and the avoidance or omission relationship by region E. P(S/R) — probability of a stimulus given a response; P(S/R̄) — probability of a stimulus given no response.

reinforcement or as punishment, depending on the stimulus that is involved. If stimulus probability increases with responses but nevertheless remains low, as in the part of region B that lies below region A, the relationship becomes one involving intermittency (e.g., as in variable-ratio schedules of reinforcement).

At the other extreme, stimuli may occur in the absence of responding, but their probabilities may be reduced whenever responses occur. If the stimuli are aversive, such an arrangement is spoken of as an avoidance procedure. If the stimuli are reinforcers, such an arrangement is spoken of as an omission procedure or as the differential reinforcement of other behavior (the DRO schedule of Reynolds, 1961).

Procedures in which stimuli occur with substantial probabilities in the absence of responses and in which responses modify the probabilities only to some degree, corresponding to regions B and D, are available in the literature (e.g., as when unavoidable response-independent shocks are superimposed on a baseline avoidance performance: Sidman, Herrnstein, and Conrad, 1957). Such procedures, however, would simply have to be enumerated here, because they are not conveniently categorized within the current available vocabulary of behavioral procedures.

Those cases in which stimulus probabilities are independent of responses, i.e., in which the stimulus probability given a response is the same as the stimulus probability given no response, are represented in region C. The procedures, because they involve stimulus presentations that occur independently of behavior, are fundamentally respondent. Yet examples of such procedures include not only such traditionally respondent cases as Pavlovian temporal conditioning, but also operant cases such as the establishment of an experimental superstition. In fact, instances of temporal conditioning and of experimental superstition have differed as procedures only in their temporal parameters; the empirical differences rest predominantly with the responses that experimenters have chosen to look at. The resulting behavior has been dealt with in respondent terms if observed responses have been related in some way to the responses elicited by the stimulus; it has been dealt with in operant terms if the behavior has been variable from one organism to another and has not been obviously related to responses elicited by the stimulus.

But the relationships in Fig. 7-2 do not help with respect to the handling of the classical Pavlovian case. There is no direct way to move from these R-S relationships to those involved in the fourth, stimulus-stimulus or S-S, case, without introducing still another set of dimensions. Yet to marshall a series of descriptive relationships that does no more than enumerate the logical possibilities is not likely by itself to be a fruitful endeavor.

Stimuli may be correlated with stimuli, that is, the probability relationships among stimuli may be specified. Rescorla (1967) has discussed some properties of such relationships in terms of S-S contingencies, and Seligman, Maier, and Solomon (in press) have proposed a Pavlovian-conditioning space analogous to those in Figs. 7-1 and 7-2, with S-S relationships substituted for S-R or R-S relationships. But a more complete account of experimental procedures demands a different type of specification of the possible relationships, because an exhaustive account also should be able to treat the three-term contingency of an operant discrimination. For this purpose, a somewhat modified notation will be useful. The kinds of R-S relationships illustrated in Fig. 7-2 will be noted as $R:S$, which may be read as "the effect of response R on the probability of stimulus S." Such a relationship may be arranged so that it holds at all times within a particular experimental setting, under which circumstances an analysis may proceed in terms of the coordinates illustrated in Fig. 7-2; on the other hand, the relationship may be arranged so that it holds only in the presence of a specific stimulus that is introduced into the experimental setting. In the latter case, the relationship may be represented as $S^D(R:S)$, where S^D is the stimulus in the presence of which the $R:S$-relationship holds. This S^D, of course, corresponds to the traditional discriminative stimulus in an operant discrimination, because by our definition the $R:S$-relationship holds in its presence but not in its absence.

But we have already noted that the $R:S$-relationship may take on any of the values in the coordinates of Fig. 7-2. Thus, we need not restrict our concern only to those cases in which a response raises the probability of a stimulus whenever a discriminative stimulus is present, as in the simplest operant discriminations. We may also represent as $S^D(R:S)$ those cases in which responses reduce the probability of a stimulus whenever the discriminative stimulus is present. Discriminated avoidance is an example of one such case: In the presence of the warning stimulus, S^D, a response reduces the probability of an aversive stimulus.

If the $R:S$-relationship is of the respondent type, then $S^D(R:S)$ represents a case in which, in the presence of a discriminative stimulus, a response has no effect on the probability of a stimulus. For example, in the presence of a tone, food may be presented independently of responses. This case, in which a discriminative stimulus sets the occasion on which some other stimulus occurs independently of responding, will be recognized as an instance of classical Pavlovian conditioning. At least at the formal level, the S^D or CS of the Pavlovian case stands in relation to simple elicitation as the S^D of an operant discrimination stands in relation to reinforcement or punishment.

The implications of this formal analysis lead us in the opposite direction from traditional attempts to resolve the relationship between operants and respondents. Where many attempts have been directed toward reducing either type to a special case of the other, the present account suggests that the difficulties of the traditional treatments have been created by an omission. We have been speaking of only two processes when we should have been speaking of three: elicitation, reinforcement, and stimulus control.

The simplest kinds of operations are elicitation operations: the presentation of stimuli. We know too little about elicitation, but for decades there have been hints in the literature that the properties of elicitation cannot be ignored in the analysis of behavior. These hints can be summarized by the generalization that the elicitation of responses makes these responses more probable even in the absence of the eliciting stimulus (we no longer speak often of practice, but the prevalence of this term in the lay vocabulary of behavior may indicate some recognition of the importance of the phenomenon). Examples are provided in observations of spontaneous salivation after salivation has been elicited by food, and in the reliance, in generating the first instance of an avoidance response in avoidance conditioning, on topographical similarity of avoidance responses and responses elicited by the aversive stimulus. The various instances of Pavlovian temporal conditioning, and contemporary analogues such as Morse, Mead, and Kelleher's (1967) studies of the temporal patterning of responses elicited by periodic shock in the squirrel monkey, provide additional cases. In these cases, it is sometimes argued that the control of responding in the absence of the eliciting stimulus depends on CS-properties that are acquired by the experimental environment. Throughout the history of respondent conditioning, the consequences of procedures that are operationally simple (periodic presentations of a single stimulus) have been dealt with in terms of principles derived from procedures that are operationally complex (periodic presentations of two or more stimuli in combination). But it must be noted that such a characterization in terms of established S-S procedures carries with it the very assumptions that a resolution of the respondent-operant dichotomization of behavior must question. (Analogous developments are evident in the analysis of schedules of reinforcement, in which concern is shifting from interpretations in terms of the discriminative properties of schedule performances to reassessment in terms of more elementary processes. For example, the fixed-interval schedule is simpler than some other schedules that involve changing exteroceptive stimuli, and yet the findings in the more complex schedules have often been invoked in accounts of fixed-interval performance. Dews [1962] points out, however, that fixed-interval performance may be dealt with more economically in terms of the relatively simple process of delayed reinforcement than in terms of the more complex process of temporal discrimination.)

It will be useful at this point to illustrate the coordination of the relationships that have been considered here within a somewhat different context, simply because the variety of conditioning procedures makes it impractical to present them conveniently within the context of coordinate systems such as those in Figs. 7-1 and 7-2. Given the present status of our understanding, we must make several assumptions and can deal with relevant dimensions of behavior only to a first approximation. It is therefore important to emphasize that the presentation that follows is concerned solely with a tentative organization of experimental procedures that takes into account historical distinctions; it says nothing of the behavioral outcomes that may follow from these procedures, nor does it defend the historical bases of the distinctions. Thus, it is a classification of behavioral operations rather than a classification of behavioral processes.

The account is also tentative with respect to the quantitative status of the dimensions it considers. There do not exist adequate metrics for specifying unambiguously the kinds of stimulus properties and the relationships between behavior and environment that will be necessary for elaborating the account. Nevertheless, the organization provides a way of dealing with a variety of traditional and novel behavioral procedures within a fairly exhaustive operational system.

Three dimensions are needed to fully treat the respondent and the operant procedures that this account sets out to consider. These dimensions are illustrated in Fig. 7-3. The first is a stimulus dimension, represented along the abscissa and corresponding to the widely accepted classification of environmental events into appetitive, neutral, and aversive stimuli. The second is a dimension summarizing the R:S-relationship, represented along the ordinate and corresponding to a range of effects that responses may have on the environment: Responses may increase stimulus probability, have no effect on stimulus probability, or reduce stimulus probability. The third is a dimension related to discriminative control, represented by the difference between the front and rear surfaces of the coordinates and corresponding to the relationship of R:S-contingencies to discriminative stimuli.

The abscissa, which represents certain properties of stimuli along a continuum, has considerable historical precedent, but it has already been noted that historical precedent must be accepted only with caution. Appetitive or reinforcing stimuli and aversive or punishing stimuli have been classified by appeal to their effects when they are made consequent on behavior, but it has been amply demonstrated (as in Premack's analysis

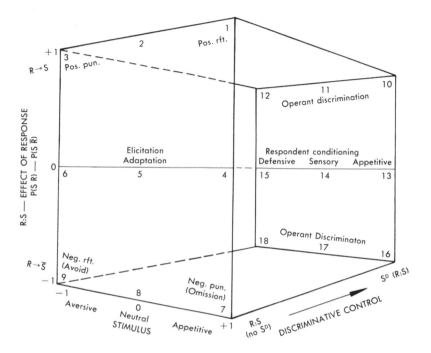

FIGURE 7-3. A coordinate system for representing behavioral procedures. The three dimensions include a stimulus-property continuum, a continuum representing the consequences of responding, and the presence or absence of discriminative control. This figure is of interest mainly because of its relationship to historical distinctions among procedures; the essential behavioral operations are illustrated less ambigiously in Fig. 7-2.

of the relativity of the reinforcement relationship) that the reinforcing properties of stimuli cannot be defined in absolute terms; instead, these properties must be dealt with relative to the responses that produce these stimuli as consequences.

Nevertheless, there are certain behavioral properties of these classes of stimuli that suggest it may be possible to deal consistently with this stimulus dimension. For example, most stimuli that are regarded as reinforcers have the property that the responses they elicit increase in probability with deprivation, and decrease in probability with successive presentations (satiation). The temporal parameters of deprivation and satiation effects may vary considerably from reinforcer to reinforcer (e.g., as in the different time courses for alimentary and for sexual reinforcers), but the existence of these processes provides at least a rough basis for classification. (It may be noted in passing that one interpretation of reinforcing brain stimulation, for which deprivation and satiation effects have not been convincingly demonstrated, is the suggestion that such stimulation involves only weak reinforcing effects; Pliskoff, Wright, and Hawkins, 1965.) Most stimuli that are regarded as aversive, however, have opposite effects. The elicitation of responses by aversive stimuli tends to increase with successive presentations (sensitization) and to decrease with time since the last presentation (e.g., Badia, Suter, and Lewis, 1966; Azrin, Rubin, and Hutchinson, 1968.) These relationships may be related to the ubiquitous phenomenon of warm-up in many aversive-control procedures. In any case, the opposite direction of these effects from those of reinforcing stimuli may again provide a rough basis for classification.

The stimulus continuum along the abscissa of Fig. 7-3, then, ranges from $+1$, representing reinforcing stimuli, through zero, representing neutral stimuli, to -1, representing aversive or punishing stimuli. (For the present purposes, it will not be a matter of concern that the reinforcing properties, and therefore the numerical representation, of a given stimulus may be varied by deprivation operations.) Some events are not easily incorporated into this continuum, because every environmental event necessarily involves a change from one set of conditions to another. For example, it is not clear whether the demonstration that heat may reinforce the responses of an organism in the cold (Weiss and Laties, 1961) should be regarded as positive reinforcement, because heat is added to the organism's environment, or as negative reinforcement, because the aversive effects of cold on temperature receptors in the organism's skin are removed. Nevertheless, the continuum takes into account distinctions that have been widely accepted in the historical treatment of conditioning procedures, although it may not follow that it puts stimuli into the most effective empirical order.

The second dimension, the ordinate in Fig. 7-3, is a derivative of the R:S-relationship of Fig. 7-2. The relationship has been expressed in terms of the difference between the two probabilities of Fig. 7-2: $P(S/R) - P(S/\bar{R})$, or the stimulus probability given a response minus the stimulus probability given no response. For example, if stimulus probability is 1.0 whenever a response occurs but is otherwise zero, this statistic equals $+1$ and represents the case in which a response reliably produces a stimulus; if stimulus probability is the same whether or not a response occurs, this statistic equals zero and represents the case in which stimuli are presented independently of responding; and, if stimulus probability

is zero after a response occurs but is otherwise 1.0, this statistic equals
− 1 and represents the case in which a response reliably prevents or avoids
a stimulus.

This dimension, like the stimulus dimension, may need a more precise
and unequivocal formulation to put it in good empirical order. For example, it assumes that 1.0 − 0.5 is operationally equivalent to 0.5 − 0.
That assumption is likely to be incorrect. But at least it provides a convenient way to reduce the coordinates of Fig. 7-2 to a single dimension.
In addition, the manner in which it would deal with both escape and
avoidance procedures would depend critically on the way in which stimulus probabilities are calculated. Nevertheless, because the dimension is
concerned with experimental procedures rather than with behavioral processes, it should be possible in any particular case to specify the relevant
dimensions adequately in terms of concrete experimental operations.

The third dimension involves the correlation between a discriminative
stimulus, S^D, and an R:S-relationship. It would be possible to represent
this dimension in terms of a continuum of correlations or contingencies,
but because the subsequent treatment will be more convenient and because the continuity between various regions along this dimension will
not be a substantial concern, only two points on the continuum are represented in Fig. 7-3: the front surface of the coordinate system, which
corresponds to the case in which there is no S^D correlated with R:S, and
the rear surface, which corresponds to the case in which an S^D is perfectly
correlated with R:S. (In fact, every experimental situation provides correlated and uncorrelated stimuli, such as the experimental chamber itself,
and in some respects the relevant distinctions may not be behaviorally
significant in any sufficiently generalized formulation.)

It is now possible to explore the correspondence between various
regions of Fig. 7-3 and traditional learning and conditioning procedures.
The regions of the figure have been systematically numbered for convenience of exposition. The front surface, which does not involve discriminative control by an S^D, will be considered first. Regions 1, 2, and 3 include
cases in which a response raises the probability of a stimulus. Region 1,
in which the stimulus is a reinforcer, corresponds to the familiar operation of positive reinforcement. Procedures concerned with sensory reinforcers, which are typically weak reinforcers, may be located between
regions 1 and 2. Region 2, in which the stimulus is neutral, corresponds
to an operation that is involved in a number of experimental designs. For
example, in one type of latent-learning experiment, a response produces
a neutral stimulus that is subsequently paired with a reinforcer independently of behavior; later procedures, in extinction, test whether learning occurred during the first condition. The operation represented by

region 2 has also served often as a control condition in experiments on conditioned reinforcement. Even certain perceptual learning experiments may be interpreted in terms of the operations represented by region 2. For example, experiments with inverting lenses change the stimulus consequences of motor responses, and yet these consequences are presumably not to be regarded as strong reinforcers or strong punishers. Finally, region 3, in which the stimulus is aversive, corresponds to the operation of punishment. Because the operation involves the presentation of a stimulus when responses occur, it is convenient to refer to this operation as positive punishment. In practice, this operation is usually superimposed upon a baseline of reinforced responding, but the operations must be distinguished even if they are combined.

In each of these cases, responses need not raise the probability of a stimulus to 1.0. Stimulus presentations may be scheduled, in which case the increment in the probability of the stimulus may be considerably less than 1.0. Such operations are represented in the area between regions 1, 2, and 3 and regions 4, 5, and 6 (according to a strict interpretation of the probability relationships of R:S, this area represents only variable-ratio schedules, but accounts of other schedules in terms of probability relationships are possible, as in the t system of Schoenfeld, Cumming, and Hearst, 1956).

Regions 4, 5, and 6 include cases in which stimulus presentations occur independently of responding. When the stimuli are reinforcers, in region 4, we speak of the operation in terms of experimental superstition or in terms of respondent cases such as temporal conditioning, depending on temporal parameters and on the responses that we choose to observe. When the stimuli are neutral, in region 5, we speak of adaptation; the operation of extinction also may be represented in this region. Finally, when the stimuli are aversive, in region 6, we speak of respondent procedures such as defensive temporal conditioning.

Regions 7, 8, and 9 include cases in which a response reduces the probability of a stimulus or, in other words, avoids or prevents stimulus presentations. In region 7, when the stimulus is a reinforcer, the operation corresponds to an omission procedure usually referred to as differential reinforcement of zero behavior or of other behavior: Reinforcement occurs only in the absence of the specified response. An example is Miller and Carmona's (1967) demonstration that a thirsty dog's salivation can be reduced by delivering water only after periods of no salivation. Because the procedure ordinarily involves the reduction of responding by withdrawal of reinforcers, it may be referred to as negative punishment, by analogy to the usual distinction between positive and negative reinforcement in terms of whether a stimulus is presented or withdrawn. Obvious examples of procedures represented by region 8, in which the stimulus is neutral, are not common in the literature, but it is possible to design procedures incorporating such an operation. For example, a latent-learning experiment that involved aversive control might include an initial stage in which a response prevented the occurrence of a neutral stimulus, as in region 8, and a subsequent stage in which, independently of behavior, the neutral stimulus was paired with an aversive stimulus. Finally, region 9, in which the stimulus is aversive, includes cases of negative reinforcement. In free-operant shock avoidance (Sidman, 1953), for example, shocks are delivered in the absence of responding, and each response reduces the probability of shock to zero for a specified period of time. Again, schedules are represented in the area between regions 7, 8, and 9 and regions 4, 5, and 6.

It is important to note that regions 1 through 9 are arranged along continua; the figure does not simply represent a 3-by-3 table of procedures. Procedures corresponding to any point on the surface can be designed, and examples of a number of instances that are intermediate to those enumerated above are available in the literature. For example, the range of aversive-stimulus procedures that extends from region 3 through region 6 to region 9 includes those in which every response is punished; those in which responses are punished according to a schedule or in which aversive stimuli are presented with some probability independently of behavior but increase in probability if responses occur (as in studies of schedules of shock delivery in the squirrel monkey by Morse, Mead, and Kelleher, 1967); those in which aversive stimuli are completely independent of behavior; those in which responses only partially reduce the probability of aversive stimuli (as in the schedules of shock-rate reduction studied by Herrnstein and Hineline, 1966); and those in which every response is effective as an avoidance or escape response. The dimensions represent only experimental operations, however, and the question of whether the outcomes of these operations involve different behavioral processes is an empirical one. The answer will depend on whether, for particular stimuli and responses, behavioral measures show discontinuities as one moves from one region to another along these continua.

The general properties of the procedures illustrated by the front surface in Fig. 7-3 have been exhausted, but the classical respondent procedures have not yet been represented. To deal with these, it is necessary to examine the same set of S:R-relationships when they hold only in the presence of a discriminative stimulus. Consider now the rear surface of the coordinate system, in which an S^D is superimposed upon the R:S-relationship.

Regions 10, 11, and 12, like regions 1, 2, and 3, represent cases in which a response produces a stimulus. Region 10, therefore, corresponds to a simple operant discrimination, in which a response is reinforced in the presence but not in the absence of a particular discriminative stimulus. Region 11 may be interpreted as an operation corresponding to one stage of a latent-learning experiment. One of many possible examples is the following: In the presence of a discriminative stimulus, such as a particular choice point in a maze, a response may be followed by a neutral stimulus, such as a distinctive goal-box. Region 12 corresponds to an operant discrimination based on punishment in the presence but not in the absence of a particular discriminative stimulus. (Like the undiscriminated case, in region 3, this procedure is ordinarily superimposed on a baseline of reinforced responding, as in Brethower and Reynolds [1962] study of the effect of punishment on unpunished responding.)

In regions 13, 14, and 15, one stimulus, the S^D, serves as a discriminative stimulus in the presence of which another stimulus, S, is presented independently of responding. It is here, in region 13, that we may put Pavlov in his place. If S^D is a tone and the stimulus that occurs in its presence is a reinforcer such as food in the mouth, the procedure corresponds to the classical case of respondent appetitive conditioning. But it is not wholly restricted to the Pavlovian case. For example, Brown and Jenkins' autoshaping of pigeons' key-pecks involves key-illumination in the presence of which food is presented independently of behavior. Other procedures (e.g., Rescorla and Solomon, 1967) involve the superimposition of discriminative stimuli that precede reinforcers on baseline performances maintained by positive or negative reinforcement. If, however, one stimulus serves as a discriminative stimulus in the presence of which a neutral stimulus is delivered independently of behavior, as in region 14, the procedure corresponds to the preconditioning stage of experiments on sensory preconditioning. Finally, if the discriminative stimulus is correlated with presentations of an aversive stimulus, as in region 15, the procedure corresponds to cases such as respondent defensive conditioning, or such as conditioned suppression (Estes and Skinner, 1941). It may be interesting to note that such classical procedures as trace conditioning can be regarded as cases in which the correlation of S^D with R:S is not perfect.

Regions 16, 17, and 18, like regions 7, 8, and 9, represent cases in which a response prevents or avoids the occurrence of a stimulus. When the stimulus is a reinforcer, as in region 16, the procedure corresponds to discriminated omission training (as in the unsuccessful attempt by Sheffield, 1965, to reinforce the absence of salivation with food in the presence of a discriminative stimulus). When the stimulus is neutral, as in region 17, the procedure may correspond to a preliminary condition of a latent-learning experiment (though no obviously representative cases are available in the literature). When the stimulus is aversive, as in region 18, the procedure corresponds to discriminated avoidance.

The relationships in Fig. 7-3 represent a variety of experimental procedures for which extensive data are already available in the literature. The formulation could also be extended easily to more complex procedures. For example, the S of a given R:S-relationship could be the S^D with respect to still another R:S-relationship, and therefore the same set of dimensions could be used to describe the features of chained schedules, higher-order conditioning, and other complex cases in which various S^D (R:S) relationships are nested within or combined with each other. Thus, the coordinate system provides a reasonably comprehensive description of behavioral operations (even though Fig. 7-2, which does not attempt to deal with historically differentiated procedures, is preferable because of its less ambiguous specification of relationships.)

The system, however, says nothing about the behavioral consequences of these operations. Generalizations about behavioral consequences must appeal to other dimensions of behavior, and at the present time it is possible only to hint at the kinds of dimensions that may be relevant. Several lines of evidence suggest the importance of the relationship between the response, R, of the R:S relationship and the response, R_S, that is elicited by S. These responses may be similar or identical, they may be independent in the sense that each may be emitted without interfering with or facilitating the other, or they may be incompatible. Various procedures involving R:S-relationships appear to be more effective in increasing the probability of R if R and R_S are similar than if R and R_S are incompatible. Many examples are available. Food reinforcers typically elicit increases in activity in the pigeon, and Blough (1958) has shown that it is difficult to reinforce the maintenance of a posture, which is incompatible with activity, with food reinforcement. Omission training with respect to salivation is ineffective in reducing salivation with food as a reinforcer, as in Sheffield's (1965) experiments, but the procedure is effective with water as a reinforcer, as in Miller and Carmona's (1967) experiments; food as a reinforcer elicits salivation which is incompatible with decreased salivation, whereas water as a reinforcer does not. Avoidance responding is more easily established and maintained if the response is similar to that elicited by the aversive stimulus (witness the frequent use of a locomotor response in avoidance procedures) than if the response has no special relationship to that elicited by the aversive stimulus (witness the often-noted difficulty of establishing key-pecking as an avoidance response in the pigeon). And, finally, to come full circle, the hallmark of classical respondent procedures has been the relationship of the response elicited by the CS to that elicited by the US. These examples point once again to the importance of studying elicitation, because the involvement of elicited responses in the effects of various R:S-relationships makes it unlikely that these effects can be understood without taking elicitation into account. The analysis of elicitation must consider not only the responding that is produced by successive stimulus presentations, but also responding in the absence of the eliciting stimulus (comparison of the effects of periodic and aperiodic schedules of stimulus presentation may also be of particular interest, as suggested in studies by Kelleher and Morse, 1968, of the effects of periodic shock).

But none of this follows from the coordinate system of Fig. 7-3. To the extent that the system does have implications, they bear not on the character of behavioral processes, but rather on the way in which we talk about these processes. It is only in this regard that the system may contribute to our understanding of the traditional distinction between operants and respondents. Perhaps the most important feature of the account is what it suggests about the relationship of discriminative control to other processes.

We began this account with a distinction between S-S or respondent and R-S or operant procedures. With reference to simple elicitation in the dimensions of Fig. 7-3, these procedures are orthogonally related. Comparisons between them (such as in terms of the effectiveness of partial reinforcement) do not seem legitimate because the procedures are not dimensionally equivalent and therefore cannot be discussed in terms of analogous operations. The issue of reduction disappears because they do not have enough in common on which a reduction can be based.

As we have already indicated, instead of attempting reduction, we might more effectively introduce another process; elicitation. We can superimpose upon this process the effects of response consequences: reinforcement or punishment. And we can superimpose upon these processes the third: stimulus control. The coordinate system of Fig. 7-3 suggests that discriminative control in an operant discrimination bears the same type of relationship to simple reinforcement or punishment as respondent conditioning bears to elicitation. In both cases, an S^D sets the occasion for a particular R:S-relationship, and in both cases the typical effect is that the responding generated by this R:S-relationship becomes distributed in time so that it is concentrated in the presence of the S^D. The literature includes many instances of correspondences between data obtained with respondent and with operant discrimination procedures to support this suggestion, and the similarities hold despite the many parametric differences in the temporal patterning of presentations of S^D in the two cases.

With the present emphasis on the process of elicitation, we are nevertheless not so far from many extant accounts of behavioral processes. We continue to deal with the reinforcing or punishing effects of response consequences, typically discussed in terms of R-S or response learning, and with the controlling effects of discriminative stimuli, typically discussed in terms of S-S or stimulus or perceptual learning. We have, nevertheless, ordered these processes somewhat differently, and indicated a different way in which they may be related to traditional learning and conditioning procedures. The data are, in many cases, already available and will not change, but we must reconsider the way in which we speak of behavior and behavioral relationships. We have inherited a vocabulary that may not correspond in the most effective way to the behavioral events that we observe. Even the present account was made difficult because it could be presented only in terms of the behavioral vocabulary that was already available. (The vocabulary of elicitation, for example, has served a different function in some behavioral accounts than the simple descriptive usage that has been emphasized here.) It is the present view that there is no such thing as a class of responses to be called respondent and another class, perhaps even overlapping the first, called operant. Rather, there are respondent relationships characterized in terms of the process of elicitation, and there are operant relationships characterized in terms of the consequences of behavior (the processes of reinforcement and punishment). And because the former involves stimuli followed by responses, and the latter responses followed by stimuli, these processes are not incompatible: There is no reason why an elicited response cannot also be reinforced. Superimposed on either or both of these processes may be a third, stimulus control, characterized in terms of the correlation between discriminative stimuli and the response-stimulus relationship. But although these processes may be distinct and different, it must be recognized that they can be represented in terms of a complex continuum of behavioral relationships, and that discontinuities in procedure do not necessarily call for dichotomizations of behavior. The relationships that have been considered can be spoken of in terms of response learning, stimulus learning, conditioning, perceptual learning, or any of a number of other vocabularies; we must take care that these vocabularies do not obscure the fundamental behavioral operations on which they are based.

REFERENCES

Azrin, N. H., Rubin, H. B., and Hutchinson, R. R. Biting attack by rats in response to aversive shock. *Journal of the Experimental Analysis of Behavior*, 1968, *11*, 633–639.

Badia, P., Suter, S., and Lewis, P. Rat vocalization to shock with and without a CS. *Psychonomic Science*, 1966, *4*, 117–118.

Blough, D. S. New test for tranquilizers. *Science*, 1958, *127*, 586–587.

Breland, K., and Breland, M. The misbehavior of organisms. *American Psychologist*, 1961, *16*, 681–684.

Brethower, D. M., and Reynolds, G. S. A facilitative effect of punishment on unpunished behavior. *Journal of the Experimental Analysis of Behavior*, 1962, *5*, 191–199.

Brown, P. L., and Jenkins, H. M. Auto-shaping of the pigeon's key peck. *Journal of the Experimental Analysis of Behavior*, 1968, *11*, 1–8.

Chomsky, N. Formal properties of grammars. In R. D. Luce, R. R. Bush, and E. Galanter (Eds.), *Handbook of mathematical psychology*. Vol. II. New York: Wiley, 1963. Pp. 323–418.

Dews, P. B. The effect of multiple SΔ periods on responding on a fixed-interval schedule. *Journal of the Experimental Analysis of Behavior*, 1962, *5*, 369–374.

Estes, W. K., and Skinner, B. F. Some quantitative properties of anxiety. *Journal of Experimental Psychology*, 1941, *29*, 390–400.

Green, D. M., and Swets, J. A. *Signal detection theory and psychophysics*. New York: Wiley, 1966.

Herrnstein, R. J., and Hineline, P. N. Negative reinforcement as shock-frequency reduction. *Journal of the Experimental Analysis of Behavior*, 1966, *9*, 421–430.

Hull, C. L. *Principles of behavior*. New York: Appleton-Century-Crofts, 1943.

Kelleher, R. T., and Morse, W. H. Schedules using noxious stimuli. III. Responding maintained with response-produced electric shocks. *Journal of the Experimental Analysis of Behavior*, 1968, *11*, 819–838.

Konorski, J., and Miller, S. On two types of conditioned reflex. *Journal of General Psychology*, 1937, *16*, 264–272.

Lashley, K. S. The problem of serial order in behavior. In L. A. Jeffress (Ed.), *Cerebral mechanisms in behavior*. New York: Wiley, 1951. Pp. 112–136.

Miller, N. E., and Carmona, A. Modification of a visceral response, salivation in thirsty dogs, by instrumental training with water reward. *Journal of Comparative and Physiological Psychology*, 1967, *63*,1–6.

Morse, W. H., Mead, R. N., and Kelleher, R. T. Modulation of elicited behavior by a fixed-interval schedule of electric shock presentation. *Science*, 1967, *157*, 215–217.

Pavlov, I. P. *Conditioned reflexes*. (Tr. G. V. Anrep) London: Oxford University Press, 1927.

Pliskoff, S. S., Wright, J. E., and Hawkins, T. D. Brain stimulation as a reinforcer: intermittent schedules. *Journal of the Experimental Analysis of Behavior*, 1965, *8*, 75–88.

Premack, D. Toward empirical behavior laws: I. Positive reinforcement. *Psychological Review*, 1959, *66*, 219–233.

Rescorla, R. A. Pavlovian conditioning and its proper control procedures. *Psychological Review*, 1967, *74*, 71–80.

Rescorla, R. A., and Solomon, R. L. Two-process learning theory: Relationship between Pavlovian conditioning and instrumental learning. *Psychological Review*, 1967, *74*, 151–182.

Reynolds, G. S. Behavioral contrast. *Journal of the Experimental Analysis of Behavior*, 1961, *4*, 57–71.

Schoenfeld, W. N. Some old work for modern conditioning theory. *Conditional Reflex*, 1966, *1*, 219–223.

Schoenfeld, W. N., Cumming, W. W., and Hearst, E. On the classification of reinforcement schedules. *Proceedings of the National Academy of Sciences*, 1956, *42*, 563–570.

Sechenov, I. M. *Reflexes of the brain.* Cambridge, Mass.: M. I. T. Press, 1965.

Seligman, M. E. P., Maier, S. F., and Solomon, R. L. Unpredictable and uncontrollable aversive events. In F. R. Brush (Ed.), *Aversive conditioning and learning.* New York: Academic Press, in press.

Sheffield, F. D. Relation between classical conditioning and instrumental learning. In W. F. Prokasy (Ed.), *Classical conditioning: A symposium.* New York: Appleton-Century-Crofts, 1965. Pp. 302–322.

Sherrington, C. S. *The integrative action of the nervous system.* New Haven: Yale University Press, 1906.

Sidman, M. Two temporal parameters in the maintenance of avoidance behavior by the white rat. *Journal of Comparative and Physiological Psychology*, 1953, *46*, 253–261.

Sidman, M., Herrnstein, R. J., and Conrad, D. G. Maintenance of avoidance behavior by unavoidable shocks. *Journal of Comparative and Physiological Psychology*, 1957, *50*, 553–557.

Skinner, B. F. The concept of the reflex in the description of behavior. *Journal of General Psychology*, 1931, *5*, 427–458.

Skinner, B. F. Two types of conditioned reflex and a pseudotype. *Journal of General Psychology*, 1935, *12*, 66–77.

Skinner, B. F. Two types of conditioned reflex: A reply to Konorski and Miller. *Journal of General Psychology*, 1937, *16*, 272–279.

Smith, K. Conditioning as an artifact. *Psychological Review*, 1954, *61*, 217–225.

Weiss, B., & Laties, V. G. Behavioral thermoregulation. *Science*, 1961, *133*, 1338–1344.

Wyrwicka, W. An experimental approach to the problem of mechanism of alimentary conditioned reflex, Type II. In G. A. Kimble (Ed.), *Foundations of conditioning and learning.* New York: Appleton-Century-Crofts, 1967, Pp. 260–268.

Zener, K., and McCurdy, H. G. Analysis of motivation factors in conditioned behavior: I. Differential effect of change in hunger upon conditioned, unconditioned and spontaneous salivary secretion. *Journal of Psychology,* 1939, *8,* 321–350.

SOME OBSERVATIONS
ON DESCRIPTIVE ANALYSIS

JOHN W. DONAHOE

University of Massachusetts

Professor Catania has provided us with a perceptive re-examination of the origin and the utility of the operant-respondent distinction in the light of a descriptive analysis of the procedures employed in instrumental and classical conditioning. His analysis indicates that operants and respondents need not be viewed as members of two qualitatively different response classes and, moreover, that such a view arises from procedural differences having their beginnings in experimental expediency rather than theoretical substance. In place of the bifurcation of behavior into operants and respondents, three conditional relationships between stimuli and responses — elicitation, stimulus control, and reinforcement — are proposed which permit the development of a scheme for the classification of a wide range of conditioning procedures. The classificatory system, in turn, has the effect of emphasizing the continuities, similarities, and interrelationships among procedures rather than any assumed differences among processes. The cogency of the operant-respondent distinction is diminished while, in its stead, other issues relating particularly to the effects on response strength of elicitation per se rise to the fore.

Because of the potential for a parsimonious treatment of instrumental- and classical-conditioning data and because of the encouragement of the investigation of new research paths, the paper represents a contribution which should have a salutary effect on research. However, because the theoretical contribution is as yet only a potential one and because any new path awaits empirical exploration lest it prove to be a cul-de-sac, the paper presents special problems for a discussant. Accordingly, I shall confine my remarks to a few observations on the general orientation expressed in the analysis of the operant-respondent distinction and to some suggestions concerning the direction in which future theoretical work might move.

The Necessity for a Descriptive Analysis

In a discussion concerned with the metaphysics of science, Henry Margenau (1950) noted an important difference between the layman and the scientist regarding the manner in which they view unexpected or discrepant findings:

> In the eyes of the nonscientist, the greatness of a discovery is often commensurate with its strangeness, with the amount of public surprise which it occasions. To the scientist, however, this is a clear misapprehension, for he distrusts great departures from expectation and suspects error or incompleteness in a strange discovery [p. 79].

Too often, however, the psychologist has not shared this attitude with his fellow scientists, but has preferred to magnify and to make permanent the unruly result by enshrining it in a monument of theory rather than by examining the procedural differences which antedate the discrepant finding. Thus, instead of a detailed analysis of the differing observable antecedents of the phenomenon and a subsequent manipulation of these antecedents to determine which antecedent or combination of antecedents is responsible for the discrepancy, the psychologist "solves" the problem by postulating some theoretical, and frequently untestable, respect in which the phenomena are said to differ. For a variety of reasons (see Skinner, 1966), examples of such theorizing abound in psychology (see Ritchie, 1965) and have occurred with varying frequency within all theoretical camps. The operant-respondent distinction has been a particularly fertile field for such activity, and the following will serve as but one of many possible illustrations:

It was observed experimentally that partial reinforcement during the acquisition of a classically conditioned eyelid response in human subjects led to a lower frequency of blinking than found with continuous reinforcement, whereas partial reinforcement during the acquisition of an instrumental running response in rats produced no comparable performance decrement. The procedural differences antedating the discrepant effects of partial reinforcement in the two situations are myriad — the nature of the reinforcement and a host of differences correlated with the reinforcing stimulus, such as deprivation level; the nature of the response and a multitude of differences correlated with the response, such as baseline frequency and the nature of the experimental subject. Instead of investigating the effects of these procedural differences, the scientist chose to interpret the result as indicating that reinforcement is necessary in classical aversive conditioning but that contiguity alone is sufficient in instrumental reward learning and, then, to commence research — albeit ingenious and programmatic — to test this hypothesis (Spence, 1960, 1966).

Now consider the approach taken in "Elicitation, reinforcement, and stimulus control." The strategy of the analysis consists of the subdivision of nature into two classes of events — stimuli and responses — and the suggestion is made that the variance in behavior may be associated with conditional relationships among these molar events. The conclusion reached following such a descriptive analysis indicates that operants and respondents need not be viewed as members of two nonoverlapping response classes governed by different laws, but rather as two loci of procedures described within a three-dimensional space defined by differing conditional relationships among stimuli and responses. The implications of the analysis for research point toward investigations which seek to discover how performance changes as the coordinates within the procedural space are varied and, then, to determine the form of the functions describing the changes.

Within psychology, the theoretical position which is most closely identified with descriptive analysis is operant conditioning, and the method associated with this position is termed "the experimental analysis of behavior." A basic orienting attitude of the position is summarized in the following admonition from an eminent investigator in another field.

> It is a capital mistake to theorize before one has data. Insensibly, one begins to twist facts to suit theories, instead of theories to suit facts.

— A. C. Doyle
A Scandal in Bohemia

In "Elicitation, reinforcement, and stimulus control," the foregoing advice by Sherlock Holmes has been heeded and the fundamental distinction which many theorists have erected between operant and respondent behavior has been effectively undermined. An interesting turnabout in the present instance is the origination of a descriptive analysis of the operant-respondent distinction within the context of operant methodology. Historically, the experimental analysis of behavior has been supportive of a descriptive analysis while simultaneously maintaining the basic importance of the operant-respondent dichotomy (Skinner, 1938). In Professor Catania's paper, the principles of the experimental analysis of behavior have, in a real sense, been turned upon themselves, and one may speculate concerning the implications of the new analysis for the fate of other distinctions such as are customarily made between emitted and elicited behavior, between respondents and discriminated operants, and so forth. Do these terms refer to fundamentally different classes of behavior or do they now allude simply to different loci on a set of common descriptive continua? Professor Catania's analysis would seem to favor the latter alternative.

The Insufficiency of a Descriptive Analysis

While a descriptive analysis of the empirical antecedents of events is clearly an indispensable component of the science of behavior, it is equally clearly not the entirety of the scientific enterprise. Brief reflection will yield the conclusion that the very existence of a purely descriptive analysis — in the sense of a completely objective and theoretically neutral treatment of events — is never realized within the scientific endeavor. The terms "stimulus," "response," and "reinforcement" which form the basis of Professor Catania's re-analysis of the operant-respondent distinction have been in existence with essentially the same meanings for approximately forty years, and yet it is only now that the suggestion is made that operants and respondents differ only quantitatively with respect to a number of common dimensions and not qualitatively as had been previously emphasized (e.g., Skinner, 1938).

What accounts for the change from the old "descriptive" analysis in which differences were highlighted to the new "descriptive" analysis in which similarities are highlighted? The answer, in agreement with Professor Catania, lies in the recent demonstrations of the control by response-contingent reinforcement of response systems which had previously been controlled only by respondent procedures (Miller and DiCara, 1967; Trowill, 1967) and the control by response-independent reinforcement of response systems which had previously been controlled only by operant procedures (Brown and Jenkins, 1968). Thus, the emergence of new data which increase the difficulty of maintaining "operant" and "respondent" in their original status as discriminative stimuli correlated with different scientific laws has led to the extinction of that discrimination and the establishment of a new discrimination in which "elicitation," "reinforcement," and "stimulus control" are developed as new discriminanda which hopefully will permit the development of new, more comprehensive laws. In other contexts, behaviors which are acquired on the basis of a fortuitous correlation with reinforcement are known as superstitions. Similarly, discarded scientific laws have the status of superstitions which are abandoned when new laws are formulated which lead to behavior on the part of the scientist that is more highly correlated with reinforcement.

The proposed three-dimensional system is designed to elucidate the interrelationships between operant and respondent conditioning, and it accomplishes this important heuristic and pedagogic function admirably. But, because taxonomy invariably has implication for theory, and in spite of Professor Catania's statement that the system is "a classification of behavioral operations rather than a classification of behavioral processes" (p. 208), there may well be a strong tendency to translate the procedural dimensions into dimensions of process. Indeed, it would be a very strange subject matter for science if procedure and process were not intimately related. It is readily apparent, however, that many conceptual and empirical problems would arise in an effort to use the system as the foundation for a theoretical structure. The R:S-axis, $P(S/R) - P(S/R)$, assumes a combination rule whereby behavior is a function of the difference in probabilities independent of the absolute values of the constituent probabilities — a very strong assumption for which there is, at present, insufficient support. The stimulus axis, which ranges from aversive to appetitive, begs the question before us by assuming that which we are supposed to be examining — the nature of reinforcement. The discriminative-control axis, S^D (R:S), represents only one of the many conditional probabilities — namely, $P(S/R, S^D)$ — which is of potential interest to the student of behavior. Other conditional probabilities, such as $P(S/R_1, R_2)$ which is concerned with what Professor Catania aptly terms the structure of behavior, are not capable of representation within this space. Finally, the dimensions of the system may not be independent, as the behavioral effects of elicitation may be dependent upon the stimulus-control dimension, e.g., the preference of rats for signaled over unsignaled shock (Lockard, 1963). Thus, while the system performs its intended function of displaying the salient features of the operant-respondent distinction, it is not apt to evolve directly into a general system from which theoretical predictions may be derived.

What the system does convey that is of theoretical import is the potential power of the analysis of the conditional probabilities among stimuli and responses devoid of any special assumptions concerning such postulated entities as drive reduction, fear, contiguity of implicit events, and the like. Other work, notably that of Premack presented herein (pp. 121–149) and elsewhere (1959), strengthens the proposition that a peripheralistic probabilistic approach offers great promise. Premack's empirical laws of positive reinforcement and punishment in which the strength of a response is determined by the rate of responding which occurs in the presence of stimuli produced by the response is clearly consistent with the position outlined in "Elicitation, reinforcement, and stimulus control." Moreover, Premack's approach to unconditioned, or primary, reinforcement is congruent with other analyses of conditioned, or secondary, reinforcement (Wyckoff, 1959). In both instances, the reinforcing effect of a stimulus is proportional to the control which that stimulus exerts over a subsequent response. Only the origin of the control differs between unconditioned and conditioned reinforcement, with the former emphasizing such operations as deprivation and the latter focusing upon the operation of prior conditioning.

If the analysis of behavior into the probabilistic nexus between stimulus and response events is to ultimately generate a quantitative, predictive theory, some rules for operating on probabilities, i.e., probability theory, must be introduced. Sufficient data are now available in some areas such as the effects of schedules of reinforcement on behavior to warrant serious efforts in this direction (e.g., Norman, 1966; Shimp, 1969). Likewise, the problem of the effects of spontaneous responding on subsequent behavior to which Professor Catania has referred has undergone preliminary evaluation within the context of stimulus-sampling theory (Atkinson and Estes, 1963; Estes, 1958). The implications of differences in the rate of spontaneous responding on respondents and discriminated operants following comparable experimental operations would appear to represent a particularly fruitful direction for empirical and theoretical research. Premack's analysis of reinforcement would lend itself readily to this treatment while providing a firm empirical foundation for the undertaking. In summary, while a verbal descriptive analysis is an essential part of science, attempts to deal with the effects of multiple antecedents on behavior in dynamic situations by purely verbal means and without recourse to the mapping of these events into formal theories, such as those developed for the description of stochastic processes, are destined to remain forever plausible but never compelling. The results of recent theoretical work of this general sort are quite encouraging (Catania, 1963; Herrnstein, 1970).

REFERENCES

Atkinson, R. C., and Estes, W. K. Stimulus sampling theory. In R. D. Luce, R. R. Bush, and E. Galanter (Eds.), *Handbook of mathematical psychology*. Vol. II. New York: Wiley, 1963. Pp. 121–268.

Brown, P. L., and Jenkins, H. M. Auto-shaping of the pigeon's key peck. *Journal of the Experimental Analysis of Behavior*, 1968, *11*, 1–8.

Catania, A. C. Concurrent performances: Reinforcement interaction and response independence. *Journal of the Experimental Analysis of Behavior*, 1963, *6*, 253–263.

Estes, W. K. Stimulus-response theory of drive. In M. R. Jones (Ed.), *Nebraska symposium on motivation*. Vol. 6. Lincoln: University of Nebraska Press, 1958. Pp. 35–69.

Herrnstein, R. J. On the law of effect. *Journal of the Experimental Analysis of Behavior*, 1970, *13*, 243–266.

Lockard, J. S. Choice of a warning signal or no warning signal in an unavoidable shock situation. *Journal of Comparative and Physiological Psychology*, 1963, *56*, 526–530.

Margenau, H. *The nature of physical reality*. New York: McGraw-Hill, 1950.

Miller, N. E., and DiCara, L. Instrumental learning of heart rate changes in curarized rats: Shaping, and specificity to discriminative stimulus. *Journal of Comparative and Physiological Psychology*, 1967, *63*, 12–19.

Norman, M. F. An approach to free-responding in schedules that prescribe reinforcement probability as a function of interresponse times. *Journal of Mathematical Psychology*, 1966, *3*, 235–268.

Premack, D. Toward empirical behavior laws: I. Positive reinforcement. *Psychological Review*, 1959, *66*, 219–233.

Ritchie, B. F. Concerning an incurable vagueness in psychological theories. In B. Wolman (Ed.), *Scientific psychology*. New York: Basic Books, 1965.

Shimp, C. P. Optimal behavior in free-operant experiments. *Psychological Review*, 1969, *76*, 97–112.

Skinner, B. F. *The behavior of organisms*. New York: Appleton-Century-Crofts, 1938.

Skinner, B. F. Operant behavior. In W. K. Honig (Ed.), *Operant behavior: Areas of research and application*. New York: Appleton-Century-Crofts, 1966. Pp. 12–32.

Spence, K. W. *Behavior theory and learning*. Englewood Cliffs, New Jersey: Prentice-Hall, 1960.

Spence, K. W. Cognitive and drive factors in the extinction of the conditioned eyeblink response in human subjects. *Psychological Review*, 1966, *73*, 445–458.

Trowill, J. A. Instrumental conditioning of the heart rate in the curarized rat. *Journal of Comparative and Physiological Psychology*, 1967, *63*, 7–11.

Wyckoff, L. B. Toward a quantitative theory of secondary reinforcement. *Psychological Review*, 1959, *66*, 68–79.

8

VICARIOUS- AND SELF-REINFORCEMENT PROCESSES[1]

ALBERT BANDURA

Stanford University

A large body of evidence has accumulated over the years demonstrating that behavior is controlled by its consequences. Until recently, however, investigations of reinforcement processes have been essentially confined to operations in which experimenters imposed particular contingencies upon subjects and administered reinforcing stimuli to them whenever the appropriate responses were performed. As a result, reinforcement has been generally equated with the performance-regulating functions of directly experienced conseqences arising from external sources.

Under naturalistic conditions, reinforcement typically occurs within a social context. That is, people continually observe the behavior of others and the occasions on which it is rewarded, ignored, or punished. As will

[1] The preparation of this paper and research by the author which is reported here was facilitated by Grants M-5162 and 1F03MH42658 from the National Institute of Mental Health, U.S. Public Health Service. The author also gratefully acknowledges the generous assistance of the staff of the Center for Advanced Study in the Behavioral Sciences.

228

be shown later, observed rewards and punishments can play an influential role in regulating behavior. Observed consequences also provide a reference standard that determines whether a particular reinforcer that is externally administered will serve as a reward or as a punishment. Thus, for example, the same compliment is likely to be punishing for persons who have seen similar performances by others highly acclaimed, but positively reinforcing when others have been less generously praised.

Traditional research on reinforcement has established the relational character of reinforcing events by demonstrating that the same stimulus can have rewarding or punishing effects on behavior depending upon the nature, frequency, or magnitude with which subjects' performances were previously reinforced. However, incentive-contrast effects, resulting from discrepancies between observed and directly experienced consequences, have received relatively little attention. Most human behavior, of course, is not controlled by immediate external reinforcement. Rather, people regulate their own actions to some extent by self-generated anticipatory consequences. This provides the stimulus for foresightful behavior. Homeowners, for instance, do not wait until they experience the discomfort of a burning house to buy fire insurance; housewives do not rely on painful hunger pangs to prompt them to purchase groceries; and usually, motorists do not wait until inconvenienced by a stalled automobile to replenish gasoline. Alternative courses of action are often initially performed covertly and either discarded or retained on the basis of anticipated outcomes. By engaging in symbolic trial and error, people are spared the hazards and travail involved in the enactment of ineffectual or detrimental modes of response. Thus, through representational mechanisms, future consequences can be converted into current stimuli that are functionally similar to external physical stimuli in their capacity to influence behavior.

Behavior can be self-regulated, not only by anticipated social and other external consequences, but also by self-evaluative responses to one's own behavior. In preparing manuscripts, for example, authors engage in extensive self-corrective editing of their own writing performances until they are satisfied with what they have written. The self-editing often exceeds external requirements of what would be satisfactory to others. Similarly, in most other areas of functioning, people set themselves certain performance standards and respond to their own behavior in self-rewarding and self-critical ways in accordance with their self-imposed demands. Anticipation of self-disapproval for personally devalued actions provides an additional motivating influence to keep behavior in line with adopted standards. Such self-monitoring reinforcement mechanisms can serve to alter and to maintain behavior when external reinforcing feedback is absent or operates in conflicting directions. The present paper examines in some detail the functional properties of vicarious and self-reinforcing events and the psychological mechanisms through which they regulate human behavior.

Vicarious Reinforcement

Vicarious reinforcement is defined as a change in the behavior of observers as a function of witnessing the consequences accompanying the performances of others. It should be emphasized here that vicarious reinforcement is simply a descriptive term referring to response changes produced by observed consequences; it does not contain any explanation of their effects. Relevant evidence will be cited later to support five different mechanisms through which vicarious reinforcement can operate to modify behavior.

Vicarious punishment is indicated when observers show either decrements in the modeled class of behavior or a general reduction of responsiveness as a result of seeing performers experience negative response consequences. The effects of observed punishment are difficult to evaluate because it contains two major stimulus components that generally operate in opposing directions: When modeled actions are subsequently punished, the power of modeling stimuli to increase matching behavior in observers is counteracted by the suppressive effects of adverse outcomes. Under conditions where these opposing influences are of comparable strength, persons who have observed modeled behavior punished and those who have had no exposure to the model may display an equally low incidence of response. Indeed, in experiments involving novel modeled behavior that is rarely performed by control subjects, vicarious punishment that produced complete response suppression would equal the zero control baseline but exceed it if the facilitative effects of modeling were only partially nullified. The capacity of vicarious punishment to reduce matching behavior is sometimes mistakenly questioned (Rosekrans and Hartup, 1967) on the grounds that model-punished and no-model conditions produce equally low rates of imitative behavior. Clarification of the influence of observed punishment, therefore, requires a comparison condition in which subjects observe the same modeled behavior without any evident consequences to assess the contribution of the modeling component. Nor can the reductive effects of seeing others experience negative outcomes be revealed in studies where control subjects, for one reason or another, fail to perform the relevant responses even though they exist in their repertoires and are situationally prompted (Stein, 1967).

The inhibitory effects of observed punishment have been assessed by several different methods. Crooks (1967) measured response decrements from baseline levels after subjects had observed a model punished for performing one set of responses but experienced no adverse outcomes for alternative behavior. Differential vicarious punishment virtually eliminated in observers the negatively sanctioned behavior, whereas responses that incurred no consequences were performed at an undiminished rate.

Several experiments have been conducted (Bandura, 1965b; Bandura, Ross, and Ross, 1963) in which observers were shown a film depicting a model engaging in novel aggressive behaviors that were either rewarded, punished, or unaccompanied by any consequences. Postexposure tests revealed that subjects who had witnessed aggression punished performed significantly fewer matching responses than subjects in the aggression-rewarded or the no-consequence groups (Fig. 8-1). These differences were especially marked among girls for whom physical aggression is generally labeled sex-inappropriate and negatively sanctioned. In order to determine whether the obtained differences reflected response inhibition or learning deficits, subjects in all three groups were later given highly attractive incentives contingent upon their reproducing the aggressive responses that they had previously seen modeled. Boys who had previously observed the model either rewarded or experience no consequences performed under

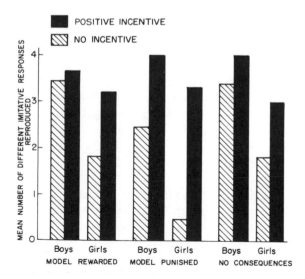

FIGURE 8-1. Mean number of different matching responses performed by children as a function of response consequences to the model and positive incentives for reproducing the model's behavior. (Bandura, 1965b.)

positive reinforcement all of the aggressive responses that they had learned, and no additional matching responses emerged. On the other hand, boys who had observed the model punished, and girls in all three treatment conditions, displayed significant increments in imitative behavior when they were rewarded for performing matching responses. The inhibitory effects of observed punishment are thus revealed in both the intergroup and the intrasubject differences in imitative aggressive behavior.

The foregoing studies demonstrate the inhibitory influence of observed adverse consequences to a model on the aggressive behavior of viewers. Walters and his associates (Walters, Leat, and Mezei, 1963; Walters and Parke, 1964; Walters, Parke, and Cane, 1965) have likewise shown that witnessing peer models punished for transgressive behavior increases observers' inhibition of deviant behavior when tempted with prohibited objects, as compared with conditions in which modeled transgressions are either rewarded or go unpunished. Results of a comparative study by Brenton (1967) indicate that, under some conditions, observed and directly experienced punishment may be equally efficacious in reducing deviant behavior. Children who observed peers punished for engaging in prohibited activities later showed the same amount of response inhibition as the punished performers.

Another method of assessing the effects of observed punishment is to use compound procedures in which different types of vicarious reinforcement serve as successive components. Rosekrans and Hartup (1967) measured imitative aggression in children who had observed the aggressive behavior of a model consistently rewarded, consistently punished, or successively rewarded and punished. Observation of successive reward and punishment of modeled aggression produced significantly less imitative behavior than consistent reward, but more than consistent punishment. These findings show that observed punishment attenuates the behavioral enhancement effects of rewarding consequences to the model. In accord with previous findings, consistent vicarious punishment reduced imitative responses to the near zero baseline of control subjects who had observed no model.

All of the preceding studies employed externally administered punishment to a model in the form of verbal reprimands or physically aversive consequences. In many instances, persons respond with self-punitive and self-devaluative reactions to their own behavior that may be considered permissible, or even rewardable, by external agents. Numerous experiments, which will be discussed in detail later, demonstrate that witnessing punishments self-administered by a model have inhibitory effects on observers with respect to devalued achievements. Observation of self-produced consequences by a model have also been shown by Porro (1968) to have similar effects on transgressive behavior. For children who viewed a filmed model exhibiting self-approving responses to her transgressions, 80 per cent subsequently handled toys that were forbidden to touch, whereas the transgression rate was only 20 per cent for children who had observed the same model responding self-critically toward her own transgressions.

Behavior can be enhanced as well as reduced by observed outcomes. *Vicarious positive reinforcement* is evident when observers display an increase in matching behavior as a function of observing rewarding consequences to a model. It is of interest to note that, when models exhibit modes of behavior that are ordinarily inhibited, the absence of anticipated punishing consequences increases matching behavior in observers to the same degree as witnessing models rewarded (Bandura, 1965b; Marlatt, Jacobsen, Johnson, and Morrice, 1970; Walters and Parke, 1964; Walters, Parke, and Cane, 1965). The disinhibitory effects of observing transgressions going unpunished have also been convincingly demonstrated by, among others, Blake (1958), Ross (1971), and Wolf (1969). These findings indicate that to the extent that omission of anticipated punishment conveys permissiveness and produces vicarious fear extinction, behavioral restraints are thereby reduced and formerly inhibited responses are performed more freely. For this reason, experiments modeling prohibited behaviors that can be readily disinhibited through absence of consequences provide no clear evidence for the occurrence of positive vicarious reinforcement.

Results of numerous experiments involving neutral or positively sanctioned behaviors generally show that observed rewards augment matching responses compared to conditions in which exemplified actions produce no evident consequences. Thus, for example, vicarious positive reinforcement, either independently or in interaction with other variables, has been found to increase adoption of high performance standards of self-reinforcement (Bandura, Grusec, and Menlove, 1967a); novel food preferences (Barnwell, 1966); object preferences (Liebert and Fernandez, 1970); and choice behavior (Clark, 1965). Observation of the response outcomes of others also tends to enhance diverse psychological functioning, including motor responding (Kelly, 1966); verbal conditioning (Kanfer, 1965; Marlowe, Breecher, Cook, and Doob, 1964; Marston, 1966); and acquisition of conceptual behavior (Flanders and Thistlethwaite, 1969).

There are certain conditions, of course, under which observed reinforcement may have opposite effects upon recipients and observers. In an experiment conducted by Sechrest (1963), pairs of subjects solved similar problems concurrently, and, although both achieved correct solutions, the performance of only one of the pairmates was either praised or criticized. A subsequent test on a related task revealed that witnessing others rewarded for equivalent performances operates as a punisher in decreasing the efforts of ignored participant observers. Conversely, seeing others criticized for comparable performances that are accepted without comment in observers is functionally similar to a positive reinforcer. Sechrest speculated that these "implicit" reinforcement effects are most likely to obtain in competitive situations where small groups of people engage concurrently in similar activities and where they achieve roughly comparable levels of performance that are plainly evident. Likeness in status and performance would undoubtedly create anticipation of similar response outcomes.

Implicit reinforcment should be distinguished from vicarious reinforcement. In the latter phenomenon, observers do not perform any responses during the influence period and, therefore, the model's outcomes have no immediate personal consequences for observers. By contrast, in implicit reinforcement, individuals perform responses that are explicitly reinforced in some members and implicitly rewarded or punished in others. When the same deserving performances are praised in one case and ignored in the other, the slighted person is not only exposed to observed outcomes, but he experiences immediate direct consequences to his own behavior, which can have rewarding, punishing, or extinctive effects.

Relative effects of direct and vicarious reinforcement.   Several experiments have been conducted in which behavioral changes in performers whose responses are directly rewarded are compared with those of observers who simply watch the reinforced performances. Results of some of these investigations are difficult to interpret, however, because they fail to include a group of observers who witness the model's behavior without consequences which can, in itself, significantly increase appropriate responding (Bandura, 1962; Marston, 1965a; Phillips, 1968; Simon, Ditrichs, and Jamison, 1965). When the necessary control conditions are employed, exposure to modeled responses combined with reinforcing consequences to the model generally produces greater response changes in observers than modeling alone.

One would ordinarily expect direct reinforcement to exceed vicarious reinforcement in its capacity to maintain responsiveness. However, in some studies comparing discriminative responding under direct and vicarious reinforcement (Berger, 1961; Hillix and Marx, 1960; Marlatt, 1968; Rosenbaum and Hewitt, 1966), observers surpass reinforced performers on the same task. This somewhat surprising finding is attributed to the detrimental effects of interfering responses evoked by overt performance and associated consequences. The interference may take several different forms. Persons who are absorbed in the task of creating, selecting, and enacting responses are slower to discern the response-reinforcement contingencies operative in the situation than the observers (Kanfer, 1965). Given valued incentives, knowledge of the responses required to produce reinforcement results in substantial increments in performance. When reinforcing stimuli have strong affective properties, anticipation of consequences by the performer can increase emotional arousal beyond optimal levels. Finally, direct experience of rewarding or punishing stimulation may be temporarily distracting, or it may create emotionally disruptive effects. Observers, on the other hand, can give their undivided attention to discovering the essential performance requirements of the situation.

Evidence supporting the relative superiority of vicarious reinforcement should be accepted with reservation for several reasons. The experiments on which this evidence is based simply require subjects to learn to discriminately perform responses that already exist in the repertoires of observers and performers. Consequently, selective vicarious reinforcement mainly serves an informational function in helping observers to identify the types of responses that bring rewards or punishments. As previously noted, this form of discrimination learning is apt to be hindered rather than aided by overt performance. However, on tasks involving the acquisition of new complex skills, reinforced performance would probably prove more efficacious than observation alone, particularly in response learning that requires abstracting subtle common properties from otherwise different instances and in developing skills containing important motoric components. It should also be noted that the studies have not demonstrated that vicarious reinforcement alone can sustain effortful behavior over a long period, which is usually the major function of direct reinforcement. One would not recommend to employers, for example, that they maintain the productivity of their employees by having them witness a small group of workers receiving paychecks at the end of each month. The overall findings indicate that vicarious reinforcement alone can have strong short-term behavioral effects. Moreover, as will be shown next, observation of other people's outcomes can have a continuing influence on the effectiveness of direct reinforcement by providing a standard for judging whether the reinforcements one customarily receives are equitable, beneficial, or unfair.

Since both direct and vicarious reinforcement inevitably occur together under natural conditions, the interactive effects of these two sources of influence on human behavior are of much greater social significance than their independent controlling power. It has been convincingly demonstrated (Premack, 1965) that reinforcement value is a relational rather than an absolute property of contingent events. Findings based on studies of contrast of reinforcement, which are especially pertinent to the issue under discussion, lend further support to the view that the potency of a given reinforcer is largely determined by its relational rather than by its intrinsic properties. Buchwald (1959a,b) has shown that nonreward following punishing outcomes functions analogously to a positive reinforcer, whereas nonreward subsequent to a series of rewards operates as a negative reinforcer. In fact, even a weak positive reinforcer, when contrasted with more rewarding prior events, assumes negative reinforcing value (Buchwald, 1960).

The incentive-contrast effects demonstrated through variation in magnitude of reward that the same individual receives at different times also occur between individuals on the basis of social-comparison processes. In most situations, the consequences that individuals consider appropriate or equitable for given performances are not defined by the characteristics of the behavior itself. Rather, the outcomes experienced by others create expectations in observers about the type, the rate, and the magnitude of outcomes that will accompany similar performances. Hence, the effects of observed outcomes may serve as important determinants of the efficacy of directly administered reinforcers. As a rule, the reinforcing value of received rewards should be enhanced by favorable contrast with previously observed reinforcement, and decreased by unfavorable comparison.

Research is lacking on the behavioral effects of discrepancy between magnitude of observed and experienced outcomes. However, findings of several studies that are reviewed later demonstrate that observed schedules of reinforcement influence the persistence and vigor with which observers subsequently perform similar behavior under conditions of zero reinforcement. A number of experiments have been reported, however, in which the independent and interactive effects of vicarious and direct reinforcement are compared. In a study conducted by Kanfer and Marston (1963b), groups of subjects heard a tape recording of a model expressing in a free interview progressively more human nouns (e.g., hand, mouth, ear, leg, face and so forth) which were either consistently socially reinforced or were not accompanied by approving remarks. Later, subjects participated in a similar verbal-conditioning situation during which their verbalizations of human nouns were reinforced with social approval or accepted without comment. A control group performed the same task without any vicarious or direct reinforcement to furnish a baseline response rate. As shown in Fig. 8-2, performance of the appropriate response was unaffected by direct reinforcement alone, but was significantly increased by vicarious reinforcement. The combination of vicarious and direct reinforcement, however, produced the highest response rate and

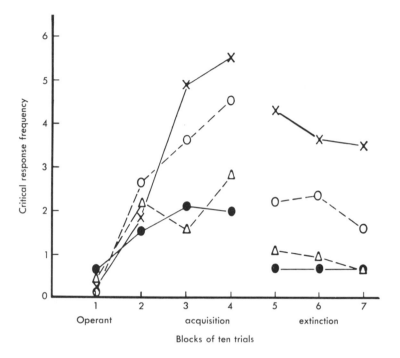

FIGURE 8-2. Frequency of correct responses performed during baseline, acquisition, and extinction periods by subjects under different conditions of reinforcement. (Kanfer and Marston, 1963b.)

the slowest extinction after approval for human nouns was discontinued. The authors attributed the ineffectiveness of direct reinforcement alone to the fact that most subjects never exhibited any of the required responses that could be reinforced.

Marlatt (1968) investigated the relative influence of vicarious and direct reinforcement, in the form of either positive, negative, or neutral feedback, when administered alone and in all possible combinations of these different types of reinforcement. The findings are summarized in Fig. 8-3. Positive vicarious reinforcement produced greater and more enduring changes in verbal behavior than did direct positive reinforcement. In the case of punishing consequences, however, both direct and vicarious negative reinforcement had comparable reductive effects on behavior. The data furthermore revealed that prior vicarious reinforcement, depending on its nature, can augment or diminish the behavior changes subsequently

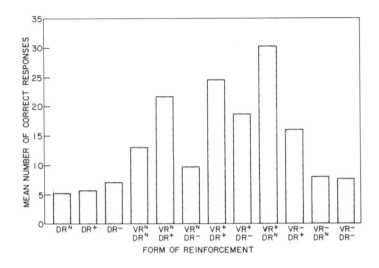

FIGURE 8-3. **Mean number of correct responses performed by subjects who received vicarious (VR) or direct reinforcement (DR) either independently or in various combinations. The symbols +, −, and n refer to approving, disapproving, and neutral feedback, respectively. (Marlatt, 1968.)**

achieved through direct reward or punishment. Condrell (1967) and Ditrichs, Simon, and Greene (1967) similarly found that responsiveness to direct reinforcement was dependent upon previous vicarious reinforcement.

The foregoing results, and additional findings reported later, support the conclusions that the influence of direct reinforcement administered under social conditions cannot be understood fully without considering the effects of vicarious reinforcement. Social-comparison variables may alter the reinforcing value of given outcomes in more complex ways than has been investigated so far. The degree to which observers are influenced by witnessing the outcomes accruing to others undoubtedly depends upon the social rank, status, or role occupied by reinforced performers. Observers are more apt to be affected by comparison of their own outcomes with those of others whom they consider comparable to themselves than with the reinforcement schedules of persons who possess a dissimilar status. One would expect observed consequences to be least influential under conditions where observers have reason to believe that the model's contingencies do not apply to themselves. It is unlikely, for example, that witnessing social approval for physical aggression performed by a person occupying a unique role, such as a soldier, would enhance imitative aggressiveness in observant citizens to any great extent. Therefore, experiments are needed that test the magnitude of vicarious-reinforcement effects as a function of comparability of the contingencies and amount of reinforcement customarily applied to models and to observers.

Interpretation of vicarious-reinforcement effects. The previously reported research provides ample evidence that, like the effects of direct reinforcement, responses in observers can be increased by observed reward and decreased by observed punishment. Moreover, vicarious-reinforcement effects are partly determined by incentive variables such as the percentage, intermittency, and magnitude of reinforcement in essentially the same manner as when they are administered directly to performers. Witnessing others experiencing rewarding or punishing consequences can create diverse psychological effects and, hence, several mechanisms may be responsible for the changes accompanying vicarious-reinforcement operations (Bandura, 1965a). These alternative explanations are discussed in the sections that follow.

Informational function. Reinforcing stimuli not only function as rewards but they also convey information. By observing the differential consequences produced by variations in their behavior, performers develop and confirm hypotheses about the types of responses required to obtain or to avoid punishment. The acquired information can result in substantial increases in appropriate responding given adequate incentives (Dulany, 1968; Spielberger and De Nike, 1966).

One possible explanation of vicarious reinforcement is in terms of the discriminative or informational function of reinforcing stimuli presented to the model. Response consequences experienced by performers undoubtedly also convey information to observers about the probable reinforcement contingencies associated with analogous performances in similar situations. Knowledge concerning the types of responses that are likely to meet with approval or disapproval can, through self-instructional influences, later aid in facilitating or inhibiting matching behavior. Information gained from observed outcomes would be particularly influential in regulating behavior when ambiguity exists as to what actions are permissible or punishable, and where the observer believes that the models' contingencies apply to himself as well.

It would be predicted from the informational interpretation of vicarious reinforcement that under conditions where the correct responses are easily discernible and subjects are either required or willing to perform the selected behavior, observed consequences are unlikely to serve as a contributing influence to behavior change. The findings of Flanders and Thistlethwaite (1969) and Liebert and Fernandez (1970) that vicarious reward does not facilitate accurate performance when subjects are required to select responses in simple discrimination tasks support this assumption. The fact that observers may identify the relevant responses from witnessed differential consequences does not necessarily mean that observers will subsequently perform what they have learned. An informational explanation alone cannot account for the differential effects that vicarious reinforcement has on observers who are equally aware of the proper behavior. Observed reinforcement is not only informative, but it can also have important motivational effects which are discussed later.

When modeled behavior is repeatedly reinforced, observers gain information about the manner in which people respond to social influence as well as what responses are considered appropriate. An experiment by Ditrichs, Simon, and Green (1967), in which models increased, decreased, or did not alter rewarded behavior, reveals that depicted influenceability subsequently affects observers' responsiveness to direct reinforcement. Children who observed models giving progressively more hostile responses for social approval later substantially increased their own output of hostile responses under positive reinforcement, whereas when models either progressively reduced their performance of rewarded behavior or responded in random fashion, observers did not modify their expression of similar responses even though they were positively reinforced.

Stimulus enhancement effects.   In most studies of vicarious reinforcement, models are preinstructed to display certain responses at designated times, but no environmental cues are provided to signify the likely consequences for performing similar behavior under different stimulus conditions. Hence, in nondiscriminated modeling, observers can gain information only about the likelihood that given responses may be either rewarded, punished, or ignored. Under natural circumstances, however, the same modeled behavior is often differentially reinforced depending upon the persons toward whom it is directed, the social settings in which it is expressed, and other environmental factors. When differential consequences are correlated with different stimulus conditions, the model's responses and reinforcing outcomes may enhance the distinctiveness of the relevant environmental stimuli by drawing the observers' attention to them (Miller and Dollard, 1941). This attention-directing function of vicarious reinforcement enables observers to more readily identify the situations in which the modeled behavior is considered appropriate and reinforceable. The resultant discrimination learning can later facilitate performance of matching responses in the presence of the cues to which the model previously had been responding with favorable consequences.

The development of stimulus control through discriminated modeling has been investigated in numerous studies (Church, 1957; McDavid, 1962, 1964; Miller and Dollard, 1941; Wilson, 1958). These experiments typically employ discrimination tasks in which the correct-choice responses of the model are associated with distinctive environmental cues. During the imitation phase of the study, observers are exposed to the compound stimulus containing both the social cue of the model's rewarded choices and the environmental cue to which the model responds. Later, observers are tested for the extent to which they use the environmental cue alone to guide their choice behavior when the model is absent from the situation. The results generally show that, when models always respond to the reinforced stimulus, and hence modeling and environmental cues are perfectly correlated, observation of reinforced performances facilitates discrimination learning as compared to selective reinforcement of trial-and-error responding without the benefit of prior vicarious reinforcement (Miller and Dollard, 1941; Wilson, 1958). On the other hand, discrimination learning may be retarded when modeling cues and the relevant environmental stimuli are only partially correlated (McDavid, 1962, 1964). As long as models are successful most of the time, observers may become excessively dependent on modeling cues and less disposed to attend to pertinent environmental stimuli.

Taken together, the findings just discussed and those reported in the preceding section disclose that vicarious reinforcement can serve an informative function not only by singling out reinforceable responses, but also by identifying the specific social and environmental situations in which it is appropriate to perform the behavior.

Incentive-motivational effects.   After certain actions have been repeatedly reinforced, a performer ordinarily comes to anticipate the rewarding or aversive outcomes. Anticipation of reinforcement can serve a motivating function that has incremental or decremental effects on behavior depending on the forms the anticipatory outcomes take. Countless studies of performance changes arising from variations in the amount, quality, delay, and probability of reinforcement have convincingly demonstrated that incentives function as motivators (Bolles, 1967; Logan and Wagner, 1965). In fact, under some conditions, expected rewards can exercise more powerful control over behavior than the conditions of reinforcement that are actually in effect.

Kaufman, Baron, and Kopp (1966) gave students either accurate or erroneous information concerning the schedule according to which their behavior would be rewarded. One group of students was accurately informed that rewards would be forthcoming each minute on the average (VI-1), whereas other groups were misled into believing that their behavior would be reinforced either on a fixed interval of one minute (FI-1), or after they had performed 150 responses on the average (VR-150). Subjects then performed the task and their responses were in fact reinforced on a variable-interval schedule with reinforcements being administered one minute on the average. The illusory schedules governed students' responsiveness in much the same way as they do in reality: Anticipated fixed-interval reinforcement produced exceedingly low rates (median responses = 6); expected variable-ratio reinforcement maintained an extremely high-response output (median = 260); and anticipation of reinforcement on a variable-interval schedule generated intermediate rates of response (median = 66). Alleged schedules thus outweighed the influence of the program of reinforcement that was actually imposed on students' behavior.

Observation of another person's reinforcing outcomes may affect the motivation of observers in much the same way as incentives activate and sustain the behavior of performers. To the extent that the sight of desired reinforcers arouses in observers expectation of similar reward, one would expect their imitative performances to be enhanced. Thus, for example, witnessing a performer rewarded with a culinary treat for executing a given sequence of responses will convey the same amount of information about the probable reinforcement contingencies to a famished and to a satiated observer, but their subsequent imitative performances will, in all likelihood, differ radically because of the differential effects of deprivation state on the activating power of the anticipated rewards. As shown in the findings discussed next, incentive-generated motivation in observers is most likely to affect the speed, intensity, and persistence with which matching responses are executed.

An experiment reported by Bruning (1965) illustrates how variations in the magnitude of observed rewards, while providing equivalent information about the matching responses required for reinforcement, produce different motivational effects on observers. Children who observed a performer generously rewarded, subsequently responded more rapidly when they received smaller rewards for performing the same responses, whereas when observed rewards were smaller than the ones observers later received, they decreased their rate of responding. Shifts in magnitude of reinforcement produced analogous changes in the speed with which the performing models accomplished the responses. These unexpected effects that reversal in the amount of reinforcement had on performance were attributed by Bruning to frustrative motivational effects in the decremental-reward condition, and to satiation effects in the treatment involving incremental reward.

Several experiments have been conducted in which performing models are reinforced during acquisition either continuously or on a partial schedule, after which response strength is measured in both models and observers on nonreinforced trials. Results of these studies show that variations in percentage of reinforcement have similar effects on performers and observers. Rosenbaum and Bruning (1966) found that, when subjects were required to complete a fixed number of responses, those who had previously experienced 100 per cent reinforcement, either directly or observationally, increased the speed with which they responded on successive nonrewarded trials, whereas subjects in the 50 per cent condition showed little change in the vigor of their behavior. Rosenbaum and Bruning explained the intensification of responding as due to frustrative emotional effects created by marked disparity between high expectancy of reward and omission of positive reinforcement. Under conditions where subjects are free to discontinue responding whenever they wish, observers who witness performers reinforced on an intermittent schedule display greater resistance to extinction than observers who have seen the model's behavior continuously (Berger and Johansson, 1968). It has been further shown by Hamilton (1970) that the behavioral effects of vicarious partial reinforcement can persist for a relatively long period.

Vicarious emotional-conditioning effects. In a vicarious reinforcement event, performers generally exhibit emotional responses while undergoing rewarding or punishing experiences. Observers can become highly aroused by the emotional experiences of others. The manner in which social affective cues serve as stimuli for emotional arousal in observers has been demonstrated most clearly by Miller and his colleagues (Miller, Banks, and Ogawa, 1962, 1963; Miller, Murphy, and Mirsky, 1959) through the use of an ingenious cooperative avoidance-conditioning procedure. In this experimental paradigm, monkeys are first trained to avoid an electric shock by pressing a bar whenever a light appears. Following the avoidance training, the animals are seated in different rooms, with the bar removed from the chair of one monkey and the light from the other. Thus, the animal having access to the light stimulus has to communicate by means of affective cues to his partner, equipped with the response bar, who can then perform the appropriate instrumental response that will enable both animals to avoid painful stimulation. Distress cues exhibited by the stimulus monkeys in anticipation of shock are highly effective in eliciting fear in their observing partner as reflected in increased heart rate and rapid performance of discriminated avoidance responses (Miller, 1967). The finding that color slides showing the stimulus animal in fear or pain elicited more avoidance responses than pictures of the same animal in nonfearful poses indicates that simple facial and postural expressions alone are sufficient cues for eliciting emotional responses. It was further shown that emotional responses in monkeys could be vicariously aroused not only by the sight of their fearful experimental counterparts but also, through stimulus generalization, by another monkey who was never involved in the original aversive contingencies. Moreover, mere exposure to a monkey reacting in an apprehensive manner could reinstate avoidance responses in the observer after they had been extinguished.

Church (1959) has provided some evidence that social cues signifying affective arousal acquire emotion-provoking properties through essentially the same process of classical conditioning that is involved in the establishment of positive or negative valence to nonsocial environmental stimuli. That is, if affective expressions of others have been repeatedly paired with emotional consequences for observers, affective social cues alone gradually attain the power to instigate emotional reactions in observers. Vicariously elicited emotional responses in observers can become conditioned to formerly neutral stimuli through contiguous stimulation. Both direct and vicarious conditioning are governed by the same basic principle of associative learning, but they differ in the source of the emotional arousal. In the direct prototype, the learner himself is the recipient of pain- or pleasure-producing stimulation, whereas in vicarious forms, somebody else experiences the reinforcing stimulation and his affective expressions, in turn, serve as the arousal stimuli for the observer.

In laboratory investigations of vicarious classical conditioning (Bandura and Rosenthal, 1966; Berger, 1962), the model typically undergoes an aversive conditioning procedure in which a neutral stimulus is presented, and shortly thereafter, the model displays pain cues and other emotional reactions supposedly in response to shock stimulation. After witnessing the model's emotional responses in conjunction with the neutral stimulus, observers begin to exhibit emotional responses to the conditioned stimulus alone, even though they have not themselves experienced the aversive stimulation directly. In a further extension of socially mediated conditioning, Craig and Weinstein (1965) found that observation of a performer experiencing repeated failure produces vicarious emotional arousal that becomes conditioned to previously neutral environmental cues.

The foregoing results indicate that emotional responses evoked in observers through vicarious reinforcement can become conditioned either to the modeled responses themselves or to environmental stimuli that are regularly correlated with the performer's distress reactions. As a consequence, the later initiation of matching responses by the observer or the presence of the negatively valenced environmental cues are likely to evoke aversive emotional arousal and behavioral suppression.

A study reported by Crooks (1967) illustrates how discriminative response suppression can be established solely on the basis of differential vicarious fear conditioning. After being tested for the extent to which they handled play objects, monkeys observed distress vocalizations sounded (through a tape recorder) whenever a model monkey touched a particular object. Later the observers also received a control-conditioning procedure wherein they witnessed the model's contacts with different objects paired with the distress vocalizations played backwards, thus obliterating the distressing value of the sounds. In a subsequent test, the observers played freely with the control items, but actively avoided objects that accompanied supposedly painful experiences for another animal.

Fear arousal can be extinguished as well as acquired on a vicarious basis. Vicarious extinction of fears and behavioral inhibitions is achieved by having persons observe models performing fear-provoking behavior without any adverse consequence accruing to the performers (Bandura, Grusec, and Menlove, 1967b; Bandura and Menlove, 1968). In a detailed analysis of vicarious extinction, Bandura, Blanchard, and Ritter (1969) found that observers' fear arousal progressively declined with each successive exposure to the modeled approach behavior. Blanchard (1970) furthermore revealed that the more thoroughly fear arousal was vicariously extinguished in phobic subjects, the greater was the reduction in avoidance behavior and the more generalized the increase in formerly inhibited approach responses. These findings lend support to the view that vicarious conditioning and extinction of emotional arousal may partially account for the behavioral suppression or facilitation that results from observing the affective consequences accruing to a model.

In their interpretation of vicarious reinforcement, Lewis and Duncan (1958) also assigned importance to the emotional-conditioning function of observed consequences. According to these authors, during the acquisition phase the model's responses elicit in observers analogous covert verbalizations, and the observed outcomes are also experienced vicariously. As a result of contiguous occurrence, the pleasurable effects of observed rewards and the frustrative effects of observed nonreward become conditioned to the observer's covert verbalizations. It is further assumed that these vicariously established emotions are transmitted from verbalizations to similar motor actions on the basis of prior associations between these two modes of responding.

As was previously shown, observers can develop conditioned emotional reactions as a result of seeing others enduring painful consequences. It remains to be demonstrated, however, whether observed nonreward is emotionally arousing to observers; whether observers covertly verbalize the model's instrumental responses while observing them performed; and whether emotional properties are, in fact, conditioned to verbalizations. In the more cognitive interpretation of classical conditioning (Bandura,

1969a), when a stimulus is paired with aversive experiences, the stimulus alone produces emotional responses, not because it is invested with emotional properties but because it tends to elicit emotion-arousing thoughts. In other words, the emotional responses are to a large extent cognitively induced rather than automatically evoked by the conditioned stimuli. From this perspective, performance of responses that individuals had previously seen punished can instigate anticipatory self-arousal without requiring emotional responses to be conditioned initially to covert verbalizations which then serve as the vehicle for connecting emotions to overt actions.

Modification of model status. It has been abundantly documented (Bandura, 1969b; Blake, 1968; Campbell, 1961) that models who possess high status in prestige, power, and competence hierarchies are emulated to a considerably greater degree than models of subordinate standing. The influence of model status on matching behavior is generally explained in terms of differential reinforcement and generalization processes (Miller and Dollard, 1941). According to this interpretation, the behavior of high-status models is more likely to be successful in achieving favorable outcomes, and hence have greater utilitarian value for imitators, than the behavior of models who possess relatively low vocational, intellectual, and social competencies. As a result of repeated differential reinforcement for matching models who possess diverse attributes, the identifying characteristics and status-conferring symbols assume discriminatory functions in signifying the probable consequences associated with behavior modeled by different social agents. Moreover, the effect of a model's prestige tends to generalize from one area of behavior to another and to unfamiliar persons to the extent that they share similar characteristics with past reward-producing models.

Status can be conferred on performers by the manner in which their behavior is reinforced. In a series of studies conducted by Hastorf and his colleagues (1965), a subject who initially gained a subordinate status in group discusssions was generously rewarded for whatever contributions he made, while his associates were reinforced on a less favorable schedule. Under these conditions of reinforcement, the ineffectual member increased his responsiveness and was attributed higher status by his colleagues not only in the experimental phase but even after arbitrary contingencies had been discontinued. Bandura, Ross, and Ross (1963), in addition, provided evidence that reinforcements administered to the model alone have important effects on both social evaluation and imitative performance. Punishment devalues the model and his behavior, whereas the same model assumes emulative qualities when his actions are rewarded. These changes in model status, in turn, are accompanied by corresponding differences in the degree to which observers imitate the model's behavior. The generality of the latter findings was further extended by Shafer (1965), who measured imitative behavior as a function of reversal of model status. Children displayed high imitation of models presented as prestigious figures but later discarded matching behavior after the models' superior status was lowered through new information.

None of the foregoing explanations assumes that vicarious reinforcement produces its effects by strengthening responses or S-R associations. Such a mechanism of operation would require observers not only to perform covert matching responses concurrently with the model, but also to experience indirectly the internal events activated by reinforcing stimuli. A reinforcement process of this type is not implausible, though it seems highly improbable. An associative-strengthening explanation of vicarious reinforcement would be especially hard-pressed to account for response changes in observers when models perform a variety of responses that extend over a long time and the consequences are not administered until after the entire set of responses has been completed.

Although the material presented in preceding sections is primarily concerned with possible mechanisms through which vicarious reinforcement produces its effects in observers, it should be noted in passing that the alternative explanations apply equally to interpretation of the effects of direct reinforcement on performers. Reinforcing stimuli convey information to performers about the types of responses that are reinforceable; selective reinforcement directs performers' attention to correlated environmental stimuli and thus increases their effectiveness in regulating behavior; previous reinforcements create anticipated consequences that serve a motivating function in augmenting and sustaining reinforceable responses; punishments administered to performers can endow associated environmental stimuli or the responses themselves with emotion-arousing properties that have behavior-suppression effects; and finally, a given history of positive or negative reinforcement can alter persons' self-evaluations in ways that affect the frequency with which they exhibit behaviors that are discrepant with their self-attitudes and the determination with which they perform them. Explanations of reinforcement processes usually conceptualize vicarious reinforcement as though it possessed only informational content, and direct reinforcement as though it had only automatic associative-strengthening effects.

The conditions under which direct reinforcement is employed, and the specific forms it takes, largely determine the mechanisms through which it can affect behavior. In most human learning experiments, achievement-oriented college students are required to respond to stimulus material for a brief period during which they receive correctness feedback in the form of lights, tones, or verbal cues that lack affective properties. In such situations, reinforcing stimuli can affect performance only through their informational value. In most behavior-modification programs, on the other hand, reinforcers influence behavior primarily through their incentive-motivational effects. Here, subjects are informed in advance as to what performances are required, and valued incentives are used to activate and to sustain a desired level of responding over a given period of time. An employer would soon be deserted by his staff members if their sole reinforcement was information indicating the number of production units that they successfully completed during each month.

Most of the experimental paradigms used to study the behavioral effects of direct reinforcement operations are suitable for assessing the informational value of feedback stimuli, but they are inadequate to establish whether response consequences have direct associative-strengthening effects. The question of whether performance changes must be symbolically mediated can be answered most decisively by studies in which the reinforced responses or the reinforcing events are unobservable to the performer and therefore fail to convey sufficient information to produce changes on a cognitive basis. Either of the latter conditions effectively precludes recognition of the response-reinforcement contingency employed. It has been shown that correct responding in food-deprived animals can be significantly increased by unnoticeable intravenous presentation of nutritive solutions contingent upon correct performances (Chambers, 1956; Coppock and Chambers, 1954). And Hefferline and his associates (Hefferline and Keenan, 1963; Hefferline, Keenan and Harford, 1959; Sasmor, 1966) have successfully conditioned covert responses in adult humans without their observing the rewarded response. In these experiments, visually imperceptible thumb contractions of a preselected magnitude (detected by the experimenter through electromyographic amplification) are increased substantially when reinforced with monetary points or termination of aversive stimulation, whereas they decline abruptly after reinforcement is withdrawn. Such changes are reliably achieved even though subjects are unable to identify the response that produces reinforcement.

Self-Reinforcement Processes

Most human behavior is altered and maintained in the absence of immediate external reinforcement. It is generally assumed that people can, and indeed, do, exercise some degree of control over their own actions by utilizing self-generated stimulation. Experimental investigations of self-regulatory processes have primarily focused on the manner in which self-produced verbal and imaginal representations of events serve a performance-guiding function. Another major aspect of self-control is concerned with whether people can regulate their own behavior through self-produced consequences. Until recently, self-reinforcement phenomena have been virtually ignored in psychological theorizing and experimentation, perhaps due to the strong set established by studies conducted with infrahuman subjects. Unlike humans, who generally respond to their own behavior in self-approving or self-criticizing ways, rats and chimpanzees are disinclined to pat themselves on the back for commendable performances, or to berate themselves for getting lost in cul-de-sacs. By contrast, people typically set themselves certain standards of behavior and self-administer rewarding or punishing consequences depending on whether their performances fall short of, match, or exceed their self-prescribed demands.

A self-reinforcing event includes several subsidiary processes, some of which have been extensively investigated in their own right. First, it involves a self-prescribed standard of behavior which serves as the criterion for evaluating the adequacy of one's performances. The standard-setting component has been explored in some detail in studies of aspiration level. Most performances do not provide objective feedback of adequacy, and consequently, the attainments of other persons must be utilized as the norm against which meaningful self-evaluation can be made. Thus, for example, a student who achieves a score of 160 points on a given examination, and who aspires to exceed modal performances, would have no basis for either self-approving or self-disparaging reactions without knowing the accomplishments of others who are selected as the appropriate comparison group. As a second feature, a self-reinforcing event, therefore, often entails social-comparison processes. Third, the reinforcers are under the person's own control, and fourth, he serves as his own reinforcing agent. The significance of the two latter defining characteristics should be underscored because in some studies designed to investigate self-reinforcement processes, subjects do not have free access to the rewards; hence, the procedures essentially represent variations on externally managed reinforcement systems. Johnson and Martin (1970), for example, report a study in which subjects activated a reward signal after making responses they judged correct, but only a small proportion of the signaled correct responses was actually reinforced by the experimenter. Although subjects in this study judged when their performances deserved to be rewarded, the reinforcement was, nevertheless, externally controlled.

Investigations of self-reinforcement processes involve two separate lines of research. One set of studies is primarily designed to identify the conditions under which self-reinforcing responses are acquired and modified. In these experiments, self-rewarding and self-punishing responses constitute the dependent variables. The second line of research is principally concerned with whether self-administered rewards and punishments serve a reinforcing function in controlling the person's own behavior. In testing for reinforcing effects, self-reinforcement serves as the independent variable that is measured in terms of its power to influence performance.

Determinants of self-reinforcing responses.   Several paradigms have been used to explore the acquisition of self-reinforcing responses. In the procedure typically employed by Kanfer and Marston, subjects perform a task in which their performances remain ill-defined; they are instructed to press a button that flashes a light or dispenses a token whenever they think their responses are correct. These accuracy judgments are interpreted as self-reinforcing responses.

In some of the studies conducted within this approach (Kanfer and Marston, 1963a; Marston, 1970a) subjects were presented with a pseudo-subliminal perception task in which the same unrecognizable nonsense syllable was flashed on the screen on each trial, and subjects were required to guess which of several designated words they saw; in other studies (Kanfer and Marston, 1963b; Marston, 1964a) subjects selected what they considered to be the correct nonsense syllable from among alternatives that were randomly chosen as right; in other experiments (Marston, 1970b), subjects took tokens when they believed that they had hit the bull's-eye with darts tossed while blindfolded, when they assumed that they had judged the length of lines correctly, or when they judged their responses to projective-test stimuli as accurate or popular (Marston, 1964b); and in still other investigations (Kanfer, 1966), the number of times that children claimed they guessed correctly the number ranging from 0 to 100 that the experimenter would pick on each trial was used as an index of self-reward. Considering the extremely low probability of correct matches, high responses on the latter task more likely reflect fabrication than positive self-evaluation.

Certain interpretive problems arise when self-reinforcing responses are defined in terms of accuracy judgments. The major difficulties stem from the fact that correctness evaluations and self-commendations may be only partially correlated. There are many occasions when people evaluate their performances as accurate but not deserving of self-praise. The lack of relationship between these two sets of responses is most likely to obtain when individuals are required to perform tasks that they regard as simple or trivial, or that they personally devalue. Similarly, people may designate their responses on a particular task as inaccurate, but these judgments are unaccompanied by self-disparagment if the assignment is viewed as excessively difficult, irrelevant, or inappropriate to their background training. A mathematician, for example, who is asked to solve elementary arithmetic problems would undoubtedly judge his calculations to be accurate but hardly worthy of self-reward; conversely, a humanities enthusiast might rate most of his responses on tests of engineering competence inaccurate without engaging in any self-condemnation.

The necessity for distinguishing between the two types of responses would readily become evident if the experimental procedures previously described included two sets of response buttons, one signifying accuracy judgments and the second measuring self-approving reactions. The mathematician solving elementary arithmetic problems would frequently press the "accurate" button, but he might rarely, if ever, press the "commendable" button. The dual-response arrangement would also provide information on whether procedures in which subjects' performances remain ill-defined produce an adequate amount of self-reinforcing behavior. Under conditions of performance ambiguity, people may be willing to make tentative guesses about their responses but view the situation as providing insufficient basis for engaging in self-reward.

The foregoing comments, while questioning the substitution of accuracy estimates for direct measures of self-reinforcing behavior, are not meant to imply that categorization of one's responses on an accuracy dimension under low-feedback conditions is irrelevant to self-reinforcement processes. Performance designation serves as one of several factors determining whether individuals will respond with self-praise or self-reproof. Research conducted within this general paradigm (Kanfer, 1970) has identified many variables that influence the incidence with which ambiguous performances are self-defined as accurate.

Ordinarily, self-reinforcement occurs in response to performances that are clearly discernible. That is, golfers see the distance and direction of their drives; students receive explicit scores on their academic tests; and authors can recognize the amount of material that they have written within a given period. In investigating the determinants of self-reinforcing responses, one must, of course, avoid performances that either produce distinct evaluative feedback or for which there are pre-existing norms. When self-evaluative responses are already linked to differential performance levels, subjects' covert self-reinforcement may obscure the influence of experimentally manipulated variables. It is therefore advantageous to choose tasks which produce performances that have no pre-established, self-evaluative significance. In other words, subjects can observe their attainments, but they have no basis for judging their adequacy. A person who receives a score of thirty on an unfamiliar motor task, for example, cannot determine whether it represents a mediocre, an adequate, or a superior achievement. By eliminating evaluative feedback, it is possible to study the conditions under which self-reinforcing responses can be established to particular performances. The paradigm originally employed by Bandura and Kupers (1964) was selected with the above requirements in mind.

Establishment of self-reinforcing responses through differential reinforcement. Self-reinforcing responses are undoubtedly developed to some extent through selective reinforcement. In this learning process, an agent adopts a criterion of what constitutes a worthy performance and consistently rewards persons for matching or exceeding the adopted criterion level, but nonrewards or punishes performances that fall short of the minimum standard. When persons subsequently respond to their own behavior they are likely to reinforce themselves in a similarly selective manner. The effects of differential reinforcement of qualitative variations in performance on patterns of self-reward have not as yet been investigated experimentally. Kanfer and Marston (1963a) have shown that miserly and indulgent pretraining can influence the rate at which subjects administer tokens to themselves for responses they judge to be correct. The performances of some adults were generously rewarded with token reinforcers accompanied by an approving attitude toward self-reward, whereas with others the experimenter parted grudgingly with a few tokens and cautioned subjects against requesting rewards for performances of questionable accuracy. Those who received lenient training later rewarded themselves more frequently on a different task than subjects who were stringently trained, even though the achievements for both groups were comparable.

Establishment of self-reinforcing responses through modeling. There exists a substantial body of evidence that modeling processes play a highly influential role in the transmission of self-reinforcement patterns. In the standard paradigm (Bandura and Kupers, 1964; Bandura, Grusec, and Menlove, 1967a), subjects observe a model performing a bowling task in which he adopts either a high-performance standard or a relatively low criterion of self-reinforcement. On trials in which the model attains or exceeds the self-imposed demand, he rewards himself with candy or exchangeable tokens and expresses positive self-evaluations, but when his attainments fall short of the adopted requirement he denies himself available rewards and reacts in a self-derogatory manner. Later, observers perform the task alone, during which time they receive a predetermined set of scores and the performances for which they reward themselves are recorded. The results show that people tend to adopt standards for self-reinforcement displayed by exemplary models, they evaluate their own performances relative to that standard, and then they serve as their own reinforcing agents. In the study by Bandura and Kupers (1964), children who observed a model setting a high standard of self-reinforcement later rewarded themselves sparingly and only when they achieved superior performances, whereas children exposed to models who considered low achievements deserving of self-reward later tended to reinforce themselves generously for mediocre performances (Fig. 8-4). A control group

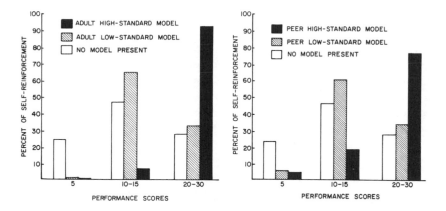

FIGURE 8-4. Frequency with which children rewarded themselves at three performance levels after observing models reinforce themselves either according to a high standard (score of 20 points) or a low criterion (10-point score) of achievement. Control subjects had no prior exposure to models. The figure on the left depicts the patterns of self-reward for children who observed adult models; the figure on the right presents the distribution of self-reward for children who were exposed to peer models. (Bandura and Kupers, 1964.)

of children, who had no exposure to models, did not reward themselves selectively for differential levels of achievement. Subjects in the experimental conditions not only adopted the modeled standards of self-reinforcement, but they also matched variations in the magnitude with which the models rewarded their own performances.

In laboratory studies, a self-reinforcing response typically combines self-administration or self-denial of available tangible rewards with verbal self-praise or self-criticism. The verbal self-evaluation is an important defining component of a self-reinforcing event. The fact that a person passes up available edibles or exchangeable tokens does not by itself signify a self-punishing response. The absence of a response may be due to satiation, to disinterest in the material objects, or to any number of extraneous factors. However, when a model refrains from taking rewards and derogates his performances, there is no question that he is engaging in self-punitive behavior. Some investigators have either deleted (Colle and Bee, 1968) or varied (Liebert, Hanratty, and Hill, 1969) the verbal self-evaluation component on the assumption that it represents a "rule structure."

Verbal self-commendation and self-derogation following differential attainment provide the basis for inferring the guiding standard, but the specific modeled examples do not constitute the rule. In fact, in experiments in which performances vary over a relatively wide range, postexperimental interviews disclose that the standard of self-reinforcement children derive from the models' performances does not always correspond to the one that was actually modeled. One must distinguish between a rule statement that defines the minimum criterion for self-reinforcement from self-critical and self-approving verbalizations accompanying specific performances. There is a marked difference between derogating oneself for a particular performance (e.g., "That's poor; it doesn't deserve a treat") and verbalizing a rule for self-reinforcement that applies to all instances (e.g., "I reward myself only when I get a score of twenty points or above"). To delete the verbal self-reinforcing reactions is to remove an important feature of the very phenomena being studied. As might be expected, matching self-rewarding behavior is more effectively established when verbal self-evaluative responses are modeled than when they are not.

Manipulation of verbal self-reinforcement also tends to introduce other unintended variations in treatment conditions. It is difficult to make changes in verbal self-reinforcement without producing corresponding variations in the emotional intensity with which self-reinforcing responses are modeled. Results are therefore not easily interpretable from studies where self-reinforcing responses are performed enthusiastically when accompanied by verbal self-evaluations and perfunctorily when verbal self-reinforcers are omitted (Liebert, Hanratty, and Hill, 1969).

It will be recalled that social-comparison processes were assigned a prominent role in self-reinforcement. In the preceding experiment by Bandura and Kupers (1964), both the model and the subjects obtained a wide and overlapping range of scores; consequently, subjects had no reliable basis for judging their ability level. Ordinarily, social groups contain models of clearly differing abilities so that a given individual must select the modeled standards against which to evaluate his own performances. According to social-comparison theory (Festinger, 1954), persons tend to choose reference models who are similar in ability, and to reject those who are too divergent from themselves. One might also expect a history of negative reinforcement of achievement behavior to lower people's evaluation of their own performances (Stotland and Zander, 1958) and hence reduce the frequency and generosity with which they reward themselves.

To test the above propositions, an experiment was conducted (Bandura and Whalen, 1966) in which children underwent a series of success or failure experiences, following which they were exposed to either a superior model adopting a high criterion for self-reward, an inferior model displaying a very low standard of self-reinforcement, an equally competent model exhibiting a moderately high self-reward criterion, or they observed no models. Children who witnessed the inferior model subsequently rewarded themselves more frequently at low-performance levels and more generously than subjects who observed competent models adopting higher criteria of self-reinforcement. Upward discrepancies from adult models thus enhanced children's evaluation of their attainments. In accord with social-comparison theory, children rejected the self-imposed reinforcement contingencies of the superior model and adopted a lower standard commensurate with their achievements. Experimental subjects who had undergone failure experiences generally rewarded themselves less frequently than their successful counterparts. However, superior attainments outweighed the effect of reinforcement history so that subjects in all modeling conditions exhibited equally high rates of self-reward for outstanding performances regardless of whether they had previously met with repeated success or failure.

Although the exacting norms of highly divergent models tend to be rejected, nevertheless it is not uncommon for people to adopt stringent standards of self-reinforcement. An experiment by Bandura, Grusec and Menlove (1967a) investigated some of the social conditions under which persons emulate austere standards of self-reinforcement even though the self-imposition of such contingencies produces negative self-evaluative consequences. Children were exposed to an adult model who performed the bowling task at a consistently superior level and adopted a high criterion of self-reward. Half the subjects experienced a prior rewarding interaction with the model, whereas with a second group of children the same model behaved in a nonnurturant manner. This relationship variable was selected on the assumption that the rewarding quality of the model, which tends to increase interpersonal attraction, would facilitate emulation of the model's norms. Adherence to high standards of achievement is generally rewarded and publicly recognized. Therefore, with half the subjects in each of the two levels of nurturance, the adult model was praised for adopting stringent standards of self-reinforcement, but with the remaining children the model received no social recognition for high standard-setting behavior.

Ordinarily, individuals are exposed to a multiplicity of modeling influences, many of which operate in opposing directions. Speculations about the influence of multiple modeling on social learning generally assign importance to conflicting identification with adult and peer models. In order to determine the effects of simultaneous exposure to antagonistic modeling influences, half the children in each subgroup observed both the stringent adult and a peer model who displayed a low standard of self-reward. When faced with a conflict between adult and peer standards, children would be predisposed toward peer modeling because emulation of high aspirations results in frequent negative self-reinforcement of one's performances. It was assumed, however, that the tendency for peer modeling to reduce the impact of adult modeling might be counteracted by the operation of opposing influences arising from positive ties to the adult model, and from vicarious positive reinforcement of high standard-setting behavior.

Figure 8-5 presents the per cent of trials in which children rewarded themselves for performances below the minimum criterion adopted by the adult model. As shown graphically, children exposed to conflicting modeling influences were more inclined to reward themselves for low achievements than children who had observed only the adult model consistently adhere to a high standard of self-reinforcement. Children were also more likely to impose severe criteria of self-reward on themselves when the adult model received social recognition for his high standard-setting behavior than when the model's stringent achievement demands went unrewarded. However, contrary to expectation, subjects who had experienced a highly nurturant interaction with the adult model were more likely to accept the low-performance standard set by the peer than if the adult model was less beneficent. Apparently, a nurturant relationship was interpreted by the children as permissiveness for lenient self-demands.

Comparison of subgroups containing various combinations of variables revealed that the influence of the peer's liberal self-reward was effectively negated by social reinforcement of the adult's high standard-setting behavior. The most austere pattern of self-reinforcement was displayed by children who experienced a relatively nonnurturant relationship with the adult model, who had no exposure to conflicting peer norms, and who witnessed the adult receive social recognition for adhering to high standards (see Fig. 8-5). These children, who rarely considered performances that fell below the adult's criterion worthy of self-reward, displayed unyielding self-denial. The adoption and continued adherence to unrealistically high self-evaluative standards is especially striking, considering that the self-imposition of rigorous performance demands oc-

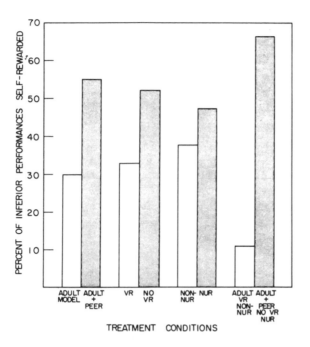

FIGURE 8.5 Per cent of trials in which subjects rewarded themselves for performances below the minimum standard adopted by the adult model as a function of model nurturance, vicarious reinforcement of high standard-setting behavior, and exposure to conflicting peer-modeling influences. (Bandura, Grusec, and Menlove, 1967a.)

curred in the absence of any social surveillance, under high permissiveness for self-gratification, and the modeled standards resulted in considerable self-devaluation and self-forbiddance of freely available rewards.

Comparative studies (Liebert and Allen, 1967; Liebert and Ora, 1968) disclose that modeling and direct training, in which experimenters judge which of the performer's attainments are deserving of reward, are equally effective in transmitting high standards of self-reinforcement. Under naturally occurring conditions, modeling and reinforcement practices often operate concurrently in ways that either supplement or counteract each other. Findings of research in which both of these sources of influence are varied simultaneously (McMains and Liebert, 1968; Mischel and Liebert, 1966; Rosenhan, Frederick, and Burrowes, 1968) show that rewards are most sparingly self-administered when stringent standards have been consistently modeled and imposed, whereas social-learning conditions in which persons both model and reinforce lenient performance demands produce generous self-reward patterns of behavior. Discrepant practices, on the other hand, in which models prescribe stringent standards for others but impose lenient ones upon themselves, or who impose austere demands on themselves and lenient ones on others, reduce the likelihood that high standards will be adopted.

The transmission of self-reward patterns through a succession of models has been demonstrated by Mischel and Liebert (1966). Children who adopted the standards of reinforcement of adults subsequently both modeled the same self-rewarding behavior with peers and applied the same reinforcement contingency to their performances. Marston (1965a) has likewise shown in an experiment with adults that witnessing models reinforcing their own performances at either high or low rates not only affected the self-reinforcing behavior of the observers, but also influenced the frequency with which they later reinforced another person performing the same task. Results of these laboratory experiments are in accord with field studies demonstrating that, in cultures where austerity is consistently modeled and reinforced as the dominant social norm, not only are positive reinforcements sparingly self-administered, but because of the emphasis on personal responsibility for high standards of conduct, self-denying, self-punitive, and depressive reactions occur with high frequency (Eaton and Weil, 1955). By contrast, in societies in which generous self-gratification patterns predominate, self-rewards are usually made contingent upon minimal performances (Hughes, Tremblay, Rapoport, and Leighton, 1960).

Self-reinforcement, self-concept, and achievement behavior.   In the aforementioned laboratory studies, individuals who had been exposed to models favoring lenient standards of self-reinforcement were highly self-rewarding and self-approving for comparatively mediocre performances. By contrast, persons who observed models adhering to stringent performance demands later displayed self-denial and self-dissatisfaction for objectively identical accomplishments. These contrasting self-reactions illustrate how self-esteem, self-concept, and related self-evaluative processes can be conceptualized within a social-learning framework. From this perspective, self-esteem is the result of discrepancies between a person's behavior and the standards that he has selected as indices of personal merit. When behavior falls short of one's evaluative standards, the person judges himself negatively or holds himself in low self-esteem. On the other hand, when performances coincide with, or exceed, a person's standards, he evaluates himself positively, which is considered indicative of high self-esteem.

The self-concept, which is assigned a prominent role in some theories of personality, also reflects the phenomenon of self-reinforcement. Self-concept usually signifies a person's disposition toward positive and negative self-evaluation of different aspects of his behavior. In measuring this personality characteristic, individuals are presented with a set of evaluative statements in adjective check lists, Q-sorts, or inventories, and asked to rate which statements apply to them. The individual responses are then summed to provide a global index of self-evaluation. Within a social-learning approach, a negative self-concept is defined in terms of a high frequency of negative self-reinforcement of one's behavior and, conversely, a favorable self-concept is reflected in a relatively high incidence of positive self-reinforcement (Marston, 1965b).

Dysfunctions in self-reinforcement systems often assume major importance in psychopathology through their capacity to create excessive self-punishment and aversive conditions that can maintain other forms of deviant behavior. Many of the people who seek psychotherapy are highly competent and free of debilitating anxiety, but they experience a great deal of personal distress stemming from excessively high standards of self-evaluation that are often supported by unfavorable comparisons with models noted for their extraordinary achievements. Talented individuals who have high aspirations that are possible but difficult to realize are especially vulnerable to self-dissatisfaction despite their notable achievements. As Boyd (1969) graphically describes this phenomenon, "Each violinist in any second chair started out as a prodigy in velvet knickers who expected one day to solo exquisitely amid flowers flung by dazzled devotees. The 45-year-old violinist with spectacles on his nose and a bald spot in the middle of his hair is the most disappointed man on earth."

In its more extreme forms, an austere system of self-reinforcement gives rise to depressive reactions, chronic discouragement, and feelings of worthlessness and lack of purposefulness. Excessive self-disparagement, in fact, is one of the defining characteristics of psychotic depression. As Loeb, Beck, Diggory, and Tuthill (1967) have shown, depressed adults evaluate their performances as significantly poorer than do nondepressed subjects, even though their actual achievements are the same. People also suffer from considerable self-devaluation when they experience loss in ability due to age or physical injury but continue to adhere to their original standards of achievement. In the latter instances, most of their performances are negatively self-reinforced to the point where eventually they become apathetic and abandon significant aspects of their behavioral

repertoire. When a person's behavior produces self-punishing consequences, any activities that avert or reduce these aversive outcomes are
thereby strengthened and maintained. Many forms of deviant behavior,
such as alcoholic self-anesthetization, grandiose ideation, and reluctance
to engage in activities that may have self-evaluative implications, serve
as means of escaping or avoiding self-generated aversive stimulation.

The discussion thus far has emphasized the personal negative by-
products of stringent self-reinforcement. Social problems can arise from
deficient or deviant self-reinforcement systems. Individuals who have
failed to develop well-defined standards necessary for adequate self-
regulating reinforcement, and those who make self-reward contingent
upon skillful performance of antisocial behavior, readily engage in transgressive behavior unless deterred by externally imposed controls. Similarly, individuals who set lax behavioral standards for themselves are
inclined to display low achievement strivings.

There is reason to assume, from findings reported later, that self-
reinforcement serves both a motivating and a reinforcing function with
respect to achievement behavior. It has been repeatedly demonstrated
(Locke, Cartledge, and Koeppel, 1968) that performance standards are
a major determinant of level of productivity. The higher the standards
that people set for themselves, the higher their attainments. Setting performance goals by itself does not automatically produce achievement behavior. Rather, the motivational effects of goal-setting are most likely
mediated by self-reinforcement. After a person has committed himself to
a specified level of performance, his self-approval becomes contingent
upon goal attainment. This leads him to intensify his efforts in order to
exceed self-disappointing performances. Having achieved a given performance, people are usually no longer content with it and make self-reward
contingent upon progressively more difficult accomplishments. In the present interpretation, motivational effects derive not from the goals themselves but from the fact that people respond evaluatively to their own
achievements and, therefore, regulate their level of effort accordingly.

Conditions maintaining self-reinforcing responses.   In preceding sections, processes have been examined whereby evaluative and reinforcing
functions performed by others are transferred to the individual himself
so that he serves as the reinforcer of his own actions. An interesting, but
inadequately explored, question is what maintains discriminative self-
reinforcing responses after they have been acquired through modeling and
direct training. No elaborate theory is needed to explain why people engage in self-rewarding behavior. The more challenging question requiring

explanation is why people deny themselves available rewards over which they have full control, and why they punish themselves.

Conditioned relief. One possible interpretation is that self-evaluative responses acquire secondary reinforcing properties through repeated association with primary or social reinforcement. According to this classical-conditioning view, which has been advanced by Aronfreed (1964), transgressive behavior arouses anticipatory anxiety as a result of past association with punishment. Under conditions where social disapproval occurs contiguously with termination of anxiety or punishment, verbal criticism attains anxiety-attenuating value. The subject therefore applies critical labels to his own behavior because they serve as automatic anxiety reducers. To test this notion, Aronfreed (1964) conducted an experiment in which children performed an ambiguous task; on designated trials a buzzer sounded, signifying a transgression, following which the children were verbally reprimanded for behaving the "blue" way and deprived of some candy. For one group of subjects, the critical label "blue" was expressed when the buzzer and punishment were terminated; for a second group the label coincided with the onset of buzzer and punishment; while with control children the blue label was verbalized as the buzzer was turned off, without any accompanying punishment. On two test trials, during which the buzzer signaled a transgression, children who experienced labeling at the termination of punishment were more inclined to verbalize the critical label than either the controls or the children receiving labeling at the onset of punishment, who did not differ from each other.

The above findings are consistent with a conditioned-reinforcement view, although interpretation of the data is complicated by the fact that children rarely uttered the critical label on their own and did so only after being verbally prompted by the punishing agent through a series of questions concerning their actions. Given anxiety arousal, one would expect an anxiety reducer to be performed rapidly and spontaneously. An alternative interpretation of the data is that the verbal response was performed because of its anticipated functional value rather than for its conditioned mollifying effects. That is, by uttering the critical label, the children could terminate the experimenter's verbal probing. Subjects who had earlier learned that a particular verbalization discontinues punishment by the experimenter should be more willing to produce it when prompted to do so than children for whom the verbal response brought on the punishing experiences. The differential expectations established through prior training might be expected to persist over more than two trials. The conditioned-reinforcement theory of self-punishment would also require several complicated assumptions to explain how children adopt self-punishing responses by observing punishments self-administered by a model for devalued behavior without observers experiencing any direct aversive consequences.

Self-arousal. There is a growing body of evidence (Bandura, 1969a) that in humans the effects of paired stimulation are largely governed by an intervening self-stimulation mechanism. These findings indicate that a stimulus is not automatically endowed with emotion-arousing or emotion-reducing properties through association with primary reinforcement. Rather, as a result of paired experiences, a conditioned stimulus assumes informative value that is capable of activating emotion-provoking or calming thoughts. The self-stimulation view of conditioning based on thought-produced arousal suggests a somewhat different mode of operation of self-punishment than is assumed in the conditioned-reinforcement explanation.

In everyday situations, the performance of punishable behavior creates anticipatory arousal that is likely to persist in varying degrees until the person is reprimanded. Punishment not only terminates distressing thoughts about impending discovery of the transgression and possible social condemnation, but it also tends to restore the favor of others. Thus, punishment can provide relief from self-generated aversive stimulation that is enduring and often more painful than the actual reprimand itself. This phenomenon is most vividly illustrated in extreme cases where people torment themselves for years over relatively minor transgressions and do not achieve equanimity until after making reparations of some type. Self-punishment may serve a similar distress-relief function. Having criticized or punished themselves for undesirable actions, individuals are likely to discontinue further upsetting ruminations about their behavior.

The way in which self-punishing responses can be maintained by averting anticipated punishing consequences is strikingly demonstrated by Sandler and Quagliano (1964). After monkeys learned to press a lever to avoid being shocked, a second contingency involving self-administered painful stimulation was introduced. A lever-press prevented the occurrence of the original shock, but it also produced an electric shock of lesser magnitude. As the experiment progressed, the self-administered shock was gradually increased in intensity until it equalled the aversive stimulation being avoided. However, the animals showed no reduction in the frequency of self-punishing responses although this behavior no longer served as a "lesser of two evils." Even more interesting, after the avoided shock was permanently discontinued but lever-pressing responses (which had now become objectively functionless) still produced painful consequences, the animals continued to punish themselves needlessly with shock intensities that they had previously worked hard to avoid. This experiment reveals how self-punishment can become autonomous of contemporaneous conditions of reinforcement and be maintained through its capacity to forestall anticipated aversive experiences.

Further support for the emotion-reducing function of self-punitive behavior is furnished by Stone and Hokanson (1969). When adults could avoid painful shocks by administering to themselves shocks of lesser intensity, self-punitive responses not only increased but they were accompanied by reduction in autonomic arousal. Self-punishing responses continued to be performed at an undiminished rate, though with increased autonomic arousal, after conditions were altered so that self-administered punishment was only partially effective in avoiding painful stimulation.

The preceding analysis of self-punishment can be applied as well to self-disappointing performances as to transgressive behavior. The valuation of performances which fall short of, match, or exceed a reference norm is partly achieved through differential reinforcement. For example, parents who expect their children to exceed the average performance of their group in whatever tasks they undertake will selectively reward superior achievements and find fault with average and lower-level attainments. Differential achievement levels thus take on positive and negative value, and the performance standard common to the various activities is eventually abstracted and applied to new endeavors. That is, a person for whom average performances have been repeatedly devalued will come to regard modal achievements on new tasks as inadequate and attainments that surpass modal levels as commendable. It is assumed that, like transgressive behavior, inferior performances can be a source of disconcerting thoughts and social disapproval that individuals will strive to reduce by criticizing or punishing themselves.

As shown earlier, specific patterns of self-reinforcement can be acquired observationally without the mediation of direct external reinforcement. Once the evaluative properties of differential accomplishments are well established, favorable or inadequate matches with adopted standards are likely to elicit self-reactions that, in turn, give rise to self-rewarding or self-punishing behavior. At this stage the whole process becomes relatively independent of external reinforcement, but remains dependent upon cognitive evaluations based on the match between self-prescribed standards, performance, and the attainments of reference models.

External reinforcement.   Although self-punishment can operate autonomously to some extent by reducing self-generated aversive stimulation, self-reinforcing responses are partly sustained by periodic external reinforcement. Adherence to high standards of self-reinforcement is actively supported through a vast system of rewards involving praise, social recognition, and a variety of awards and honors, whereas few accolades are bestowed on people for rewarding themselves on the basis of mediocre performances. To the extent that people choose a reference group whose members share similar behavioral norms for self-reinforcement, a given individual's self-evaluations are undoubtedly influenced by the actual or anticipated reactions of members whose judgments he values highly. Once established, patterns of self-reinforcement are thus intermittently reinforced and upheld through selective association.

In everyday life, high evaluative standards are not only favored, but negative sanctions are frequently applied to discourage inappropriate positive self-reinforcement. Rewarding oneself for inadequate or undeserving performances is more likely than not to evoke critical reactions from others. Similarly, lowering one's performance standards is rarely considered praiseworthy. As a result of extensive social training, performances that are self-defined as failures come to elicit self-devaluative reactions that are incompatible with self-rewarding behavior and thus reduce its occurrence.

Finally, it should be noted that self-punishment often serves as an effective means not only of lessening negative consequences administered by others, but in eliciting commendations from them as well. By criticizing and belittling themselves, people can predictably get others to enumerate their noteworthy accomplishments and abilities, and to issue reassuring predictions that continued effort will produce future triumphs.

Reinforcing function of self-administered consequences.   The studies reported earlier were designed primarily to identify some of the variables governing the acquisition of self-rewarding and self-punishing responses. Given that individuals can be influenced to engage in self-reinforcing activities, the basic question remains whether self-generated consequences serve a reinforcing function in regulating behavior. Demonstrations of the behavioral effects of self-produced response consequences require experimental situations in which self-reinforcing events serve as the controlling variables in relation to other forms of behavior.

To test the relative efficacy of self-monitored and externally imposed systems of reinforcement, Bandura and Perloff (1967) conducted an experiment that proceeded in the following manner: Children worked at a manual task in which they could achieve progressively higher scores by performing increasingly more effortful responses. Eight complete rotations of a wheel were required to advance 5 points so that, for example, a total of 16 cranking responses was necessary to achieve a 10-point score, 24 responses to attain a 15-point score, and so on. Children in the self-reinforcement condition selected their own achievement standards and rewarded themselves with tokens whenever they attained their self-prescribed level of performance. Children assigned to an externally imposed reinforcement condition were individually matched with partners in the self-reward group so that the same performance standard was externally set for them and the reinforcers were automatically delivered whenever they reached the predetermined level. To ascertain whether subjects' behavioral productivity was due to the operation of contingent reinforcement or to gratitude for the rewards that were made available, children in an incentive control group performed the task after they had received the supply of rewards on a noncontingent basis. A fourth group worked without any incentives to estimate the amount of behavior generated by the characteristics of the task itself. Because the capacity to maintain effortful behavior over time is one of the most important attributes of a reinforcement operation, the dependent measure was the number of responses the children performed until they no longer wished to continue the activity.

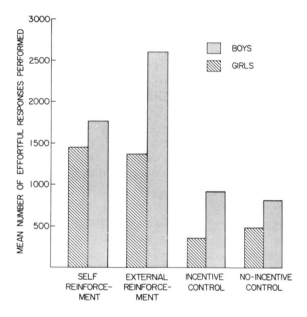

FIGURE 8-6. Mean number of responses maintained by self-monitored, externally imposed, and noncontingent systems of reinforcement. (Bandura and Perloff, 1967.)

As shown graphically in Fig. 8-6, both self-monitored and externally imposed reinforcement systems sustained substantially more behavior than either the contingent reward or the nonreward condition, which did not differ from each other. In the case of boys, externally administered rewards generated more behavior than self-reinforcement, but otherwise the two systems of reinforcement proved equally efficacious. Of even greater interest is the prevalence with which children in the self-monitored condition imposed upon themselves highly unfavorable schedules of reinforcement. Not a single child chose the lowest score which required the least effort, while approximately half of them selected the highest achievement level as the minimal performance meriting self-reward. Moreover, a third of the children subsequently altered their initial standard to a higher level, without a commensurate increase in amount of self-reward, thereby imposing upon themselves a more unfavorable work-to-reinforcement requirement. This behavior is all the more striking because the self-imposition of stringent performance demands occurred in the absence of any social surveillance and under high permissiveness for self-reward.

It can be reasonably assumed that most older children have acquired standards of achievement through modeling and differential reinforcement, and that they have undergone experiences in which rewarding oneself for performances judged to be unworthy has been socially disapproved. Hence, under conditions where persons are provided with opportunities to optimize their material outcomes by engaging in behavior which has low self-regard value, conflicting tendencies are likely to be aroused. On the one hand, individuals are tempted to maximize rewards at minimum-effort costs to themselves; they can achieve this by simply lowering their performance standards. On the other hand, low-quality performances produce negative self-evaluative consequences, which, if sufficiently strong, may inhibit undeserving self-compensation. Apparently, subjects were willing to deny themselves rewards over which they had full control rather than risk self-disapproval for unmerited self-reward. Many of the children, in fact, set themselves performance requirements that incurred high-effort costs at minimum material recompense. These findings are at variance with what one might expect on the basis of reward-cost theories, unless these formulations include the self-esteem costs of rewarding devalued behavior. The desire to avoid aversive self-devaluative consequences may also partly explain why children willingly give up rewards they possess in response to substandard performances after having observed models relinquished rewards and criticize themselves for behavior they judged inadequate (Herbert, Gelfand, and Hartmann, 1969).

In recent years, self-reinforcement procedures have begun to be employed to modify and to maintain response patterns in treatment programs. These studies usually measure the frequency with which deviant responses occur during baseline conditions and after self-administered consequences are made explicitly contingent upon selected behaviors. Goodlet and Goodlet (1969), for example, compared the incidence of aggressively disruptive behavior in boys during a baseline period, when teachers rewarded the children with exchangeable tokens for reductions in aggressiveness, and when the boys evaluated their own performances and reinforced their own behavior accordingly. The mean amount of disruptive behavior displayed by the boys under these three conditions was 35.33, 8.92, and 9.95, respectively. These findings indicate that self-administered consequences can aid in controlling one's own behavior; but the comparative data should be accepted with reservation because the sample size is small and the two systems of reinforcement were not administered in counterbalanced order. Lovitt and Curtiss (1969) and Glynn (1970) also provide evidence that when behavioral objectives and contingency systems are clearly specified, children are able to manage their own behavior as well as more effectively by self-reinforcement than is achieved through similar externally administered consequences.

Several studies have been reported in which self-administered, aversive consequences were used with some degree of success to reduce disfluencies (Goldiamond, 1965), obsessional ruminations (McGuire and Vallance, 1964), craving for addictive drugs (Wolpe, 1965), and deviant sexual behavior (McGuire and Vallance, 1964). The preliminary findings of these studies, while most interesting, require further validation through systematic manipulation of self-reinforcement procedures.

Recent investigations of techniques of self-control also assign a principal role to self-managed reinforcement. In these treatment programs (Ferster, Nurnberger, and Levitt, 1962; Harris, 1969; Stuart, 1967), changes in highly refractory behavior are induced by having subjects regulate the stimulus conditions that ordinarily control undesired and competing response patterns. However, unless positive consequences for self-controlling behavior are also arranged, the well-intentioned practices are usually short-lived. Self-controlling behavior is difficult to maintain because it tends to be associated, at least initially, with relatively unfavorable conditions of reinforcement. Prepotent activities such as heavy drinking by alcoholics and excessive eating by obese people are immediately rewarding, whereas their detrimental consequences are not experienced for some time. Conversely, self-control measures usually produce immediate unpleasant effects while the personal benefits are considerably delayed. Self-reinforcement practices are, therefore, employed to provide immediate support for self-controlling behavior until the benefits that eventually accrue take over the reinforcing function. This is achieved by having individuals select a variety of activities that they find rewarding and make them contingent upon the performance of self-controlling behavior. Successsful results have been achieved with self-managed programs of behavioral change. However, self-reinforcement is only one component in a multiple method, and its relative contribution to the measured outcomes has not been adequately assessed.

Covert self-reinforcement.   All of the preceding studies involved self-administration of tangible reinforcers. Of considerable interest is the question of whether symbolically produced consequences can serve a reinforcing function in regulating overt behavior. Weiner (1965) reports some evidence that symbolized outcomes may possess reinforcing properties that are similar to their physical equivalents. Inappropriate motor responses by adults were either punished by withdrawal of monetary points or by having the subjects imagine the same loss of monetary points, or their performances had no consequences. Weiner found that imagined aversive consequences and the actual occurrence of the same negative outcomes both reduced responding compared to the condition involving no feedback. Covert self-punishment, however, produced somewhat weaker reductive effects. These findings suggest that overt behavior can be partly regulated by covert self-reinforcement operations.

To the extent that covert self-reinforcement can substitute for, supplement, or reduce the effects of extrinsic consequences (Kanfer, 1968), this factor may partly account for intersubject variability in the degree of control exercised over human behavior by external reinforcement. It is also likely that covert self-reinforcement mediates the effects of many extrinsic events that are attributed reinforcing properties. For example, informative feedback of performance can enhance and maintain responding even when the information signifies level of attainment rather than accuracy which can improve performance through its response-guidance functions. Confirmation of correctness by itself does not have inherent rewarding value. Performance knowledge assumes positive or negative qualities only when evaluated by the performer in relation to his intrinsic standards. In other words, it is not the lights or the tones signifying correct responses that are reinforcing; rather, they serve as cues for subjects to apply to themselves positive or negative self-evaluations which function as the critical reinforcing events. Hence, correctness feedback on tasks that are personally devalued or regarded as trifling is unlikely to operate as a reward. On the other hand, confirmation of attainments that exceed personal standards of what constitutes a worthy performance will tend to activate positive self-reinforcement. Knowledge of past achievements may also lead subjects to raise their performance standards for positive self-evaluation, thus increasing their level of effort on the task. The motivational and goal-setting effects of knowledge of results are well documented by Locke, Cartledge, and Koeppel (1968).

Possible applications of covert self-reinforcement are discussed by Homme (1965) in a paper concerned with implicit psychological activities. In reducing detrimental behaviors that produce immediate and automatic reinforcing effects, the individual selects numerous aversive consequences of the behavior which can be employed as covert negative reinforcers. Whenever he is instigated to perform the undesired behavior, he immediately symbolizes the aversive effects or revivifies other unpleasant experiences. Miller (1951) and Grose (1952) have shown that negatively valenced thoughts generate strong emotional responses. In fact, imagined painful stimulation can produce subjective distress and physiological arousal similar to those responses induced by actual painful stimulation (Barber and Hahn, 1964). To the extent that sufficiently strong affective consequences can be symbolically produced contingent upon undesired behavior, its occurrence may be significantly reduced. Covert self-reinforcement is likely to exert greatest controlling power when applied to weaker incipient forms of the behavior than when the response tendency is quite compelling, or after the undesired behavior and its attendant reinforcement have already occurred.

Thought-induced affective experiences have been most extensively employed in aversive counterconditioning for the purpose of controlling injurious addictive behavior or intractable response patterns that can create serious social consequences (Bandura, 1969a). In the application of this procedure, the objects to which individuals are markedly attracted are repeatedly paired with aversive reactions that are symbolically induced. The negative contents are usually drawn from disagreeable, painful, or revolting experiences that the individuals have previously undergone either in connection with the pleasurable objects and activities or in other contexts. Preliminary results based upon clinical applications reveal that aversions can be established in this manner for modifying alcoholism (Anant, 1967; Ashem and Donner, 1968; Miller, 1959); obesity (Cautela, 1966); deviant sexual behavior (Davison, 1968; Miller, 1963); and drug addiction (Kolvin, 1967).

The foregoing procedure gains support from experimental investigations of classical conditioning that rely upon symbolically induced emotional responses. Subjects are informed that the CS will sometimes be followed by shock; they are given a sample shock or a single confirmation trial during the acquisition series, but otherwise the CS is never paired with any externally administered aversive stimulation. Subjects develop conditioned autonomic responses in the absence of an external UCS by generating fear-producing thoughts in conjunction with the occurrence of the CS (Dawson and Grings, 1968; Grings, 1965). Bridger and Mandel (1964), in fact, report that autonomic conditioning was similar regardless of whether the CS was associated with threat of shock alone, or with threat and actual shock stimulation. Some suggestive evidence for the influential role of self-stimulation in symbolic conditioning is provided by Dawson (1966) who found that the degree to which subjects believed that shock would follow a certain signal and the severity of the shock they anticipated were positively correlated with the extent of autonomic conditioning.

Modification of thought processes through self-reinforcement.   The preceding section discussed how symbolically produced effects can be employed as reinforcing events to control overt behavior. Often, certain trains of thought produce strong emotional responses that are subjectively distressing or behaviorally disruptive, in which case the problem becomes one of controlling the covert events themselves. Assuming that symbolic activities obey the same psychological laws as overt behavior, it should be possible to significantly influence the nature, incidence, and potency of covert events. The difficulties in detecting the presence of implicit responses present a major obstacle to their control by reinforcement practices if one adheres to the conventional paradigm in which an external agent monitors the occurrence of the desired behavior, imposes the contingencies on subjects, and administers the reinforcers to them. However, as Homme (1965) points out, the occurrence or absence of covert events can be easily and reliably detected by the person doing the thinking. Consequently, such responses can be most easily influenced through self-reinforcement. In this type of approach, implicit events are self-monitored, the contingencies are self-prescribed, and the consequences are self-produced.

Homme suggests that Premack's (1965) differential-probability principle (i.e., any highly preferred activity has reinforcing capabilities) might be utilized in the contingency arrangement and selection of self-reinforcers. In this approach, the strength and incidence of certain classes of thoughts are modified by making preferred activities contingent upon their occurrence. If thought processes are controllable by this means, then depressive, infuriating, and other vexatious ruminations could be reduced by self-reinforcement of more constructive lines of thought. The results of both clinical and laboratory studies are sufficiently promising to warrant further investigation of self-reinforcement processes and their role in the self-regulation of behavior.

REFERENCES

Anant, S. S. A note on the treatment of alcoholics by a verbal aversion technique. *Canadian Psychologist*, 1967, *8*, 19–22.

Aronfreed, J. The origin of self-criticism. *Psychological Review*, 1964, *71*, 193–218.

Ashem, B., and Donner, L. Covert sensitization with alcoholics: A controlled replication. *Behaviour Research and Therapy*, 1968, *6*, 7–12.

Bandura, A. Social learning through imitation. In M. R. Jones (Ed.), *Nebraska symposium on motivation: 1962*. Lincoln: University of Nebraska Press, 1962. Pp. 211–269.

Bandura, A. Vicarious processes: A case of no-trial learning. In L. Berkowitz (Ed.), *Advances in experimental social psychology*. Vol. 2. New York: Academic Press, 1965. Pp. 1–55. (a)

Bandura, A. Influence of models' reinforcement contingencies on the acquisition of imitative responses. *Journal of Personality and Social Psychology*, 1965, *1*, 589–595. (b)

Bandura, A. *Principles of behavior modification*. New York: Holt, 1969. (a)

Bandura, A. Social-learning theory of identificatory processes. In D. A. Goslin (Ed.), *Handbook of socialization theory and research*. Chicago: Rand McNally, 1969. Pp. 213–262. (b)

Bandura, A., Blanchard, E. B., and Ritter, B. The relative efficacy of desensitization and modeling approaches for inducing behavioral, affective, and attitudinal changes. *Journal of Personality and Social Psychology*, 1969, *13*, 173–199.

Bandura, A., Grusec, J. E., and Menlove, F. L. Some social determinants of self-monitoring reinforcement systems. *Journal of Personality and Social Psychology*, 1967, *5*, 449–455. (a)

Bandura, A., Grusec, J. E., and Menlove, F. L. Vicarious extinction of avoidance behavior. *Journal of Personality and Social Psychology*, 1967, *5*, 16–23. (b)

Bandura, A., and Kupers, C. J. The transmission of patterns of self-reinforcement through modeling. *Journal of Abnormal and Social Psychology*, 1964, *69*, 1–9.

Bandura, A., and Menlove, F. L. Factors determining vicarious extinction of avoidance behavior through symbolic modeling. *Journal of Personality and Social Psychology*, 1968, *8*, 99–108.

Bandura, A., and Perloff, B. Relative efficacy of self-monitored and externally imposed reinforcement systems. *Journal of Personality and Social Psychology*, 1967, *7*, 111–116.

Bandura, A., and Rosenthal, T. L. Vicarious classical conditioning as a function of arousal level. *Journal of Personality and Social Psychology*, 1966, *3*, 54–62.

Bandura, A., Ross D., and Ross, S. A. Vicarious reinforcement and imitative learning. *Journal of Abnormal and Social Psychology*, 1963, *67*, 601–607.

Bandura, A., and Whalen, C. K. The influence of antecedent reinforcement and divergent modeling cues on patterns of self-reward. *Journal of Personality and Social Psychology*, 1966, *3*, 373–382.

Barber, T. X., and Hahn, K. W., Jr. Experimental studies in "hypnotic" behavior: Physiological and subjective effects of imagined pain. *Journal of Nervous and Mental Disease*, 1964, *139*, 416–425.

Barnwell, A. K. Potency of modeling cues in imitation and vicarious reinforcement situations. *Dissertation Abstracts*, 1966, *26*, 7444.

Benton, A. A. Effects of timing of negative response consequences on the observational learning of resistance to temptation in children. *Dissertation Abstracts*, 1967, *27*, 2153–2154.

Berger, S. M. Incidental learning through vicarious reinforcement. *Psychological Reports*, 1961, *9*, 477–491.

Berger, S. M. Conditioning through vicarious instigation. *Psychological Review*, 1962, *69*, 450–466.

Berger, S. M., and Johansson, S. L. Effect of a model's expressed emotions on an observer's resistance to extinction. *Journal of Personality and Social Psychology*, 1968, *10*, 53–58.

Blake, R. R. The other person in the situation. In R. Tagiuri and L. Petrullo (Eds.), *Person perception and interpersonal behavior*. Stanford, Calif.: Stanford University Press, 1958. Pp. 229–242.

Blanchard, E. B. Relative contributions of modeling, informational influences, and physical contact in the extinction of public behavior. *Journal of Abnormal Psychology*, 1970, *76*, 55–61.

Bolles, R. C. *Theory of motivation*. New York: Harper & Row, 1967.

Boyd, L. M. Most disappointed men in the world. *San Francisco Chronicle*, March 15, 1969.

Bridger, W. H., and Mandel, I. J. A comparison of GSR fear responses produced by threat and electric shock. *Journal of Psychiatric Research*, 1964, *2*, 31–40.

Bruning, J. L. Direct and vicarious effects of a shift in magnitude of reward on performance. *Journal of Personality and Social Psychology*, 1965, *2*, 278–282.

Buchwald, A. M. Extinction after acquisition under different verbal reinforcement combinations. *Journal of Experimental Psychology*, 1959, *57*, 43–48. (a)

Buchwald, A. M. Experimental alterations in the effectiveness of verbal reinforcement combinations. *Journal of Experimental Psychology*, 1959, *57*, 351–361. (b)

Buchwald, A. M. Supplementary report: Alteration in the reinforcement value of a positive reinforcer. *Journal of Experimental Psychology*, 1960, *60*, 416–418.

Campbell, D. T. Conformity in psychology's theories of acquired behavioral dispositions. In I. A. Berg and B. M. Bass (Eds.), *Conformity and deviation*. New York: Harper & Row, 1961. Pp. 101–142.

Cautela, J. R. Treatment of compulsive behavior by covert sensitization. *Psychological Record*, 1966, *16*, 33–41.

Chambers, R. M. Effects of intravenous glucose injections on learning, general activity, and hunger drive. *Journal of Comparative and Physiological Psychology*, 1956, *49*, 558–564.

Church, R. M. Transmission of learned behavior between rats. *Journal of Abnormal and Social Psychology*, 1957, *54*, 163–165.

Church, R. M. Emotional reactions of rats to the pain of others. *Journal of Comparative and Physiological Psychology*, 1959, *52*, 132–134.

Clark, B. S. The acquisition and extinction of peer imitation in children. *Psychonomic Science*, 1965, *2*, 147–148.

Colle, H. A., and Bee, H. L. The effects of competence and social class on degree of modeling of self-reward patterns. *Psychonomic Science*, 1968, *10*, 231–232.

Condrell, K. N. Vicarious learning of a discrimination learning problem as a function of reinforcement and set. *Dissertation Abstracts*, 1967, *28*, 1221.

Coppock, H. W., and Chambers, R. M. Reinforcement of position preference by autonomic intravenous injections of glucose. *Journal of Comparative and Physiological Psychology*, 1954, *47*, 355–357.

Craig, K. D., and Weinstein, M. S. Conditioning vicarious affective arousal. *Psychological Reports*, 1965, *17*, 955–963.

Crooks, J. L. Observational learning of fear in monkeys. Unpublished manuscript, University of Pennsylvania, 1967.

Davison, G. C. Elimination of a sadistic fantasy by a client-controlled counterconditioning technique: A case study. *Journal of Abnormal Psychology*, 1968, *73*, 84–90.

Dawson, M. E. Comparison of classical conditioning and relational learning. Unpublished master's thesis, University of Southern California, 1966.

Dawson, M. E., and Grings, W. W. Comparison of classical conditioning and relational learning. *Journal of Experimental Psychology*, 1968, *76*, 227–231.

Ditrichs, R., Simon, S., and Greene, B. Effect of vicarious scheduling on the verbal conditioning of hostility in children. *Journal of Personality and Social Psychology*, 1967, *6*, 71–78.

Dulany, D. E. Awareness, rules, and propositional control: A confrontation with S-R behavior theory. In T. R. Dixon and D. L. Horton (Eds.), *Verbal behavior and general behavior theory*. Englewood Cliffs, N. J.: Prentice-Hall, 1968. Pp. 340–387.

Eaton, J. W., and Weil, R. J. *Culture and mental disorders*. Glencoe, Ill.: Free Press, 1955.

Ferster, C. B., Nurnberger, J. I., and Levitt, E. B. The control of eating. *Journal of Mathetics*, 1962, *1*, 87–109.

Festinger, L. A theory of social comparison processes. *Human Relations*, 1954, *7*, 117–140.

Flanders, J. P., and Thistlethwaite, D. L. Effects of informative and justificatory variables upon imitation. Unpublished manuscript, Vanderbilt University, 1969.

Glynn, E. L. Classroom applications of self-determined reinforcement. *Journal of Applied Behavior Analysis*, 1970, *3*, 123–132.

Goldiamond, I. Fluent and nonfluent speech (stuttering): Analysis and operant techniques for control. In L. Krasner and L. P. Ullmann (Eds.), *Research in behavior modification*. New York: Holt, 1965. Pp. 106–156.

Goodlet, G. R., and Goodlet, M. M. Efficiency of self-monitored and externally imposed schedules of reinforcement in controlling disruptive behavior. Unpublished manuscript, University of Guelph, Ontario, 1969.

Grings, W. W. Verbal-perceptual factors in the conditioning of autonomic responses. In W. F. Prokasy (Ed.), *Classical conditioning: A symposium*. New York: Appleton-Century-Crofts, 1965. Pp. 71–89.

Grose, R. F. A comparison of vocal and subvocal conditioning of the galvanic skin response. Unpublished doctoral dissertation, Yale University, 1952.

Hamilton, M. L. Vicarious reinforcement effects on extinction. *Journal of Experimental Child Psychology*, 1970, *9*, 108–114.

Harris, M. B. A self-directed program for weight control: A pilot study. *Journal of Abnormal Psychology*, 1969, *74*, 263–270.

Hastorf, A. H. The "reinforcement" of individual actions in a group situation. In L. Krasner and L. P. Ullmann (Eds.), *Research in behavior modification*. New York: Holt, 1965. Pp. 268–284.

Hefferline, R. F., and Keenan, B. Amplitude-induction gradient of a small-scale (covert) operant. *Journal of the Experimental Analysis of Behavior*, 1963, *6*, 307–315.

Hefferline, R. F., Keenan, B., and Harford, R. A. Escape and avoidance conditioning in human subjects without their observation of the response. *Science*, 1959, *130*, 1338–1339.

Herbert, E. W., Gelfand, D. M., and Hartmann, D. P. Imitation and self-esteem as determinants of self-critical behavior. *Child Development*, 1969, *40*, 421–430.

Hillix, W. A. and Marx, M. H. Response strengthening by information and effect on human learning. *Journal of Experimental Psychology*, 1960, *60*, 97–102.

Homme, L. E. Perspectives in psychology: XXIV. Control of coverants, the operants of the mind. *Psychological Record*, 1965, *15*, 501–511.

Hughes, C. C., Tremblay, M., Rapoport, R. N., and Leighton, A. H. *People of cove and woodlot: Communities from the viewpoint of social psychiatry*. New York: Basic Books, 1960.

Johnson, S. M., and Martin, S. Self-evaluation as conditioned reinforcement. Unpublished manuscript, University of Oregon, 1970.

Kanfer, F. H. Vicarious human reinforcement: A glimpse into the black box. In L. Krasner and L. P. Ullmann (Eds.), *Research in behavior modification*. New York: Holt, 1965. Pp. 244–267.

Kanfer, F. H. Influence of age and incentive conditions on children's self-rewards. *Psychological Reports*, 1966, *19*, 263–274.

Kanfer, F. H. Verbal conditioning: A review of its current status. In T. R. Dixon and D. L. Horton (Eds.), *Verbal behavior and general behavior theory*. Englewood Cliffs, N. J.; Prentice-Hall, 1968. Pp. 254–290.

Kanfer, F. H. Self-regulation: Research, issues and speculation. In C. Neuringer and J. L. Michael (Eds.), *Behavior modification in clinical psychology*. New York: Appleton-Century-Crofts, 1970.

Kanfer, F. H., and Marston, A. R. Conditioning of self-reinforcing responses: An analogue to self-confidence training. *Psychological Reports*, 1963, *13*, 63–70. (a)

Kanfer, F. H., and Marston, A. R. Human reinforcement: Vicarious and direct. *Journal of Experimental Psychology*, 1963, *65*, 292–296. (b)

Kaufman, A., Baron, A., and Kopp, R. E. Some effects of instructions on human operant behavior. *Psychonomic Monograph Supplements*, 1966, *1*, 243–250.

Kelly, R. Comparison of the effects of positive and negative vicarious reinforcement in an operant learning task. *Journal of Educational Psychology*, 1966, *57*, 307–310.

Kolvin, I. "Aversive imagery" treatment in adolescents. *Behaviour Research and Therapy*, 1967, *5*, 245–248.

Lewis, D. J., and Duncan, C. P. Vicarious experience and partial reinforcement. *Journal of Abnormal and Social Psychology*, 1958, *57*, 321–326.

Liebert, R. M., and Allen, M. K. Effects of rule structure and reward magnitude on the acquisition and adoption of self-reward criteria. *Psychological Reports*, 1967, *21*, 445–452.

Liebert, R. M., and Fernandez, L. E. Imitation as a function of vicarious and direct reward. *Developmental Psychology*, 1970, *2*, 230–232.

Liebert, R. M., Hanratty, M., and Hill, J. H. Effects of rule structure and training method on the adoption of a self-imposed standard. *Child Development*, 1969, *40*, 93–101.

Liebert, R. M., and Ora, J. P., Jr. Children's adoption of self-reward patterns: Incentive level and method of transmission. *Child Development*, 1968, *39*, 537–544.

Locke, E. A., Cartledge, N., and Koeppel, J. Motivational effects of knowledge of results. *Psychological Bulletin*, 1968, *70*, 474–485.

Loeb, A., Beck, A. T., Diggory, J. C., and Tuthill, R. Expectancy, level of aspiration, performance, and self-evaluation in depression. *Proceedings of the 75th Annual Convention of the American Psychological Association*, 1967, *2*, 193–194.

Logan, F. A., and Wagner, A. R. *Reward and punishment.* Boston: Allyn and Bacon, 1965.

Lovitt, T. C., and Curtiss, K. Academic response rate as a function of teacher- and self-imposed contingencies. *Journal of Applied Behavior Analysis,* 1969, *2*, 49–53.

McDavid, J. W. Effects of ambiguity of environmental cues upon learning to imitate. *Journal of Abnormal and Social Psychology,* 1962, *65*, 381–386.

McDavid, J. W. Effects of ambiguity of imitative cues upon learning by ob- servation. *Journal of Social Psychology,* 1964, *62*, 165–174.

McGuire, R. J., and Vallance, M. Aversion therapy by electric shock: A simple technique. *British Medical Journal,* 1964, *1*, 151–153.

McMains, M. J., and Liebert, R. M. Influence of discrepancies between suc- cessively modeled self-reward criteria on the adoption of a self-imposed standard. *Journal of Personality and Social Psychology,* 1968, *8*, 166–171.

Marlatt, G. A. Vicarious and direct reinforcement control of verbal behavior in an interview setting. Unpublished doctoral dissertation, Indiana Uni- versity, 1968.

Marlatt, G. A., Jacobsen, E. A., Johnson, D. L., and Morrice, D. J. Effect of exposure to a model receiving varied informational feedback upon con- sequent behavior in an interview. *Journal of Consulting and Clinical Psy- chology,* 1970, *43*, 104–114.

Marlowe, D., Breecher, R. S., Cook, J. B., and Doob, A. N. The approval mo- tive, vicarious reinforcement, and verbal conditioning. *Perceptual and Motor Skills,* 1964, *19*, 523–530.

Marston, A. R. Response strength and self-reinforcement. *Journal of Experi- mental Psychology,* 1964, *68*, 537–540. (a)

Marston, A. R. Variables affecting incidence of self-reinforcement. *Psycho- logical Reports,* 1964, *14*, 879–884. (b)

Marston, A. R. Imitation, self-reinforcement, and reinforcement of another person. *Journal of Personality and Social Psychology,* 1965, *2*, 255– 261. (a)

Marston, A. R. Self-reinforcement: The relevance of a concept in analogue research in psychotherapy. *Psychotherapy: Theory, Research and Prac- tice,* 1965, *2*, 1–5. (b)

Marston, A. R. Determinants of the effects of vicarious reinforcement. *Jour- nal of Experimental Psychology,* 1966, *71*, 550–558.

Marston, A. R. The effect of external feedback upon the rate of positive self- reinforcement. *Journal of Experimental Psychology,* in press. (a)

Marston, A. R. Self-reinforcement and external reinforcement in visual-motor learning. *Journal of Experimental Psychology,* in press. (b)

Miller, M. M. Treatment of chronic alcoholism by hypnotic aversion. *Journal of the American Medical Association,* 1959, *171*, 1492–1495.

Miller, M. M. Hypnotic-aversion treatment of homosexuality. *Journal of the National Medical Association*, 1963, *55*, 411–415.

Miller, N. E. Learnable drives and rewards. In S. S. Stevens (Ed.), *Handbook of experimental psychology*. New York: Wiley, 1951. Pp. 435–472.

Miller, N. E., and Dollard, J. *Social learning and imitation*. New Haven: Yale University Press, 1941.

Miller, R. E. Experimental approaches to the physiological and behavioral concomitants of affective communication in rhesus monkeys. In S. A. Altmann (Ed.), *Social communication among primates*. Chicago: University of Chicago Press, 1967. Pp. 125–134.

Miller, R. E., Banks, J. H., Jr., and Ogawa, N. Communication of affect in "cooperative conditioning" of rhesus monkeys. *Journal of Abnormal and Social Psychology*, 1962, *64*, 343–348.

Miller, R. E., Banks, J. H. Jr. and Ogawa, N. Role of facial expression in "cooperative avoidance conditioning" in monkeys. *Journal of Abnormal and Social Psychology*, 1963, *67*, 24–30.

Miller, R. E., Murphy, J. V., and Mirsky, I. A. Nonverbal communication of affect. *Journal of Clinical Psychology*, 1959, *15*, 155–158.

Mischel, W., and Liebert, R. M. Effects of discrepancies between observed and imposed reward criteria on their acquisition and transmission. *Journal of Personality and Social Psychology*, 1966, *3*, 45–53.

Phillips, R. E. Vicarious reinforcement and imitation in a verbal learning situation. *Journal of Experimental Psychology*, 1968, *76*, 669–670.

Porro, C. R. Effects of the observation of a model's effective responses to her own transgression on resistance to temptation in children. *Dissertation Abstracts*, 1968, *28*, 3064.

Premack, D. Reinforcement theory. In D. Levine (Ed.), *Nebraska symposium on motivation: 1965*. Lincoln: University of Nebraska Press, 1965. Pp. 123–180.

Rosekrans, M. A., and Hartup, W. W. Imitative influences of consistent and inconsistent response consequences to a model on aggressive behavior in children. *Journal of Personality and Social Psychology*, 1967, *7*, 429–434.

Rosenbaum, M. E., and Bruning, J. L. Direct and vicarious effects of variations in percentage of reinforcement on performance. *Child Development*, 1966, *37*, 959–966.

Rosenbaum, M. E., and Hewitt, O. J. The effect of electric shock on learning by performers and observers. *Psychonomic Science*, 1966, *5*, 81–82.

Rosenhan, D., Frederick, F., and Burrowes, A. Preaching and practicing: Effects of channel discrepancy on norm internalization. *Child Development*, 1968, *39*, 291–301.

Ross, S. A. A test of the generality of the effects of deviant preschool models. *Developmental Psychology*, 1971, in press.

Sandler, J., and Quagliano, J. Punishment in a signal avoidance situation. Paper read at the Southeastern Psychological Association, Gatlinburg, Tennessee, 1964.

Sasmor, R. Operant conditioning of a small-scale muscle response. *Journal of the Experimental Analysis of Behavior*, 1966, *9*, 69–85.

Sechrest, L. Implicit reinforcement of responses. *Journal of Educational Psychology*, 1963, *54*, 197–201.

Shafer, J. Self-reinforcement and the devaluation of a model. Unpublished master's thesis, Stanford University, 1965.

Simon, S., Ditrichs, R., and Jamison, N. Vicarious learning of common and uncommon associations in children. *Psychonomic Science*, 1965, *3*, 345–346.

Spielberger, C. D., and De Nike, L. D. Descriptive behaviorism versus cognitive theory in verbal operant conditioning, *Psychological Review*, 1966, *73*, 306–326.

Stein, A. H. Imitation of resistance to temptation. *Child Development*, 1967, *38*, 157–169.

Stone, L. J., and Hokanson, J. E. Arousal reduction via self-punitive behavior. *Journal of Personality and Social Psychology*, 1969, *12*, 72–79.

Stotland, E., and Zander, A. Effects of public and private failure on self-evaluation. *Journal of Abnormal and Social Psychology*, 1958, *56*, 223–229.

Stuart, R. B. Behavioral control of overeating. *Behaviour Research and Therapy*, 1967, *5*, 357–365.

Walters, R. H., Leat, M., and Mezei, L. Inhibition and disinhibition of responses through empathetic learning. *Canadian Journal of Psychology*, 1963, *17*, 235–243.

Walters, R. H., and Parke, R. D. Influence of response consequences to a social model on resistance to deviation. *Journal of Experimental Child Psychology*, 1964, *1*, 269–280.

Walters, R. H., Parke, R. D., and Cane, V. A. Timing of punishment and the observation of consequences to others as determinants of response inhibition. *Journal of Experimental Child Psychology*, 1965, *2*, 10–30.

Weiner, H. Real and imagined cost effects upon human fixed-interval responding. *Psychological Reports*, 1965, *17*, 659–662.

Wilson, W. C. Imitation and learning of incidental cues by preschool children. *Child Development*, 1958, *29*, 393–397.

Wolf, T. M. The effects of multiple modeling on resistance to deviation. Paper read at the Biennial Meeting of the Society for Research in Child Development, Santa Monica, California, 1969.

Wolpe, J. Conditioned inhibition of craving in drug addiction: A pilot experiment. *Behaviour Research and Therapy*, 1965, *2*, 285–288.

THE ROLES OF OVERT RESPONDING AND EXTRINSIC REINFORCEMENT IN "SELF-" AND "VICARIOUS-REIN- FORCEMENT" PHENOMENA AND IN "OBSERVATIONAL LEARNING" AND IMITATION[1]

JACOB L. GEWIRTZ
National Institute of Mental Health

In recent years, issues of both practical and theoretical significance have been raised concerning the roles of overt responding and extrinsic

[1] The author appreciates the dedicated editorial assistance of Laura Rosenthal and Danielle Spiegler in the preparation of this paper. The suggestions made by Donald M. Baer, Albert J. Caron, and Frederick H. Kanfer for improving an early version are also acknowledged with thanks. The opinions expressed herein are those of the author, and do not necessarily represent the position of the NIMH.

reinforcement in behavior acquisition and maintenance. Professor Bandura's work of the past decade (as exemplified by his paper in this volume) has occupied a central place in this literature, generating conceptually provocative examples of human behavior in social contexts. Some of these behavior-change phenomena, including those termed "observational learning," "vicarious reinforcement," "imitation," and "self-reinforcement," have seemed anomalous in terms of the consensual adaptive-learning paradigm of instrumental conditioning that has given the term "reinforcement" much of its contemporary tone. Specifically, on the basis that they appear to involve neither overt responding nor extrinsic reinforcement (or responding without extrinsic reinforcement in the case of "self-reinforcement"), such seemingly anomalous behavior phenomena have sometimes been thought to create conceptual difficulties for contemporary S-R reinforcement-learning approaches and to imply that a theoretical approach using some cognitive terms might somehow better order the phenomena at issue.

In discussing some examples from Professor Bandura's creative and prolific research program, I shall therefore attempt to deal constructively with the larger issue that they imply: In what ways can apparently anomalous, "hyphenated-reinforcement" phenomena such as "vicarious-" and "self-reinforcement" effects (and those of apparent learning through observation and imitation) be explained efficiently and plausibly in a reinforcement-learning approach? I recognize that the heuristic approach I favor is not the only one that in principle could order Professor Bandura's experimental cases, and that conditioning approaches have up to now devoted far too little attention to such topics. All the same, I shall propose that many such phenomena which appear anomalous for a reinforcement-learning conception may, in fact, be readily explicable in terms of routine conditioning concepts, in particular instrumental responding, extrinsic reinforcement and acquired stimulus control. Where possible, I have attempted to integrate my own theoretical assumptions with those of Professor Bandura. However, because I have had difficulty in understanding some assumptions underlying the experimental demonstrations reported in his paper for this volume, I have attempted to approach certain key issues in terms of his earlier works as well. I fear that as a consequence I may have misrepresented Professor Bandura's position on certain points. If this is in fact so, I apologize in advance. I hope the reader will keep in mind that my main purposes in this endeavor are to present a constructive line of reasoning with differential implications for theoretical analysis and research and, where possible, to relate some of the issues involved to the wider theoretical context.

Moreover, it should be made clear at the outset that I do not intend to argue that the instrumental-conditioning approach I have found most useful is necessarily the heuristic panacea for ordering the entire range of systematic response-change phenomena that are conventionally termed learning. Clearly, the controversies of the past four decades on the mechanisms of learning suggest that it is unlikely that a single theoretical model could be applied plausibly at the present time to explaining such diverse phenomena. In this context, there are apparent learning phenomena that cannot readily be ordered with the notions of overt responding and extrinsic reinforcement, just as there are phenomena that are difficult to explain plausibly with a conception (S-S or other) that does not include the role of responding and reinforcement.

At the very least, attempting such an encompassing conceptual solution could preclude an effective focus upon "self-" and "vicarious-reinforcement" processes as well as upon observational, imitative learning. Indeed, I fear that in my attempts to focus on some key conceptual issues raised by Professor Bandura's important program of research, I may not have sufficiently emphasized some of his most interesting results and interpretations, for example, his treatment of the role of contextual conditions in controlling reinforcing stimulus efficacy (and sometimes even directionality). This topic has all too often been neglected in experimental reports, particularly of learning procedures. (My own consideration of the range of contextual factors that can control momentary stimulus function in evoking, cueing, and reinforcing behavior is presented elsewhere [Gewirtz, 1969a].)

On "hyphenated-reinforcement" conceptions. In the context of the open-ended *empirical law of effect* (cf., e.g., McGeoch and Irion, 1952), the operational emphasis of Skinner (e.g., 1938, 1953), and the explicitness of operant-conditioning technology, any identified extrinsic event correlated with a change in the rate of the response upon which it has been made contingent is (defined) a "reinforcer."[2] The basic instrumental-conditioning paradigm has been derived from a wide array of research in simple settings. It has facilitated the discovery of and emphasis on basic principles of acquisition and performance, as well as various qualifying conditions. Moreover, that basic paradigm and those derived from it (e.g., discriminative stimulus control and conditional discrimination) have shown their heuristic utility in ordering a great variety of relatively complex animal and human behavior patterns whose explanation earlier seemed (and to some may still seem) to require more complex principles or processes, or even principles discontinuous with those that govern the

---

[2] Such events have often routinely been termed "reinforcers," regardless of "setting" (i.e., performance context) determinants, the implication being that reinforcers function through the entire range of setting conditions. However, the possibility must be kept in mind that events may operate as reinforcers only for particular responses, in certain discriminative contexts, and/or under very special setting conditions (Gewirtz, 1967, 1969b,c).

simpler behaviors of lower organisms. Even so, approaches that have emphasized the instrumental-conditioning paradigm must be open to the possibility that some behaviors might be acquired or maintained in the absence of what are termed reinforcing stimuli. While it focuses a powerful and ubiquitous class of behavior-influence conditions, the extrinsic-reinforcement conception (that subsumes the empirical law of effect) implies only that there exist stimuli which, when placed in a specified contingency with responses, will increase the rate of some of them. Thus, reinforcers need not exist under all conditions for every response, the contingency described in the definition of "reinforcer" is not the only mechanism associated with changes in instrumental-response strength, and the fact that a stimulus functions as a reinforcer in one context does not preclude its functioning in other stimulus roles in other contexts. As a simple descriptive statement, therefore, the empirical law of effect would be untouched by experimental demonstrations of high-rate responses with no obvious extrinsic (reinforcing) consequences, and most certainly is untouched by observations on the complexity of stimulus control possible in human affairs.

Yet, even in this open-ended frame there are researchers who would attempt to modify the operational-reinforcement conception, via a process of "hyphenation," to encompass cases where the rate of an instrumental response changes systematically (or is maintained) in the apparent absence of extrinsic reinforcing consequences. Qualifiers meant to communicate the essential feature of a set of behavior phenomena in which extrinsic contingencies appear to play no role are appended to the reinforcement term. The result is a set of hyphenated terms like "vicarious-reinforcement," "self-reinforcement," and "intrinsic-reinforcement" (whose usage in the literature has often overlapped such terms as "vicarious-," "imitative-," and "observational-learning," and even "self-control" and "self-evaluation"). Even if these reinforcement qualifiers are meant only to serve as descriptive and not as explanatory concepts, they emphasize the absence rather than the presence of observed consequences. That the very context in which these "hyphenated-reinforcement" terms are used implies flight from the consensual reinforcement notion need not, in itself, preclude their potential utility. However, their use can also de-emphasize the role of acquired discriminative stimulus control, particularly in a context where extrinsic-reinforcement history is not assessed. It is this control that may be the key to understanding many of the phenomena grouped ahistorically under hyphenated-reinforcement concepts.

Professor Bandura has clearly stated in his paper prepared for this volume that he has used the term "vicarious reinforcement" only to describe a phenomenon and not to explain it. However, when considered in terms of the usual instrumental-conditioning approach, a modifier like "vicarious" can suggest that when a model's response is reinforced, an unemitted matching "response" of an observer is also somewhere, somehow, "reinforced," and that the process is thereby explained. Hence, even when a researcher's intention is neither to use those terms to stand for new explanatory concepts nor to imply that an issue has been solved, the use of such hyphenated appellations for seemingly nonextrinsic (reinforcement) phenomena can obscure some potentially relevant features of a phenomenon, especially its relations to standard processes, and specifically the possible dependence of the behavior involved on learned cues from the subject's extrinsic-reinforcement history. The use of such hyphenated terms often seems to suggest that entirely new theories are required to order the phenomena thought to be anomalous, or that it will prove necessary to modify markedly the instrumental-conditioning conception in common use insofar as the concept of reinforcement (and responding) is involved. Both solutions may be premature if they are being sought merely in response to a failure to identify an extrinsic reinforcing event within the range of settings that happen to have been sampled, particularly when there have been remarkably few attempts to manipulate experimentally, or even just to assess, possible antecedent or concurrent extrinsic events in that context to see if the relationships at issue could thereby be explained. Only through a close consideration of the possible dependence of the apparently anomalous phenomena on the wider extrinsic-reinforcement context can the likely continuity of "vicarious-" and "self-reinforcement" phenomena with traditional learning conceptions be demonstrated or ruled out. Serious efforts to apply conditioning concepts can only be catalytic for advances in both theory and research.

For these reasons, our heuristic posture in approaching such hyphenated-reinforcement effects must be a conservative one: to explore the extent to which basic conditioning conceptions of acquired stimulus control can explain contemporaneous behavior-change phenomena that, when considered ahistorically, often appear to have occurred in the absence of overt responding and extrinsic reinforcement. Specifically, earlier learned behavior systems may have relevance to the impact on behavior of stimuli provided under experimental conditions like those of Bandura's studies. A conservative analysis would give attention to such possibly relevant conditioning-history details. However, there have been very few attempts to do so. In this discussion, therefore, I shall emphasize a twofold issue that may be critical to interpreting such phenomena as those of "self-" and "vicarious-reinforcement" and observational learning:

1. the characteristic failure of experimenters working with human

subjects in complex situations (and, indeed, even with infrahuman organisms in relatively simple settings) to implement some
of the necessary controls for relevant past experience; and

2. the apparent continuity of many of the functional relations under-
    lying "self-" and "vicarious-reinforcement" with the basic par-
    adigm of instrumental conditioning in which the operation of
    overt responding and extrinsic reinforcement is fundamental and
    the conception of acquired stimulus control is integral.

My approach throughout will be compatible with earlier attempts to
outline how behavior systems (including seemingly autonomous ones)
depend upon maintaining conditions, considered in the framework of
conditioning histories (Gewirtz, 1961, 1968, 1969c).

"Self-Reinforcement"

"Self-reinforcement" as confounded with responses.   Professor Bandura has proposed that after responses develop through (a) the differential reinforcement, by an environmental agency, of a child's instrumental
response or (b) the observation by the child of the differential "self-
reinforcing" behaviors of a model, subjects are subsequently likely to
reinforce themselves, either overtly (verbally or materially) or covertly,
in a similar selective way when they respond to their own behavior. Thus,
he assumes that both direct reinforcement and modeling can be effective
in transmitting performance standards for self-reinforcement, and that
self-evaluation is an important defining component of self-reinforcing
events.[3] Specifically, he conceives that more than the simple acquisition
of a response class is involved, that the instrumental response is defined
as *worthy* of reinforcement. He assumes that reinforced or modeled responses, insofar as they reflect group norms, will acquire "positive value"
and that nonreinforced or nonmodeled responses (that reflect lower-than-
norm achievement levels) will acquire "negative value." The performance standard (in reference to specific norms) common to various acts

---

[3] In the discussion that follows I shall deal only in passing with the usage of "self-
reinforcement" which implies that the responses at issue occur "for their own sake"
(e.g., Harlow, 1950; Kohlberg, 1963). Some theorists have written that such responses are "intrinsically motivated," based on what appears to be a gratuitously
postulated "motive" to exhibit the behavior (e.g., the motive of exploration, or curiosity, or the "manipulation drive" of Harlow, Harlow, and Meyer, 1950), and that
organisms have a "need" for the sensory stimulation which ensues as a consequence.
Other theorists have postulated that such responses are based upon an "effectance"
or "competence-mastery" motive for "interesting" events or for successful mastery
of a seemingly difficult task (e.g., White, 1959; Kohlberg, 1966, 1969). The issues involved have been more extensively discussed in earlier analyses (e.g., Gewirtz, 1969c).

will eventually be ". . . abstracted and applied to new endeavors."

Professor Bandura has written further: "At this stage the whole process becomes relatively independent of external reinforcement, but remains dependent upon cognitive evaluations based on the match between self-prescribed standards, performance, and the attainments of reference models."[4] Such self-evaluation appears to stand for some sort of complex, intra-psychic, cognitive comparison activity, or at the very least for a simple, covert, self-reinforcing response. However, Bandura's notion of "relative" independence may be nothing more than the notion of intermittent extrinsic reinforcement, for he states: "Once established, patterns of self-reinforcement are thus intermittently reinforced and upheld through selective association [see Bandura, this volume, pp. 263–264]." In this context, an emphasis on the cognitive term "self-evaluation," and even on the term "self-reinforcement," which tends to negate the importance of extrinsic-reinforcement contingencies provided by environmental agencies, seems inconsistent and may be entirely unnecessary.

It is thus my contention that use of a self-reinforcement conception, or the use of inexplicit cognitive terms like "self-evaluation," would be unwarranted in a conditioning analysis. This is because "self-reinforcing" responses (verbal or nonverbal, overt or covert), and those involved in what are generally termed "self-regulatory" processes, self-prescribed behavior standards, the self-administration of extrinsic reinforcers and/or the self-establishment of appropriate setting conditions for them, are readily explicable with the routine conditioning conception of functional response classes (and S-R chains) acquired and maintained under intermittent, extrinsic reinforcement from some environmental agency. Under a conservative conditioning posture, both instrumental training and modeling (i.e., conditional responding in our approach) can be conceived simply as a means by which a discriminated response, defined as reinforceable by an environmental agency, enters the child's repertory. If the response (class) is consistently defined by the reinforcing agency in relation to some group norm, then cues denoting such norms could become part of the definition of the response and therefore discriminative for reinforcement. The notions that a response is discriminated by a subject, that it takes on value connoting worthiness of extrinsic reinforcement, and that performance standards are abstracted and applied to new endeavors are all encompassed in the conception of a functional response class (comprised of diverse yet functionally equivalent behaviors insofar as they all lead to the same consequences in a given context).

---

[4] Aronfreed (1969) has similarly conceived that, in the internalization process, the behavior becomes "independent to some extent" of its external consequences.

The purely conceptual analysis advanced here concerning "self-reinforcement" processes might be interpreted as negating the possible utility of a focus upon overt responses connoting "self-reinforcement," whether or not that term, or terms like "self-control" or "self-evaluation," are actually employed in such attempts. However, I have in no way intended to devalue the considerable importance of Professor Bandura's research on such processes. Regardless of the adequacy of the terms that have been applied to explain or label "self-reinforcement" phenomena, a focus on verbal and other overt responses involved in such processes may be useful for understanding important human behavior patterns and for attempting to modify behavior. For example, overt evaluative responses might be programmed into S-R chains for some purposes. In this context, I would like to close my comments on "self-reinforcement" by considering some general questions about the utility and parsimony of postulating hypothetical concepts that stand for what appear to be unindexed, implicit mediating processes.

Mediating representational events and covert self-reinforcement. Psychological theorists differ on how they would attempt to bridge the conceptual gap between experience and later response outcomes. Thus, theorists may differ on: the nature and number of concepts to employ in this venture; the labels and heuristic flavor to assign to those concepts (for instance, objective or subjective-cognitive); the concepts' levels of abstraction (in the sense of being differentially remote from the observable events to which they are tied); and even the utility of postulating mediating gap-bridging processes at all.

Professor Bandura has employed a number of terms like "covert responses" to stand for sequential aspects of the mediating process he postulates between experience with stimuli and subsequent responding. He has assumed that perceptual and symbolic responses representing the sequence of stimuli provided during the occurrence of the model's response can be acquired during observation. These "internal representational processes" mediate subsequent behavior reproduction and therefore play a prominent role in observational learning. However, these hypothetical terms seem only loosely tied to antecedent and consequent operations, and to each other.[5] When independent operations are not specified for defining a concept, or for indexing values of implicit, intervening representational or cognitive processes, the parsimony and heuristic utility

---

[5] My comments here could apply also to the "internal representational responses" ("motoric" and "verbal") or "mediating responses" employed by a number of conditioning researchers and theorists of molar processes (e.g., Berlyne, 1965; Kendler and Kendler, 1962; Miller, 1948; Osgood, 1953) and to the "representational cognitions" and "cognitive templates" employed by some theorists who favor cognitive terms (e.g., Aronfreed, 1968, 1969).

of positing such terms or processes may be questioned. Thus, when intra-psychic cognitive-act euphemisms, phrased in an immediate-experience or common sense flavored language, are used to characterize the bases for a subject's behavior in a given context, it is often difficult to determine whether the locus of such heuristic terms is meant to be the head of the subject or (the theory) of the researcher. To be sure, the use of such concepts may reflect only that a researcher feels the organism's actions are governed by concepts (e.g., "schema," "cognitive structure") that are more abstract or complex than that of an "S-R bond." Even so, in line with Reichenbach's (1938, 1951) distinction, these terms often seem relevant more to the researcher's operations within his own, informal prescientific "context of discovery" than to the required scientific "context of verification."

In an earlier paper, Bandura (1965b) had assumed that implicit cue-producing response mediators could be experimentally manipulated, that they could be conditioned and extinguished according to the same laws as those governing explicit forms of behavior. He has shown that various instructional setting conditions can be implemented during prior training (observation) to facilitate subsequent test performance. These setting operations include attentional-highlighting or dimensional-appreciation procedures, or even an observer's attempts to code into "vivid images" or to describe in concrete verbal terms the details of a model's behaviors while he is viewing them (e.g., Gerst, 1968, as cited in Bandura, 1969b). The functional relations into which these operations enter with behaviors may constitute a contribution to the experimental lore about the imitative process, and thus may have a utility independent of any particular theory. Nevertheless, the only "indices" of implicit response processes seem to be the very imitative-behavior outcomes the implicit responses are postulated to explain, or the differential instructional operations that established them. If this is so, it would be difficult to see how the instructional sets can be said to constitute the experimental manipulation of implicit, symbolic mediating responses. Further, such operations do not necessarily show that the particular imaginal or representational processes hypothesized are the processes that mediate the recall of copying responses. Indeed, attempts to explain the effects on behavior of instructional-set conditions in terms of implicit representational or cognitive responses could seem gratuitous, however intuitively plausible such processes might seem to a researcher operating within the "context of discovery."

Moreover, explanations that merely hypothesize mental processes or events to mediate between molar behaviors and overt controlling stimuli may even be detrimental to the search for the relevant functional relations. This could be the case if those explanations lead to research that does not increase our knowledge of the ways stimulus variables control behavior, but rather that attempts to validate or define the hypothesized mediating events themselves. An alternative approach would hold that statements of functional relations involving controlling stimuli, qualifying setting conditions (e.g., instructions), and repertory behaviors can stand independently, and parsimoniously, as an adequate first-order explanation (e.g., Gewirtz, 1969b). Of course, these functional relations might be grouped under more general relations or propositions for particular purposes of theory or application.

"Vicarious-Reinforcement"

Professor Bandura has found that extrinsic positive reinforcement administered to a demonstrator-model contingent upon a particular behavior can increase the likelihood that an observer will match that behavior. He and others have termed this phenomenon "vicarious reinforcement" (Hill, 1960; Bandura, Ross, and Ross, 1963). Professor Bandura's survey indicates that greater response changes occur under vicarious reinforcement than under a condition in which the observed response of the model is not reinforced. Further, greater response changes have been found under vicarious-reinforcement than under direct extrinsic reinforcement. In light of what he has termed its informational and its stimulus-enhancement functions, Professor Bandura considers the vicarious-reinforcement procedure to be particularly effective, relative to instrumental training, when there is ambiguity concerning the appropriate response and situational context for reinforcement. However, he assumes that instrumental conditioning might be more effective for the acquisition of responses connoting complex skills, having in mind, I suppose, the response-shaping procedure that would facilitate bringing a topographically new response into the subject's repertory. Furthermore, Bandura suggests that effortful behaviors cannot be sustained by vicarious-reinforcement procedures for more than brief periods in the absence of their extrinsic reinforcement.

Professor Bandura has attributed the short-term superiority of vicarious-reinforcement effects over direct instrumental conditioning to the temporarily distracting effects of interfering responses under direct extrinsic reinforcement, for instance the anticipation of reinforcement or attending to it upon its receipt. Further, the experiments involved required that the subject learn to discriminatively perform responses already in his repertory. Thus, Bandura has noted that reinforcement to a model may serve an informational or cueing function by identifying for the observer-imitator those responses (in his repertory) that lead to positive or negative reinforcement in given discriminative contexts, as well as an incentive-motivation function by evoking in the observer the anticipation of (similar) reinforcement. Under an instrumental-conditioning conception, it would be expected that after the child-observer has been routinely reinforced for the imitative matching of various demonstrator-models' reinforced responses, reinforcement provided contingent upon a model's behavior could come to function as a generalized cue for a high probability of extrinsic reinforcement to the observer when he matches that behavior or as a cue indicating the permissibility of reproducing that behavior.

Another possible explanation of some vicarious-reinforcement phenomena in terms of an instrumental-learning conception is that the child-observer's responses, like those for which a demonstrator-model is reinforced, may have been extrinsically reinforced in the same settings, whether emitted independently or matched to a model's responses; whereas the child-observer's responses, like those for which a model is not reinforced, or for which he is punished, are *not* likely to have been reinforced there. Often, therefore, the reinforced response that is to be "matched" may already be in the observer's repertory under the control of the very same cues as those which occasioned the model's response. In such contexts, the demonstrator-model's presence may facilitate the discriminative control process, but would otherwise be irrelevant (except perhaps in that it could obscure the process at issue). This conception constitutes a recurring theme in the extensive animal literature on learning by observation (cf., e.g., Hall, 1963).

Professor Bandura has observed that direct extrinsic reinforcement and vicarious-reinforcement procedures inevitably occur together under natural conditions, and that their joint effects may be of greater importance than their independent effects. Indeed, I would imagine that the combination of instrumental training and "vicarious-reinforcement" procedures may well account for the relatively rapid socialization learning that often occurs in natural settings. However, a procedure providing direct reinforcement for responding and the vicarious-reinforcement procedure that provides discriminative cues for matching responses would seem to represent only the difference between obvious reinforcing stimulus control and discriminative stimulus control that necessarily implies extrinsic reinforcement for matching. Indeed, the mechanisms outlined by Professor Bandura to account for response changes that accompany vicarious-reinforcement operations would seem to depend on at least occasional extrinsic reinforcement for the matching responses. Thus, it appears that the instrumental-conditioning paradigm plays a key role in vicarious-reinforcement behavior changes under both Bandura's conception in this volume and the one I shall detail in the next section. However,

the use of such an hyphenated-reinforcement label may obscure the underlying processes and may even imply that a process discontinuous with
instrumental conditioning is involved.

Although Bandura's conceptualization of the conditions under which
vicarious reinforcement operates must inevitably rely on the assumption
of relevant prior learning, the role of an organism's reinforcement history
is only implied in his treatment of vicarious reinforcement. The details
of reinforcement history are important not only because vicarious-
reinforcement effects seem to represent the functioning of learned discriminative stimulus control, but also because Bandura assumes that
vicarious-reinforcement procedures influence only those responses that
are already in an observer's repertory. Bandura has conceived that new
responses can enter an observer-learner's repertory via mere observation
of the model's response and that, once acquired, response performance
can change as a function of observing reinforcement provided contingent
upon the model's response. That is, mere observation (as in observational
learning) provides the basis for the acquisition of a new response, and
viewing of the reinforcement of a model's response (as in vicarious reinforcement) represents a basis for the performance of a response already
in the observer's repertory.

I realize that few theoretical approaches have articulately, or even
consistently, handled the traditional distinction between performance and
acquisition (on this issue, cf., e.g., Estes' survey — 1971). Indeed, some
of them may not even emphasize such a distinction. For instance, under
an operant approach like that outlined in this chapter, the term *conditioning* has been used to encompass (a) the entry of a new response into
the subject's repertory (as via a shaping procedure), (b) the acquisition
of initial or new (e.g., through "stimulus fading") discriminative control
over a repertory response, as well as (c) responding at the asymptotic
level for stimulus control. Momentary contextual-setting (i.e., performance) conditions can operate to make stimuli salient for behavior in
each of these three cases. However, there are conceptualizations concen-
trating upon overt responding and reinforcement that have more formally
distinguished between acquisition and performance factors, for instance
in terms of longer-term associative-learning factors and momentary performance (e.g., "drive") factors that interact to predict responding (cf.,
e.g., Hull, 1943, 1952). Thus, the distinction between acquisition and
performance apparently made by Bandura (e.g., 1969b; Bandura and
Walters, 1963) does not take incisive hold of the issue that the acquisition-
performance distinction has typically implied for theorists. In particular,
his distinction emphasizes not the momentary performance (e.g., "energizing") conditions for repertory behaviors, but rather the occurrence of
repertory responses in a new discriminative context, as in the vicarious-

reinforcement case. This usage converges on the operant case of the acquisition of new discriminative stimulus control over a repertory response — conditioning type (b) above. In this context, it is hard to see the meaningfulness of Bandura's distinction.

The conditioning approach to imitative-matching behavior, that I shall detail in the next section, is that vicarious reinforcement can be conceived to be simply a subcase of apparent observational learning. The reinforcement provided contingent upon the model's response in vicarious reinforcement is thought to represent a special case of conditional responding, where reinforcement to the model would indicate to the observer that his matching response in that context is very likely to be reinforced. This emphasis on discriminative stimulus control is very much like Bandura's notion of an informational mechanism. Further, Professor Bandura's observation that vicarious-reinforcement procedures alone cannot sustain effortful behavior over more than brief periods, while extrinsic reinforcement usually can, is compatible with a key feature of the conception I shall emphasize: The entire conditional-responding system of the observer that can connote observational learning, and vicarious reinforcement as well, must be maintained by at least intermittent extrinsic reinforcement for matching responses. What follows is a historical and functional analysis of some phenomena of observational or imitative learning, including those of vicarious reinforcement.

Observational Learning, Vicarious Reinforcement, and Conditional Responding

Observational learning: a pervasive and focal issue. The phenomenon of vicarious reinforcement involves some operational overlap with those phenomena that have been grouped under the broader heading of "observational learning." A subject is reported to match the behavior of a demonstrator-model in an experimental setting after he has simply observed that behavior, even when he has not overtly performed the matching response, when reinforcers are administered neither to him nor to the model, and when the first appearance of the matching response is delayed for lengthy periods of time. A discussion of this more general case of "observational" or "imitative" learning can provide the conceptual frame for some of the issues I have noted about the vicarious-reinforcement phenomena reported by Professor Bandura and others, and for an alternative conception that I shall propose.

Although few would question that the phenomenon descriptively termed observational learning is a common occurrence, theorists differ on how they would explain this phenomenon. In different ways, Bandura

(1965b, 1969b),[6] Hilgard and Bower (1966), and John, Chesler, Bartlett, and Victor (1968) appear to assume that learning by observation is a primary, prepotent acquisition process, a capacity of the organism as it were, rather than an outcome of a conventional learning process, a possibility that, for instance, this writer and some others have suggested (Gewirtz and Stingle, 1968; Gewirtz, 1969c; Rosenbaum and Arenson, 1968).[7] Bandura has recently held that, while conceptions that emphasize instrumental conditioning and reinforcement can account for the acquired control over previously learned matching responses, they fail to explain how new responses are acquired through observation alone. On the basis mainly of Bandura's earlier work (1962, 1965b), Hilgard and Bower (1966) have emphasized that observational (imitative) learning is a more efficient and ubiquitous means for establishing new responses than shaping via differential extrinsic reinforcement (but that an optimal application might be to use both methods in conjunction). Indeed, compared to routine instrumental-training procedures, the efficiency of apparent learning by observation, in experienced organisms in certain training contexts, has prompted the conclusion by John et al. (1968) that instrumental conditioning ". . . may well be a phenomenon of limited relevance, utilizing relatively unnatural mechanisms [p.1491]."

The controversy among learning approaches as to whether or not a primary form of learning can occur through exposure or observation in the absence of explicit responses by a viewing organism (and reinforcement) began even before the turn of this century. The underlying issue has been appearing almost routinely through the years in diverse comparative analyses performed with a variety of infrahuman species under such overlapping headings as *imitation, observational learning, suggestibility*, and *social facilitation* (cf., e.g., Thorndike, 1898; Berry, 1908; Haggerty, 1909; Yerkes, 1934; Warden and Jackson, 1935; Crawford

---

[6]To account for this phenomenon, Bandura (e.g., 1969b) has applied a stimulus-contiguity conception of observational learning. Specifically, during exposure to the sequence of stimuli controlling and representing a model's exemplary behavior, perceptual and symbolic responses standing for those stimuli can be acquired by the observer-learner. The presumed recall of these "internal representational processes" will mediate-guide subsequent imitative behavior reproduction. Such a contiguity conception of observational, imitative learning would thus depend upon postulated "internal processes" whose utility I have questioned earlier. Furthermore, it fails to emphasize the case when an observer does not acquire a response that matches the model's, although Bandura does specify some conditions under which a subject's behaviors will be matched to a model's. In the context of this very general S-S contiguity explanation for the acquisition of imitative behaviors through observation, Bandura appears to have emphasized the conditions under which matching *performance* will occur rather than how such behaviors are originally *acquired*.

[7]To be complete here, it should be noted that the logical possibility that a primary observational-learning process may be a precondition for instrumental conditioning has also not been heretofore considered.

and Spence, 1939; Miller and Dollard, 1941; Herbert and Harsh, 1944; Adler, 1955; Church, 1957a,b, 1959; Hall, 1963). This issue has appeared, as well, in analyses of (generalized) *imitation* and *identification* in humans, and recently also of *observational learning, social facilitation, social influence, vicarious experience,* and *vicarious reinforcement* (e.g., Humphrey, 1921; Miller and Dollard, 1941; Sears, 1957; deCharms and Rosenbaum, 1960; Mowrer, 1960; Bandura and Walters, 1963; Bandura, 1965b; Kanfer, 1965; Baer, Peterson and Sherman, 1967; Allport, 1968; Gewirtz and Stingle, 1968; Rosenbaum and Arenson, 1968; Gewirtz, 1969c). The very same issue appears to have come to a focus also in what has seemed to be the methodologically indeterminate controversy on *latent learning* that began in the late 1920's, and is by now a traditional one in psychology (Tolman, 1959; see Kimble, 1961, for a brief summary of the issues). It may also occasionally have been involved in discussions comparing simple stimulus exposure with overt responding (and reinforcement) in *perceptual learning* (e.g., Gibson, 1969), as well as of such phenomena as *incidental learning* and the acquisition of *superstitious* behavior.

In my discussion of observational learning, I shall first consider the possibility that instances of apparent learning by observation may represent highly efficient but straightforward forms of instrumental conditioning. I shall next consider the possibility that apparently rapid, even errorless, learning by observation may be the outcome of various types of prior learning. Finally, I shall detail how a conditional-responding process based upon instrumental-conditioning principles can account for many apparent observational-learning and imitative phenomena. In this context, I shall emphasize the assumption (much like Bandura's) that extrinsic reinforcement of another's response, the basis for the concept of vicarious reinforcement, may be conceived as representing to an observer only a discriminative cue that his own matching response is likely to be extrinsically reinforced. The conceptual tack I shall follow in my analysis details implications for differential, theoretical, and experimental analyses. At the very least, I hope to contribute to bringing about a better balance between alternative theoretical conceptions of the bases of observational-learning phenomena.

Observational learning as an efficient form of instrumental conditioning. Researchers of observational learning, even those who appear to have argued for its primacy, have rarely attempted to rule out the possibility that the phenomena so labeled may not warrant a learning classification that is distinct from instrumental conditioning. Compared to a routine trial-and-error procedure, apparent learning by observation may often represent only a case of instrumental conditioning that has been made more efficient by the presence and actions of a demonstrator-model. The demonstrator-model's actions may:

1. highlight for the observer-learner the relevant (functional) discriminative stimulus features in the situation;
2. make more likely the initial occurrence of the appropriate response of the observer-learner (through a process like "guidance" or "shaping"); and/or
3. preclude the observer-learner from exhibiting irrelevant responses or sequences.

The possibility that a demonstrator-model's presence may simply constitute a highly efficient instrumental-response training procedure has been noted by a number of writers over the years (e.g., Thorndike, 1898; Spence, 1937; Miller and Dollard, 1941; Church, 1957a; deCharms and Rosenbaum, 1960; Hall, 1963). This learning-through-observation case would thus conform to the "same-behavior," rather than the "matched-behavior," paradigm of Miller and Dollard (1941) (whose work under the heading of *imitation* has represented an important focus, within the S-R tradition, on the phenomena of apparent learning via observation). This possible interpretation may apply particularly when the demonstrator-model has some special relationship to an observer-learner. For example, even for young organisms with limited experience (such as the nine- to ten-week-old kittens of Chesler, 1969), stimuli associated with a mother demonstrator-model may differentially evoke orienting and interactive responses which could facilitate the selection and initial occurrence of the correct response that might then appear (but would not functionally be) matched to the model's response. Moreover, responses not clearly in the observer's repertory are rarely evidenced in the observational learning of animals (Hall, 1963). Thus, a modeled response may often already be in an observer's repertory, and some of the stimuli in the situation may already control the observer's "matching" response. The case for a primary acquisition process based on demonstrations of apparent learning-through-observation phenomena in animal species can almost routinely be impeached by failure to take account of such characteristically uncontrolled considerations.

Observational learning as an outcome of prior learning.   There is an overlapping issue that may be even more critical for the analysis of observational-learning and vicarious-reinforcement phenomena like those that have been reported by Professor Bandura: A predictable outcome of straightforward acquired stimulus control might appear to be an instance of rapid, often instantaneous, learning through observation to those unfamiliar with an organism's learning history. Hence, it is thought that only through the close scrutiny of the possible dependence of observational-learning effects on the extrinsic reinforcement histories of experienced organisms can the continuity or discontinuity of those phenomena with traditional learning conceptions be demonstrated definitively. However, I have noted that none of the many researchers in the area has as yet implemented the necessary experimental controls (or assessments) for possibly relevant experience, to rule out the possibility that much of what has been termed observational learning may represent a derived rather than a primary acquisition process. This seems to be due only in part to the fact that such controls are typically difficult to implement methodologically.

There are at least three ways in which past learning experiences may be capable of affecting performance in subsequent observational contexts to give the appearance of learning-by-observation:

1. An observer's response like that of a demonstrator-model may have been extrinsically reinforced in the same setting whether emitted independently or matched to the model's response. Thus, the response may already be in an observer's repertory, under the control of the very cues that occasioned the model's response.
2. Stimuli that have earlier acquired discriminative value in a given context may rapidly come to control an observer's responses in a new but not very different experimental situation. That is, an event which functions as a discriminative stimulus in one context may be salient in another, similar, context. Such an event may acquire control of a new response more rapidly there than may other, initially unfamiliar events, giving the appearance of learning by observation. This earlier learning and that under number 1 above may have occurred routinely under instrumental conditioning or some corollary paradigm, like adventitious, spurious, or incidental learning (cf., Church, 1957a, b; Herrnstein, 1966; Skinner, 1948, 1953).[s]
3. An organism may have acquired a *learning set* across exposure occasions, i.e., he may have learned to learn-by-observation. On

[s]In connection with incidental learning, which involves the pairing or confounding of a previously nonfunctional stimulus with a functional discriminative stimulus, a dominant response can often be acquired error-free (as via Terrace's [1966] fading method). As the number of response alternatives increases, this procedure becomes increasingly more efficient than instrumental training (Church, 1957b). A response may also be acquired and maintained on the basis of an accidental response-reinforcer contingency ("superstitious" learning), for instance by the intermittent extrinsic reinforcement of an independent, but concurrent, response. The rapid, often errorless, acquisition of control over an observer's response, following earlier exposure to an obscure incidental- or similar adventitious-learning procedure, can give the appearance of learning by observation.

the basis of similar relations among stimuli in a series of diverse simultaneous-discrimination problems, correct responding on later problems may occur more rapidly over successive trials than on earlier problems, even to the point where correct responding occurs when new problems are first presented. Termed "learning-to-learn" (Harlow, 1959) and "rule" and "strategy learning" (Gagné, 1968, 1970), this process may constitute a case of transfer in which one set of discriminative stimuli has been substituted for another, and at least partial discriminative control over responding is maintained.

Thus, on the bases either that rapid, often errorless, behavior changes (giving the appearance of learning by observation) may simply be the result of routine instrumental conditioning, adventitious learning, or a "learning-to-learn" pattern acquired in earlier situations, *or* that the presence and actions of a demonstrator-model may merely expedite the process of routine instrumental conditioning, there exist ample grounds for caution when emphasizing the primacy of an observational-learning process.

In this context, it is puzzling that neither Bandura, in his various writings, nor authors like Hilgard and Bower (1966) and John et al. (1968), have taken into account much of the extensive literature of the past half-century on apparent learning by observation and the issues (and caveats) therein. For instance, in their important text on learning theories, Hilgard and Bower have documented a good part of their argument against the adequacy or generality of stimulus-response approaches to learning almost entirely on the basis of Bandura's conceptual analysis of observational learning (and its distinction from shaping and instrumental conditioning) and his research into some of the variables that influence it. Yet, those researches have been carried out with *experienced* (if young) humans whose possibly relevant conditioning histories were uncontrolled and unassessed (e.g., Bandura, 1962, 1965b).

The questions concerning the relation between apparent learning through observation and instrumental learning can therefore be considered open, almost as open perhaps as when Thorndike (1898) reported his pioneering analysis of associative and imitative processes in animals at the end of the last century. In this context, more than a tentative conception of the primacy of observational learning, much less a conclusion about its generality, would be premature at this time. What follows is a brief outline of a heuristically plausible conditioning approach to what has been termed observational learning (including the subcase of vicarious reinforcement).

Observational learning as a conditional-responding process. In the framework of the matched-behavior (copying) imitation paradigm (Miller and Dollard, 1941; Skinner, 1953), the behavioral changes connoting observational learning in children can be explained in terms of basic instrumental-conditioning procedures routinely involved in adult-child interaction, in particular as they are focused in a matching-to-sample, conditional-responding conception (Lashley, 1938; Cumming and Berryman, 1965). Under this paradigm it is thought that a functional imitative response class containing a potentially unlimited number of instrumental responses *matched* to diverse reinforced and nonreinforced responses of models (or one model) can be acquired through the routine intermittent, extrinsic reinforcement of some members of that response class in the discriminative contexts controlling the models' responses (Gewirtz, 1969c; Gewirtz and Stingle, 1968).

The first matching responses by the subject will occur either through physical assistance or through instrumental training. This training could be via shaping procedures in the case of responses not already in an individual's repertory or via stimulus fading or more conventional procedures for responses already in the repertory but not yet under the desired discriminative stimulus control. Subsequently, these responses are likely to be strengthened and maintained by direct extrinsic reinforcement from environmental agents. The result is a class of diverse but functionally equivalent matching behaviors that is maintained by extrinsic reinforcement provided on an intermittent schedule. Additions to that matching-response class routinely occur, and differences in response content are thought to play a minimal role as long as the responses are members of the imitative-response class as defined functionally by reinforcing agents. As reinforced responses in this functional matching-response class are diverse, and under intermittent extrinsic reinforcement, discrimination between matched behaviors that have been reinforced and those that have not is unlikely to occur, and some matching responses that are never directly reinforced will therefore persist unless they are specifically punished or are incompatible with stronger responses in the subject's repertory (Baer and Sherman, 1964; Lovaas, Berberich, Perloff, and Schaeffer, 1966; Baer, Peterson, and Sherman, 1967). On this basis, novel matching responses (in terms of content) will continue to enter the functional imitative class of the subject. Instances where the observer-imitator does not immediately exhibit the matching response, and/or it appears that he has not received extrinsic reinforcement when he has imitated, can be explained by the facts that:

1. The matching-response class can vary in content.
2. The extrinsic maintaining reinforcement (from various environmental agencies) can be intermittent.
3. There can be many models.

4.   The matching response can be reinforced even when there are lengthy delays between the demonstrator-model's response and the observer's imitation of it, or when the model is not present.

Individuals' responses can thus come under a complex type of conditional stimulus control in which both cues from the demonstrator-model's response and contextual cues indicate that matching the model's response will lead to reinforcement. Initially, cues for extrinsic reinforcement are likely to be identical with the discriminative context in which the demonstrator-model emits his response. However, after the matching-response class is acquired by an individual in the same discriminative context as that for the demonstrator-model's responding, it will often be reinforced extrinsically in other discriminative contexts, for instance when the model is absent or when he has not emitted the response. These additional contexts can also come to control subsequent responding (a process similar to that of stimulus fading). The matching-response class thus can become subject to the same contingencies as are other instrumental-response classes; and given that a discrimination is established between contexts in which matching will be reinforced and those in which it will not, the matching-to-sample conditional-responding paradigm would seem to provide a parsimonious and useful analogy to the acquisition and maintenance of the (functional) matching-response class (also termed imitation) Gewirtz and Stingle, 1968; Sherman, Saunders, and Brigham, 1970).

Both observational learning and conditional responding under intermittent extrinsic reinforcement involve an observer-imitator's matching his response to the response of a model in a given discriminative context and, in my view, therefore, may be functionally equivalent in the range of settings considered. (Moreover, the theoretical approach outlined here can also order many phenomena that, to some, have connoted "intrinsic reinforcement" or "intrinsic motivation" [Gewirtz, 1969b].) Nevertheless, there are some differences to be considered between the imitative-matching paradigm that apparently characterizes much of the socialization process in the life setting and the matching-to-sample paradigm for conditional responding often used in the laboratory (Gewirtz and Stingle, 1968).

In the matching-to-sample discrimination paradigm, a subject ("observer-imitator") is reinforced when he routinely employs a simple standard response (like a lever-press) to "select" from an *array* of stimuli the one that exactly matches the conditional, sample stimulus (usually displayed concurrently or just prior to the presentation of the comparison-stimulus array). In the imitative-matching paradigm there are no obvious comparison stimuli, but a *single* stimulus is presented to which the response match is or is not made by the subject. The stimulus to be matched in the imitation situation is provided by a response of a demonstrator-model, and the observer-imitator matches it by making a similar response that is reinforced. In natural settings, the demonstrator-model's response may be one of a potentially unlimited number, the observer-imitator's response may vary along many stimulus dimensions from the demonstrator-model's, and the criteria for reinforcement of an adequate match may vary with each reinforcing agency and with aspects of the wider context. Furthermore, there can be delays between presentation of the stimulus to be matched and the observer's matching response.

However, these differences are in no way conceived to impeach the heuristic analogy I have proposed between the imitative-matching and the matching-to-sample paradigms. Instead, they appear merely to reflect a methodological distinction: The imitative case has been studied mostly in life settings, whereas the matching-to-sample case has typically been studied in contrived experimental situations (involving formal constraints, where, for instance, variations in response content are minimized and a precise match to the sample is usually possible). It appears reasonable to assume that the matching-to-sample situation could be designed so that the content-meaning of the standard response (denoted by the stimulus to which it corresponds) could approximate the range of topographic content values that can characterize an imitative response in a natural setting. (This will be particularly so when the stimuli of the comparison array are graded to represent instances along a physical-stimulus dimension.) Conversely, an imitative-response situation could be established to limit the number of content alternatives, even to include a case where responses can vary along a single topographic dimension of response similarity. Indeed, it is likely that many natural situations contain implicit situational constraints that limit the number of responses in the array of the observer-subject's alternatives. (More could be done to assess such constraining conditions in experiments conducted in life settings.)

It is therefore my assumption that the conditional-responding paradigm can constitute a credible model for approaching the general case of imitative matching, including outcomes connoting learning through observation. However, Professor Bandura (1969a, p. 123) has suggested that modeling and matching-to-sample performances cannot be equated as we have proposed (Gewirtz and Stingle, 1968). He has held that although a person can make errorless choices on a matching-to-sample comparison (for example, between a sample Wagnerian recital and a comparison array of operatic arias), that person may not be able to perform the (vocal) behavior exhibited in the sample. Therefore, he has written that accurate stimulus discrimination is a precondition for, but not equivalent to, observational learning. I shall attempt to show here that the distinction Bandura has emphasized in no way impeaches the heuristic analogy between the imitative-matching and the matching-to-sample paradigms that I have proposed.

An observer-imitator's inability to perform certain responses with the content or quality of the demonstrator-model does not imply that an imitative response cannot be made. What the matching-to-sample analogy emphasizes is the *attempt* of the observer-imitator to match the demonstrator-model's response. Deficiencies in the matching response (along dimensions of quality, amplitude, latency, etc.) due simply to limitations in the ability of the observer-imitator to match the demonstrator-model's response are often to be expected, and are thought irrelevant to demonstrating the essentials of the process of conditional stimulus control that is at issue. Thus, when a young child puffs a candy cigarette or turns the pages of a book after viewing his father smoking a cigarette or reading a book, it would seem that, to the best of his ability, the child is matching his behaviors to those of the model. The matching-to-sample paradigm de-emphasizes the skill and knowledge of the observer-imitator in making the conditional matching response, while it emphasizes entirely the process whereby the matching response (however similar to the demonstrator-model's response it might be) comes systematically under the control of the cues provided by the demonstrator-model's behavior.

It has been noted that relating the various observational-learning and vicarious-reinforcement researches to our theoretical conceptions can be complicated by the fact that animal and human subjects will have extensive reinforcement histories relevant to the conditions of an experiment. While this pertinent experience will typically confound a simple interpretation of the functional relations reported, I have noted that it could also tempt a researcher to seek a new explanatory concept to rationalize a set of possibly anomalous results. For example, a response being conditioned may already be contained in the subject's repertory, and it may have been extrinsically reinforced in the very same setting as the demonstrator-model's; or the imitative response class may be under the control of the same discriminative stimuli as those setting the occasion for the model's response. Hence, when the relationship between subjects' reinforcement histories and the training and test conditions of an experiment are not known, straightforward discriminative stimulus control may erroneously be thought to merit a "motivational" (or setting condition — Gewirtz, 1967, 1969a) interpretation; and learning that is simply an end result of a conventional instrumental-training or conditional-responding process may erroneously be conceived to constitute a prepotent learning-by-observation process.

Bandura (1965a) himself has commented on the inevitability of extrinsic reinforcement of matching responses during human social development, since models typically exhibit responses from cultural repertories proved effective in stimulus settings. As he then noted, observational learning (and vicarious reinforcement), purportedly demonstrated in experimental work with children, may simply reflect prior instrumental learning for which the requisite experimental control conditions unfortunately are impractical. Thus Bandura suggested, in that 1965a paper, that definitive tests of this theoretical issue might require the use of infrahuman subjects whose reinforcement histories could be more readily controlled. (As our earlier brief survey of the literature on learning by observation in diverse infrahuman species has shown, the relevant controls have rarely been attempted, even with animal subjects.) It is simply such an emphasis on the importance of relevant earlier experience for observational learning and "vicarious reinforcement" that is recommended here, following from the argument that it is quite plausible to assume that humans (and other mammalian species) must *learn* to learn by observation (modeling). It has been seen that some of Bandura's previous writings and his paper in this volume permit one to assume that common learning experiences could predispose a group of experienced children toward learning by observation in familiar situations.

It has been argued that the imitative behavior conception of conditional-responding can account for most, perhaps all, of the phenomena grouped under observational learning in children. Because extrinsically reinforced imitative performance is likely in life settings prior to a subject's exposure to a model in observational-learning or vicarious-reinforcement research designs, the conditional-responding conception would seem to be a parsimonious one for an (initial) approach to the general problem of explaining behavioral matching in children. This concept can provide a useful framework for much of the research that remains to be done and, at the very least, a frame for the controls that are yet to be implemented. Only when appropriate controls are exercised over subjects' prior experiences relevant to experimental conditions does it become possible to begin to uncover the mechanism underlying observer-matching behaviors.

It is recalled that imitation and identification phenomena, which overlap those termed observational learning and vicarious-reinforcement, have been widely thought to represent a very different type of socialization learning than that of direct tuition (e.g., Aronfreed, 1967, 1968, 1969; Bandura, 1967, 1969b; Sears, 1957; and Sears, Rau, and Alpert, 1965). In contrast, my thesis has been that observational learning and vicarious-reinforcement may be conceived as representing only a derivative of instrumental conditioning (specifically, a conditional-responding process), and that it would be illusory to hold that this type of learning takes place outside a context of direct instrumental training and extrinsic reinforcement from socializing agents. The only other difference between the two processes appears to be that socializing (i.e., reinforcing) agents tend to focus less on immediate socialization goals and hence to be somewhat less explicit about the responses the child may acquire through imitative learning than through instrumental training, where their focus is on clearly specified outcomes, i.e., single overt responses and discriminable reinforcing stimuli in a well-defined discriminative context.

Vicarious-reinforcement.   In the preceding section I detailed the assumption that a child will often be directly reinforced in life settings for matching (imitating) various demonstrator-models' reinforced and nonreinforced responses. Vicarious-reinforcement phenomena can be conceived simply as a subcase of the conditional-responding matching-to-sample behavior pattern that can be acquired and maintained on this basis. Under the assumption (much like Bandura's) that the child's behaviors that are similar to those for which a demonstrator-model is reinforced are generally also likely to be reinforced, reinforcement provided contingent upon a model's response, that characterizes the vicarious-reinforcement procedure, could come to function as a cue for a high probability of extrinsic reinforcement to the child when he matches that behavior (Gewirtz and Stingle, 1968). Alternatively, reinforcement to a model could function as a cue indicating the permissibility of reproducing behaviors that are not generally sanctioned (Walters, Parke, and Cane, 1965).

However, no matter how often the model's response is reinforced in the child-observer's presence, that observer would not be expected to match his response to the model's unless he himself has been at least occasionally extrinsically reinforced for such matching. It would be expected that if the pattern of discriminative conditions were reversed, that is, if the observer-learner were reinforced relatively less often for matching behaviors for which the model is reinforced and more often for alternative behaviors (or if matching responses were punished), reinforcement to the model could come to serve as a discriminative stimulus for alternative behaviors (as illustrated recently in a matching-to-sample study with young children by Sherman, Saunders, and Brigham, 1970).

Recapitulation

This paper has considered some empirical and theoretical issues critical to the interpretation of "self-" and "vicarious-reinforcement" phenomena like those reported by Professor Bandura. Insofar as "self-reinforcement" appears to involve overt responding without extrinsic reinforcement from environmental agencies and "vicarious-reinforcement" to involve neither overt responding nor extrinsic reinforcement, such behavior-change phenomena may appear anomalous under the instrumental-conditioning paradigm (from which the term "reinforcement" has derived much of its contemporary tone). In some cases, it has even been thought that new theories, for example those containing cognitive terms, may be required to order the seemingly anomalous phenomena. However, my heuristic posture in this paper has been that such pessimism about S-R theory is premature, and may be due in part to the fact that the behavior-change phenomena at issue have been considered mostly in an ahistorical frame. When considered in the context of a subject's earlier conditioning history and the overall maintaining stimulus context, such phenomena may be readily explicable in terms of routine conditioning concepts, in particular instrumental responding, extrinsic reinforcement, and acquired stimulus control. My main intention in this endeavor has been to present a constructive line of reasoning with differential implications for theory and research, as well as to relate some of the issues involved to the wider theoretical context.

Professor Bandura has stated that most human behavior is altered and maintained in the absence of immediate external reinforcement. It has been my assumption that a unique conception of "self-reinforcement" to explain what appears to be response occurrence in the absence of extrinsic reinforcement and the use of inexplicit cognitive terms like "self-evaluation" as central to that process, would be entirely unnecessary in a conditioning analysis. "Self-reinforcing" responses (verbal or nonverbal, overt or covert) and those involved in what are generally termed "self-regulatory" processes, self-prescribed behavior standards, or the self-administration of extrinsic reinforcers, may be explained plausibly in an operational-learning analysis with the conception of functional response classes (and S-R chains) acquired and maintained by intermittent, extrinsic reinforcement from environmental agencies. Furthermore, unless independent empirical operations are specified that define a theoretical term or that index some features of a postulated implicit-response, representational or cognitive process, the parsimony and heuristic utility of positing such terms or processes (to bridge the gap between experience and subsequent performance) is questionable. Even so, attention to verbal and other overt responses connoting "self-reinforcement" or "self-control" may be useful in providing a greater understanding of important human behavior patterns.

Professor Bandura and others have reported that children exhibit matching responses following observation of models' reinforced responses, when there has been no apparent opportunity for the occurrence (practice) of the observing child's matching responses and therefore no possibility for extrinsic reinforcing stimuli to be provided contingent on those responses. Under an instrumental-conditioning conception, it would be expected that after the child-observer has been routinely reinforced for the imitative matching of various demonstrator-models' reinforced responses, reinforcement provided contingent upon a model's behavior could come to function as a generalized cue for a high probability of extrinsic reinforcement to the observer when he matches that behavior or as a cue indicating the permissibility of reproducing a behavior not generally sanctioned. Furthermore, the models' reinforced response that is matched may already be in an observer's repertory, under the control of the very cues as those which occasioned the model's response.

It has appeared to this writer that such vicarious-reinforcement phenomena could be considered merely a subcase of the more general phenomenon of apparent observational learning, in which an observer is said to match the behavior of a demonstrator-model regardless of whether or not he has witnessed the model's behavior reinforced. I have noted that there are theorists who appear to assume that learning by observation is a primary, prepotent acquisition process, a capacity of the organism as it were. However, it seems that few of the many researchers on what is taken to be learning by observation have even attempted to rule out the possibility that such phenomena may represent a case of routine instrumental conditioning where the presence of a demonstrator-model only functions to expedite the conditioning procedure. Furthermore, there have been rather few attempts to implement the necessary controls (or assessments) for possibly relevant experience, to rule out either the possibility that an organism may have learned to learn by observation or the possibility that stimuli provided under an experimental condition may earlier have been conditioned to control the relevant response.

It has been my contention in this context that vicarious-reinforcement phenomena, as well as the more general case of apparent observational learning, can be explained plausibly and efficiently by a matching-to-sample, conditional-responding learning conception for the acquisition of functional response classes. It is conceived that a functional imitative-response class can be acquired (and maintained) through the routine occurrence of intermittent, extrinsic reinforcement (from environmental agencies) of responses matched to diverse reinforced and nonreinforced responses of demonstrator-models (or of one model). This class would include matching responses emitted even when there are lengthy delays between the demonstrator-model's response and the observer's imitation of it, or when the model is not present. Moreover, particular matching responses of this class may never themselves be reinforced for a subject.

Without knowing the relation of a subject's reinforcement history to the training and test conditions of an experiment, systematic response change reflecting straightforward discriminative stimulus control occurring in an experiment may erroneously be thought to merit a "motivational" interpretation; and learning that is merely the end result of a conventional instrumental-learning or conditional-responding process, or a "learning-to-learn" process, may erroneously be conceived to represent a prepotent process of learning by observation (or "vicarious-reinforcement").

REFERENCES

Adler, H. E. Some factors of observational learning in cats. *Journal of Genetic Psychology*, 1955, *86*, 159–177.

Allport, G. W. The historical background of modern social psychology. In G. Lindzey and E. Aronson (Eds.), *The handbook of social psychology*. (2nd ed.) Vol. 1. Reading, Mass.: Addison-Wesley, 1968. Pp. 1–80.

Aronfreed, J. Imitation and identification: An analysis of some affective and cognitive mechanisms. Paper presented at the biennial meeting of the Society for Research in Child Development, New York, March, 1967.

Aronfreed, J. *Conduct and conscience: The socialization of internalized control over behavior*. New York: Academic Press, 1968.

Aronfreed, J. The concept of internalization. In D. A. Goslin (Ed.), *Handbook of socialization theory and research*. Chicago: Rand McNally, 1969. Pp. 263–323.

Baer, D. M., Peterson, R. F., and Sherman, J. A. The development of generalized imitation by reinforcing behavioral similarity to a model. *Journal of the Experimental Analysis of Behavior*, 1967, *10*, 405–416.

Baer, D. M., and Sherman, J. A. Reinforcement control of generalized imitation in young children. *Journal of Experimental Child Psychology*, 1964, *1*, 37–49.

Bandura, A. Social learning through imitation. In M. R. Jones (Ed.), *Nebraska symposium on motivation: 1962*. Lincoln: University of Nebraska Press, 1962. Pp. 211–269.

Bandura, A. Influence of models' reinforcement contingencies on the acquisition of imitative responses. *Journal of Personality and Social Psychology*, 1965, *1*, 589–595. (a)

Bandura, A. Vicarious processes: A case of no-trial learning. In L. Berkowitz (Ed.), *Advances in experimental social psychology*. Vol. 2. New York: Academic Press, 1965. Pp. 1–55. **(b)**

Bandura, A. The role of modeling processes in personality development. In W. W. Hartup and N. L. Smothergill (Eds.), *The young child: Reviews of research*. Washington, D. C.: National Association for the Education of Young Children, 1967. Pp. 42–58.

Bandura, A. *Principles of behavior modification*. New York: Holt, 1969. (a)

Bandura, A. Social-learning theory of identificatory processes. In D. A. Goslin (Ed.), *Handbook of socialization theory and research*. Chicago: Rand-McNally, 1969. Pp. 213–262. (b)

Bandura, A., Ross, D., and Ross, S. A. Vicarious reinforcement and imitative learning. *Journal of Abnormal and Social Psychology*, 1963, *67*, 601–607.

Bandura, A., and Walters, R. H. *Social learning and personality development*. New York: Holt, 1963.

Berlyne, D. *Structure and direction in thinking*. New York: Wiley, 1965.

Berry, C. S. An experimental study of imitation in cats. *Journal of Comparative Neurology*, 1908, *18*, 1–26.

Chesler, P. Maternal influence in learning by observation in kittens. *Science*, 1969, *166*, 901–903.

Church, R. M. Transmission of learned behavior between rats. *Journal of Abnormal and Social Psychology*, 1957, *54*, 163–165. (a)

Church, R. M. Two procedures for the establishment of imitative behavior. *Journal of Comparative and Physiological Psychology*, 1957, *50*, 315–318. (b)

Church, R. M. Emotional reactions of rats to the pain of others. *Journal of Comparative and Physiological Psychology*, 1959, *52*, 132–134.

Crawford, M. P., and Spence, K. W. Observational learning of discrimination problems by chimpanzees. *Journal of Comparative Psychology*, 1939, *27*, 133–147.

Cumming, W. W., and Berryman, R. The complex discriminated operant: Studies of matching-to-sample and related problems. In D. Mostofsky (Ed.), *Stimulus generalization*. Stanford, Calif.: Stanford University Press, 1965. Pp. 284–330.

deCharms, R., and Rosenbaum, M. E. The problem of vicarious experience. In D. Willner (Ed.), *Decisions, values and groups*. New York: Pergamon Press, 1960. Pp. 267–277.

Gagné, R. M. Contributions of learning to human development. *Psychological Review*, 1968, *75*, 177–191.

Gagné, R. M. *The conditions of learning*. (Rev. ed.) New York: Holt, 1970.

Gewirtz, J. L. A learning analysis of the effects of normal stimulation, privation and deprivation on the acquisition of social motivation and attachment. In B. M. Foss (Ed.), *Determinants of infant behaviour*. London: Methuen (New York: Wiley), 1961. Pp. 213–299.

Gewirtz, J. L. Deprivation and satiation of social stimuli as determinants of their reinforcing efficacy. In J. P. Hill (Ed.), *Minnesota symposia on child psychology.* Vol. 1. Minneapolis: University of Minnesota Press, 1967. Pp. 3–56.

Gewirtz, J. L. The role of stimulation in models for child development. In L. L. Dittmann (Ed.), *Early child care: The new perspectives.* New York: Atherton, 1968. Pp. 139–168.

Gewirtz, J. L. Contextual determinants of discriminative and reinforcing stimulus efficacy. Paper presented at the biennial meeting of the Society for Research in Child Development, Santa Monica, Calif., March 1969. (a)

Gewirtz, J. L. Levels of conceptual analysis in environment-infant interaction research. *Merrill-Palmer Quarterly of Behavior and Development,* 1969, *15,* 7–47. (b)

Gewirtz, J. L. Mechanisms of social learning: Some roles of stimulation and behavior in early human development. In D. A. Goslin (Ed.), *Handbook of socialization theory and research.* Chicago: Rand-McNally, 1969. Pp. 57–212. (c)

Gewirtz, J. L., and Stingle, K. G. Learning of generalized imitation as the basis for identification. *Psychological Review,* 1968, *75,* 374–397.

Gibson, E. J. *Principles of perceptual learning and development.* New York: Appleton-Century-Crofts, 1969.

Haggerty, M. E. Imitation in monkeys. *Journal of Comparative Neurology,* 1909, *19,* 337–445.

Hall, K. R. L. Observational learning in monkeys and apes. *British Journal of Psychology,* 1963, *54,* 201–226.

Harlow, H. F. Learning and satiation of response in intrinsically motivated complex puzzle performance by monkeys. *Journal of Comparative and Physiological Psychology,* 1950, *43,* 289–294.

Harlow, H. F. Learning set and error factor theory. In S. Koch (Ed.), *Psychology: A study of a science.* Vol. 2. New York: McGraw-Hill, 1959. Pp. 492–537.

Harlow, H. F., Harlow, M. K., and Meyer, D. R. Learning motivated by the manipulation drive. *Journal of Experimental Psychology,* 1950, *40,* 228–234.

Herbert, M. J., and Harsh, C. M. Observational learning by cats. *Journal of Comparative Psychology,* 1944, *37,* 81–95.

Herrnstein, R. J. Superstition: A corollary of the principles of operant conditioning. In W. K. Honig (Ed.), *Operant behavior: Areas of research and application.* New York: Appleton-Century-Crofts, 1966. Pp. 33–51.

Hilgard, E. R., and Bower, G. H. *Theories of learning.* (3rd ed.) New York: Appleton-Century-Crofts, 1966.

Hill, W. F. Learning theory and the acquisition of values. *Psychological Review,* 1960, *67,* 317–331.

Hull, C. L. *Principles of behavior.* New York: Appleton-Century-Crofts, 1943.

Hull, C. L. *A behavior system.* New Haven: Yale University Press, 1952.

Humphrey, G. Imitation and the conditioned reflex. *Pedagogical Seminary,* 1921, *28*, 1–21.

John, E. R., Chesler, P., Bartlett, F., and Victor, I. Observation learning in cats. *Science,* 1968, *159*, 1489–1491.

Kanfer, F. H. Vicarious human reinforcement: A glimpse into the black box. In L. Krasner and L. P. Ullmann (Eds.), *Research in behavior modification.* New York: Holt, 1965. Pp. 244–267.

Kendler, H. H., and Kendler, T. S. Vertical and horizontal processes in problem solving. *Psychological Review,* 1962, *69*, 1–16.

Kimble, G. A. *Hilgard and Marquis' conditioning and learning.* New York: Appleton-Century-Crofts, 1961.

Kohlberg, L. Moral development and identification. In H. W. Stevenson (Ed.), *Child psychology: The sixty-second yearbook of the National Society for the Study of Education.* Chicago: University of Chicago Press, 1963. Pp. 277–332.

Kohlberg, L. A cognitive-developmental analysis of children's sex-role concepts and attitudes. In E. E. Maccoby (Ed.), *The development of sex differences.* Stanford, Calif.: Stanford University Press, 1966. Pp. 82–173.

Kohlberg, L. Stage and sequence: The cognitive-developmental approach to socialization. In D. A. Goslin (Ed.), *Handbook of socialization theory and research.* Chicago: Rand-McNally, 1969. Pp. 347–480.

Lashley, K. S. Conditional reactions in the rat. *Journal of Psychology,* 1938, *6*, 311–324.

Lovaas, O. I., Berberich, J. P., Perloff, B. F., and Schaeffer, B. Acquisition of imitative speech by schizophrenic children. *Science,* 1966, *151*, 705–707.

McGeoch, J. A., and Irion, A. L. *The psychology of human learning.* New York: Longmans, Green, 1952.

Miller, N. E. Studies of fear as an acquirable drive: I. Fear as motivation and fear reduction as reinforcement in the learning of new responses. *Journal of Experimental Psychology,* 1948, *38*, 89–101.

Miller, N. E., and Dollard, J. *Social learning and imitation.* New Haven: Yale University Press, 1941.

Mowrer, O. H. *Learning theory and the symbolic process.* New York: Wiley, 1960.

Osgood, C. E. *Method and theory in experimental psychology.* New York: Oxford University Press, 1953.

Reichenbach, H. *Experience and prediction.* Chicago: University of Chicago Press, 1938.

Reichenbach, H. *The rise of scientific philosophy.* Berkeley, Calif.: University of California Press, 1951.

Rosenbaum, M. E., and Arenson, S. J. Observational learning: Some theory, some variables, some findings. In E. C. Simmel, R. A. Hoppe, and G. A. Milton (Eds.), *Social facilitation and imitative behavior.* Boston: Allyn and Bacon, 1968. Pp. 111–134.

Sears, R. R. Identification as a form of behavioral development. In D. B. Harris (Ed.), *The concept of development.* Minneapolis: University of Minnesota Press, 1957. Pp. 149–161.

Sears, R. R., Rau, L., and Alpert, R. *Identification and child rearing.* Stanford, Calif.: Stanford University Press, 1965.

Sherman, J. A., Saunders, R. R., and Brigham, T. A. Transfer of matching and mismatching behavior in preschool children. *Journal of Experimental Child Psychology,* 1970, 9, 489–498.

Skinner, B. F. *The behavior of organisms.* New York: Appleton-Century-Crofts, 1938.

Skinner, B. F. "Superstition" in the pigeon. *Journal of Experimental Psychology,* 1948, *38,* 168–172.

Skinner, B. F. *Science and human behavior.* New York: Macmillan, 1953.

Spence, K. W. Experimental studies of learning and the higher mental processes in infra-human primates. *Psychological Bulletin,* 1937, *34,* 806–850.

Terrace, H. S. Stimulus control. In W. K. Honig (Ed.), *Operant behavior: Areas of research and application.* New York: Appleton-Century-Crofts, 1966. Pp. 271–345.

Thorndike, E. L. Animal intelligence. An experimental study of the associative processes in animals. *Psychological Review Monograph Supplement,* 1898, 2(4, Whole No. 8).

Tolman, E. C. Principles of purposive behavior. In S. Koch (Ed.), *Psychology: A study of a science.* Vol. 2. New York: McGraw-Hill, 1959. Pp. 92–157.

Walters, R. H., Parke, R. D., and Cane, V. A. Timing of punishment and the observation of consequences to others as determinants of response inhibition. *Journal of Experimental Child Psychology,* 1965, *2,* 10–30.

Warden, C. J., and Jackson, T. A. Imitative behavior in the rhesus monkey. *Journal of Genetic Psychology,* 1935, *46,* 103–125.

White, R. W. Motivation reconsidered: The concept of competence. *Psychological Review,* 1959, *66,* 297–334.

Yerkes, R. M. Suggestibility in chimpanzee. *Journal of Social Psychology,* 1934, *5,* 271–282.

9

REINFORCEMENT: APPLIED RESEARCH[1]

MONTROSE M. WOLF and TODD R. RISLEY

University of Kansas

Research in the practical application of reinforcement is a fairly recent phenomenon. About a decade ago, Ayllon and Michael (1959), using a straightforward application of reinforcement, reported dramatic modifications in the behavior of institutionalized psychotics. They described how powerful relationships, as regular and lawful as those found in the laboratory, existed between the abnormal behavior and the reinforcement even in the sometimes chaotic setting of a mental hospital ward. The implication was clear: Significant human behavior occurring in natural environments may not be sufficiently complex or capricious to preclude research in the practical application of reinforcement. The applied research which has resulted from this implication has exerted profound effects in a very brief period of time. These effects are most apparent in programs for children.

[1]The preparation of this manuscript was supported in part by Public Health Service grants MS 16609 from the Center for Studies of Crime and Delinquency of the National Institute of Mental Health and HD 03144 from the National Institute of Child Health and Human Development to the Bureau of Child Research and the Department of Human Development at the University of Kansas. The authors wish to thank Robert Hoyt for his valuable editorial assistance in the preparation of the manuscript.

The discipline of special education, for example, has incorporated reinforcement techniques as standard procedures in the management of the classroom behavior of severely retarded and disturbed children. This is reflected in the recent announcement by the U. S. Office of Education that funds are available to train special-education teachers in behavior modification. Also, numerous institutions for the retarded and the delinquent have incorporated reinforcement procedures in their regular programs, and dramatic results have been reported by therapists who train parents to apply reinforcement techniques to modify the behavior of their deviant children.

One result of the growing popularity of applied reinforcement research has been the appearance of a group of skeptics. They say that such research is discovering nothing really new — that effective teachers and parents have always known about reinforcement as common sense. And these critics are right, with one qualification. People have applied common-sense reinforcement just as they have applied common-sense physics. Sir Isaac Newton's grandmother no doubt understood and used the principle of gravity before Newton precisely described its parameters. She probably applied her knowledge of trajectory if she had occasion to throw a spoon at young Newton when he was stealing a bite of pie before dinner. She most certainly could have told him that apples fall down and not up. Thus, the practical contribution of the early physicists was not in the discovery of the more obvious principles of physics — everyone applied them in a common-sense fashion already. Instead, the great practical impact came from the powerful experimental methodology that early physicists developed to produce precise descriptions of physical principles. This methodology was then applied to analyze the relative importance of these principles under specific practical conditions, and to exclude that part of the common-sense physics which was only superstition.

In the same manner, the initial contribution of researchers in applied reinforcement has not come from the discovery of genuinely new phenomena. Many grandmothers, teachers, and parents apply, as common sense, the reinforcement procedures that we are studying today. Instead, the greatest practical contribution of applied reinforcement research is coming from the experimental model which the researchers in this field have developed. It is a simple and elegant model that allows a researcher, practitioner, or parent to objectively measure and analyze the problem behaviors of an individual child.

The model incorporates accepted rules of measurement and experimental design. The measurement is usually carried out by a human observer, since in many instances human observation is the only feasible technique for recording significant behavior. This means that particular attention must be devoted to the description of the response that is given to the observer. In order for the measurement of the behavior to be replicable, the response description must be sufficiently objective and detailed to allow an independent observer to record the same behavior with a high degree of agreement with the principal observer. Fortunately, there was a well-developed methodology of human observation already established which we could apply (Bijou, Peterson, and Ault, 1968). On the other hand, problems of experimental design for research with individual children have been more difficult. Our starting point was baseline logic for research with individual subjects, as described by Sidman (1960). Baseline logic comprises one question: Does a treatment condition substantially affect the baseline rate of a subject's behavior? Unfortunately, this is not a simple question. To "affect a behavior" means not only that a change in the behavior occurs but also that we have sufficient information to attribute that change in behavior to our treatment condition. Our thinking about this problem has evolved through several phases.

A-B Experimental Design

Originally, the most popular experimental design was the two-stage A-B design. We would measure a behavior during the baseline condition (A) and then watch for a change in the behavior during the treatment condition (B) as shown with hypothetical data in Fig. 9-1. Figure 9-2

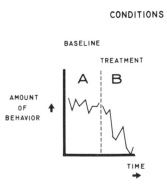

FIGURE 9-1. Hypothetical data presented in an A-B (baseline-treatment) experimental design.

represents the baseline and treatment measures of the actual crying behavior of a normal four-year-old nursery school child who was studied by our nursery-school-teacher colleagues Betty Hart, Eilleen Allen, Joan Buell, and Florence Harris (1964). Traditionally, nursery school teachers have depended upon internal variables such as fear, lack of confidence, or regression to explain excessive crying. These teachers decided to look at this child's social environment for an explanation of his behavior. The teachers attempted to analyze whether their attention was acting as a social reinforcer and thus maintaining the crying. They recorded the frequency of the child's cries. The crying response was defined as "(a) loud enough to be heard at least fifty feet away and (b) of five seconds or more duration." Each dot represented the number of crying episodes in one day. During baseline, the child averaged about eight episodes in one day. Each time the child cried, a teacher approached and comforted him. After ten days of baseline, the treatment (which involved extinction) was introduced and the teachers ignored the cries, ". . . neither going to him, speaking to him, nor looking at him while he was crying, except for an initial glance in order to assess the situation [Hart, Allen, Buell, Harris, and Wolf, p. 149]." As shown in Fig. 9-2, within five days after extinction was introduced, the crying decreased to between zero to two episodes.

While these results were dramatic, they were difficult for us to evaluate. What was the chance of coincidence? Did we really have sufficient information to indicate that the change in the crying behavior was due to our extinction condition and not the result of some unknown coincidental variable? After all, many preschool children cry excessively for awhile and

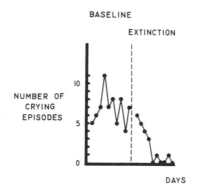

FIGURE 9-2. Number of crying episodes of a nursery school child which occurred each day during baseline and extinction. This is an example of an A-B design. (Hart, Allen, Buell, Harris, and Wolf, 1969.)

then seem to decrease their crying as they establish friendships or interests in play. It was true that the baseline behavior seemed stable. But could we afford to rely on the information given by the baseline as our only means of estimating what the natural course of the behavior would have been if we had not intervened? The same question applies to all research using an A-B design.

This problem also arose in the evolution of experimental medicine. Claude Bernard warned physicians a century ago of the danger of being misled by a coincidental change in a simple A-B analysis:

> A physician who tries a remedy and cures his patients, is inclined to believe that the cure is due to the treatment. Physicians often pride themselves on curing all their patients with a remedy that they use. But the first thing to ask them is whether they have tried doing nothing, i.e., not treating other patients; for how can they otherwise know whether the remedy or nature cured them"? Gall wrote a little known book on the question as to what is nature's share and what is the share of medicine in healing disease, and he very naturally concludes that their respective shares are quite hard to assign. We may be subject daily to the greatest illusions about the value of treatment, if we do not have recourse to comparative experiment. I shall recall only one recent example concerning the treatment of pneumonia. Comparative experiments showed, in fact, that treatment of pneumonia by bleeding, which was believed most efficacious, is a mere therapeutic illusion [quoted from pp. 194 and 195 of the 1957 edition of the English translation of the book originally published in 1865].

In applied reinforcement research, we can be misled as easily about the effectiveness of a reinforcement technique assessed in an A-B design. Bernard's solution for medicine was to use experimental-group control-group comparisons. In applied reinforcement research, however, we often do not have an opportunity to use group designs. We usually deal with a specific child or at most a few children. Until recently, no methodology existed for the scientific study of individual children. As recently as 1963, the same year as we were carrying out the study with the crying child, Mussen, Conger, and Kagan (1963, p. 24) concluded that ". . . methods for dealing with groups and group data are readily available, whereas methods for dealing with the individual case scientifically, are not." Thus, our aim has been to develop designs which will allow believable conclusions to be drawn from an analysis of the behavior of individual cases. In the case of the crier, he was the only child in our nursery school who cried so excessively that year. We conceded that the A-B analysis was incomplete. The analysis provided no information about what the natural course of the behavior would have been had we not intervened with our treatment condition.

A-B-A-B Reversal Design

While we can never know what would have happened had we not altered the baseline conditions, two classes of designs have emerged which do give us sufficient information to make a believable estimate (Baer, Wolf, and Risley, 1968). One we have referred to as the *reversal* or the A-B-A-B design illustrated in Fig. 9-3. If the behavior "reverses" back to something approximating the baseline level when the treatment is withdrawn, we can make a reasonable estimate about what the natural course of the uninterrupted baseline behavior would have been. Once a reversal in behavior has occurred, the treatment condition is usually reinstated in order to replicate the original-treatment effect and also to leave the child in the improved state. The reversal design was actually employed (see Fig. 9-4) by the nursery school teachers when we carried out the research with the crier. "When continuous adult attention was again given to all cries and approximations to cries, the baseline rate of crying episodes was soon re-established. Then, four days after the reintroduction of extinction for operant crying, the behavior was practically eliminated [Hart et al., 1964]."

CONDITIONS

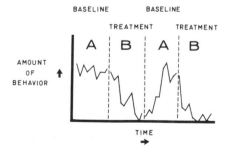

FIGURE 9-3. **Hypothetical data presented in a reversal, A-B-A-B, (baseline-treatment-baseline-treatment) experimental design.**

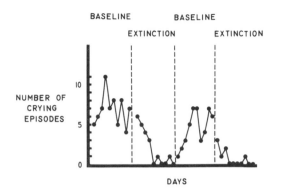

CONDITIONS

FIGURE 9-4. Number of daily crying episodes of a nursery school child during baseline, extinction, baseline, and extinction conditions. This represents an example of a reversal (A-B-A-B) design. (Hart, et. al., 1969.)

Multiple-Baseline Design

Reversal designs, on the other hand, can present problems. Sometimes the modified behaviors do not reverse in the "reversal" phase. Also, there are many occasions when reversals are undesirable, as when the target behavior is dangerous or self-destructive, or when the pleased parent or teacher does not want the undesirable behavior to return. In these instances, we employ a second strategy that we call a *multiple-baseline* design. Two or more behavioral baselines are recorded simultaneously as shown in Fig. 9-5. The treatment condition is then introduced for one of the behaviors but not for the second. The second behavior acts as a control for coincidence being responsible for any change in the first behavior. The second baseline allows us to estimate what the treated behavior might have looked like had we not intervened. A second replication of the effect with the second behavior also serves to increase our confidence in the reliability of the treatment effect. The greater the number of baselines used in a multiple-baseline analysis, the greater our confidence can be in the reliability of the relationship. While a study involving two baselines can be very suggestive, a set of replications across three or four baselines may be almost completely convincing.

There are several considerations in setting up a multiple-baseline study. One possibility is that there will be *induction* from one baseline to the next; that is, the change that a treatment condition seems to produce

CONDITIONS

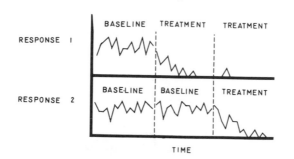

FIGURE 9-5. Hypothetical data presented in a multiple-baseline design. Two or more behavioral baselines are recorded simultaneously. Treatments are then introduced sequentially, first for one behavior and then for the second.

in the treated behavior may also appear in the second baseline that is intended to act as a control. The fact that change occurs across both behaviors diminishes the usefulness of the second baseline as a control. Another consideration is that multiple-baseline analysis may be quite convincing when carried out (1) across two or more different responses under the same environmental condition(s) and on the same subject(s), or (2) across two or more environmental conditions with the same response(s) and on the same subject(s), or (3) across two or more subjects with the same response(s) and under the same environmental condition(s).

A study involving multiple baselines across two different environmental conditions with the same responses and the same subjects was carried out by Barrish, Saunders, and Wolf (1969). This study is unusual in that the experimental design also involved a combination of reversal and multiple-baseline comparisons. Furthermore, the unit of analysis, rather than being an individual child, was an entire classroom of children. Out-of-seat and talking-out behaviors were studied in a regular fourth-grade classroom which included several "problem children" whom the teacher reportedly could not manage. Baseline rates of the inappropriate behaviors were recorded for a few weeks in math and reading periods. The reversal design was carried out in the math period. After baselines were obtained in math, the students were divided into two teams "to play a game." Each out-of-seat and talking-out response by an individual child resulted in a mark on the chalkboard which meant a possible loss of privileges by all the members of his team. If neither team obtained more than five marks, everyone received the privileges. If both teams received more than five marks, the team with the fewest marks earned the privileges. The privileges included extra recess, being first to line up for lunch, time for special projects, stars and name tags, as well as winning the game.

As a matter of fact, both teams received fewer than five marks and thus won more than 85 per cent of the time. Figure 9-6 shows the suppressive effects of the game on out-of-seat and talking-out behaviors. When the conditions were reversed back to baseline, the inappropriate behaviors came back immediately, and when the game was reintroduced, order in the classroom was restored. Meanwhile, as a multiple-baseline control we had been recording concurrently the same behaviors in the reading period as shown in Fig. 9-7. If the reversal-design analysis had not worked properly, that is, if the behavior had not reversed when we returned to the baseline conditions, we could have relied on the multiple-baseline control condition and the second replication of the game condition that were carried out during the reading period to help us reach a conclusion about the effectiveness of the game treatment. On the other hand, while these data from the reading period show a change in the responses from the baseline condition to the game condition, by themselves they represent only an A-B demonstration. Thus, the data in Fig. 9-7 alone would have been insufficient to allow a proper conclusion about the role of the game. As it turned out, the game had a substantial and reliable influence on the two responses each time it was introduced. The results of the reversal condition

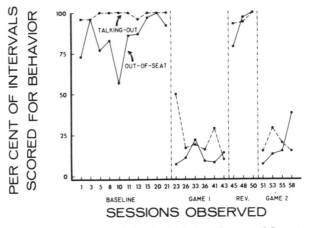

FIGURE 9-6. Per cent of 1-minute intervals scored by an observer as containing talking-out and out-of-seat behaviors occurring in a classroom of 24 fourth-grade school children during math period. During the game condition, out-of-seat and talking-out responses by a student resulted in a possible loss of privileges for the student and his team. The data were collected according to a reversal, A-B-A-B, design (baseline-treatment-baseline-treatment). (Barrish, Saunders, and Wolf, 1969.)

indicated that the game had a continuing role in the maintenance of order in the classroom.

As in the study just described, the subject-matter periods of the typical school day lend themselves to a multiple-baseline experimental design. Simultaneous baselines of the behavior of one student or of an entire class can be obtained in two or more subject-matter periods. The modification technique can then be introduced successively into each of the periods. If in each instance there is a change in behavior (and the behavior during the remaining baseline periods remains essentially unchanged), the investigator will have achieved a believable demonstration of the effectiveness of his technique. And he will have done so without depending upon or requiring a reversal of the behavior. A substantial increase in the number of behavior-modification studies using a multiple-baseline design can be expected in the future. Since we have only recently begun employing these designs, the other examples in this chapter will involve A-B-A-B (reversal) designs and their variations.

Token Reinforcement

Our next example of applied reinforcement research is a study carried out by our colleague Elery Phillips and his wife Elaine (Phillips, 1968; Phillips, Wolf, Bailey, and Fixsen, 1970). The Phillips are the houseparents at Achievement Place, a family-style treatment program for predelinquent boys who have been committed there by the county court. The treatment and research are administered by the houseparents who apply

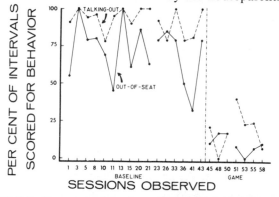

FIGURE 9-7. Per cent of 1-minute intervals scored by an observer as containing talking-out and out-of-seat behaviors occurring in a classroom of 24 fourth-grade school children during reading period. The baseline and game conditions were the same as during math period. The data represent a simple A-B analysis. (Barrish et al., 1969.)

and measure the effects of reinforcement procedures aimed at remedying a variety of the boys' social, self-care, and academic behavioral deficiencies. The six boys living at Achievement Place are thirteen to fifteen years old. Their records describe histories of aggression, thievery, truancy, and failure in school. They come from low-income families, some with long histories of criminal activity.

The treatment program of the Phillips', which incorporates relevant research as a major feature, is an example of the programmatic applied reinforcement research which should characterize more and more child-treatment programs. It also exemplifies a reinforcement technique now being broadly adopted: token reinforcement. The aim of a token economy is to arrange for immediate consequences, tokens, to bridge the delay between behavior and its scheduled reinforcer when the reinforcer cannot be made immediately contingent upon the behavior. The token economy at Achievement Place is similar in many respects to those designed by Ayllon and Azrin (1965), Staats, Staats, Schutz, and Wolf (1962), Cohen (1968), and others. The unit of the token-reinforcement system is the "point." The boys can earn points for appropriate behavior and lose points for inappropriate behavior. The points are traded for a variety of privileges. Almost everything that is important to the boys is incorporated into the system and is earned through points. At the end of each week, earned points are traded for privileges during the next week. Some of the privileges include the use of a bicycle, tools, games, TV, allowances, snacks, and freedom to go downtown or home for a visit.

The point system is arranged so that if a youth accomplishes certain tasks expected of him while losing a minimum of points in fines, he will obtain all the privileges without having to perform any extra jobs. Each boy needs about one thousand points a day to earn most of the privileges. Almost all of the boys earn more than one thousand points a day the majority of the time. Points are earned by engaging in designated social, self-care, and academic behaviors. A record of each reward or fine is made on a three-by-five "point card" which each boy carries. At the end of the day, the earned and lost points are tallied and recorded on a weekly point sheet. Most of the behaviors which earn or lose points are described and posted on the bulletin board. Rewards and fines range from ten to ten thousand points.

The daily routine at Achievement Place is similar to that of many conventional families. The boys get up about 7 A.M. They shower, dress, and clean their bedrooms and bathrooms. Following breakfast, some boys are assigned kitchen clean-up duties before leaving for school. After school, the boys come home immediately and prepare their homework. They are then free to do as they please depending, of course, on the privileges that they have earned. After dinner and clean-up chores they again may engage in their privilege activities until bedtime.

Among the first behavior problems dealt with by Mr. and Mrs. Phillips was aggressive behavior. When the first three youths were admitted to Achievement Place, physical aggression was expected to be a problem; however, almost no physical aggression has occurred. There was, on the other hand, a great deal of aggressive *verbal* behavior. The youths frequently threatened damage to property or persons, and often made such statements as "I'm going to kick your butt" and "You better watch your mouth or you won't live 'til tomorrow." Inter-observer agreement regarding the measurement of aggressive statements averaged better than ninety per cent. The behavior was recorded for three hours each evening. Under the initial baseline condition, the behavior of each of the three boys was recorded without consequence. As shown in Fig. 9-8, Don had a high rate averaging about twenty-two responses per evening. Tom averaged about seventeen and Jack about five responses.

The first experimental condition involved correction. After each response, the boys were informed that they should not make aggressive statements. This seemed to reduce Tom's rate to about five per evening. But it appeared to have almost no effect on Don's or Jack's behavior.

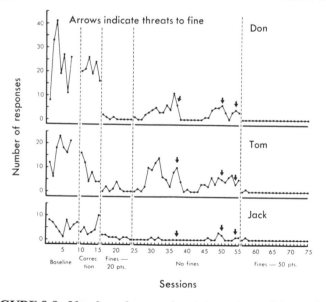

FIGURE 9-8. Number of aggressive statements per 3-hour observation session for each boy under each condition. If the correction condition is disregarded, the data represent an A-B-A-B analysis (baseline, fine, baseline, fine.) (Phillips, 1968.)

When correction did not eliminate the behavior, twenty-point fines were made contingent upon each response. In the fines condition, the response rates fell to near zero for each of the boys. After nine days, the no-fines condition was introduced unannounced. The boys no longer lost points for aggressive statements. During the third week of this condition, the houseparent threatened (designated by the arrows in Fig. 9-8) to reinstate the fines unless the aggressive statements were stopped. There was a significant reduction in the aggressive behavior, but it lasted only about a week. Then the rates again rose and the threat to fine was made a second time. There was a decrease in the behavior, but it was not as significant or as long-lasting as the previous reduction. A third threat appeared also to have very little effect. At the beginning of the fifty-sixth session, an announcement was made and the fines (fifty points this time) were reinstated. There were only two responses during the next twenty sessions. The A-B-A-B design clearly demonstrated the effectiveness of a point fine in controlling the aggressive verbal behavior.

Another problem concerned the boys' lack of cleanliness. Most of them arrived dirty at Achievement Place. Reports by probation officers suggested that in most cases the homes of these boys were extremely dirty and disarranged. Reports from teachers also contained comments about poor hygiene habits and dirty clothing. Token reinforcement contingencies were arranged for a variety of self-care behaviors and for maintenance of the home. While it was possible to arrange the reinforcement contingencies for aggressive verbal behavior to relate directly to the behavior of each individual boy, many maintenance behaviors were difficult to handle on an individual basis. Therefore, the Phillips investigated a number of systems involving individual and group reinforcement. These have been compared for their effectiveness in accomplishing the tasks as well as for their reinforcement value to the boys. The Phillips first tried arranging reinforcement contingencies for the group of boys as a whole; however, this arrangement proved to be less effective than others. A very effective system involved making a single boy responsible for the behavior of his peers. He had authority to give and take away points. In this manner, a *peer-managership system* was established. The manager's duties included seeing that a specified list of tasks such as taking showers and cleaning bathrooms, yard, and basement, were accomplished each day. The manager had the authority to give and take points depending on his judgment of the quality of the job completed. In turn, the manager earned or lost points according to whether the tasks were accomplished or not and, whenever possible, as a function of the quality of work.

Figure 9-9 shows the relative effectiveness of the manager system with its contingencies and consequences as compared to a group condition in maintaining bathroom-cleaning behavior. Explicit criteria were established for each item in the bathroom. For example, no objects were to be left on the sink, the soap was to be in the soap dish, the toothbrush in the toothbrush holder, and all other objects in the medicine cabinet. Reliability of measurement between two independent observers averaged ninety-seven per cent. Under the baseline condition, when the boys were simply instructed to clean the bathrooms, very few of the items were completed. When the manager condition was introduced for the first time,

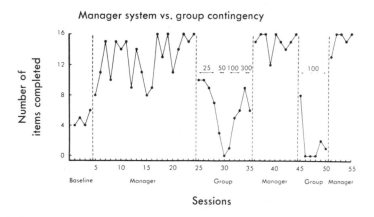

FIGURE 9-9. Number of bathroom-cleaning tasks accomplished per session for each condition. The numbers above the arrow indicate the number of points lost by each boy for the sessions indicated by the horizontal arrows. (Phillips, 1968.)

it took about two weeks for an acceptable level of bathroom cleanliness to occur. The manager condition was then discontinued and point contingencies were placed on the entire group. But the various point values which were applied did not produce a level of tidiness equal to that produced by the managership arrangement. When the manager condition was reintroduced, the cleaning behavior again improved. When the group condition was put back into effect, the behavior deteriorated. And again when the manager condition was reinstated, the cleanliness of the bathrooms increased significantly. Clearly in this instance, the group contingency and consequences were less effective than the peer-manager-arranged contingencies and consequences.

The Phillips have systematically exposed the boys to several systems involving individual or group consequences and individual or group tasks as well as variations in the manager system. The preliminary data indicate that when allowed to choose their own system, the boys will consistently vote for a manager system when they elect the manager. This system is effective in accomplishing the chores, preferred by the boys, practical from the standpoint of the houseparents, and has other obvious attributes. Thus, through research, an excellent organizational system evolved that might not have occurred naturally and that does not usually occur in other institutions for predelinquents. Using similar measurement and design procedures, the Phillips have developed reinforcement techniques which have dramatically improved the social behavior, school achievement, promptness, communication skills, and manners of their boys. And in each case, the objectively obtained data and the experimental analysis have made possible a clear evaluation of the role of the treatment variables.

Conclusion

We are only beginning to apply reinforcement procedures to practical problems of child behavior; however, we already are able to depend upon a research methodology that can objectively and precisely measure and analyze significant behavior of individual children in natural settings. The methodology should allow us to design and to evaluate more effective and preferred treatment programs for all child and adult behavior problems. At the same time it will enable us to discontinue those aspects of common-sense reinforcement which are only superstitions. Clearly, an applied science and technology of reinforcement are at hand.

REFERENCES

Ayllon, T., and Azrin, N. H. The measurement and reinforcement of behavior of psychotics. *Journal of the Experimental Analysis of Behavior*, 1965, *8*, 357–383.

Ayllon T., and Michael, J. L. The psychiatric nurse as a behavioral engineer. *Journal of the Experimental Analysis of Behavior*, 1959, *2*, 323–334.

Baer, D. M., Wolf, M. M., and Risley, T. R. Some dimensions of applied behavior analysis. *Journal of Applied Behavior Analysis*, 1968, *1*, 91–97.

Barrish, M., Saunders, M., and Wolf, M. M. Good behavior game: Effects of individual contingencies for group consequences on disruptive behavior in a regular classroom. *Journal of Applied Behavior Analysis*, 1969, *2*, 119–124.

Bernard, C. *An introduction to the study of experimental medicine.* New York: Dover Publications, 1957.

Bijou, S. W., Peterson, R. F., and Ault, M. H. A method of integrating descriptive and experimental field studies at the level of data and empirical concepts. *Journal of Applied Behavior Analysis,* 1968, *1*, 175–191.

Cohen, H. L. Educational therapy: The design of a learning environment. In J. M. Shlien (Ed.), *Research in psychotherapy.* Washington, D.C.: American Psychological Association, 1968, 21–53.

Hart, B. M., Allen, K. E., Buell, J. S., Harris, F. R., and Wolf, M. M. Effects of social reinforcement on operant crying. *Journal of Experimental Child Psychology,* 1964, *1*, 145–153.

Mussen, P. H., Conger, J. J., and Kagan, J. *Child development and personality.* New York: Harper & Row, 1963.

Phillips, E. L. Achievement Place: Token reinforcement procedures in a home-style rehabilitation setting for "pre-delinquent" boys. *Journal of Applied Behavior Analysis,* 1968, *1*, 213–224.

Phillips, E. L., Wolf, M. M., Bailey, J. S., and Fixsen, D. L. The Achievement Place model: A community-based family-style behavior modification program for pre-delinquents. Delinquency Prevention Strategy Conference, California Youth Authority, 1970.

Sidman, M. *Tactics of scientific research.* New York: Basic Books, 1960.

Staats, A. W., Staats, C. K., Schutz, R. E., and Wolf, M. M. The conditioning of textual responses using "extrinsic" reinforcers. *Journal of the Experimental Analysis of Behavior,* 1962, *5*, 33–40.

APPLYING APPLIED REINFORCEMENT

LAUREN B. RESNICK
University of Pittsburgh

Wolf and Risley's paper is more an essay on applied research methodology than it is a report on a specific body of research on reinforcement. Its central point is that we now have at our disposal a research strategy that makes it possible to conduct scientific studies in relatively natural settings. The research strategy described is experimental rather than purely observational; that is, the experimenter intervenes with special "treatments" much as he does in the laboratory. However, the setting is usually a social institution of some kind, and the behaviors studied are typically of real social concern. The studies Wolf and Risley report are excellent exemplars of the kind of careful applied research advocated in their paper; the list of such exemplars is growing rapidly, and a new journal (*Journal of Applied Behavior Analysis*) is devoted almost exclusively to reports of applied reinforcement studies.

What is important about this growing body of research is that (1) it represents an application of basic psychological principles to socially relevant problems, and (2) in so doing, it carries research itself directly into the field. This approach contrasts with the more conventional relationship between basic psychological research and application, in which "basic" scientists run laboratory studies, extract a set of principles and write a prescription for their application, but leave all concern for actual implementation to a different group of people, who are often untrained in or uninterested in research. The studies reported by Wolf and Risley move scientific methodology directly into the natural setting. Research is built directly into an intervention program; manipulations of treatment conditions are planned so that the effects of different elements of the treatment program and their interactions can be assessed. At the same time, results of the research program can be fed back into the intervention program so that treatments are changed in accord with new findings.

The importance of reversal and multiple-baseline designs to this general effort is that they permit the isolation of elements of the treatment conditions without the use of control groups. A study by Madsen, Becker, and Thomas (1968) illustrates some of the possibilities for such experimental analysis. In this study, the effects of three elements of a classroom-control system were explored. Two classrooms were studied. In each, explicit rules for classroom behavior were first stated for the children. This condition had no effect on the rate of "inappropriate" behaviors (getting out of seat, making noise, grabbing, and so forth). In the next experimental period, the teacher stated the rules and also ignored all instances of inappropriate behavior; in one classroom, inappropriate behaviors increased; in the other there was no change. Next, a condition was introduced in which rules were stated, inappropriate behavior ignored, and appropriate behavior praised. Inappropriate behaviors dropped in both classrooms. A return to baseline conditions produced a return to baseline rates of inappropriate behavior, and reintroduction of the rules + ignorance + praise condition lowered the rate again. This study, by introducing the elements of treatment one at a time, permitted the inference that praise was the effective element in the treatment. However, a study in which praising is introduced first is needed to permit a clear conclusion.

A study by Reynolds and Risley (1968) used the reverse approach, first introducing a complex treatment and then withdrawing elements one at a time. In this study, the specified reinforcement — teacher attention and access to play materials contingent on verbalization by a preschool girl — was introduced, leading to an increase in talking by a child. One element of the reinforcing event — question-asking by the teacher prior to giving the child material she requested — was then withdrawn. Verbalization fell, but recovered when questioning was reintroduced. This result demonstrates that it was not general "attention" but specifically the teacher's questioning, together with contingent access to materials, that maintained the child's behavior.

Studies of this kind represent what may be called a "second generation" of applied behavioral research. Earlier studies were content to show simply that reinforcement contingent on acceptable performance could increase the quality and frequency of that performance. Little attempt was made to isolate the effective components of the contingencies or to specify what types of contingent events were likely to be effective under what circumstances. Although their number is still small, a growing body of second-generation studies supports the Wolf and Risley claim that we now have at hand a sophisticated methodology for studying the effects of various reinforcement procedures. However, I am less convinced than Wolf and Risley appear to be that we now have a reinforcement technology suitable for immediate and widespread application. Certain crucial issues must be addressed before applied research in reinforcement can be expected to have major social impact.

A basic issue, for both theoretical and practical reasons, is the question of whether and how behavior can be maintained after special programs of reinforcement are terminated. Baer, Wolf, and Risley (1967) have called this the process of return to the "natural community of reinforcers." In addition, there is the practical problem of how to establish and maintain appropriate reinforcing behavior on the part of key personnel in natural social settings. I would like to elaborate on these two issues, considering, in the process, questions concerning the types of reinforcers and dependent variables studied, and the need for replication studies to determine the range of applicability of specific reinforcement programs.

Except in a few extreme cases, the ultimate goal of most behavior-modification programs is to prepare the individual to function in a "natural" setting, i.e., one in which external reinforcers are not systematically programmed. Reinforcers will still be present in the natural setting, but they may be of a different type, and much more "thinly" scheduled, than in the behavior-modification environment. In the natural environment, for example, the Phillips' boys would not lose points for verbal aggression, although subtle forms of reinforcement (perhaps simply the absence of negative consequences) would certainly be present in many settings. For other kinds of behavior — academic performance, for example — natural reinforcements are more visible, but they are often extremely delayed and symbolic, e.g., "grades." Systematic social and token-reward systems are designed to provide more immediate or tangible reinforcers for individuals who cannot maintain socially defined "appropriate" behavior under natural conditions. Must these special reinforcement systems remain in effect indefinitely, or can we find ways of fading out reinforcers while still maintaining the desired behaviors? Put another way, can systematic reinforcement programs be used as a means of shaping the ability to work for less favorably programmed external rewards?

Classic research on reinforcement suggests two mechanisms by which reinforcement contingencies can be modified while behavior is maintained. One is the process of gradually extending, or thinning, the reinforcement schedule. The quality of the reinforcer remains the same, but it comes less frequently, and, to be most effective in maintaining behavior, less predictably. The second process is the establishment of conditioned or secondary reinforcers. Here the schedule is not necessarily altered (although it may be), but the individual learns to work for a qualitatively different reinforcer. Examples of the application of secondary-reinforcement principles in an applied setting would be the pairing of verbal praise with a token, or the use of external praise and recognition for objectively successful academic performance. In the first case, the hope is that praise alone will eventually be sufficient to maintain the behavior originally reinforced by the token; in the second, the aim is to make the academic performance itself reinforcing enough to maintain the requisite study behaviors.

Extensive and systematic study of the relationship between "programmed" and "natural" rewards is badly needed before reinforcement principles can be widely and well used in applied settings. In conjunction with studies of methods of fading out tokens or other external reinforcers, there should be attention given to analyzing the whole range of reinforcers that may operate in an environment, how these interact with each other, and how new classes of events can become available and functional as reinforcers. In this research, it may be useful to consider reinforcers not as dichotomized into "intrinsic" and "extrinsic" classes, but as running along a continuum from reinforcers closely tied to a given task (i.e., "intrinsic to the task") to highly generalized reinforcers that have no inherent relationship to the task itself. Naturally available social reinforcers, such as attention, recognition, or winning an argument, would fall somewhere in the middle of such a continuum. Analysis in terms of such a continuum would lead to questions such as the extent to which more generalized reinforcers, which are usually easier to engineer in social settings, can be used to bring individuals into contact with task-specific reinforcers they might otherwise have missed, and how anticipation of favorable generalized consequences may help to maintain the reinforcing power of task-specific events.

Bandura's chapter reviewing research on self-reinforcement processes is extremely intriguing with regard to the latter question. If self-administered reinforcement can be shown to reliably maintain behavior, then it seems reasonable to consider the use of an overt self-reinforcement condition as a step in the process of fading out systematic external reinforcement in a substantially "thinned" external-reinforcement schedule. There is anecdotal evidence that something of this kind happens in many cases, particularly with young children. However, I know of no applied studies on processes of positive self-reinforcement.

Another possibility for fading out systematic reinforcement is to view the programmed contingencies as a means of shaping new behavior repertoires, which in turn make it possible for the individual to profit from reinforcements normally available in the environment. For example, if a teacher normally rewards only reading performance that is up to a certain arbitrary standard, and a particular child is unable to meet that standard, then he has no means of earning reinforcement in that environment. He may seek attention in disruptive ways. An intensive program in reading, together with powerful external reinforcers, at least initially, should have the effect of establishing a new repertoire which will bring him reinforcement in the classroom. Thomas et al. (1968) report precisely such an effect for an elementary school boy. In a study by Buell et al. (1968), teacher reinforcement of climbing on outdoor play apparatus served to increase time spent in contact with other children. The child thus was reinforced by other children for age-appropriate social behavior with a resultant decrease in certain collateral asocial and regressive behaviors. It is possible to interpret Wolf and Risley's example of the effectiveness of a "managership" system, as opposed to group contingencies, in these terms. The group-contingency condition required the boys to organize themselves — define what constituted "cleanliness," set up a system of policing, establish penalties for infractions. These functions required a set of social and organizational skills which the boys probably did not possess. The managership system essentially performed these functions for the boys. I wonder whether certain kinds of shaping procedures might not have succeeded in establishing skills which would have made it possible for them to perform effectively under the group condition.

With respect to actual social application of "applied" reinforcement research, it is important to emphasize that there is no simple dichotomy between laboratory and applied research. Rather, there is something like a continuum from more to less control over the range of variables that affect behavior. Each of the studies reported by Wolf and Risley was conducted in a natural social environment, and the experimenters committed themselves to study of behaviors that are educationally and socially relevant. On the other hand, in each of these studies, the reinforcement agent was committed to research and experimentation; in most of Wolf's and Risley's studies, the agents were graduate students rather than career teachers or youth workers. There is, therefore, another step from the laboratory yet to be made — to an environment in which ordinary teachers, houseparents, therapists, or ward personnel are the agents of reinforcement.

To make this step, it will be necessary, first of all, to pay serious attention to the problems of how professional and sub-professional workers are to be trained in the use of reinforcement techniques and how their reinforcing behavior is to be maintained after the initial training period. I believe the same kind of experimental analysis can be applied to these questions as is now being applied to the design of treatment and management procedures for patients, schoolchildren, and delinquents. Even the most casual armchair analysis of skills needed by reinforcement agents suggests that verbal discussion however sophisticated and theoretically sound, is unlikely to produce the kind of behavior changes in the reinforcement agents that are needed if a systematic reinforcement program is to be effective. This suggestion is supported by informal reports of psychologists who have given courses or institutes on behavior modification for teachers and then checked on these teachers' classroom behavior a few weeks or months later.

Development of effective training and maintenance programs for reinforcement agents will require several steps. The first of these is analysis and specification of the components of effective reinforcement programs. Research of the kind reported by Wolf and Risley represents a major contribution to this effort. As a result of such studies, it should be possible to specify with increasing precision the critical components of applied reinforcement programs. However, it is important that in their enthusiasm for intra-individual experimental designs, applied reinforcement researchers not overlook the need for replication studies designed to explore the range of individuals and conditions across which generalizations concerning particular reinforcement effects can be made. A recent study in a Headstart classroom revealed four distinct patterns of response to the same classroom token economy (Wrobel and Resnick, 1970). Findings of this kind highlight the need for research specifying the effects of specific types of reinforcers and reinforcement schedules on individuals with histories of various kinds. Without a body of such research, we will need to begin anew with each individual subject to develop a reinforcement program suited to his needs, with relatively little learned from past experiences except a methodology of measurement and continuous evaluation.

This in fact seems to be the current "state of the art" in the field of applied reinforcement. We can state with assurance that a broad class of contingent events which we call reinforcers, administered systematically, will enhance (or suppress) target behaviors identified by experimenters. We have a methodology for monitoring the course of treatment in applied settings. But the choice of precisely what contingencies — what reinforcers on what schedule — to apply in a given instance remains to a large degree a matter of hunch and intuition. In other words, we are in possession of a theory and methodology of behavior analysis which, when applied by sophisticated experimenters, can result in dramatic behavior changes in social settings. It is not at all clear, however, that the average "practitioner" in the field will be willing or able to use this method in its present form. A much more prescriptive approach to defining behavior-modification systems may be needed for widespread use.

A second step in training agents of reinforcement is the development of treatments designed to change adults' behavior in complex interactional settings. Again, the principles and techniques from the behavioral laboratory can be applied and systematically studied. What kinds of reinforcers are both effective and feasible in working with adults of various levels of education? Is it possible to shape behavior directly in a social environment through reinforcement of successive approximations to effective performance? If so, how can reinforcement and feedback be delivered to the treatment agent without disrupting the ongoing social interaction? How effective is "modeling" of appropriate performance in establishing complex skills? An initial study in our laboratory suggests that an expanded form of modeling that includes instances of poor performance as well as good, may allow subjects to learn to "edit" their own behavior, thus eliminating the need for direct feedback from a trainer or supervisor (Resnick and Kiss, 1970); but we need further research to determine the limits of such modeling and self-reinforcement procedures in training practitioners. All of these are critical questions for the future utility of applied reinforcement procedures. To date, there has been very little research in this direction.

Finally, for even the most careful training programs to prove of lasting social benefit, attention will have to be paid to the problem of maintaining the practitioners' reinforcing behavior over extended periods of time. Effective training programs will undoubtedly incorporate relatively dense reinforcement contingencies born of the need to shape new behaviors. Will these new behaviors on the part of teachers or other practitioners continue to be practiced when the training period is over? The problem is exactly analogous to the one raised earlier concerning the need to fade out formal reinforcement programs for children or patients and transfer control to natural contingencies in the environment. The solutions will probably be analogous as well. One hypothesis worthy of experimental investigation is that the practitioners' reinforcing behavior will maintain itself to the extent that children or patients exhibit visibly improved performance as a result of it. According to this hypothesis, reinforcement in social environments is not a "one-way" affair in which teachers or therapists control the behavior of their charges. Instead, teachers and children, therapists and patients, mutually reinforce each other, with a consequent maintenance of the behavior of both participants. This interpretation is consonant with the "social-exchange" view of reinforcement espoused by many social psychologists (Gergen, 1969). Experiments on mutual reinforcement patterns may thus mark a fruitful point of contact between social and learning psychology.

REFERENCES

Baer, D., Wolf, M., and Risley, T. The entry into natural communities of reinforcement. Paper presented at the meeting of the American Psychological Association, Washington, D. C., 1967.

Buell, J., Stoddard, P., Harris, F., and Baer, D. M. Collateral social development accompanying reinforcement of outdoor play in a preschool child. *Journal of Applied Behavior Analysis*, 1968, *1*, 167–173.

Gergen, K. J. *The psychology of behavior exchange.* Reading, Mass.: Addison-Wesley, 1969.

Madsen, C., Jr., Becker, W., and Thomas, D. Rules, praise and ignoring: Elements of elementary classroom control. *Journal of Applied Behavior Analysis*, 1968, *1*, 139–150.

Resnick, L. B., and Kiss, L. E. Discrimination training and feedback in shaping teacher behavior. Paper presented at meetings of the American Educational Research Association, March, 1970.

Reynolds, N. J., and Risley, T. R. The role of social and material reinforcers in increasing talking of a disadvantaged preschool child. *Journal of Applied Behavior Analysis*, 1968, *1*, 253–262.

Thomas, D., Nielson, L., Kuypers, D., and Becker, W. Contributions of social reinforcement and remedial instruction in the elimination of a classroom behavior problem. Unpublished manuscript, University of Illinois, 1968.

Wrobel, P. A., and Resnick, L. B. An investigation of the effects of the application and removal of a token economy on the working behavior of sixteen Headstart children. Paper presented at meetings of the American Educational Research Association, March, 1970.

10

REINFORCEMENT: IS IT A BASIC PRINCIPLE, AND WILL IT SERVE IN THE ANALYSIS OF VERBAL BEHAVIOR?

JOHN B. CARROLL

Educational Testing Service

In this paper I shall restrict my comments to two major problems that seem to have run through the conference: (1) How "basic" is the concept of reinforcement? and (2) How stands the concept of reinforcement in the study of the "higher mental processes," such as language?

How "Basic" Is the Concept of Reinforcement?

By this question I mean the following: If we assume that a principle of reinforcement is experimentally and theoretically well established (and I shall make that assumption), is this a principle that underlies all learning (in which case it is "basic"), or is it a principle that (a) applies only in a particular set of circumstances or that (b) can be derived from some more elementary principles or considerations? The (a) and (b) parts of this second alternative are not quite the same. On the one hand, it could be that a principle applicable only in special circumstances could be valid independently of any more fundamental principles; on the other, a principle of reinforcement derivable from more elementary considerations could nevertheless be valid universally for all kinds of learning. It might, for example, have a status analogous to that of the concept of force in mechanics, derivable from more elementary concepts of mass and acceleration and yet of universal application.

It is difficult and perhaps unfair to attempt to categorize the positions of the conference participants on this question. They were, after all, convened to address themselves to problems of reinforcement, and their papers do not necessarily reveal where they stand on the question of the extent to which reinforcement is a fundamental process. Nevertheless I shall try to classify the positions that seem to have been revealed.

We have, first, a group of contributors whose papers either are silent on this question, or suggest strongly that they have little interest in it. Catania, and also Premack, are concerned mainly with working out the conditions under which reinforcement phenomena manifest themselves. Catania proposes an ingenious framework into which (presumably) all operant- and respondent-conditioning phenomena could be fitted, without committing himself concerning the pervasiveness of these phenomena in behavior in general. Premack analyzes the interactions of rewards and punishments in the case where there are two competing response tendencies, thus developing in more detail his well-known "Premack principle" to the effect that any response tendency of higher strength can serve as a reinforcer of one of lower strength. We might hear him saying that since all response tendencies may be assumed to have a certain strength, his principle would have complete generality. But he does not say so explicitly. Wolf and Risley address themselves solely to the "applied" aspects of reinforcement theory. They would probably say that since they are in possession of an excellent and more or less general behavioral principle, they are interested solely in making it work for them, without caring *how* it works or whether it is a fundamental principle of learning. Within the task they set themselves, they are perfectly justified in their single-mindedness; they have enough to do without indulging in theoretical speculation. Nevertheless, one suspects that all those participants I have mentioned thus far, if pushed to the wall, would prefer to claim that reinforcement is indeed a fundamental principle; they represent the current breed of "reinforcement theorists" in the tradition of

Thorndike and Skinner (my apologies to them and to Skinner, if apologies are necessary, for suggesting that they are theorists).

We have next a group of conferees who give the impression, and in at least two cases, explicit statements, that they regard the reinforcement principle as purely derivative and subsidiary to other principles, even though it may be important and fruitful in its own right. In the following passage, for example, Logan seems to be appealing to a contiguity theory of the Guthrian type:

> People learn about stimuli, about responses, and about rewards. If stimuli occur in temporal sequence, this association is learned. If responses occur in the presence of effective stimuli, including stimuli produced by previous responses, those responses become associated with those stimuli. And if rewards or punishments follow the occurrence of a response, people learn that rewards or punishments are associated with that response [this volume, p. 53].

For Logan, associations of stimuli and responses represent processes that are more fundamental than that of reinforcement. Nevertheless, the reinforcement principle can be invoked whenever behavior is attended by some component of motivation or incentive. And since motives and incentives are dominant in much behavior, the reinforcement principle is an especially useful one.

A somewhat similar tack is implied by Bandura, but in the context of his discussion of vicarious reinforcement. When people see others being rewarded or punished for their actions, they translate these experiences into information concerning what outcomes may be expected for their own responses — sometimes, indeed, they overreact, responding as if they "get the message" in a clearer and less ambiguous form than is actually permitted by the information available to them. In any case, it is obvious to Bandura that because of the vicarious nature of the "reinforcement," it is hardly possible to assume that the strengthening effect of observed rewards operates directly upon the individual's responses — the effect must be mediated by processes in which the transfer of information, attitudes, and emotions is involved. Such transfers, then, must be processes that are more fundamental than the process of reinforcement itself.

Estes addresses himself directly to the question we have raised. He is quite explicit in doubting the "sovereignty" of the law of effect — even as an empirical principle. The law of effect, to the extent that it may be valid, is subsidiary to more fundamental principles of contiguity and association. Rewards and punishments must be viewed rather as carriers of information about outcomes than as satisfiers or castigators of drives or motives. While Estes does not seem to be as much of a contiguity theorist as he once was — perhaps because he seeks a more satisfying statement of the contiguity principle — the thrust of his remarks is clearly against assuming that reward and punishment have any special status in psychological theory, or any *direct* "strengthening" effects on behavior responses. If reward has any special effects, those effects are more likely to operate on the direction of attention or the facilitation of informational feedback.

An even stronger position of this type is adopted by Atkinson and Wickens. According to them, the basic processes in behavior, broadly defined, involve "the uses of memory," i.e., the transfer of information among three types of memory store (the sensory register, the short-term store, and the long-term store). Rewards and punishments are, in the first instance, events whose perceptual representations enter the sensory register and modulate the flow of information among the three types of memory store. (Some rewards and punishments may exist, however, as memories in either the short-term or long-term stores.) They "view reinforcement as a complex process . . . derived from other, more fundamental aspects of the learning process," and they feel that there exists no "single, unified law to explain all reinforcement phenomena." Through the use of ingenious experiments and an associated mathematical formulation, they are able to demonstrate, quite impressively, that "reinforcement" (the administration of actual or expected rewards and punishments) has varied effects that depend upon more basic conditions and that can be predicted from a number of assumptions concerning information transfer and memory phenomena.

Thus far the "box score" for reinforcement as a basic psychological process, at least among our conferees, is essentially zero. Three of the papers (or four authors) have in effect abstained from voting; there have been two somewhat indifferent negatives, and two strong negatives. If this conference had been held around 1950, there would surely have been some strong positives from representatives of the Thorndikean-Skinnerian-Postmanian position. How the times have changed!

More as compulsive pollster than as objective observer, I am going to count the work described in oral discussion by Stein (1969) on the positive side. There is nothing very explicit in Stein's discussion to suggest that he believes reinforcement to be a fundamental process, although he makes reference to traditional interpretations of the law of effect. But here we have a man who is really trying to discover the physiological and chemical mechanisms by which the law of effect operates, and he comes up with the conclusion that there are actually built-in brain functions by which rewards and punishments (i.e., satisfying and dissatisfying states of affairs, to use Thorndike's phraseology) have their effect. I would not even try — for I am not competent — to evaluate Stein's evidence, but I gather from the comments by Alan Fisher* that the evidence is solid. I am inclined to think that if it can be demonstrated that there exist special brain systems for the handling of messages concerning satisfying and aversive stimuli, controllable in quite specific ways by chemical substances, we are dealing with a biological and psychological process of fundamental significance. If such a system did not exist, the short-term and long-term memory stores postulated by Atkinson and Wickens would have to be, like homogeneous memory cores in a computer, completely neutral with respect to whether information had reward-punishment implications. Perhaps such a "neutral" system would be viable, but with Stein's evidence it becomes possible to conceptualize a rather more complicated system in which there are not only neutral memory stores but also additional brain components that control the plus-or-minus tagging and transfer of information. One wonders, therefore, whether Atkinson and Wickens' stark rejection of reinforcement as a fundamental principle is really in keeping either with the evidence or with the inherent logic of their total theory. The shoe fits also in the cases of Estes, Logan, and Bandura.

In discussion at one point in the conference, Stein made what to me was a highly significant suggestion, namely that the act of storing information (i.e., transferring information from a short-term store to a long-term store, in Atkinson and Wickens' sense) might be regarded as an operant, itself subject to reward contingencies. Now, to be sure, Atkinson and Wickens grant that reinforcement processes may "modulate" information transfer, but they still seem to relegate such processes to a secondary and incidental role. Stein's suggestion brings reinforcement into play at a basic level. If storing a piece of information is a "learnable response" (in Meehl's [1950] sense), it may be subject to Meehl's "Strong Law of Effect": "Every increment in strength involves a trans-situational reinforcer." This would imply a thorough recasting of Atkinson and Wickens' theory in terms of reinforcement influences upon information transfer. It would also imply that a reinforcement principle would underlie all learning, and hence that it is a fundamental principle.

In my view, Atkinson and Wickens should not reject such a reinterpretation of their theory out of hand. In claiming that reinforcement is a "subsidiary" phenomenon, they are really saying that a *simple* view of reinforcement whereby *any* response is strengthened or weakened by its consequences is untenable, and they have amply demonstrated this. If, however, the reinforcement principle is restricted to the process of information transfer as a molecular phenomenon, it might be possible for them to amplify their explanations of the varied effects of "reinforcement,"

*University of Pittsburgh

loosely defined, still preserving reinforcement as a basic principle applicable to information transfer.

Atkinson and Wickens operate solely within the context of verbal learning and similar settings where the "response" the subject makes is essentially a verbal report of a memory state. In the absence of any theory connecting memory states with motor responses such as bar-pressing, locomotion, and the like, it is at present difficult to foresee how their theory can be extended to cover the usual motoric operant response, but one can encourage speculation in this direction.

Thus we have possibly come back full circle to the kind of position espoused by Thorndike, that satisfying outcomes have an automatic strengthening effect on responses; now, however, we restrict the phenomenon to *covert* responses involving memory transfer, ridding ourslves of the various complications entailed when we try to apply the theory to the total class of overt responses, but at the same time getting ourselves into tremendous theoretical and experimental difficulties in identifying and measuring covert responses. It will take a very sophisticated nomothetic network to climb out of these difficulties. One is reminded, however, of the success of physicists in identifying subatomic particles by the use of such nomothetic networks.

How Stands the Concept of "Reinforcement" in the Study of the "Higher Mental Processes"?

Before discussing the second major theme that I perceive to have underlain the conference, let me introduce a personal note. The major reason I was pleased to be invited to the conference was that I hoped to find out how reinforcement theory may have fared in recent years in response to some of the criticisms that have been leveled at it by Chomsky and his followers in psycholinguistics. It was Chomsky (1959) who in his famous review of Skinner's *Verbal Behavior* (1957) asserted that Skinner's definition of reinforcement was tautological, indeed that his definition of *response* was vacuous. By implication, all stimulus-response theories of learning were held to be totally inadequate to explain the facts of language learning and language behavior. Actually, Chomsky left a few holes in the fence through which behavior theorists might crawl ("Reinforcement undoubtedly plays a significant role [in the 'strength' of linguistic behavior]" he says at one point), but the net effect has been to turn psycholinguists away from learning theory or from any attempt to reconstruct reinforcement theory to take care of linguistic behavior. The trend has been, in fact, quite the opposite, i.e., in the direction of further rejection of behavior theory (e.g., Bever, Fodor, and Weksel, 1965; Fodor, 1965). A group of psycholinguists and traditional behavior theorists convened to consider the resolution of the conflict failed, strangely enough, to take the opportunity to reconsider the role of reinforcement (Dixon and Horton, 1968). For the most part, the traditional behavior theorists were all too ready to grant that in the light of psycholinguistic "discoveries," stimulus-response theories (and even association theories) were ready for interment; reinforcement theory received only casual mention. To be sure, there have been a number of dogged stimulus-response theorists who have persisted in attempts to apply such theories of language (Salzinger, 1959; Staats, 1968), but they have remained isolated from the main stream of psycholinguistics. Staats (1968) asserts that reinforcement principles are "relatively well substantiated in laboratory research" (p. 89) and proceeds to apply them in a host of theoretical explanations of language behavior; he views psycholinguistic theory of the Chomskyan variety as misguided in that it has no contact with the "determining conditions" and hence cannot make explanatory statements (pp. 154 ff.).[1]

In view of the poor repute of reinforcement theory among psycholinguists generally, however, one would have reason to hope that a conference on reinforcement would provide at least some argumentation concerning its role in higher mental processes such as language. I must say that I have been rather disappointed in this hope, both because (as we have seen) opinion has seemed to favor the notion that reinforcement is a subsidiary and derivative process, and also because there has been little direct discussion of the role of reinforcement in language behavior. Nor has there been any direct discussion of the presumed "tautological" nature of the concept.

As for the problem of tautology, I would have assumed that the matter was pretty well disposed of, in the negative, some years ago by Meehl (1950). Psycholinguists who have been overimpressed by Chomsky's review of Skinner should read that paper, in which Meehl shows that the concept of reinforcement is not tautological, either as a matter of definition or of proof. He does show, however, that the concept has to be built up with careful prior definitions of such terms as schedule, learnable response, and classes of reinforcers. Even though Skinner's definition of reinforcement may be vulnerable to Chomsky's argmuents, I feel that Meehl's definition would stand up against them.

Among the conferees, Estes seems to be the only one to have seriously addressed himself to whether reinforcement principles can apply to higher

---

[1]Note added in proof: See now MacCorquodale's (1969, 1970) "retrospective" review of Skinner's *Verbal Behavior* and his answers to Chomsky's review. These brilliant articles will give considerable comfort to the behaviorist camp.

mental processes such as language. He does this in discussing the problem of "continuity," tending to favor the idea that whatever reinforcement principles may exist, they are perfectly general throughout biological species, including man. If the operation of reinforcement in language and other rule-governed behavior is difficult to perceive, it may be, he thinks, only because the nature of the behavorial units involved has not been adequately understood. It was not within the scope of his paper, however, to state how this might be so.

Most of the conferees made no explicit comment about reinforcement in higher mental processes, although one might argue that some were dealing with such processes in speaking of "expectancies" of reward (Logan), the ways in which people discern response-reward contingencies (Bandura), or socially-instituted point systems that control behavior (Wolf and Risley). Atkinson and Wickens, incidentally, explicitly disavow any attempt to extend their theory, derived from experiments on human learning, to lower animals. Yet, even their work on human learnings is restricted to simple tasks such as continuous paired-associate learning and concept identification — nothing approaching the complexity of language learning.

It may seem that despite the enormous effort that has been put into research on reinforcement, the time is not yet ripe to reconstruct reinforcement theory as it may apply to language learning and use. Yet one feels that there is already hope for progress in this direction. Some of the underlying ideas of the paper by Atkinson and Wickens strike me as particularly promising. Notions of information processing and memory could be used, it seems to me, in accounting for some of the phenomena of language learning. The child learning a language is constantly receiving sensory impressions having to do with language symbols and the situations in which they are used. His "imitations" are an attempt to regenerate and match these impressions by his own vocal behavior. Language learning is not all "response learning" in the Skinnerian sense; it is in large part "stimulus learning" — learning to recognize and identify stimuli (both linguistic and nonlinguistic), or what I have elsewhere (Carroll, 1968) called "epistemic" learning (the learning of information) quite apart from the learning of any discriminated overt responses associated with such stimuli. Language patterns and sequences, however complex they may be, are among the stimulus patterns that can be noticed, stored, and compared, without any necessary concomitants of immediate over response. "Reinforcement" must play a part in all this by way of directing attention to particular stimulus-response-reward contingencies, which then are stored for later use.

But these are mere speculations, hardly worked out in any useful form. On balance, one gets the impression from the conference that reinforcement theory makes little contribution, as yet, to the understanding of higher mental processes.

REFERENCES

Bever, T. G., Fodor, J. A., and Weksel, W. On the acquisition of syntax; a critique of "contextual generalization." *Psychological Review*, 1965, *72*, 467–482.

Carroll, J. B. On learning from being told. *Educational Psychologist*, 1968, *5* (2), 1, 5–10.

Chomsky, N. Review of Skinner's *Verbal Behavior. Language*, 1959, *35*, 26–58.

Dixon, T. R., and Horton, D. L. (Eds.) *Verbal behavior and general behavior theory*. Englewood Cliffs, N. J.: Prentice-Hall, 1968.

Fodor, J. A. Could meaning be an r_m? *Journal of Verbal Learning and Verbal Behavior*, 1965, *4*, 73–81.

MacCorquodale, K. B. F. Skinner's *Verbal Behavior*: A retrospective appreciation. *Journal of the Experimental Analysis of Behavior*, 1969, *12*, 831–841.

MacCorquodale, K. On Chomsky's review of Skinner's *Verbal Behavior. Journal of Experimental Analysis of Behavior*, 1970, *13*, 83–99.

Meehl, P. E. On the circularity of the law of effect. *Psychological Bulletin*, 1950, *47*, 52–75.

Salzinger, K. Experimental manipulation of verbal behavior: A review. *Journal of Experimental Psychology*, 1959, *61*, 65–94.

Skinner, B. F. *Verbal behavior*. New York: Appleton-Century-Crofts, 1957.

Staats, A. W. *Learning, language, and cognition*. New York: Holt, 1968.

Stein, L. Chemistry of reward and punishment. In D. H. Efron (Ed.), *Proceedings 1968 Meeting of Am. Coll. Neuropsychopharmacol.* Washington, D. C.: U. S. Government Printing Office, in press.

SOME RELATIONS OF REINFORCEMENT THEORY TO EDUCATION

ROBERT M. GAGNÉ

Florida State University

Surely one of the most exciting new complexes of ideas discussed in these conference papers is the proposed shift in point of view toward reinforcement as a mechanism of information processing, as contrasted with a mechanism of reward or drive satisfaction. According to Estes, this direction of thought is shared by a majority of investigators of human learning at the present time. Logan would prefer to incorporate the intellectual processing within the drive itself — a drive for learning — whereas Estes and others want to see it acknowledged that human beings store information concerning relationships that include rewards and punishments. The most thoroughly articulated point of view on the information-processing trend is that of Atkinson and Wickens, who propose that reinforcement modulates the information flow in various components of the memory process, essentially by directing the learner's attention to one aspect of the situation rather than to others.

Currently, I represent myself as an educational psychologist, and I want here to comment on the theoretical ideas presented from that point of view. As the engineer is to the physicist, the educational psychologist, in at least one of his roles, is "on the other side of the fence." He greatly admires what the experimental psychologist does, the ingenuity of his methods, the elegance of his theories. At the same time, he is usually

343

thinking hard about how this work may have to do with education, or more specifically, with learning in the school.

Theories

The initial reaction of the educational psychologist to the "information-processing" view of reinforcement must inevitably be one of applause. This new trend of thought appears to do two things. First, it takes a step away from the overly simple conception that is Thorndike's law of effect and begins to talk about different kinds of rewards and punishments, different kinds of incentives, different settings for reinforcement, and even several different functions of reinforcement. The variety of learning behavior one observes in the school has often seemed to demand this more varied treatment of such an important set of behavioral events.

Second, this new trend appears to get us a bit farther away from the humoral, homeostatic interpretations of behavior, which have always seemed somewhat incongruous when applied to students' learning of the kinds of intellectual tasks represented by algebra, chemistry, history, composition, and the like. The researcher's credulity, not to mention the teacher's, has often been somewhat strained by the analogy of drive reduction in hunger or sex, applied to the confirmation of adequate solutions of problems in analytic geometry, or the achievement of measures of electrical variables which balance the equation of Ohm's law.

These tendencies seem to be good ones, in the sense of holding promise of providing theories about learning which the educational psychologist can apply to school learning, and perhaps thereby tell others how to apply. However, there are also limitations in these promises, and these I think should be carefully noted. A responsible scientist, I believe, should be continually attentive to the question, "Have I really tackled the right problem?" All problems, of course, are worth studying in some ultimate sense. But it is sometimes better to aim for the more comprehensive theory, the larger conception, than for the smaller. We are all aware of the difference between a theory which explains little, as opposed to one which succeeds in making a great many phenomena fall into place all at once. It is the selectiveness vs. the comprehensiveness of theories of learning and reinforcement, such as those described at the conference, that seems to be worthy of further comment.

The limitations that I somewhat dimly perceive seem to me to arise from two related phenomena in the social psychology of psychological science. First is the fact that there are certain traditional prototypes of learning situations which appear to be depended upon over and over again, despite the fact that overwhelming evidence shows them to be atypical of much learning, and representative of only very special situations in which learning occurs. The first of these, of course, is animal trial-and-error learning (as it used to be called), in which the animal's behavior was interpreted as being a matter of gradual increase of strength of an associative bond or connection. Surely we have learned enough about learning by now to judge this as a most inadequate model of the animal's behavior, and therefore as a most inaccurate prototype. At least, the theories presented at this conference generally begin with the assumption that it is an inadequate prototype for human learning.

If that assumption is granted, there then seems to be a general tendency to jump to another prototype, which I judge to be equally inappropriate — the learning of verbal syllables or word pairs. Traditionally, the learning of paired-associates was studied because it was believed to be a way of investigating the characteristics of the single stimulus-response connection. But we have long since rid ourselves of that delusion. Modern investigators and theorists are well aware that there must be many different processes involved in paired-associate learning — differentiation of stimuli, mediation, coding, response familiarization — to name only a few of the most prominent ones. Despite these widely accepted facts, learning and reinforcement theorists continue to return to the paired-associate task as if it were typical of some kinds of learning. Why will we not take full cognizance of the fact that such learning is highly specialized, and extremely atypical? When does anyone learn anything like paired associates in real life? Very seldom, and if he does, it is not very important to him.

The second general kind of limitation that I see in theories of reinforcement as components of learning theories is, in a sense, an extension of the first. It lies in the comfortable idea that what we must seek are theories of "information-processing." Atkinson and Wickens, I note, are commendably careful to point out that in their discussions, this phrase is not to be given a technical meaning. But I want to speak about the phrase in its nontechnical meaning. Why should one want to think that the outcome of learning is "information processing"? What is typical about that, as a representative human task? It implies that the human being should be learning how to receive, process, store, and retrieve verbal information. In other words, educationally speaking, it implies that the typical event is that a student hears or reads a verbal communication, codes it, stores it, retrieves it, and spews it back on an examination. Has not each one of us, in his role as a college or university teacher, spent some of his time deploring this practice? Have we not pointed out, in the most vociferous terms, the triviality of such a practice as it pertains to the important learning the student must accomplish? We do not really believe, I take it, that we want the student to deliver "processed information" as a result of his educational effort. Why, then, do we choose this as a prototype of learning?

In order to clarify this point, let me list some actual learning tasks of students in school. Here are a few typical, representative examples:

1. learning to add dissimilar fractions;
2. learning to say orally unfamiliar English words;
3. learning to classify instances of abstract concepts in accordance with a definition;
4. learning to compose sentences containing a subject and predicate;
5. learning to demonstrate the application of Newton's second law to instances of rotary motion.

What these examples suggest, to me, is that they are not directly concerned with information processing. I would certainly agree that their learning *involves* information processing; but processed information is not their *outcome*. I have found no better way of describing their outcome than to say they are intellectual skills. They are inferred capabilities that make it possible for the students to *do* some things, not simply to know them in the sense of being able to talk about them.

Consider the first example, adding dissimilar fractions. Is the input "information" in the form of a set of dissimilar fractions? Possibly so, although one must not forget the directions "add." But what do we look for as output? A fraction expressing the sum. Is this "information" that has been coded, stored, and retrieved? Not at all. It is an output that represents a transformation of the input brought about by some rather complex intellectual processing. The particular information contained in the input is not stored or retrieved at all, and it is quite possible that the student could not retrieve it if we asked him to. Some would say, what has happened here is that the student has learned to use a rule. That is exactly what I mean by an intellectual skill.

In further elaboration of this point, I want to refer particularly to the theory proposed by Atkinson and Wickens. Perhaps I should say first that it seems to me an excellent theory which has been described with remarkable clarity. These authors propose that reinforcement operates at certain critical points between and within their hypothesized components — the sensory register, the short-term store, and the long-term store — all three of which are capable of retaining "information." In addition, they say, there are certain control processes which can vary from one task to the next. For example, there is a process of transfer from SR to STS; within

STS there is a rehearsal process, and also a decision process which determines whether information will enter the rehearsal buffer; another very important set of processes pertains to the coding and organizing of information, and further to the transfer of information to LTS; then there are processes of storage within LTS; and finally the very essential process of retrieval.

Let us assume for the moment that it is a reasonable question as to how an individual engages in this kind of "information processing." The theory tells us that this is done by means of a number of *control processes*. The most important question I have to ask is, where do these processes come from? Are they innately determined? Apparently not, because we have much evidence that individuals perceive situations in different ways depending on prior experience; they rehearse information in different manners, and more or less effectively; they code situations in various ways; they retrieve information more or less well, again depending on their experience. In other words, there is a good deal of suggestive evidence that these processes are learned, and that how adequately they are learned may have an enormous effect on the special task of remembering verbal information.

Educators have been saying for many years that school learning is *not* a matter of learning information, although the latter learning may be incidentally involved. School learning *is* a matter of learning process. The student must learn the processes of attending, of coding, or organizing, storing, and retrieving verbal information. He must also learn many other kinds of processes in order to be a capable person — processes of classifying, of defining, of transforming, of rule following, of problem solving.

How are such processes (or intellectual skills) learned? How are they stored, maintained, and kept available? How are they retrieved when needed? This seems to me to be the challenging problem for reinforcement theory. Can it be supposed that rehearsal processes, for example, are learned by being momentarily imaged in a sensory register? Do they then themselves become subjected to a rehearsal process before being permanently stored? Are they transferred from a short-term store to a long-term store, and then retrieved when the proper stimulus is presented? If these suppositions are true, then an "information-processing" account of reinforcement and learning may be expected to illuminate this kind of learning, the kind that the school is supposed to be concerned with. If they are not true, then such theories will take their places along with others as explanations of a relatively special variety of human learning behavior.

Applications of Reinforcement

While theoretical accounts of reinforcement, not surprisingly, continue to present difficult and complex problems, some of the conference papers serve as reminders of what an amazingly powerful means of behavioral control is provided by applications of not-so-complex reinforcement techniques. Wolf and Risley have referred to and described a number of studies of behavior modification, as well as rather dramatic results of application of these techniques to the control of children's behavior in classrooms and other social settings.

In addition, we have Bandura's thoroughgoing description and analysis of the phenomena of vicarious reinforcement and self-reinforcement, with a valuable reference to Premack's conception of reinforcement as a relational property of contingent events. It is most interesting to have a review of findings which show that vicarious reinforcement, under suitable conditions, can bring about marked changes in behavior, and that a variety of procedures exist which make it possible for such changes to be maintained. It is equally intriguing to have the evidence that modeling can establish standards for self-reinforcement which can then effectively control behavior through either rewarding or aversive consequences.

Obviously, these authors believe that additional research will add further clarification to our understanding of the practical applications of reinforcement. Undoubtedly, they are very much aware, as they have said, of the social implications of their work. As scientific investigators, I believe we have the social responsibility to see that some of these findings reach a broad audience. I cannot help but note how markedly some of these conclusions appear to conflict with what I believe to be the moral convictions of many of our reigning intelligentsia, particularly those who scoff at empirical science. Here are the kinds of generalizations I note, with undisguised glee:

1. Virtuous behavior can be learned by seeing that virtue is rewarded.
2. Virtue can come to provide its own reward.
3. Evil behavior can be reduced or eliminated by seeing that it is punished.
4. Evil behavior can come to be avoided by the establishment of conscience.
5. Punishment provides an effective means of eliminating undesirable behavior.
6. Vicarious experience of punishment can be a deterrent to antisocial behavior.

7. Standards of desirable conduct can be learned by example from human models.
8. Tokens, such as gold stars, can function effectively to establish good conduct.
9. Responsibility, when suitably rewarded, can be a means of generating socially desirable behavior.
10. Adult overpermissiveness can interfere with the learning of desirable self-control by the child.

Those who would challenge these ten propositions must come up with some pretty solid evidence!

SOME COMMENTS ON THE LANGUAGE OF THE PSYCHOLOGY OF REINFORCEMENT AS USED IN THE CONFERENCE PAPERS

ROBERT M. W. TRAVERS

Western Michigan University

A conference such as this would appear to be called on the assumption that there is some common meaning that characterizes the usage of the term "reinforcement," much as there is common meaning in the term *"electron"* when it is used in the discussion of such various topics as transistors, currents in conductors, and cathode rays. The various conference papers, however, indicate three rather different approaches to the identification of some meaning for the term "reinforcement."

(1) There is the approach that leaves the identification of the term quite open. The papers by Estes and Logan, for example, avoid the issue of pinning down the term. The Estes classification of reinforcement research assumes that the terms "reward" or "reinforcement" relate to similar phenomena in his different categories of research, but what the common essence is remains unidentified. This approach is similar to the common-language approach of discussing psychological phenomena, and

although it is one that has been frowned upon by psychologists, the physical sciences have had a history of introducing terms in this way. Chemists talked of atoms long before the atomic structure of matter was a reality and long before the attributes of atoms could be identified. The early concept of an atom was vague, but it had the function of providing a signpost indicating a direction in which to look for significant phenomena. Perhaps there is virtue in retaining a not-too-well identified concept of reinforcement at this time. Only the future can show the virtue of this strategy.

(2) A second approach is exemplified in those papers that embody the concepts of behavior modification and embrace the operationism of Percy Bridgman of nearly half a century ago. The definition of technical words in terms of operations, proposed by Bridgman and embraced by behavioral scientists of the 1930's, finds few advocates today, except among those who identify themselves as behavior-modification phychologists. The departure from traditional operationism is nowhere more evident than in the proceedings of this conference, and although I am sure that a Bridgman type of operationism is not a good model for the development of scientific language, there is controversy as to what is a good model. I am sure that none of the conferees is satisfied that each can take the term "reinforcement" and weave it into his own system of propositions, often only loosely tied to data, and that, within this matrix of statements, the term is indirectly tied to different operations than those to which it is tied in other systems of propositions developed by another scientist who also claims he is interested in reinforcement. The same term is used in both sets of propositions only because both scientists have some kind of intuitive hunch that similar variables or events are involved. The usage of the term "reinforcement" is enormously influenced by such intuitive hunches at the present time. My own intuition is, however, a little overworked when I try to find communality between Atkinson and Wicken's statement that "reinforcement is the modulation of this information flow as it influences both storage and retrieval processes" and Premack's statement that "reinforcement as a case in which the subject moves from a less to a more preferred event." In both cases "reinforcement" is tied loosely through a matrix of statements to operations, but the chain of ideas is long and the operations at the end of the chain are different. Bridgman would have been right in saying that the result of such a state of affairs would be confusion, even though his recipe for developing a scientific language never did what is promised to do, and did not represent a procedure that had been successful in the established sciences.

Operationism of the 1930's offered promise of bringing order into the confused and confusing vocabulary of the behavioral sciences, but the form in which it was applied at that time failed because of two main defects. The first was the implication that seemed to go with the procedure that the mere operational definition of a term gave it scientific standing. Philosophers such as Gustav Bergman were quick to point out this error, but behavioral scientists were much slower to recognize that a well-defined term is not necessarily a good scientific term. A second defect was a failure to recognize that statements about phenomena of any consequence cannot generally be restricted to operationally defined terms. It also should be mentioned that certain kinds of operational definitions, by their very nature represent gross categories far too crude for most scientific uses. With respect to the latter problem, consider Skinner's definition of a reinforcing event (1953, p-73). He states that an event is classified as reinforcing or not by observing the frequency of a selected response, then making an event contingent upon the response, then observing whether there is a change in frequency of the response. If there is a change, then the event is classed as a reinforcer. An event is classed as reinforcing or nonreinforcing in terms of its consequences. I doubt whether chemistry would ever have gotten anywhere if chemists had defined their key phenomena in terms of their consequences. Indeed, Lavoisier once commented bitterly on the fact that his predecessors and contemporaries classified compounds in this way. Consider, for example, the lack of utility of classifying certain compounds as corrosives, a pre-Lavoisier classification, based on the fact that corrosion is one of the consequences of their action on common materials. True, the group of chemicals that have corrosive properties can be operationally defined, but the operational definition has the unfortunate effect of grouping together chemicals, such as acids and alkalis, that should not be grouped together. Skinner's definition of a reinforcing event has this kind of difficulty attached to it. The term is beautifully and elegantly operationally defined, but in a way that inevitably leads to confusion rather than clarification.

The difficulties of developing a clarification of the concept of reinforcement, or even of developing a concept at all, stem largely from the difficulties to which a Bridgman type of operationism leads. To some degree, a conference such as this is an attempt to break from the intellectual sterility produced by rigidity of beliefs concerning the applicability of Bridgman operationalism to the development of a language of psychology when the fact is that it could never be applied to Bridgman's own area, namely, physics. The core terms of physics were never introduced through this kind of philosophical hocus-pocus at all. When J. J. Thomson introduced the concept of an electron in 1897, he produced a complex set of interrelated protocol statements about the cathode-ray phenomena he had been studying, in the language structure of which the term "electron" held a crucial role. The meaning of the term is conveyed through a set of protocol statements that are highly data-tied, but the process is complex. In terms of modern conceptions of scientific language, Thomson's term "electron" would be described as a theoretical term in that he was, at that stage, dealing with an unobservable. Later, when the cloud chamber made it possible to observe the track of an electron, it came nearer to acquiring the status of an empirical concept. This sample of scientific history also brings out the fact that there is no rigid line that can be drawn between an empirical term, that is to say one that can be operationally defined, and a theoretical term that is only indirectly tied to observables.

(3) A third approach to definition, characteristic of highly developed scientific areas, is that of embedding a word in what amounts to a network of protocol statements. This is the way in which "electron" was used in J. J. Thomson's original introduction of the term, as I have already mentioned. It is a much more complex defining process than that provided by operationism, but it is the main method by which physics has developed a technical vocabulary. In the area of reward and reinforcement it is hardly possible as yet to develop sets of protocol statements that have the utility of tying down the terms. Premack's paper comes close to this kind of procedure, but cannot go too far along these lines because of the primitive state of knowledge involved. The possibility also exists that the psychologist may never be able to utilize this kind of defining process to any marked degree because of the nature of the events he is attempting to organize.

Few would deny that we are confronted with real difficulties in the development of an adequate technical language for discussing an area such as reinforcement. Although immense progress has been made in developing rigorous experimental procedures for studying behavioral phenomena, this has not led to the development of a rigorous language for discussing the results of rigorous experiments. There is a long step between well-controlled and reproduceable experiments and the translation of the results of those experiments into compact sets of interrelated propositions. Certainly, twentieth-century psychology has shown the same proliferation of ingenious experimental techniques as was shown by nineteenth-century physics, but our language for discussing our findings is almost pre-Newtonian. Whether our experimental results can ever be translated into a concise and exact language where, for example, there will be a single precise term "reinforcement" as there is a single precise term "electron," still remains to be seen. Until such a translation takes place, we had better recognize that terms are used in particular contexts because intuition prompts us this way. The role that intuition has played in the choice of terms by the authors of these conference papers is enormous, despite the fact that the terms are used to discuss rigorously executed experiments.

What is the solution to this language problem? I am sure that just as psychologists had to work for generations on how to design rigorous experiments, so too will generations of psychologists have to work on how to discover means of developing a language permitting the rigorous discussion of rigorously conducted experiments. Mere resolve to be rigorous in this respect is not enough. Operationism was a kind of experimentation with language and was a valuable exploration of the kind I am discussing, but only a crude beginning. Hull's method of constructing and interrelating propositions has been rejected largely because of the apparent inappropriateness of the application of the Newtonian model found in the *Principia* to the development of the behavioral sciences. However, if one disregards the Newtonian conception of knowledge inherent in Hull's later writings and looks at some of the other features, one cannot help but be impressed with the advantages of departing from traditional prose in summarizing experimental findings. There are other orderly ways which also might be attempted to introduce rigor into the discussion of experimental findings, but little effort has been directed towards the problem of finding a language structure that will do for psychology what the language of physics does for physics, perhaps because the academic community has assumed that if rigorous experimentation is undertaken, then a rigorous language will follow. This seems to be quite a false assumption. That is why we have as many concepts of reinforcement at this conference as we have had speakers.

Perhaps Catania's paper comes nearest of all the contributions to representing a kind of experiment in language of the kind I am talking about. His graphs could also be reduced to a set of propositions that would look rather different from the propositions involving generalizations in other papers. Any contribution that involves experimentation with different forms of language for summarizing knowledge in the behavioral sciences is a move in the right direction.

REFERENCES

Skinner, B. F. *Science and human behavior.* New York: Macmillan, 1953.

AUTHOR INDEX

SUBJECT INDEX

A

Achievement behavior and self-reinforcement and self-concept, 258-260
Acquired
  distinctiveness
    of responses, 54, 55
    of stimuli, 54
  equivalence of responses, 54, 55
  similarity of stimuli, 54
Acquisition-performance distinction,
  see also Learning and vicarious reinforcement, 290, 291
Activation, *see* Arousal
Adaptive level, 19, 20
Adaption level theory and stimulus
  change and preference, 173
Aftereffects, representational theory of,
  25
Aggressive behavior and observed punishment, 231, 232
Analysis
  of behavior, *see* Behavior, analysis of,
    descriptive
  insufficiency of, 224-226
  necessity for, 222-224
  and operant-respondent distinction,
    223, 224
Antedating
  experience, relationship to stimulus
    change, 170, 173
  exposure
    and deprivation, 175
    effects in light-onset reinforcement,
      164, 165

Anticipatory habits, 50
Appetitive
  conditioning, 50, 51
  drives, 175, 176
  reinforcement, 157
    and sensory reinforcement
      differences, 173
      parallels with, 162
      theoretical relation to, 173, 177
  rewards, incentive-motivational interpretation, 157, 158
Applications of reinforcement, *see*
  Reinforcement, applied research in
Arousal, 29, 154, 155
  and attention, 182, 183
  changes in, as value functions, 132, 133
  and drive, 177-179
  emotional
    classical conditioning of, 244
    and social affective cues, 243, 244
  and incentive motivation and reinforcement, 177-181
  and motivation, 154, 155, 178
  as a neurophysiological reaction, 179
  optimal levels of, 154, 177, 178
  and reward value, 179, 182
  self, 261-263
Association
  habit, 47
  incentive, 47
  and law of effect, 336
Associationistic
  view of reinforcement, 2
Associative
  concepts and learning, 22